Northern Journey

A Guide to Canadian Folk Music

Gene Wilburn

RP

REFERENCE PRESS

Published in Canada by Reference Press,
7 Wragge Street, Teeswater, Ontario N0G 2S0
Telephone (519) 392-6634

Set in 10 point Times Roman

Canadian Cataloguing in Publication Data

Wilburn, Gene, 1945–
Northern journey: a guide to Canadian folk music

Includes indexes.
ISBN 0-919981-45-3

1. Folk music—Canada—Discography. 2. Folk
music—Canada—History and criticism. I. Title.

ML156.4.F5W54 1995   016.78162'00971   C95-9002237-5

To Marion and Trevor

Contents

Foreword

This is one of those books that is going to change your life. It is also, if you have any imagination at all, going to cost you a lot of money. So, if your life requires no changing and you haven't got any money to spare, and you haven't bought the book yet, I suggest you put it right back on the shelf and buy something else. Now that we've settled that, let's get to the point. This book is a treasure map. It is the first comprehensive guide to that glorious body of recorded works known as folk music. It is broad in its definition of what folk music is and limited in that it deals with CD's of Canadian folk music, or perhaps better put, folk music performed and recorded in Canada. This is not splitting hairs since there is some debate as to what exactly "Canadian" is. I share Gene's approach that if it's done in Canada it's Canadian, and that's one of the things I like about this book.

This is not an academic text. It is not a research project detailing the history of recorded folk music in this country from the first recordings done by pioneers such as Barbeau, Creighton, Fowke, Peacock and the like. It is rather a celebration of the living tradition in that if it's on CD, it's part of the cultural life of the country and not an archival relic. By excluding vinyl, this book is a contemporary tool. By excluding cassettes it is both manageable and, to some degree, discerning in that most of the good stuff is on CD. This is not to say that there aren't collections drawn from older recordings and reissues of albums that first appeared on vinyl. It is to say that most of what's here has been recorded in the last decade, the age of the CD. And, it is amazing to take a look at how much has come out on those shiny little discs.

I remember well when the first CD's started to make their appearance. I particularly remember how I and others involved in folk music bemoaned the fact that there was so little Canadian folk music in that format. It seemed that folk musicians in Canada were about to be left far behind by the latest technological revolution. Not only would a great deal of music be lost, but contemporary artists who were not on major labels would simply be sidelined, driven off the information highway onto the back roads of our time. In fact, quite the opposite has happened. Today there is both enormous democracy and diversity in the production of recorded folk music. It seems that even the most modest artist has been able to scrape together the required capital to produce a compact disc and this in turn has led to an enormous variety in what is available if only you could find it.

Years ago, in the 1960's for example, sometimes called heyday of folk music, artists pretty much recorded for the majors, i.e., those five or six big labels, or didn't record at all. Today there are hundreds of labels in Canada. Most of them are artist-owned and devoted to the production of the works of their owner. Some are a little larger, producing records by a number of artists who share a style or region. A few of them are distributed by major labels and found across the country in most record stores. Many more are carried by independent distributors but found in only the larger "flagship" stores and those independent stores that are left—the so-called "mom and pop" operations. However, as more and more artists record there are more and more recordings which are not easily available. A number of them you can really only get from the artists themselves or in local record stores near the artist's home. It's really "Catch 22". The artists can use the latest developments in DAT recording and the fairly low price of CD manufacture to make great recordings on their terms, free from the demands of the commercial marketplace, but they can't get them into the hands of their audience. Mailing lists, specialty catalogues, and even the Internet are becoming increasingly important tools to counter the restricted variety of most retail stores. However you need to know about the recordings in the first place to want to find them. That is why the publication of this book is such a long awaited event.

Recently I was in a major record store in Halifax where I discovered an entire section devoted to artists from Atlantic Canada. There were recordings that I had never come across in stores or in the catalogues of any distributor. The same is true in Vancouver, Calgary, Toronto, Montreal, and any other cities that I have visited. That is one of the great functions of this book. Gene has sat down and patiently compiled information on as many recordings of folk music on CD as he could find. He has also included the information on how you can get your hands on these gems. Not only that, he has provided a capsule review of the recording and indexed the songs of the artists. It's a heck of a thing, all the more important in a country where the combination of immense geography and small population makes access to home grown recordings a real challenge.

One important feature of the book is its function as a collective memory. The cataloguing of recordings by artists who produced their work in the days of vinyl is a great service to the increasing number of young people who are listening to folk music and for whom Ian and Sylvia or even Stan Rogers are historical figures outside their living experience. Knowing the recordings these artists made and what was on them will, I am sure, allow new generations of folk audiophiles to trace back the roots of the music.

Another strength of this book is the breadth of its approach. Gene has cast a very wide net in his research and presents many different traditions of music. This is good. In any given month I find myself listening to an amazing variety of music by Canadian artists that falls within the folk family. A casual perusal of the pile near my CD player revealed *From Paris To Kiev*—a great Ukrainian band from Winnipeg playing traditional material with a very contemporary flavour, Mary Jane Lamond—a new young singer of Gaelic songs from Cape Breton, the newest release from Quebec's La Bottine Souriante, a long-awaited reissue of Ian and Sylvia's *Great Speckled Bird*, a recent release from Vancouver's Uzume Taiko, and a strong collection of songs by

Newfoundland singer songwriter Ron Hynes. And oh yeah, an album of Yiddish theatre and folk songs sung by a Toronto woman by the name of Faye Kellerstein and finally a CD collection of work by Chilean-Canadian Winnipeg-based Hugo Torres. All of these have come out in the last year. It gives a sense, and I'm just one little person, of how much there is and how broad a spectrum is being covered these days.

There is surely more folk music being created, performed, and recorded in this country today than there has ever been before. These are the good old days for folk music. There has never been more diversity, a higher degree of technical and artistic ability, or greater opportunity to listen to folk music. From the beards-and-banjos traditionalists to the world beat bands from a dozen ports of origin, to young, edgy singer songwriters coming out of Vancouver's Commercial Drive or Toronto's Queen Street scenes, the selection is just about limitless. Atlantic Canada has produced at least a couple of dozen wonderful groups based in Celtic music. There has been a great flowering of new work by First Nations artists from the very traditional to blues and country influenced singer-songwriters. In Quebec there has been a revival of interest in traditional music, a whole slough of new chansonniers, and a stunning array of world music coming from Montreal. Pick a city, pick a region, and you can find a mit full of great folk music recordings. And Gene Wilburn, bless him, has done the dirtiest job of all and collected the information about the CD's spilling out of this musical horn of plenty and set it all down, and gone out and found a publisher.

As I said at the beginning of this little exercise, this book is a treasure map. Using it can lead you to some wonderful music. That music can change how you think and feel about yourself and the world. This is serious stuff, so serious that I suggest that you play around a little. If it sounds interesting, look for it. Try to listen to it before you buy it. You may even be blessed with a library smart enough, and still with enough of a budget, to order a bunch of these recordings. If you live in a big city, and most of us do, there is probably a university radio station that has a folk music show, and of course there's always the CBC, while it lasts. Obviously folk festivals are the most concentrated gathering of the artists listed in this book. Go to one. Not only will you hear the music live but they almost always have CD's for sale. Badger your local record store to get a copy of this book and order recordings from it. And of course, use it to track down and order CD's directly from the artists. That way you also put the most money in their pockets. This book is a great resource, it opens up vast possibilities to the culturally curious.

The rest, dear reader, is up to you.

— *Gary Cristall*

Gary Cristall was raised among folkies in Toronto. He was a founder, and, for fifteen years, the Artistic Director of the Vancouver Folk Music Festival. He hosted What The Folk *on Vancouver Co-operative Radio for seventeen years and started Festival Records, a distributor of folk and related music recordings. He is currently the Jazz, Folk and World Music Officer at the Touring Office of the Canada Council.*

Introduction

If it hadn't been for folk music I might have led a normal life. Maybe I'd have finished that degree in engineering or joined a service club. In the end there just wasn't enough time to study math *and* learn to play Ian & Sylvia and Gordon Lightfoot songs on my old, second-hand guitar, so something had to go. I chucked calculus and worked on barred chords. I never did master the guitar, but in the process I became a lifelong fan of folk music—the form of music that touches me most deeply.

I'm not alone. Each summer thousands of Canadians like myself gather together to partake in a profoundly satisfying musical ritual. We pack some snacks, grab our lawn chairs, don hats, daub on sunscreen and head out for the nearest folk festival. There, nestled on the grass among folkies of all ages—from toddlers to greysters—we listen to some of the finest music in the land. Folk music is alive, well, and thriving at a grassroots level.

What is most striking about folk music in Canada is the dedication and talent of its performers. Although some artists such as Ian & Sylvia, Stan Rogers, Joni Mitchell, Gordon Lightfoot, Leonard Cohen, Murray McLauchlan, and Bruce Cockburn are household names, most are not well known outside the festival and club circuit. This is a pity, because they are creating uncommonly good music that defines the Canadian landscape and experience in a unique way.

Fortunately, many professional Canadian folk musicians have recorded albums. Unfortunately, the albums can be hard to find. While some of the larger record shops still have a folk section, most scatter folk music across several categories—pop, rock, country, "Indie," New Age, and even world and international—if they stock it at all. Folk music, to say the least, tends to be under-represented.

Although I've been listening to folk music since the late 50's, I became most keenly aware of the richness and diversity of contemporary Canadian folk music at about the same time as I made the technology switch to compact disc on my home stereo system. As I discovered the music of James Keelaghan, La Bottine Souriante, the Rankin Family, and Natalie MacMaster, I began looking for some kind of guide to help me identify additional artists for my CD collection. Aside from spot reviews in *Dirty Linen*, *Sing Out!*, and various Canadian newspapers, I found very little to help me get a handle on the breadth and availability of folk music in Canada. In the end I decided to put together the book I wanted to buy, to help introduce others to this wonderful music. Titled *Northern Journey*, in tribute to one of my favourite Ian & Sylvia albums, this guide provides a listing of the compact disc recordings of all the Canadian folk artists I've been able to identify—nearly four hundred at the time this edition went to press.

Northern Journey is limited to albums on compact disc. Vinyl is virtually obsolete and the cassette tape bins in record shops are shrinking rapidly. Music fans have accepted the CD format overwhelmingly as their medium of choice. While there is still a significant amount of older Canadian folk music available only on vinyl or cassette tape, much of it is has already been reissued on CD. Ultimately, most of these recordings will find their way to the new format and will be included in future editions of this guide.

I sincerely hope that this book will encourage you to seek out and support the immensely talented musicians who create the very special music in this guide. I've made every attempt to ensure that the information is as accurate and complete as possible. If you discover any omissions or anomalies, or would like to make suggestions for future editions of the guide, please send me a note via my e-mail address: *72435.732@compuserve.com* on the Internet, or by regular mail: Gene Wilburn, Royal Ontario Museum, 100 Queen's Park, Toronto, Ontario, Canada M5S 2C6.

What Is Folk Music?

Folk music, Canadian or other, admits of no simple definition. The best and, perhaps, only way to understand contemporary folk music is to attend one of Canada's folk festivals and listen to the delightfully eclectic range of musical styles emanating from the stages. Festival performers embrace a broad musical spectrum, from roots and traditional music to country, bluegrass, rock, blues, jazz, gospel, honky-tonk, and musical comedy. To the probable distress of musicologists and folklorists, I've used the term *folk* to include the spectrum of music labelled, variously, "roots," "traditional," "folk/rock," "folk/pop," "aboriginal," "native," "world," "worldbeat," "worldfolk," "Maritimes," and "Celtic." The venerable term *folk* provides a simpler handle for this music, despite its unabashed ambiguity.

Canadian folk music flows from two seminal sources: traditional, ethnic-flavoured songs and instrumentation, and contemporary songwriting—the singer-songwriter tradition. Folk artists tend to emerge from one or the other of these wellsprings and often from both. When the two influences intersect, as they do in the music of Stan Rogers or Eileen McGann, the result is a sound that nearly anyone on the street, if asked, would identify as "folk."

In terms of traditional music, Canada is home to a vibrant musical heritage—the Celtic music of the Maritimes and Quebec. The traditional music of the settlers from Ireland, Scotland, Brittany and France, whether sung or performed on fiddle, accordion, bagpipe, guitar, flute, whistle, or combined instruments, is a Canadian folk-music treasure.

The definition of *folk* begins to stretch uncomfortably for traditionalists when performers, especially singer-songwriters, mix in elements like electric instruments, keyboards, synthesizers, and drums, or lyrics and melodies written in a non-formulaic country, rock, or pop style. Contemporary folk music embraces a wide range of influences as is evidenced by the singer-songwriter segment of the folk spectrum that includes such striking artists as Garnet Rogers, Stephen Fearing, Joni Mitchell, and Ferron—performers who are among festival favourites even though their styles frequently cross over to other genres.

I've taken an open, accepting stance on the question of "what is folk?" In addition to as many traditional and Celtic-oriented performers as I could locate, I've also included a large number of singer-songwriters. My basic rule of thumb was this: if "folkish" artists or groups appear regularly at Canadian folk festivals, they've been included. If a performer started his or her career primarily as a folk artist and later crossed over to other genres, I've attempted to track the artist's entire recording career. Hence you'll find listings of all the compact discs available for musicians like Joni Mitchell, Bruce Cockburn, Leonard Cohen, Spirit Of The West, and Ian Tyson.

Country, Rock, Bluegrass, French-Canadian, and World

There is clearly some overlap between folk music and country music. Both share the same roots. The pre-Nashville country music of North America—"old-time country"—can be seen as a branch of folk music. Most of today's electric-driven country music, however, is closer to rock and pop than to folk. Folksingers, on the whole, are not as influenced by Nashville-derived traditions of dress and styles of delivery. In order to keep the guide as acoustically biased as possible, I've limited country performers to those who began their careers as folk artists, or those who perform "old-time" or significantly roots-oriented country. For the same reason, I've excluded most rock groups, electric blues performers, and pop artists. Bluegrass music, with its acoustic instrumentation and traditional styles and tunes, has been included.

Although coverage is provided for all of Canada, I've written this guide for a primarily English-speaking audience. The French-language folk artists and chansonniers of Quebec and New Brunswick are represented, selectively, by historical and contemporary performers who are relatively well known to English-speaking fans—artists like Mme La Bolduc, Félix Leclerc, La Bottine Souriante, Edith Butler, and Ad Vielle Que Pourra.

All cultures in Canada are ethnic cultures, and performers from these cultures, whether they be from Canada's First Nations, descended from Irish, Scottish, English or French settlers, or newly arrived from India, Chile or the Caribbean, play folk music whenever they play traditional material. Canada is continually being settled by people from around the world who enrich our cultural mosaic with their unique, diverse musical gifts. To the extent that I've been able to locate their music, I've included Canadian native and world artists.

Folk music is, and will ever be, a moving target. Not even acoustic instruments are fixed in time. The modern, virtuoso acoustic guitar compositions of Don Ross, Mark Bracken, and Oscar Lopez, the jazz-influenced acoustic artistry of Stephen Fearing, the experimental fiddle compositions of Oliver Schroer, and the simultaneously ancient- and modern-sounding compositions of Loreena McKennitt provide reminders that folk music is an evolving process—a journey that continually takes unexpected turns.

Organization Of The Guide

The heart of *Northern Journey* is the *Artists* section, arranged alphabetically by performer. In addition to a snapshot of the style—e.g., "Folk," "Acoustic Blues," "Singer-Songwriter"—there is a brief introduction to each artist. This is followed by a list of CD recordings arranged chronologically. Each CD entry contains the album's title, date of issue, publisher, and catalogue number, if known. A dagger (†) at the end of the publisher's information indicates that the album includes printed lyrics of the songs.

A track listing displays the songs on each CD, followed by the overall duration, in minutes. In the case of anthologies (*see* Anthologies in the *Artists* section), individual artists are listed alongside the songs they perform. With the exception of a few obvious typos, song titles have been spelled the way they appear on the CD. The expression *TBA* indicates an entry that was reviewed from tape prior to its release on CD.

Each album is rated on a four-star scale. The purpose of the ratings is to help you build a folk collection with confidence. The reviews are not overly critical—folk music is a musical form in which quality of voice often plays a secondary role to quality of lyrics or musicianship. Any work that is solid musically and presented with honesty and integrity is rated as "good." A few albums are more than just good—some are "very good" and a select few are "outstanding." There are also a small number of albums that make dubious purchases. These have been rated as "poor" to "fair." A tick mark (✓) beside a CD indicates an album that is recommended as a good purchase for a "starter" collection.

The Ratings

✳✳✳✳	*Outstanding*. Albums of unqualified excellence.
✳✳✳	*Good*. Solid albums that are typical of the artist's work.
✳✳	*Fair*. Albums that may be of interest to the collector, but which lack the professionalism, conviction, spark, or creative energy that characterizes a higher-rated album.
✳	*Poor*. A misguided effort.
✓	*Recommended*. A good purchase for a "starter" collection.

Ratings that are qualified with parentheses—e.g., ✳✳✳(✳)—indicate an album with an in-between rating.

Resources and Indexes

There are two resource sections following the *Artists* section: *Record Company Addresses* lists the sources for the CD's in the guide, and *Folk Festivals In Canada* lists most of Canada's major festivals, by province, with a telephone contact number for each festival. In addition, there are two indexes: *Artist Index* and *Song Index*. The *Song Index* provides an alphabetical listing of all the songs in the guide, including the individual jigs, reels, stathspeys, and waltzes of fiddle medleys.

Acknowledgements

I have been extremely fortunate, in the preparation of this book, to be guided by some exceptional people who came to my rescue time after time when I needed information and insights. My chief mentors were Susan Martinez, Derek Andrews, Gary Cristall, Steve Fruitman, Ossie Branscombe, and Les Siemieniuk—incredibly knowledgeable individuals who gave freely and generously of their time. *Northern Journey* has been significantly enhanced by their advice, guidance, and encouragement.

For several years Steve Fruitman has granted annual Porcupine awards on his folklore radio show, *The Great North Wind*, on CIUT-FM, University of Toronto. It is my pleasure to make these thoughtful, insightful folk-music awards available to a wider audience by noting Porcupine recipients within the *Artists* section.

The book has also been strengthened by several individuals who volunteered to read through my evolving list, watching for gaps and suggesting additions. They have made an enormous contribution to the scope of the work. Thanks especially to Brian Morton, Doug Cox, Bill Gallaher, Dawn Callan, Loretto Reid, Ken Hague, Sandra Armitage, Paul Norton, and The Three BigRockateers: Jack Scown, Vic Bell, and Vic Close, for the generous help they've given me in locating additional artists.

My colleagues at the Royal Ontario Museum—Bill Pratt and Marili Moore—deserve a special badge of merit. Their sharp-eyed editing uncovered dozens of typos, grammatical lapses, and inconsistencies. Any participles left dangling are entirely my responsibility. Thanks, too, to Lilian Turner and Denise Reeve who assisted with the verification of data.

I cannot overemphasize the vital role the Internet played in the creation of this book. Through the Net I was able to tap the bountiful resources of listserves and newsgroups such as *cdnfolk, folk_music, folkdj-l, rec.music.folk, rec.music.celtic,* and *alt.music.canada.* Thanks to all on the Net who replied to my many queries so rapidly, thoroughly, and graciously.

I found two reference books to be particularly helpful during this project: *Encyclopedia of Music in Canada*, edited by Helmut Kallman, Gilles Potvin, Kenneth Winters, University of Toronto Press (ISBN 0-8020-5509-5), and *Encyclopedia of Canadian Rock, Pop and Folk Music*, by Rick Jackson, Quarry Press (ISBN 1-55082-098-2). My thanks to the authors of these fine works. And equal thanks to the editors and writers of those indispensible periodicals *Sing Out!*, *Dirty Linen*, and *Maple Roots*.

My deepest thanks of all go to my wife, Marion Wilburn, who served as editor, consultant, cheerleader, critic, and counsellor. Her faith in this project, her boundless enthusiasm, and her dedicated assistance sustained me through more than a year of collecting, research, and writing.

The Artists

1755

FRENCH-CANADIAN; CELTIC/ACADIAN ROCK; SINGER-SONGWRITERS

1755 was one of Canada's first Celtic rock bands. Combining elements of Cajun, bluegrass, and Celtic music, they created an enormous stir with their upbeat arrangements, Acadian spirit, and roots-based instrumentation, paving the way for all the Celtic bands that were to follow. Their debut album, *1755*, still sounds fresh today. From the topical, humourous "C.B. Buddie" to the bluegrass-oriented instrumental, "La Toune À Louis Arsenault," the band set high standards. The followup album, *Vivre À La Baie*, from 1979, is more rooted in traditional music and features even more adroit playing than their first album. The various members of 1755, which recombined periodically, included Roland Gauvin, Gerry Forest, Pierre Robichaud, Pete Gaudet, Kenneth Saulnier, Donald Boudreau, and Ronald Dupuis.

❋❋❋(❋)   **1755**
1978, reissued 1994 Isba (K 5003)†

> Hallo Joe; C.B. Buddie; Confession; La Toune À Louis Arsenault; Le Monde Qu'On Connait; Maudite Guerre; Rue Dufferin; Boire Ma Bouteille; U.I.C. (Unemployment Insurance Commission); Le Monde A Bien Changé; Geddap Sam; Vie De Fou; Je Chante Pour Toi *36:57*

❋❋❋(❋)✓ **Vivre À La Baie**
1979, reissued 1994 Isba (K 5004)†

> La Gang Arrive; Reel Du 375 Ième; Mon Coin De L'Acadie; Le Jardinier Du Couvent; Southville; Kouchibouguac; Je T'Aime; Vivre À La Baie; Le Pire S'En Vient; J'Ai Passé Toute La Nuit Deboute; Disco Banjo *40:53*

Tarig Abubakar & The Afro-Nubians

NUBIAN ROOTS MUSIC; COMPOSER

Toronto-based Tarig Abubakar hails from Khartoum, Sudan, at the crossroads of African and Arabic culture. Abubakar sings in Arabic, but his music is pan-African, derived from styles as diverse as shaaby-rock from Egypt, Amharic soul from Ethiopia,

rumba-soukous from Zaire, and Sudan's own traditional haqeeba music. Since set-
tling in Toronto, Abubakar has formed the Afro-Nubians, a ten-piece band with players from Ghana, Somalia, Uganda, Kenya, and Zaire. Abubakar fronts the band as
singer and sax player. On *Tour To Africa*, the title track is described in the liner notes
as "a gentle, swaying safari to 45 countries, from Algeria to Zaire." "Unity" is a plea
for pleace and harmony in his homeland. The Afro-Nubians, on this album, are Adam
Solomon, Kobena Acquaa-Harrison, Solomon Hasballa, Eshet Mengesha, Booker T.,
Misara Ghandi, Zafrino, Kobena Rueben, Bishop Okele, Godfrey Sekijoba, Hamad
Ismail, Tarig Tijani, Walid Abdelaziz, Hadi Ahmed, Joseph Ashong, and Kofi Ackah.

❋❋❋   **Tour To Africa**
      1994 Stern's Africa (STCD 1058)

      Tour To Africa; Gorba; Hawiah; Unity; Zinjeah; El Serah; Tum Tum; Jenob El
      Sudan; Gadar; Akwani; Jenob El Sudan *49:56*

John Acorn
FOLK; NATURAL HISTORY; SINGER-SONGWRITER

John Acorn is an Edmonton, Alberta naturalist who has become the host of two popular shows on Canada's Discovery TV cable channel: *The Nature Nut*, a family show
on natural history, and *Twits And Pishers*, a show about bird watching. For the *Nature
Nut* series, he has composed and recorded a series of songs and ditties that are catchy,
folksy, and zany. Kids love them, and you probably will too. This is the only CD in the
guide where you will encounter a song—"Joe Snumm, Fish-At-Large"—that was
written "as a spontaneous expression of sincere admiration for the purity of fish." Use
your kids as an excuse to buy this one for yourself if the title makes you feel self-
conscious.

❋❋❋   **The Nature Nut**
      1994 Great North (SA94631)†

      I'm A Nature Nut; Life Under The Microscope; I Could Be Your Tall Lungwort,
      Baby; Waterbug; There's Nothing Wrong With Frogs; I Saw The Butterflies;
      Telephoto Man; Bird Watching On The Beach; Munching On Aphids; Beetle
      Grabbin' Man; Tracks In The Snow; Joe Snumm, Fish-At-Large; The Ballad Of Bird
      Watcher Betty; Macro Thing *42:26*

Ad Vielle Que Pourra
FRENCH-CANADIAN; ORIGINAL COMPOSITIONS

Ad Vielle Que Pourra is a Quebec group full of surprises. Its hallmark is traditional
French instruments, but Ad Vielle plays music on them that, as the liner notes state,
"is not indigenous to the regions where the instruments come from." They intermix
Parisian waltzes, Breton sea songs, bourrées, gavottes, schottisches, and original compositions with abandon. The name Ad Vielle Que Pourra is a pun—a play on the
French expression *advienne que pourra* ("come what may"). The *vielle* is from *vielle
à roue,* a French instrument commonly known as the hurdy-gurdy.

      The founding members of Ad Vielle are Brussels-born Daniel Thonon, a luthier
who plays an intricately carved hurdy-gurdy he built himself; Alain Leroux, born in

Brittany and a fiddler specializing in traditional Breton, Scottish, and Irish melodies and songs; Clement Demers, an Ontario-born accordionist who learned Québecois tunes while living in Quebec and Cajun tunes while travelling through Louisiana; Luc Thonon, a multi-instrument musician who plays the rare Flemish bagpipes; and Gilles Plante, a Montréal-born flute, recorder, and bagpipe player who went to Brittany to study the music and culture of his ancestors.

Ad Vielle's debut album, *New French Folk Music,* will appeal to those who enjoy the sound of traditional instruments, especially the infrequently-heard hurdy-gurdy. The music is bouncy and subtly flamboyant. On *Come What May* the sound shifts slightly as accordionist Clement Demers leaves the group and is replaced by Jean-Louis Cros on guitar. There's a hint of introspection absent from their debut album. On *Musaïque*, their third album, the introspection disappears and the band is back in full flight. The sound is as infectious as ever, but also fuller. All three albums are marvellous.

✳✳✳✳ **New French Folk Music**
1989 Green Linnet (GLCD 1099)

Schottische Du Stockfish; Malloz Ar Barz Koz O Vervel; Chupad Melen/Hanterdro Tid' Poc'h; L'Agacante/Valse Du Milieu/Valse Du Faucigny; La Pucell D'Ussel; Les Filles De France; Suite De Gavottes Evit Leroux; Bourrées Dans Le Jardin; Polkas Ratées; Valse Des Coquelicots/Java Niaise; Fillettes Des Campagnes; An Dro Pitaouer/An Dro Evit Jakeza; La Malfaissante *52:14*

✳✳✳✳ **Come What May**
1991 Green Linnet (GLCD 1112)

Un Cosaque À Paris; Adagio Des Années Mornes; Evit Gabriel; Kanaouen An-Dud A Vor; Micro-Polka; Valse Minette/Les Patates Ont Germé A St. Amable; Tu Nous Les Kas-Ebarh Toi; Chanson A La Mariée; Laridé D.T./Polka D'Été; Plinn An Enaouer; À St. Malo-Sur-Mer; Le Drao Du Mao; Le Conscrit De Napoléon; Bourée En Ré *51:48*

✳✳✳✳✓ **Musaïque**
1994 Green Linnet (GLCD 4017)

Serre-Moi Plus Fort, Victor/Plant A Cao; An-Avel A Varo; Gavotte "Fair Foot"; Un Québécois À Caracas; Lou Mes De Mai Vendra; J'Ai Vu Boulou, Le Reinhardt Et La Musette; Leve La Jambe Armande; Un Garçon De Mon Village; Andropov/Polka Félix; La Tranchefoie; Javadvielle; La Complainte Des Rengaines *53:47*

Susan Aglukark
First Nations Music; Folk/Country; Singer-Songwriter

"Aglukark is one of Canada's best new artists"—Mitch Potter, *Toronto Star*. Canadian audiences have come to appreciate Inuit performer Susan Aglukark from her televised appearances on musical shows and specials. Her sweet soprano, whether she's singing in English or Inuit, makes you sit up and take notice. She received a Juno in 1995 as "New Solo Artist." The sweetness of her voice, however, is frequently belied by the starkness of the lyrics on her albums *Arctic Rose* and *This Child* which deal with hard topics such as abuse to women and people who become life's casualties. *Arctic Rose*, which received a 1995 Juno as "Music of Aboriginal Canada Recording," closes with what has become Aglukark's signature song—"Amazing Grace" sung in Inuit. *This Child* takes Aglukark a large step forward from the somewhat mundane arrangements on *Arctic Rose*. "The recording is enveloped in layer upon evocative layer of dramatic [Inuit] chants, cascading piano runs and sweeping acoustic rhythms"—Mitch Potter, *Toronto Star*. Aglukark's *Christmas* album capitalizes on her sweet voice, but a curious lack of energy prevents it from becoming a Christmas classic.

✳✳ **[Christmas]**
1993 EMI (E2 7243 8 27989 2 7)

O Come All Ye Faithful; Away In A Manger; It Came Upon A Midnight Clear; Joy To The World; Little Toy Trains; Santa Claus Is Coming To Town/Jingle Bells; The First Noel; Hark The Herald Angels Sing; O Little Town Of Bethlehem; Silent Night, Holy Night *31:39*

✳✳✳ **Arctic Rose**
1994 EMI (E2 7243 8 / 28605 25)†

Arctic Rose; Song Of The Land; Still Running; Wanderin' Child; Learn To Love Yourself; Searching; Anger And Tears; Rollin' On; Mama's Prayers; Amazing Grace *36:46*

✳✳✳✳✓ **This Child**
1995 EMI (E2 7243 8 32075 2 7)†

This Child; Shamaya; Suffer In Silence; O Siem; Dreams For You; Hina Na Ho (Celebration); Kathy I; Pond Inlet; Slippin' Through The Cracks; Breakin' Down; Casualties Of War *48:54*

Jerry Alfred & The Medicine Beat

FIRST NATIONS MUSIC; SINGER-SONGWRITER

A native artist from the Northern Tutchone Nation, Jerry Alfred blends traditional musical styles and chants with contemporary instruments to create songs that sound at once ancient and modern. *Etsi Shon/Grandfather Song* is an album that is accessible to a wide listening audience—reflecting a deep spirituality and communion with the land and its people. Alfred sings lead vocals and plays guitar and traditional drum while his band—The Medicine Beat—fills in with keyboards, accordion, harmonica, and backup vocals. The songs work as meditations that fill you with sky and cloud.

✳✳✳(✳) **Etsi Shon/Grandfather Song**
1994 Jerry Alfred (JA1-1994)†

Generation Hand Down; The Warrior Song; Caribou Stick Gambling Song; Taan Mun/Lake Laberge; The Grandfather Song/Etsi Shon; MacMillan River Love Song; Beginner Gambling Song; The Watchmen; Salaw; A Love Song; Towhata Lake *47:26*

Jenny Allen

FOLK/POP; SINGER-SONGWRITER

With a versatile voice that lends itself to folk, pop, jazz and blues arrangements, Alberta-raised Jenny Allen is a talented singer-songwriter whose lyrics intertwine themselves around her unusual guitar work. Listening to *Something To Say*—produced by Valdy—is a delight. From the hard-edged vulnerability of "Freeway Lines" to the jazz-oriented "Flesh And Bone," to the lonesome "Sail Away," she has created a contemporary folk album that should interest listeners who also enjoy early Joni Mitchell recordings. Allen's slightly countryish voice lingers on in your mind long after the album has finished.

❊❊❊(❊) **Something To Say**
1991 Strange Pagan (SPR 01-CD)†

> Freeway Lines; Seabird; Flesh And Bone; Sail Away; Shades Of Blue; So This Is Love; Voices; Over From The Start; Stuck With Me; Something To Say; Walking Away; The Fire *42:44*

Robert Amyot

FRENCH-CANADIAN; FOLK

Montreal-born Robert Amyot, who records in France, is a student of the historic material of Brittany, France, and Quebec. A piper who went abroad to study, he encountered *Gallo* traditional singing (a traditional chant from Higher-Brittany) which reminded him of the songs of his Quebec childhood. On his return to Quebec he met Danielle Martineau and Michel Faubert who introduced him to additional historic Quebec songs. On *Sur La Vignolon*, on the French Auvidis label, he sings several of these songs, and plays pipe, accompanied by French pianist and accordionist Albert Tovi. This highly satisfying recording is well worth seeking out.

❊❊❊❊ **Sur La Vignolon**
1990 Auvidis (B 6740)†

> La Veillée; Peine D'Amour; Les Filles D'Amérique; Margot Fringue; Sur Le Joli Son Du Verre; Le Petit Moine; Adieu, Je M'En Vas; Le Mai; Rencontré Mine; Sur La Vignolon; Le Curé Bon Garçon; Le Petit Moulin; Il M'A Tant Fait Plaisir; Le Rhume; Le Charbonnier *52:44*

Ancient Cultures

LATIN-AMERICAN FOLK; TRADITIONAL INSTRUMENTS

Canadian music fans are indeed fortunate. With a national culture that embraces cultural diversity, we are continually treated to the musical traditions of citizens who have moved to Canada from other countries. And, inevitably, native-born Canadians join forces with newly-arrived Canadians to form musical collaborations. Ancient Cultures is such a collaboration—a group that plays Latin American folk music.

Ancient Cultures, based in Vancouver, is composed of a mixed group of musicians. Alberto San Martin, Carlos Cortes, and Angel Araos come from Chile, but their musical roots are in jazz, folk, and classical music respectively. Fito Garcia comes from Guatemala and arranges and plays salsa music. Edward Henderson is from Vancouver Island where he grew up playing folk and classical music. Carlos Galindo Leal is from Mexico and has many years experience playing Spanish and Latin American music. Their debut album, *Acoustic Mirage/Espejismo Acustico*, combines their musical backgrounds into a deft, understated, weave of Latin American music. It is a beautiful, introspective offering. By their second album, *El Camino Real*, the group achieves full maturity. Awarded a Juno in 1994 as "Best World Beat Recording," the album displays more creative energy and a clearer sense of direction. This is a fine, sure, album that should be on every folk-music lover's play list. And for those who like Christmas albums with a twist, *The Miracle of Christmas*, which features the Vancouver Chamber Choir along with the Latin American folk instruments, is an album that is irresistible.

❋❋❋(❋) **Acoustic Mirage / Espejismo Acustico**
1992 Invincible (INVCD150)

Ventolera; Vibrations; In The Beginning/Cochabamba/Santa Cruz; The Weavers/The Water Is On; Berlin Colony; The Dream Elsewhere; Clearcut; Sustainable; Song For A Princess; Pampa Lirima; Susurro; Inner Waves; Estudio Para Zampoña; La Partida; Shattered Dreams; ¡Ay! ¡Ay! ¡Ay! *46:22*

❋❋❋❋✓ **El Camino Real**
1993 Invincible (INVCD057)

El Camino Real; Jungle Beat; Dolencias; Andean Dance In G Minor; Rio Apurimac; Persecucion De Pancho Villa; Estudio Para Charango; Serenade; La Guacamaya; Solitude; Jachauru; Ramis; Mama Chilindra; Juan Jose; Sencillo; Tinku; El Condor Pasa *51:03*

❋❋❋(❋) **The Miracle Of Christmas**
1994 GRD (GRDCD060)

We Three Kings; Deck The Hall/Christmas Bells In Summer; Angels We Have Heard On High; Reyes Morenos; O Holy Night; What Child Is This; Patapan; Bolivian Carol; Ring Christmas Bells; A La Nanita Nana; Los Reyes De Oriente; Niño Lindol; Away In A Manger; Pascua Linda; The Huron Carol; Silent Night *49:03*

Anderson & Brown

Folk/Celtic/New Age; Singer-Songwriters

Based in Stratford, Ontario, Anderson & Brown are a folk duo featuring Mary Anderson on harp and Ken Brown on guitar, flute, and vocals. Together they explore the lyrical edges of the traditional Celtic repertoire. Their work is never rushed or frenzied—this is not step-dancing music. Instead they work their way inside the loveliness and beauty of traditional music, presenting it in fresh, often mesmerizing, arrangements. On *Off On A Tangent*, they state that "like many Canadians, we were not brought up in the Celtic music tradition—we drifted into this music and fell madly in love." The album is primarily instrumental, with harp and guitar and occasionally harp and flute. Brown's soft, gentle voice accords well with Anderson's harping. *Crimson* captures Anderson & Brown in an adventurous mood. In addition to the traditional repertoire, they introduce original compositions such as "Tangent's Delight"—"one hundred and fifty pounds of Newfoundland puppy greeting the morning with boundless enthusiasm is something you just have to experience"—plus original arrangements of the poems "The Bells Of London" and "The Jabberwock." *Alone With A Dream* continues their exploration of traditional material while adding their own compositions and arrangements. As on their previous albums, there's a timeless, unhurried quality to the performances that encourages you to drift into the inner sanctum of the melodies. If you feel life is too rushed and hurried, queue up an Anderson & Brown CD, prop up your feet, and immerse yourself in these musical zephyrs.

See also Anderson & Meis; Mary Anderson.

❀❀❀(❀)　　**Off On A Tangent**
　　　　　　1990 Anderson & Brown (A&B101CD)

> Rusty Gully; The Blarney Pilgrim/The Rights Of Man; Loch Tay Boat Song (Harold Bolton); Lochaber No More/Gravel Walk; Off She Goes; Snowy Breasted Pearl; Farewell To Aberdeen/Morgan Magan; I Will Go; My Lagan Love/Lark In The Clear Air/Whelan's Jig; Eleanor Plunkett/The Flowing Tide; Willafiord; Farewell/Massacre Of Glencoe; Caitlin Triall/Morrison's Jig *58:06*

❀❀❀(❀)　　**Crimson**
　　　　　　1991 Anderson & Brown (A&B102CD)

> Tangent's Delight; The Bells Of London; Ned On The Hill; Tread Softly; One Lone Flight; Peggy Gordon; The Jabberwock; Reel De Ti-Jean; Ye Banks And Braes; Friendship; In The Bleak Mid-Winter *48:15*

❀❀❀(❀)　　**Alone With A Dream**
　　　　　　1994 Anderson & Brown (A&B103CD)

> Silkie; Virgin Carol; Fandango; Winter's Touched My Heart; Alone With A Dream; Full Moon Pacific; The Rights Of Man; Victim Of War; Lament; Waltz—Late Afternoon Late; Lord Franklin's Lament; Barham Down *49:13*

Anderson & Meis

CELTIC HARP

Ontario harpists Mary Anderson and Joanne Meis combine their talents in harp duets on *Celtic Spirit*, an easy-paced, intimate, collection of Celtic and traditional music that includes "Scarborough Fair," "Down By The Sally Gardens," "The Lark In The Morning," "Barbara Allen," and "The Ash Grove."

See also Anderson & Brown; Mary Anderson.

❀❀❀　　**Celtic Spirit**
　　　　　1992 Oasis (NHCD 201)

> Scarborough Fair; Brian Boru's March; Down By The Sally Gardens; Lark In The Morning; The South Wind; Barbara Allen; Early One Morning; Ash Grove; Gus Breo; The Star Of County Down; Garten Mother's Lullaby *44:09*

Mary Anderson
CELTIC HARP

Mary Anderson is an Ontario Celtic harpist who, in recent years, has teamed up with Ken Brown to form Anderson & Brown. She has also produced solo recordings: *Flowering Trees* and *Ballade ... Voyage*. Both albums feature Celtic and traditional material played *adagio*, squeezing every nuance out of the melodies. The result is haunting, beautiful, and relaxing, but these are not albums for those who like their Celtic music on the bouncy side.

See also Anderson & Brown; Anderson & Meis.

❋❋❋ **Flowering Trees**
1988 Anderson & Brown (FT001-CD)

Cosmic Cord; O'Carolyn's Welcome; Planxty Elora; Blackbird; Paul's Song; Munster Cloak; Humorous Of Ballyloughlin; King's Dance; Dance Of The Circle; Rathdrum Fair; Flowering Trees; Buncloudy; Wolfies Hay Day; Carrik Fergus *42:59*

❋❋❋ **Ballade ... Voyage**
1991 Anderson & Brown (A&B 201CD)

Old Chelsea Dawn: My Love Is Like A Red, Red Rose/Lark In The Clear Air; The Mill Race: Carrickfergus/Brink Of The White Rocks/The Parting Glass; Waterfall Glade: Munster Cloak/Wolfie's Farewell; Morning At Dunn's Bridge: She Moved Through The Fair/Childgrove/Ye Banks And Braes *60:37*

Faron Andrei
FOLK/POP; SINGER-SONGWRITER

"For me, a song is like an act of mercy. It comes when it is most needed and touches the soul"—Faron Andrei. A songwriter for more than fifteen years and a guitarist for more than twenty, Saskatchewan-based Andrei is a performer, guitar teacher, and session musician. *The Healing Season* is an acoustic-based album featuring Andrei's spiritually-oriented lyrics alongside his accomplished guitar licks. Highlights include "The Healing Season," "Coming Down The Road," "I'm Feeling Better," "You've Been On My Mind," and "Take Care Of Each Other."

❋❋❋ **The Healing Season**
1995 HeartSong (95501CD)†

The Healing Season; Coming Down The Road; I'm Not Turning; I'm Feeling Better; Turnaround; You've Been On My Mind; I Can Hear Someone Calling; It Doesn't Matter; Danny; Take Care Of Each Other *38:38*

The Angstones
FOLK WITH A EUROPEAN AND MIDDLE EASTERN FLAVOUR; SINGER-SONGWRITERS

The Angstones, an Ottawa band made up of musicians who also play in Fat Man Waving and Six Mile Bridge, mix European and American folk music with zany lyrics and a jumping beat on *Kommen Een Der Karz*, their first CD. The band then mixes the rhythms of Eastern Europe and the Middle East on *When Ahab Met Moishe*. The cover of the album is a takeoff of a 1950's movie poster and the liner notes describe the album as "the story of two men caught in the whirlwinds of a part of the world where no one can be trusted, let alone someone from another race. Moishe, a Jewish hockey writer for the Papaslavian Free Press, and Ahab, a waiter in an Arabic restaurant, find themselves entangled in the web of an international smuggling ring." The musicians are Peter Kiesewalter on reeds and accordion, Kurt Walther on guitar, Rob Frayne on sax, John Geggie on bass, and Ian Mackie on drums.

See also Fat Man Waving; Six Mile Bridge

✻✻✻   **Kommen Een Der Karz**
        1992 Canal (CANAL-256CD)†

> Kommen Een Der Karz; Papaslavian Variations; Old Dan Tucker; Hiroshima Sunset; Peasant Dance; Wedding In Babishjac; Maison Lafayette House; Digital Bulgarian Folkdance; Papa And I; On The Trail To Kozatzke; Swords Of Bronze *45:35*

✻✻✻   **When Ahab Met Moishe**
        1994 Canal (CANAL 265CD)†

> The Wild Boar; Breakfast In Istanbul; Ay, Ay, Ay; Ega; Wasabi Breath; Kopanitsa; The Line; Black Sea Café; Jaromir Jagr; When Ahab Met Moishe; Angst For Nothing *48:33*

Anoosh

WORLDBEAT JAZZ; ORIGINAL COMPOSITIONS

Montreal world-beat band Anoosh blends Middle-Eastern Armenian roots with North American music to create a jazz-oriented sound based on instruments as diverse as tabla, djembé, sax, flutes, guitars, ud (lute), and drums. The band has performed at venues such as the Montreal Jazz Festival, the Vancouver Folk Festival, WOMAD, and the Hamilton Earth Song Festival. The bouncy numbers on *Kess Kiss Passe*, such as the title song and tracks like "Sambra," "Finchan," and "Chameau" are sure to attract new fans to the infectious rhythms of the band.

✻✻✻   **Kess Kiss Passe**
        1991 Hima Hoss (HH-1191)

> Kess Kiss Passe; Samra; Mart Tch Kide; Mertchouni Bess; Ouzem Tchouzem; Banat Iskandaria; Finchan; Tchene Tche; Oushatsan; Chameau; Fayda Tchiga; Guessen Te; Kess Kiss Passe (Instrumental) *50:33*

Anthologies

COLLECTIONS BY VARIOUS ARTISTS, ARRANGED ALPHABETICALLY BY ALBUM TITLE

Anthologies—collections of recordings by various artists—can be either a good idea, or a bad one, depending on the quality of the collection. When they succeed, they can introduce you to interesting artists and types of music you've never heard before. If you're new to fiddle music, for instance, a good collection of fiddle pieces by various artists gives you a sense of the genre and the names of some artists you might like to pursue on solo albums. Anthologies also highlight performers who sometimes aren't available on compact disc, either because their work pre-dates the technology or because their careers haven't yet reached the point where they can afford to issue a CD.

A problem with some anthologies is that the contents are of mixed quality, with outstanding performances featured alongside lesser efforts. Among the worst are the "tribute" albums—a collection of artists paying tribute to a well-known songwriter. In most cases, you're much better off just collecting the music of the person being "honoured."

Some anthologies emphasize types of music, such as First Nations music, while others emphasize regions. The Canadian Maritime provinces, in particular, are a rich source of anthologized albums. There are also splendid historical collections, such as the incomparable Gesser material—*Canada: A Folksong Portrait* and *Folklore de Montréal*—that are essential items for every folklorist.

Anthologies frequently provide good starting points for anyone new to particular types of folk music. They also make good gifts for friends and relatives whose tastes you're unsure of.

Another Time: The Songs Of Newfoundland is a concept album, designed to feature traditional songs from Newfoundland, re-done by contemporary artists. Although they represent some of Newfoundland's leading musicians, there's a slightly artificial feeling about the result. Some vital spark is missing.

❊❊(❊)   **Another Time: The Songs Of Newfoundland**
1991 Pigeon Inlet (PIPCD-7326)

The Old Polina *(Fergus O'Byrne)*; Kelligrew's Soiree *(Anita Best)*; Squid Jiggin Ground *(Dermot O'Reilly)*; She's Like The Swallow *(Pamela Morgan)*; Tickle Cove Pond *(Ron Hynes)*; Jack Was Every Inch A Sailor *(Kim Stockwood)*; Now I'm Sixty Four *(Dave Panting)*; Hard, Hard Times *(Jim Joyce)*; Lukey's Boat *(Pamela Morgan; Anita Best)*; Petty Harbour Bait Skiff *(Roger Howse)*; The Ryans And The Pittmans *(Baxter Wareham)*; Ode To Newfoundland *(Vonnie Barron; Esther Squires)* 40:50

Atlantic Fiddles is an exception to the general rule that anthologies are frequently not as satisfying as solo albums. This outstanding collection of fiddle music by some of the greatest contemporary practitioners of the art doesn't have a weak cut on it. It is also the only current source of recordings on compact disc by artists like Brenda Stubbert and Carl MacKenzie. A great album that deserves a spot on your CD rack!

❊❊❊❊✓   **Atlantic Fiddles**
1994 Atlantica (02 77657 50222 26)

The Honourable Mrs. Moules'/The Merry Lads Of Air *(Dave MacIsaac)*; Willie Kennedy's/Traditional/Smiths Delight/Homeward Bound *(Brenda Stubbert)*; The Willow Tree/Sutherland's/Donegal *(Howie MacDonald)*; Miss Lyall's/Miss Lyall's/Sandy Cameron's/Carigon Broach *(Ashley MacIsaac)*; Autumn Leaf *(Eddie Poirier)*; Lauchie Stubbert's/Cheticamp Jig/Royal Wedding Jig *(Tara Lynn Tousenard)*; The Earl Of Jura *(Lloyd MacDonald)*; The Drunken Landlady/Shearing The Sheep *(Kim Vincent)*; Kantra To El Arish/Traditional/Christi Campbell/Mabou Coal Mines/Alan Davidson/Traditional *(Kyle MacNeil; Lucy MacNeil)*; Beautiful Lake Ainslie/Miss Grace Menzies/Mr. Bernard/Compliments To Buddy MacMaster *(Jerry Holland)*; Fram Apon Him/Miss Catherine Ann Lamey's/Charlie Hunter's/Peggy's Jig *(Richard Wood)*; Festival Reel/Jeff's Tune/Meech Lake Breakdown/McCormack's Breakdown *(Emile Benoit)*; Governor General *(Ned Landry)*; Hills Of Glenorchy/The Rovers Return/Stan's Jig *(Donny LeBlanc)*; Glen Fiddich/Neil Gows Fiddle/Celtic Ceilidh/

John Campbell's Reel/Miss Mary Stuart Of Derculich *(Carl MacKenzie)*; John Campbells/Ann Moirs Birthday/Lady Georgina Campbell/Angus On The Turnpike/ Sheehan's Reel *(Natalie MacMaster)*; La Reel Du Brae *(Eddy Arsenault) 61:12*

The Best Cree Fiddle Players Of James Bay will delight the collector of Canadian fiddle music. The Cree of James Bay have developed a fiddle tradition of their own with a unique style and sound and this collection brings together a representative sample of that tradition. This album received a Porcupine Award in the "Native Canadian" category in 1993.

❋❋❋❋✓   **The Best Cree Fiddle Players Of James Bay**
1993 Hughboy Records [no catalogue number]

Father's Reel *(Roger Weapenicappo)*; The 8th of January *(Mathew Mukash)*; Wemindji Bridge Reel *(Bobby Georgekish)*; Soldiers Joy *(Malcolm House)*; James Bay Doings *(Sinclair Cheechoo)*; Wemindji Reel *(Clarence Louttit)*; Civil Service Breakdown *(David Sam)*; Big Muskeg Reel *(Peter Bosum)*; Mamoweedow Minshtukch *(James Stewart)*; Soldiers Joy *(All) 26:36*

The Best Of Saskatchewan Indian Cultural Centre is a collection of traditional and contemporary pow-wow and dance music of Northern Plains First Nations. Anyone seeking a deeper understanding of First Nations traditions will find this album essential. The excellent liner notes provide an invaluable introduction to the music and its continuing evolution and development.

❋❋❋❋✓   **The Best Of Saskatchewan Indian Cultural Centre**
1993 Saskatchewan Indian Cultural Centre [no catalogue number]

Women's Fancy *(Edmund Bull; Red Bull)*; Crow Hop *(Elk's Whistle)*; Traditional *(Whitefish Jrs.)*; Grass Dance *(Whitefish Jrs.)*; Eagle Whistle Song *(Hawk River)*; Intertribal *(Hawk River)*; Darling Don't Cry *(Red Bull)*; Intertribal *(Dance To Red Bull)*; Oh My Sweetheart *(Grey Eagle)*; Fancy Dance *(Northern Eagle)*; White Swan Blues *(Mosquito Singers)*; Macho Man *(Mosquito Singers)*; Intertribal *(Stoney Eagle)*; Men's Traditional *(Little Island Cree)*; Theme Song *(Little Island Cree)*; Intertribal *(Southern Cree)*; Intertribal *(Southern Cree)*; Going Home Broken Hearted *(Elk's Whistle) 74:54*

Bittersweet Canada: Songs Of The New Depression is an anthology of songs that focus on the "hard times" currently being experienced by a large number of Canadians. The idea behind the anthology is solid, but the result is disappointing. With a few exceptions, such as the songs by Kate & Anna McGarrigle, Eileen McGann, and Cate Friesen, most of the songs are not particularly gripping or memorable, despite their message. This is a good collection for music libraries that provide theme material, but individual collectors are better off concentrating on solo albums by the artists they like.

❋❋(❋)   **Bittersweet Canada: Songs Of The New Depression**
1992 Word Of Mouth (WOMCD-1005-2)†

The Great Depression Of '92 *(Norm Hacking)*; First Signs Of Spring *(Grievous Angels)*; Petite Annonce Amoureuse *(Kate & Anna McGarrigle)*; A Ship Is Sinking *(Jim Payne; Christina Smith)*; Litany Of The Saints *(Lazy Grace)*; My Name Is Martha *(Rhythm Activism)*; Windigo *(Eileen McGann)*; Saying Goodbye To PEI *(Kevin J. Arsenault)*; A Mile Outside Of Kirkland *(Grievous Angels)*; Caroline (Ode To Rural Manitoba) *(Cat Eat Dog)*; Wrong Side Of The Hill *(Great Western*

Orchestra)*; Think Of Me *(Cate Friesen)*; Kira *(Diana Braithwaite)*; Eastern Avenue *(Lazy Grace)*; Surplus Value *(Jamie Dopp)*; Lost My Way *(Kathleen Yearwood)*; Canada's Sweetheart (The Karen Magnussen Song) *(Swinghammer)* 62:34

Canada: A Folksong Portrait / Un portrait folklorique provides a splendid collection for the folklorist or anyone interested in the historical folk music of Canada. Originally compiled by Samuel Gesser for the Folkways label, this important and long out-of-print collection of Canadian folk music has been reissued on compact disc on the Mercury label, courtesy of Smithsonian-Folkways. The 94 songs in the anthology span the entire country from the Maritimes to British Columbia and the Yukon. The selections include songs by native people that offer glimpses of First Nations music as it existed before the influence of European instruments and singing styles. *Canada: A Folksong Portrait* also captures the voices of several seminal Canadian artists— Alan Mills, Wade Hemsworth, Tom Kines, Karen James, Stanley G. Triggs, Jacques Labrecque, and Jean Carignan—rarely heard today. One of the many jewels in this three-CD boxed set is Hemsworth's rendition of his "Little Black Fly Song." Because several of the songs are field recordings of ordinary people singing songs they remember, some of the tracks are rough-edged. This is music to study and appreciate for its historical significance as much as for its intrinsic entertainment. The extensive, and essential, liner notes complement the music. A must purchase for the serious collector as well as for any budding folk artist looking for interesting material. This collection received a Golden Porcupine award in 1994, and its editor, Samuel Gesser, was inducted into the Porcupine Awards Hall of Fame for his lifetime achievements in the field of Canadian folk music.

✳✳✳✳✓   **Canada: A Folksong Portrait / Un Portrait Folklorique**
1994 Mercury / Smithsonian-Folkways (769748000-2)

CD1: Lord Gordon Reel *(Kenneth Faulkner)*; The Squid-Jiggin' Ground *(Alan Mills)*; I'm Going To Get Married *(Mrs. Edward Gallagher)*; The Bad Girl's Lament *(Wade Hemsworth)*; Chin Music *(Angelo Dornan)*; 'N Uair Nighidh Tu (When You Wash); À La Claire Fontaine *(Hélène Baillargeon; Alan Mills)*; Le Petit Moine *(Allan Kelly)*; Boys Of The Island *(Alan Mills)*; Lady Gowrie *(Fred Redden)*; The False Knight Upon The Road *(Edmund Henneberry)*; Lots Of Fish In Bonavist' Harbor *(Ken Peacock)*; Anti-Confederation Song *(Alan Mills)*; Pretty Susan *(Angelo Dornan)*; The Welcome Table *(Charles Owen)*; Old Tune *(Edmund Henneberry)*; Galop De La Malbaie *(Joseph Jean; Alfred Jean)*; Laquelle Marieons-Nous *(Jacques Labrecque)*; Chanson De Mesonges *(Mme William Beavan; Monique Beauchamps)*; Auprès De Ma Blonde *(Hélène Baillargeon; Alan Mills)*; Violon En Discorde *(Jean Carignan)*; Tous Les Gens Du Plaisir *(Mme William Beavan)*; À La Claire Fontaine/ Ah Tu Danses Bien Madeleine *(Mme Jean-Louis Audet)*; Vive La Canadienne *(Alan Mills)*; She Was Poor But She Was Honest *(Derek Lamb)*; A Young Man Lived In Belfast Town *(Tom Kines)*; The Wee, Wee German Lairdie *(Max Dunbar)*; Horch Was Kommt Von Draussen Rein? *(Erika Vopel; Elsa Vopel)*; Gey Ich Mir Shpatzirin *(Raasche Singerman; Tassy Singerman)*; Tell Me, Tell Me *(West Indian Society Of McGill University)*; Me'Savo Va Zi Var Dous O Tont En-Dro *(Jacques Conan)*; Pastoral *(Lucie de Vienne Blanc)*; À Paris, Sur Le Petit Pont *(Jacques Labrecque)*; Danse Carre *(Aldor Morin)* 68:25

CD2: Shining Birch Tree *(Wade Hemsworth)*; The Shantyboys' Alphabet *(Sam Campsall)*; When The Shantyboy Comes Down *(Jim Doherty)*; The Gypsy Daisy *(O.J. Abbott)*; My Irish Polly *(Tom Kines)*; Johnny Doyle *(Joe Kelly)*; The Franklin Expedition *(Wade Hemsworth)*; The Jam On Gerry's Rocks *(Tom Brandon)*; The Murder of F.C. Benwell *(Lamont Tilden)*; The Foot Of The Mountain Brow *(Tom*

Kines); The Poor Little Girls Of Ontario *(Mrs. Hartley Minnifie)*; The Black Fly Song *(Wade Hemsworth)*; An Indian Sat In His Little Bark Canoe *(Mrs. Tom Sullivan)*; The Northern Trappers Rendezvous *(Loewen Orchestra)*; The Little Old Sod Shanty *(Alan Mills)*; O Bury Me Not On The Lone Prairie *(Herbert Sills)*; Barbara Allen *(Molly Galbraith)*; Johnny Sands *(Grace Carr)*; Our Ukraine *(Paul Konoplenko)*; Chanson De Riel *(Joseph Gaspar Jeannotte)*; Un Canadien Errant *(Alan Mills)*; When The Ice Worms Nest Again *(Loewen Orchestra)*; Funky Jim *(Mel Bowker)*; The Alberta Homestead *(Alan Mills)*; A Poor Lone Girl In Saskatchewan *(Anne Halderman)*; Saskatchewan *(Jim Young)* 70:56

CD3: The Oda G. *(Stanley G. Triggs)*; The Dark-Eyed Sailor *(Karen James)*; Pretty Peggy O *(Barry Hall)*; So Long To The Kicking Horse Canyon *(Stanley G. Triggs)*; The Klondike Gold Rush *(Alan Mills)*; The Velvet Band *(Stanley G. Triggs)*; Swedish Melody *(Barry Hall)*; Land of Treasure *(The Doukhobors)*; The Lookout In The Sky *(Stanley G. Triggs)*; Willie Moore *(Barry Hall)*; The Story of Weldon Chan *(Karen James)*; Lake of Crimson *(Stanley G. Triggs)*; War Dance *(William Paul; Marin Sack; John Knockwood)*; Hunting Black Bear *(Sebastian MacKenzie)*; I Hunt With My Sons *(Joseph MacKenzie)*; Lullabye *(Dorothy Francis)*; Victory Song *(Mrs. Roderick Thomas)*; The Whipping Song *(Gertrude Murray)*; War Song (World War II) *(George Nicotine)*; Warrior's Death Song (For Sitting Bull); Grass Dance Song; Owl Dance *(Adam Delaney; Wallace Delaney)*; Lucky Stone Song *(One Gun)*; War Song *(Wilfred Calf Robe; Albert Scalp Lock)*; Wolf Song *(Billy Assu)*; Wolf Song *(Mungo Martin)*; Headdress Song *(Mungo Martin)*; Little Woman Doctor Song *(Mary Wamiss)*; Baby Song *(Dan Cramer)*; Children's Game *(Kasugat; Ishmatuk)*; Bird Imitations *(Harry Gibbons)*; I Sing About A Dance *(Uluyok; Tutinat)*; Before We Came To Religion *(Eevaloo)*; Girl's Game *(Angutnal; Matee)* 70:53

Canadian Fiddle is a pleasant anthology of fiddle music. Some of the material sounds as if it has been remastered from 78's or vinyl. Unfortunately the absence of liner notes prevents the collection from achieving its potential as an introduction to the artists and their historical impact.

❋❋❋   **Canadian Fiddle**
        [no date]   Holborne (HCD 3302)

Mom's Waltz *(Johnny Mooring)*; Joys Of Quebec *(June Eikhard)*; Little Burnt Potato *(Johnny Mooring)*; Crooked Stove Pipe *(June Eikhard)*; Blue Skirt Waltz *(June Eikhard)*; Lightning Hornpipe *(Graham Townsend)*; St. Ann's Reel *(Stan Rodgers)*; Sugar In The Gourd *(Vic Mullen)*; Morning Star Waltz *(Bill Guest)*; Medley Of Antigonish Polkas *(Winston "Scotty" Fitzgerald)*; Westphal Waltz *(Vic Mullen)*; Pat Leonard's Breakdown *(Reg Hill)*; Buckingham Reel *(Graham Townsend)*; Highland Jig *(June Eikhard)*; Little Judique Reel *(Joe Murphy)*; Alex And Maureen's Two Step *(Graham Townsend)*; The Devil's Dream *(Reg Hill)*; Carol Kennedy's Waltz *(Johnny Mooring)*; Mrs. Douglas Henderson Strathspey *(Winston "Scotty" Fitzgerald)* 41:38

Children Of The World, according to the liner notes, "is a compilation of some of Native Canada's best music." Featuring contemporary recording artists such as Kashtin, Don Ross, Shingoose, and Willie Dunn, the album spotlights several contemporary performers. A good introductory album.

❋❋❋(❋)   **Children Of The World**
          1994 Musicor (PPFC-2023)

Cree Grass Dance *(Gerry Saddleback)*; The First Ride *(Don Ross)*; Spirit Wars *(Don Ross)*; August On The Island *(Don Ross)*; Indian Time *(Shingoose)*; Nowhere Tonight *(Shingoose)*; Pakuakumit *(Kashtin)*; Tshinanu *(Kashtin)*; Sumac Nuista

(Willie Dunn); Little Charlie *(Willie Dunn)*; The Pacific (Excerpt) *(Willie Dunn)*; Children Of The World *(Susan Aglukark; Willie Dunn; Fara; Don Ross; Shingoose)*; Messages *(Various)* 40:44

Close To The Floor is another of those anthologies that works. With a focus on Newfoundland dance music, the album is a merry romp through accordion and fiddle sets by some of today's best dance-music performers. Great for your step-dancing practise and guaranteed to put a smile on your face even when you're driving home through rush-hour traffic.

❋❋❋❋✓ **Close To The Floor: Newfoundland Dance Music**
1992 Pigeon Inlet (PIP CD 7327)

Mac Master's Tune/Herb Reid's Tune *(Baxter Wareham)*; Kissing Dance Medley *(Figgy Duff)*; Midnight Waltz *(Minnie White)*; Le Reel De La Pistroli/Arriving To St. John's *(Emile Benoit)*; Arriving To St. John's *(The Crowd)*; Bridgett's Reel/Jim Hodder's Reel *(Tickle Harbour)*; Strip The Willow *(Ron Felix)*; Half Penny Reel *(Ray Johnson)*; Up The Pond *(The Quidi Vidi Ceili Band)*; I Got A Bonnet Trimmed With Blue *(Nellie Musseau)*; The Growling Old Man *(Joseph Aucoin)*; Running The Goat *(Frank Maher)*; The Portuguese Waltzes *(Art Stoyles)*; Set Dance Tunes *(Rufus Guinchard)*; Centennial Highway Reel *(Red Island)*; The Four Poster Bed *(The Wonderful Grand Band)* 48:32

Folklore de Montréal / Montreal Folklore, like *Canada: A Folksong Portrait*, is a vital Gesser collection. When Samuel Gesser collected Canadian folk music for the Folkways label in the 1950's and 60's, he amassed a large amount of material by performers based in his native Montreal for the Folkways label. Analekta has reissued a two-CD boxed set of this collection as *Folklore de Montreal / Montreal Folklore*, with Gesser material licensed from Smithsonian-Folkways. While both Gesser collections are similar in concept and sound, this set is more tuneful—more of the selections are performed by professionals. The anthology also contains a short poem read by a young Leonard Cohen. A must for serious collectors.

❋❋❋❋✓ **Folklore de Montréal / Montreal Folklore**
1994 Analekta / Smithsonian-Folkways (AN 2 9221-2)

CD1: Sun Dance Chant *(Marius Barbeau)*; Noël Huron (The Huron Carol) *(Alan Mills)*; Au Chant De L'Alouette *(Hélène Baillargeon; Alan Mills)*; Sur Le Bord De La Seine *(Jacques Labrecque)*; Le Songe *(Alain Grandbois)*; The Fair Maid On The Shore *(Karen James)*; The Barsted King Of England *(Derek Lamb)*; General Wolfe *(Alan Mills)*; Reel With Harmonica And Spoons (Reel Avec Harmonica Et Cuillères) *(Robert Beavan)*; Le Mariage Anglais *(Marius Barbeau)*; La Fille Maigre *(Anne Hébert)*; Nous N'Irons Plus Au Bois *(Mme Jean-Louis Audet)*; Le Papier D'Éping' *(Karen James)*; Paper Of Pins *(Karen James)*; Daniel O'Connell *(Tom Kines)*; Pis Ote-Toé Donc! *(Mme William Beavan)*; Montreal *(A.M. Klein)*; Travelers' Reel (Reel Du Voyageur) *(Jean Carignan)*; Un Canadien Errant *(Alan Mills)*; Lord Randall *(Max Dunbar)*; The Miner's Dream Of Home *(Derek Lamb)*; The Parting Glass *(Tom Kines)*; Le Roi Louys *(Jacques Labrecque)*; Ti-Jean And The Devil *(Jean Carignan; Alan Mills)* 58:58

CD2: Reel Du Bon Vieux Temps (Old Time Reel) *(Jean Carignan)*; À La Claire Fontaine *(Jacques Labrecque)*; En Passant Par Le Bois *(Lucie De Vienne Blanc)*; L'Ombre Rouge *(Rina Lasnier)*; Greensleeves *(Barry Hall)*; The Sun Rises Bright In France *(Max Dunbar)*; I Don't Want To Play In Your Yard *(Derek Lamb)*; J'Ai Tant Dansé, J'Ai Tant Sauté! *(Mme Jean-Louis Audet)*; Les Vieux (The Elders) *(Leonard Cohen)*; Tum-Balalaika *(Raasche Singerman; Tassy Singerman)*; Komm Lieber Mai

(Erika Vopel; Elsa Vopel); Lou Bailero *(Lucie De Vienne Blanc)*; Chumm Mit I D'Berge *(Fritz Liechti)*; Son Ar Martolod Yaouank (The Young Sailor's Song) *(Conan Family)*; Khalliha'Ala-Allah *(George Sawaya)*; El Sol Y La Luna *(Karen James)*; Mrs. Jacob *(Caribbean Chorus of McGill University)*; Voici Venir Le Temps *(Gilles Hénault)*; Reel *(Robert Beavan)*; Son Voile Qui Volait *(Mme William Beavan)*; Little Maggie *(Barry Hall)*; Cod Liver Oil *(Tom Kines)*; Reel Du Pendu (Hangman's Reel) *(Jean Carignan; Pete Seeger)*; I Went To The Market *(Hélène Baillargeon; Alan Mills)*; Donkey Riding *(Wade Hemsworth)*; Road To Grand'mere *(Art Samuels)*; À Paris, Sur Le Petit Pont *(Jacques Labrecque)*; Les Fraises Et Les Framboises *(Aldor Morin)*; La Bastringue *(Aldor Morin)* 57:53

The Gathering: A Compilation Of Toronto World Music won a Juno award in 1992 for "Best World Beat Recording." This collection makes a good starter CD for anyone venturing into "world" music because it offers a range of artistic styles and a brief introduction to each group in the liner notes. The album includes tracks by Mother Tongue, Nu Black Nation, and The Flying Bulgar Klezmer Band.

❄❄❄(❄)✓ The Gathering: A Compilation Of Toronto World Music
1991 Gathering Productions [no catalogue number]

Bellema *(Mother Tongue)*; Mishomis *(Leland Bell)*; Respect 1 *(Nu Black Nation)*; Arpa Ektum *(Dostlar)*; El Brujo *(Ramiro's Latin Orchestra)*; Rock A Talk *(Special Ice)*; Tsoga *(Siyakha)*; Hora Hora Hora *(The Flying Bulgar Klezmer Band)*; Father It's Time *(Joseph Maviglia)*; Hoy Vive El Recuerdo *(Banda Brava)*; Mahal Kita *(Dante)* 51:38

Golden Fiddle is a fiddle collection that is great for the listening and poor for the learning. The absence of any liner notes can only leave you guessing at the focus of the collection and the background of some of the performers. A pity, because it contains some excellent fiddling.

❄❄❄ Golden Fiddle
[no date] Condor (CD 501)

Angus Campbell *(Graham Townsend)*; Rosebud Of Avondale *(Eleanor Townsend)*; Salt Water Jig *(Bill Sawyer)*; Maple Sugar *(Bunty Petrie)*; St. Patrick's Jig *(Carl Elliott)*; Golden Wedding *(Carl Elliott)*; Smash The Window *(Bill Sawyer)*; Siege Of Innis *(Eddie Poirier)*; Belfast Reel *(Johnny Wilmot)*; Fuddle Duddle Hornpipe *(Chuck Joyce)*; Waylon's Breakdown *(Rick Cormier)*; High Level Hornpipe *(Eddie Poirier)*; Scottish Medley *(Eddie Poirier)*; McDowell's Breakdown *(Eleanor Townsend)*; The Waltz You Saved For Me *(Carl Elliott)*; Irish Washerwoman *(Bill Sawyer)*; Cotton-Eyed Joe *(Bill Sawyer)*; The French Reel *(Smiley Bates)*; Concert Reel *(Carl Elliott)*; Joys Of Quebec *(Bill Sawyer)*; Liverpool Hornpipe *(Gaetan Poirier)*; Heather On The Hill *(Chuck Joyce)*; Way Down Yonder *(Rick Cormier)*; Faded Love *(Bunty Petrie)*; Pat The Budgie *(Bob Ranger)* 54:04

Héritage Québécois is a charming collection of historical recordings featuring a number of key Québec artists. This CD makes a good introductory album for those exploring the folk-music heritage of Québec. Sadly, there are no liner notes, but MCA has reissued solo CD's of the artists on this anthology. Check under the individual artists in this guide.

❄❄❄(❄) Héritage Québécois
1990 MCA (MCAMD-10159)

Le Petit Sauvage Du Nord *(La Bolduc)*; L'Adieu Du Soldat *(Roland Lebrun)*; Reel

Du Pendu *(Tommy Duchesne)*; Quand Le Soleil Dit Bonjour Aux Montagnes *(Marcel Martel)*; Set Canadien *(Isidore Soucy)*; Passant Par Paris *(Aimé Major)*; Reel De L'Oiseau Moqueur *(Gérard Lajoie)*; Le Rapide Blanc *(Oscar Thiffault)*; Reel Blanchette *(Louis Blanchette)*; La Bastringue *(La Bolduc)*; Chevaliers De La Table Ronde *(Aime Major)*; Reel Du Carnaval De Québec *(Gérard Lajoie)*; La Cabane À Sucre *(Oscar Thiffault)*; Reel Des Noces D'Argent *(Louis Blanchette)*; Valse De Québec *(Tommy Duchesne)*; Les Agents D'Assurance *(La Bolduc)*; Amour, Victoire, Liberté *(Roland Lebrun)*; Reel Des Patineurs *(Tommy Duchesne)*; Allo Ma Prairie *(Marcel Martel)*; Valse De La Cuisine *(Isidore Soucy)* 56:06

I Am An Eagle: The Music From The Legends Project is part of a larger recording— *Legends*—on which native actors tell legends between musical selections. The *Eagle* album features some first-rate singing from First Nations artists living on both sides of the Canada-US border. This album provides a good introduction to contemporary native artists.

✲✲✲✲ **I Am An Eagle**
[no date] First Nations Music (Y2-77621-10017-2-2)†

I Am An Eagle *(Tammy Pierce; Murray Porter)*; Ashtum *(Legends Band)*; Midnight Strongheart *(Legends Band)*; Thunder Warrior *(Elizabeth Hill)*; Wenabeg *(Legends Band)*; Medewin Kwe *(Leland Bell)*; Indian Giver *(Murray Porter)*; Grandmother *(Legends Band)*; Oo-Wa Gitchi Manitou *(Lawrence Martin)*; Seven Generations *(Elizabeth Hill)* 42:38

Jigs & Reels, like Holborne's *Canadian Fiddle* is an anthology of fiddle music una-dorned by liner notes. This defeats the purpose of this kind of collection which in-cludes historical recordings re-mastered for compact disc.

✲✲✲ **Jigs & Reels**
[no date] Holborne (HCD 3305)

Pembroke Reel *(Johnny Mooring)*; Kiddy Car Reel *(Reg Hill)*; East York Jig *(Graham Townsend)*; Blind Man's Reel *(Cye Steele)*; Logger's Jig *(Reg Hill)*; Musty Muldoon's Irish Jig *(Reg Hill)*; Ploughboy's Reel *(John Wood)*; Sleigh Ride Reel *(Reg Hill)*; Short Grass Jig *(Reg Hill)*; Trapper's Jig *(Johnny Mooring)*; Timber Raft Jig *(Reg Hill)*; Rippling Water Jig *(Graham Townsend)*; Big John McNeill *(Joe MacIsaac)*; Buckingham Reel *(Graham Townsend)*; Sunset Jig *(Graham Townsend)*; St. Anne's Reel *(Rodgers Bros.)*; Clayton Poirier Reel *(Johnny Mooring)*; Grace McPherson's Reel *(Jimmy Chapman)*; Nellie's Jig *(Jim Mayhew)*; Journeyman's Jig *(June Eickhard)*; Prince County Jig *(Graham Townsend)* 45:16

Kick In The Darkness: Songs Of Bruce Cockburn demonstrates why tribute albums are scary. While perhaps not the worst of tribute albums on the market, these perform-ances simply do not do justice to the music for anyone weaned on the Cockburn originals. Unless you have a particular interest in one of the artists or groups on this album, save your money for the real thing.

✲✲ **Kick In The Darkness: Songs Of Bruce Cockburn**
1991 Intrepid (N21S 0008)

Lovers In A Dangerous Time *(Barenaked Ladies)*; A Long Time Love Song *(Martin Tielli; Jane Siberry)*; Lord Of The Starfields *(Swing Gang)*; Feet Fall On The Road *(Five Guys Named Moe)*; Silver Wheels *(All Her Brothers Are Drummers)*; All The Diamonds In The World *(Rebecca Jenkins)*; Wondering Where The Lions Are *(B-Funn)*; Stolen Land *(Chris Bottomley)*; Waiting For The Moon *(Fat Man Waving)*; If

I Had A Rocket Launcher *(Cottage Industry)*; Call It Democracy *(Jellyfishbabies)*; One Day I Walk *(Skydiggers)*; Red Ships Take Off In The Distance *(Bobby Wiseman)* 54:26

The Mariposa Folk Festival has been one of the leading folk festivals in North America since its glory days in the early 60's when it featured performers like Joni Mitchell, Joan Baez, Bob Dylan, Gordon Lightfoot, and Ian & Sylvia. But along the way it changed its location several times, as well as its focus. When the folk music revival of the 1960's began to wane, organizers changed the basic makeup of the festival to include more rock, blues, country, and other electric-based bands. Renaming itself as *The Mariposa Festival*, Mariposa has even sought to downplay its identity as a "folk" festival. *Mariposa '93* is a collection of material that doesn't quite hold together to make a convincing, coherent album. Unlike the Mariposa albums of the 1970's, this collection was not recorded live at the festival. Although there are some individual gems on the album, these studio-recorded tracks don't have any compelling reason for hanging out together.

❋❋   ### Mariposa '93: A Compilation Of Canadian Musicians
1993 Mariposa Folk Foundation (MAR093)

Still A Fool *(Roy Forbes)*; Hold Your Ground *(James Keelaghan)*; The Shores Of Newfoundland/Traveller's Reel *(TIP Splinter)*; Philosophy *(Arlene Bishop)*; Virgenes Del Sol *(Giovanni Ruiz)*; Streetlights *(Susan Hookong)*; Big House *(Sandy Scofield)*; Toronto Volunteers *(Anne Lederman)*; Blue Line *(Stephen Fearing)*; Double Solitaire *(Valdy)*; Little Sister's Gonna Be Alright *(Jackson Delta)*; What You Got *(Karen Gamble; The Cimarron Band)*; À La Cubaña *(Luis Mario Ocha)*; Running The Human Race *(Tight Little Island)*; Lonesome And Hurting *(Vern Cheechoo)*; Darn Folksinger *(Bob Snider)* 62:15

Moose: The Compilation was put together by ex-Torontonian Richard Chapman who founded Moose Records in 1989. Originally meant as a vehicle for the bands he was managing, Chapman formed a loose connection of artists with campaigns like "Save The Rails," which saw over thirty musicians tour together through northern Ontario. Moose Records has since disbanded but many of the artists featured on this compilation have since gone on to make their mark.

❋❋❋   ### Moose: The Compilation
1991 Moose/PolyGram (510 806 - 2)

Saturday Night In A Laundromat *(Grievous Angels)*; Old Nova Scotian *(Bob Snider)*; Sittin' On Top Of The World *(Celtic Gales)*; I'll Follow The Rain *(Pretty Green)*; Slag Heap Love *(Polka Dogs)*; You Don't Know How Much *(Lazy Grace)*; Drinkin' Ex And Askin' Why *(Allen Baekeland)*; Venez À Louisiane *(Cajun Ramblers)*; Woodstuck *(Rheostatics)*; Clothes *(Big Smoke)*; Huggin' At My Pillow *(The Bookmen)*; Memory Haunts Me *(Donkey)*; All Consuming Mistress *(Lost & Profound)*; Evangeline *(Anne Bourne)*; You Are My Sunshine *(The Jack Family)*; Jump On My Wheels *(Positively Stompin')* 59:37

Music Of The Inuit: The Copper Eskimo Tradition / Musique Des Intuit: La Tradition Des Eskimos Du Cuivre is an album of field recordings. The Inuit people of the Northwest Territories have sustained a long history of song and music and the album captures some of the essence of this tradition. The extensive liner notes explain the importance of songs and dance songs during trade exchanges, and how even Inuit children were expected to create and perform their own songs. Serious folklorists should consider this Unesco recording.

✴✴✴✴ **Music Of The Inuit / Musique Des Inuit**
1983, reissued 1994 Auvidis (Unesco D 8053)

Three Connected Songs/Trois Chants Liés; Two Connected Songs/Deux Chants Liés; Joy/Joie; The Boat Of The "Big Brows"/Le Bateau Des "Grands Sourcils"; My Song/Mon Chant; Song Of The Minto Inlet/Chant De Minto Inlet; Two Dances From The Mackenzie Delta/Deux Danses Du Delta Du Mackenzie; Two Connected Songs/ Deux Chants Liés; I Am Happy/Je Suis Tout Heureux; Boundless Joy/Joie Infinie; Coffee, Tea And Jam/Café, Thé, Confiture; Two Connected Songs/Deux Chants Liés; Agnes Nanogak's Song/Le Chant D'Agnès Nanogak; Birth Of Earthworms/ Naissance De Vers De Terre; The Song Floats Up Within Me/Le Chant Flotte En Moi *37:28*

Musique Multi-Montréal is a retrospective collection of the best of Multi-Montréal from 1991 to 1993. The collection includes traditional Québécois music such as the opener, "Belle Étoile Du Nord," plus a generous dollop of the multicultural music for which Montréal has become famous. For world music fans, a great collection.

✴✴✴✴✓ **Musique Multi-Montréal**
1994 Musique Multi-Montréal (MMM00012)

Belle Étoile Du Nord *(Karen Young; Michel Faubert)*; Kélé Fàbà *(Boubacar Diabaté)*; Kitka Ot Tangra *(Tangra)*; More Zajenise *(Tangra; Karen Young; Gisèle Savaria)*; Chacarera Tuerta *(Gisèle Duo Cabili/Savaria)*; Namthar *(Groupe Musical De L'Association Culturelle Tibétaine)*; Zompa Namsum *(Groupe Musical De L'Association Culturelle Tibétaine)*; Ghangchen Jong *(Groupe Musical De L'Association Culturelle Tibétaine; Karen Young)*; Ce Sont Les Garçons De Par Icitte/Derrière Chez Nous Y A T'Un Étang *(Les Charbonniers De L'Enfer)*; La Luette En Colère *(Les Charbonniers De L'Enfer)*; Par Un Dimanche Au Soir *(Les Charbonniers De L'Enfer; Karen Young)*; Kereshmé Dastgah Shour *(Saba)*; Charmezrab Shahnaz *(Saba)*; New Shoes *(The Immigrants)*; The Immigrants *(The Immigrants)*; Honor Song *(Norman Achneepineskum)*; Le Mariage Anglais *(Karen Young; Michel Faubert)* *69:00*

Nunavik Concert is a live recording made in Inukjuak, Nunavik on August 5, 1993. The Nunavik Concert has been formed as an annual concert at which Inuit artists are invited to participate in the yearly celebration of Inuit music. The 1993 concert features a variety of musical styles which include fiddling, country, western, accordion, folk, rock, jew's harp, and throat singing. The range is astonishing and the musicians deserve widespread exposure.

✴✴✴(✴)✓ **Nunavik Concert**
1995 Sunshine (SSCD-4236)

Tukunnanguarit *(Salluit Band)*; Umiujarmit *(Charlie Tumic)*; Kuuvvalak/Anuri/ Kiukiukallak *(Minnie Palliser)*; Ammaaq/Ujurumiaq/Pingasuiliqi/Qimmiguluapik/ Qanngavavaaq/Sanguajug/Aaqammamma *(Annie Alaku; Sarah Sivuarapik)*; [Story] *(Takuginai)*; Taanisirutialuk *(Rebecca Qumarluk)*; Ukiurtatummiugujugut *(Charlie Iqaluk)*; Inu Tuuvunga *(Kinguvaat)*; The Hunt *(André Brassard)*; Inngiluttaasunga *(Charlie Takatak; Mina Arragutainaq)*; Pulaariannguaka *(Charlie Ningiuk)* *38:38*

Our Labrador is extraordinary for its ordinariness. Few albums today have the ingenuousness of the old-style country songs in this collection—songs that celebrate, in simple words with simple chord progressions, a disappearing lifestyle in which settlers, Innu, and Inuit all relied heavily on the land as a means of subsistence. These songs, sung in English, Innu-Aimun, and Inuktitut, are a treasure.

✳✳✳✳✓ Our Labrador
1995 Butter and Snow (RDRCD-722)†

The Grand River Song *(Shirley Montague)*; Old Mokami *(Gerald Mitchell)*; Nainimut *(Margaret Metcalfe)*; Take Me To The Country *(Harry Martin)*; We Sons Of Labrador *(Gerald Mitchell)*; Atatab Kilangmitub *(Margaret Metcalfe)*; Shanty Town *(Harry Martin)*; Nantem Minuataman *(Gregory Penashue)*; Woman Of Labrador *(Shirley Montague)*; Pearl River *(Gerald Mitchell)*; Labrador Rose *(Dick Gardiner)*; Inutokaunerme *(Margaret Metcalfe)*; The Ode To Labrador *44:11*

Songs Of The Sea is a good, if less than inspired, collection of sea songs by some outstanding Maritimes performers. While pleasant, it omits some of the best sea songs in the repertoire.

✳✳(✳) Songs Of The Sea
[no date] Stephen MacDonald Productions (SMPCD1006)

Silver Sea *(The Garrison Brothers)*; Fisherman's Song *(Rankin Family)*; Bay Of St. Ann's *(Max MacDonald)*; Black Rock *(Rita MacNeil)*; Let Me Fish Off Cape St. Mary's *(Denis Ryan)*; Rollin' On The Sea *(Brakin' Tradition)*; Flow Time *(Barra MacNeils)*; Atlantic Blue *(Ron Hynes)*; Sea People *(Richard Burke)*; Believing In Better *(Lennie Gallant)*; Make And Break Harbour *(Stan Rogers)*; Atlantic Queen *(Tom Leadbetter)* *44:10*

The Sounds Of Nova Scotia is an example of what the locals call "tourist albums"— albums made for people who travel through the region and want to take home a musical memoir. While the album has some good cuts on it, it also has some rough ones.

✳✳(✳) The Sounds Of Nova Scotia
[no date] Stephen MacDonald Productions (SMPCD-1001)

Good Times *(John Allan Cameron)*; Song For The Mira *(The Garrison Brothers)*; Atlantic Chorus *(Heather Rankin)*; She's Called Nova Scotia *(Rita MacNeil)*; Skye Boat Song *(Howie MacDonald)*; Rise Again *(Raylene Rankin)*; The Bluenose *(Miller's Jug)*; Long Way From Texas *(Matt Minglewood)*; Jigging Medley *(Rankin Family)*; Bienvenue En Clare *(Les Tymeux De La Baie)*; Seabird's Cry *(John Cracie)*; Coaltown Road *(The Barra MacNeils)*; Farewell To Nova Scotia *(Catherine MacKinnon)* *43:30*

A Taste Of Atlantic Canada: The Music Of New Brunswick, Nova Scotia, Prince Edward Island, Newfoundland and Labrador, produced by Brian Doherty, of Evans & Doherty, is a Maritimes collection that works better than many similar anthologies. The difference is that the album contains some of the better works of some of the better Maritime performers. With the exception of the energetic fiddle set by Natalie MacMaster, however, the recording is a bit too middle-of-the-road and subdued. A little more energy would have made it a significantly better CD.

✳✳✳ A Taste Of Atlantic Canada
[no date] Ground Swell (GSR-59)

Wild Mountain Thyme *(Evans & Doherty)*; How Many Bridges *(Lennie Gallant)*; MacPherson's Lament *(Rawlins Cross)*; Headin' For Halifax *(Brakin' Tradition)*;

> When You And I Were Young, Maggie *(Phyllis Morrissey)*; As Long As There Is A Sail *(McGinty)*; High Germany *(Quigley Ensemble)*; Coal By The Sea *(Men Of The Deeps)*; Come By The Hills *(Sons Of Erin)*; Bonnie Annie Anderson/The Devil's Elbow/The Waterfall *(Dave MacIsaac)*; The Shearing *(Teresa Doyle)*; Calling Me Home *(Kenzie MacNeil)*; To Daun't On Me/Cameron Chisholm's/Haughs Of Cromdale/Johnny Wilmot's Fiddle/Mrs. Kennedy Of Greenan/Down The Broom *(Natalie MacMaster)*; Fiddler's Green *(Cricklewood)* 49:47

Thank You Lord! is a collection of gospel tunes performed by some of the outstanding gospel artists located in Toronto. Produced by Ken Whiteley, the album was recorded in three studios and two different churches. "Although at one time Toronto might not have been considered a hot bed for this kind of music, the diverse group on this recording is in many ways just the tip of the iceberg for what is a vibrant and growing musical community"—Ken Whiteley, liner notes.

❋❋❋ **Thank You Lord!**
1994 Pyramid (PD 009)

> If We Ever Needed The Lord Before *(The Richardsons)*; Never Alone *(Alphanso Burke Jr.)*; The Love Of God *(David Wall)*; Child Of God *(Ken Whiteley)*; Over & Over *(Youth Outreach Mass Choir)*; There Is No Way *(Youth Outreach Mass Choir)*; Everything You Touch *(The Richardsons)*; I'm Gonna Wait On The Lord *(The Toronto Mass Choir)*; Jesus Is All The World To Me *(The Toronto Mass Choir)*; Golden *(Ken Whiteley; Youth Outreach Mass Choir; Jackie Richardson)*; Who Made It So *(Alphanso Burke Jr.)*; Greatest Is Your Love *(John T. Davis; The Richardsons)* 60:41

Jann Arden
FOLK/POP; SINGER-SONGWRITER

Jann Arden, from Calgary, is an immensely popular singer-songwriter who, in the early stages of her career, performed on the folk circuit at venues like the Edmonton Folk Festival. Her atmospheric, moody, love songs are characterized by simple arrangements that bring her expressive voice front and centre. Arden's first two CD's, *Time For Mercy* and *Living Under June* appeal to a broad audience. Arden is the recipient of numerous Juno awards, including "Songwriter of the Year" and "Female Vocalist of the Year" in 1995.

❋❋❋(❋) **Time For Mercy**
1993 A&M (31454 0071 2)†

> I Would Die For You; Waiting For Someone; Will You Remember Me; We Do Some Strange Things; I'm Not Your Lover; Give Me Back My Heart; The Way Things Are Going; Kitchen Window; I Just Don't Love You Anymore; Time For Mercy; Over You 50:48

❋❋❋(❋) **Living Under June**
1994 A&M (314540248-2)†

> Could I Be Your Girl; Demolition Love; Looking For It; Insensitive; Gasoline; Wonderdrug; Living Under June; Unloved; Good Mother; It Looks Like Rain 43:22

Holly Arntzen
FOLK; SINGER-SONGWRITER

The tradition of political and social protest songs is one of the enduring legacies of folk music. British Columbia singer-songwriter Holly Arntzen embraces the tradition—putting her fine voice and writing energy into songs about contemporary situations and conditions. On *Holly Arntzen* she sings about the environment, corporate greed, changing times, and the shallowness of contemporary life. Throughout her work, however, is a thread of optimism and hope. Arntzen is a talented singer-songwriter whose work stands up well to repeated listening.

✳✳✳(✳) **Holly Arntzen**
1991 Artist Response Team / WEA (CD 74829)†

I Believe; Rushing River; Born In The Country; Stand Up; Deep In My Heart; Tracktown; 3 Minute Culture; Feeling Like A Stranger; Blade And Flame; Forget And Forgive *45:09*

Arrandale
FOLK

Based in Owen Sound, Ontario, Arrandale is a folk group whose *Arrandale* CD is a mix of old favourites, with a Celtic bias, plus some odd material such as "New Orleans." Arrandale has an engaging, clean-cut sound with pleasant voices and arrangements that keep you humming along. The banjo, mandolin, and whistle accompaniments form excellent bridges between the vocals. While it doesn't break any new ground, *Arrandale* is an album you can enjoy listening to repeatedly. The members of Arrandale are Derek Cunningham, vocals, guitar; Dave Comber, vocals, banjo, autoharp, bodhran; Brian Davidson, bass, mandolin, percussion, vocals; Bill Farrar, vocals, whistle; Dave Farrar, drums, vocals; Gillian McManaman, vocals, whistles.

✳✳✳ **Arrandale**
1992 Arrandale [no catalogue number]†

Foggy Dew; Molly Malone; Leaning Stone; New Orleans; Garten Mother's Lullaby; I Know Where He Is; Johnny I Hardly Knew Ya; Come Ye Ore Frae France; John Anderson; Sarah; John McLean's March; Tiree Love Song; John Barleycorn; The Piper O' Dundee *46:32*

The Arrogant Worms
FOLK/SATIRE/HUMOUR; SINGER-SONGWRITERS

At the edges of folk festivals you'll encounter the clowns and jesters. Sometimes they make music and end up on stage. On their debut album, *Arrogant Worms*, the group presents a mix of off-the-wall lyrics done in a variety of styles from folk ("The Last Saskatchewan Pirate") to reggae ("The Credit Song") to rock ("Let's Go Bowling"). *Russell's Shorts*, their second CD, delivers the zaniness of songs such as "Carrot Juice Is Murder" and "Killer Robots From Venus." The album also achieves a more respectable duration. These CD's are fun to listen to when you need to freshen your outlook.

The Arrogant Worms consist of Mike McCormick, Trevor Strong, John Whytock, and Steve Wood.

✳✳✳   **Arrogant Worms**
[no date] Festival (AW-444)

The Last Saskatchewan Pirate; The Credit Song; Let's Go Bowling; Goin' Huntin'; Don't Go Into Politics; No Sale/No Store; The Canadian Crisis Song; The Ballad Of Dan; Jesus' Brother Bob; I Want To Look Like Arnold; Car Full Of Pain; The Christmas Song *29:38*

✳✳✳(✳)   **Russell's Shorts**
1994 Festival (AW-555)

Tokyo Love Song; Carrot Juice Is Murder; Rippy The Gator; Killer Robots From Venus; Having Fun Is Bad For You; The Fishing Song; William Shakespeare's In My Cat; A Night On Dildo; The Last Sensitive Cowboy; Losing Hair Under God; Big Fat Road Manager *41:19*

Robert Atyeo & The Friendly Giants
FOLK/COUNTRY/BLUES; SINGER-SONGWRITER

Ontario-based singer-songwriter Robert Atyeo, who bills himself as "Robert Atyeo & The Friendly Giants," has been a long-time favourite at folk festivals. His album *Songs For Your Face*, with tunes like "Swimming In Love," introduces his folk/blues style. This solid album, with expressive lyrics and good arrangements, shows a strong, developing songwriter. *Angels On A Cliff* moves Atyeo and his band into another gear altogether. The songwriting has matured and the arrangements reach a higher level. The Friendly Giants on *Angels* include Tony Quarrington on lead guitar, Jeff Bird on bass guitar, Willie P. Bennett on harmonica and mandolin, plus several guest musicians.

✳✳✳   **Songs For Your Face**
1993 Here And Now (RAFG-2-9301)

Swimming In Love; Heart In Two; Famous For Nothing; The Wishing; Calm Down; Don't Wanna Be Late; Picture Of You; After Everybodies Gone; Out Of Control; Poison Jane *38:27*

✳✳✳✳✓   **Angels On A Cliff**
1994 Here And Now (RAFG-8-9402)

The Floor Is Closer Than You Think; Best Friends Again; Neil's Guitar; The Song; Angels In The Backseat #1; Chickens On A Cliff; Distance Between Us; Shave The Monkey; Leaving The Body (2nd Movement); Push Comes To Shove; Flash In The Pan; Suck It In; Who Decides; Leaving The Body (1st Movement); Welded; Angels In The Backseat #2 *52:02*

Back Alley John
ACOUSTIC BLUES; SINGER-SONGWRITER

Calgary-based blues artist Back Alley John (John Wilson), rolls out an excellent set of original and traditional numbers on *Out On The Highway*. Playing harmonica, acoustic guitar, and electric slide guitar, he joins his backup musicians on fine songs like

"Out On The Highway," "Yo-Yo String," "Pork Chop," and "No Place In Mind"—all Wilson compositions. Acoustic blues enthusiasts will thoroughly enjoy this album.

✳✳✳(✳)   **Out On The Highway**
1992 Back Alley John [no catalogue number]

> Out On The Highway; Yo-Yo String; 9/8 Nervous Man; Careless Love; Pork Chop; You Don't See The Blues Like Me; Ham Bone Boiled; The Blues Is A Memory; Need My Baby; No Place In Mind; Pickin' The Blues; Cold Blue Moon *45:20*

Brenda Baker
FOLK/POP; DRAMA; SINGER-SONGWRITER

"Wow! Zap! Pow! This is like no other recording you'll ever own"—*Sing Out! Daughter Of Double-Dare*, by Saskatoon native Brenda Baker, inspires this kind of comment. A combination spoken/sung recording, its feminist lyrics and sentiments exude energy and creativity. There are some great songs on the album, but some listeners may find the interspersing of readings among the music somewhat distracting.

✳✳✳(✳)   **Daughter Of Double-Dare**
1993 Brazen Hussy (BB3-DDD93)†

> Daughter Of Double-Dare; Whatcha Call Insane?; What We're Capable Of; Letter By Letter; This Room; Barcelona Bridge; Love I Can Live With; Bye-Bye Becky; The Riot Girls; Cindy; Call Yourself A Woman; The F-Word; On Tattoos, Poetry, Genius, And The Natural Order Of Things; Man Of My Dreams; Songwriters In Love; Boyland; God Wears Sunglasses; If I Was Madonna *72:53*

The Barra MacNeils
CELTIC SONGS AND INSTRUMENTALS

Another of the musical families from Nova Scotia, the Barra MacNeils consist of Sheumas MacNeil on keyboard and vocals, Kyle MacNeil on guitars, violin, mandolin, and vocals, Stewart MacNeil on electric bass, accordion, whistles, and vocals, and Lucy MacNeil on violin, celtic harp, bodhran, and vocals. Their first album, *The Barra MacNeils,* is a solid debut effort, featuring a mix of instrumental and vocal music. Their second album, *Rock In The Stream*, continues the pattern of Celtic instrumentals alongside vocal numbers. *Timeframe* alternates between traditional and contemporary material with the two types of music slightly at odds. *Closer To Paradise* continues the swing towards contemporary songs by songwriters such as John Sebastian, Dougie MacLean, Tony Arata, plus some original works by the MacNeils. The middle-of-the-road sound is pleasant, but the infectious quality of their traditional music is missing. *The Traditional Album* is easily the Barra MacNeils' best album to date. By eschewing vocals altogether, the Barra MacNeils have put together an entirely convincing and satisfying album based on dance music. The Barra MacNeils received the "Roots/Traditional Artist of the Year" East Coast Music Award in 1995.

✳✳✳(✳)   **The Barra MacNeils**
1986 Polydor (314 519 027-2)

> Playhouse Medley: Eating Bonnach/Drowsy Maggie/Drunken Landlady; No More Good Times; One For Jeffy/Lovat's Restoration/Jig Of Slurs/Angela Cameron/Mrs.

George Johnstone Of Byker; The Marquis Of Huntly's Snuff Mill; Three Reels: Traditional/Traditional/Jenny Picking Cockles; Willie C.; Trip To Sligo/Murdo MacKenzie Of Torridon; Highland Queen/Sweep's Hornpipe/Traditional Hornpipe/ Devil And The Dirk; Proud Spirit *34:41*

❄❄❄(❄) **Rock In The Sun**
1989 Polydor (314 519 028-2)†

Rattlin, Roarin Willie; Glenpark Medley; The Island; The Lone Harper; Red Ice; High Bass Tunes; Coaltown Road; Highland Exchange Medley; Kitty Bawn O'Brien; Standing By The Subway; Beautiful Point Aconi *41:58*

❄❄❄(❄) **Timeframe**
[no date] Polydor (314 519 029-2)†

Banks Of The Roses; Flow Time; Didn't Hear The Train; Flower Basket Medley; Song For Peace; Isle Of My Dreams; Looking Back; Row Row Row; Ian Hardie Set; My Heart's In The Highlands *41:10*

❄❄❄ **Closer To Paradise**
1993 Polydor (314 521 016-2)

We Celebrate; Darling Be Home; When I'm Away From You; Closer To Paradise; Chase The Man; Dancing We Would Go; In The Wink Of An Eye; Frostbite; Caledonia; Jigs: The Dusty Windowsill/The O'Keefe's Of Dublin; Mo Nighean Dubh (My Black Haired Girl); Am Pige Ruadh (Mouth Music) *44:33*

❄❄❄❄✓ **The Traditional Album**
1994 Polydor (314 523 251-2)

Clumsy Lover Set; Celtic Harp; Tribute To Robert Stubbert; The Visit Medley; The Maids Of Arrochar; The Brolum Set; Twice A Year Fiddler; March-Strathspeys-Reels; Memories Of Mary Ann MacKenzie; Wedding Party Medley; Toonik Tyme; Twin Fiddles; Neil Gow's Lament For The Death Of His Second Wife *52:59*

Willie P. Bennett

Folk/Country/Blues; Singer-Songwriter

A longtime veteran of the folk circuit, Ontario-based Willie P. Bennett delivers his emotionally-charged music in a slightly down-and-out voice that reflects a performer who has lived what his songs are about. A talented songwriter whose early work has long been out of print, it's a pleasure to see some of the best of his early work gathered together in the retrospective CD, *Collectibles*—a mix of musical influences, highlighting Bennett's wide-ranging styles. There's a countryish quality to many of his early hits—songs like "Willie's Diamond Joe" and "Blackie And The Rodeo King." "Summer Dreams, Winter Sleep" is a strong bluegrass, instrumental track. A particular gem is "Music In Your Eyes," which Garnet Rogers selected for his debut album. Its unusual cadences and melody remain fresh and captivating. *The Lucky Ones*, a later album, features Bennett in a more country/blues vein with a full electric backup band. The songwriting is a little less inspired and, by folk standards, the album is over-produced and somewhat monotonous. *Take My Own Advice* features Bennett in another heavily produced album, but the musicians are more interesting and the backup vocals by Colleen Peterson are noteworthy. While the lyrics are not vintage Bennett, they carry the album reasonably well.

❋❋❋(❋)✓ **Collectibles**
1975-78, reissued 1991 Dark Light Music (DL 12001)†

You; Lace And Pretty Flowers; Come On Train; Willie's Diamond Joe; Blackie And The Rodeo King; If You Have To Choose; Me And Molly; Summer Dreams, Winter Sleep; Storm Clouds; Country Squall; My Pie; Music In Your Eyes; Down To The Water; Hobo's Taunt; Pens And Paper *57:53*

❋❋(❋) **The Lucky Ones**
1989 Duke Street (DSRD 31059)†

Train Tracks; The Lucky Ones; Ain't Got No Notion; Cryin' The Blues; Goodbye, So Long, Hello; Tryin' To Start Out Clean; Reckless Baby; Don't Have Much To Say; Patience Of A Working Man; Andrew's Waltz *33:02*

❋❋❋ **Take My Own Advice**
1993 Dark Light Music (DL 12003)†

L.A.D.T. (Livin' In A Dirty Town); Jukebox; (If I Could) Take My Own Advice; Step Away; You Care; Sometimes It Comes So Easy; Katie's Tune; Breaking The Silence; Blood Brother; Push On; Red Dress; Why'd I Go Zydeco *47:59*

Emile Benoit

FRENCH CANADIAN; MARITIMES FIDDLE

"Benoit's influence on Newfoundland folk music can't be understated. His capacity for writing tunes was nothing short of amazing"—*Dirty Linen*. Emile Benoit was born and raised in Black Duck Brook, on the Port-au-Port peninsula of Newfoundland. A many-sided man who listed fisherman, farmer, healer, dentist, part-time veterinarian, blacksmith, storyteller, raconteur, musician, and composer among his careers, Benoit began playing fiddle at age nine. Full of *joie de vivre*, Benoit entertained audiences at many of Canada's major festivals. In later years, he toured with Figgy Duff and, fittingly, *Viva La Rose* was produced by Figgy Duff's founding members: Noel Dinn, Gary Furniss, and Pamela Morgan. This fine album is a tribute to the ultimate victory of spirit and music. Benoit has been inducted into the Porcupine Hall of Fame.

❋❋❋❋✓ **Viva La Rose**
1992 Amber Music (ACD 9014)

Christina's Dream/Tootsie Wootsie; Neil Murray's Dinner Jig/Go To The Cape Uncle Joe/Forgotten Note; Noel Dinn/Pamela's Lonely Nights; Vive La Rose; Waltz In The House; The Land We're Walking On; Skipper and Company/On The Road Again/ Claudine; Festival Reel/Jeff's Tune/Meech Lake Breakdown/McCormack's Breakdown; Sally's Waltz/Wedding Waltz; Fight For Your Rights; Jerry's Red Mountain Jig/Le Papier 'Le Gaboteur'; Lady Margaret; Brother's Farewell/Caribou Skin Nailed Around The Circle/Wayne And The Bear *40:39*

Jennifer Berezan

FOLK/POP; SINGER-SONGWRITER

"Jennifer Berezan is a bright rising folk star, evoking the vocal strength of Mary Chapin Carpenter as she keenly observes life, love, politics and injustice"—*Dirty Linen.* Jennifer Berezan, who has taken up residence in California, is a contemporary Canadian singer-songwriter who layers her work with electric instrumentation over lyrics and acoustic guitar. *Borderlines* is a good, if heavily produced, album that contains some strong moments, such as the introspective look back at Canada in "Borderlines." A solid early album from this songwriter.

※※※ **Borderlines**
1992 Flying Fish (FF70615)†

Shadows On The Street; Borderlines; State Of The Union; While We Are Here; When You're Young; You're Gone; Katie's River; One And One Makes Three; Calling; Angel Boots *43:29*

Anita Best & Pamela Morgan

TRADITIONAL FOLK

Anita Best, folklorist and singer has combined with fellow Maritimer Pamela Morgan of Figgy Duff to create *The Colour Of Amber*, one of the most haunting and beautiful Canadian folk albums ever recorded. In the early style of Figgy Duff (the producers of the album were Figgy Duff'ers Noel Dinn and Gary Furniss), Best and Morgan take traditional material and deliver it in a freshened-up format. Their perfectly blended voices float through the material carrying you into the sadness, sorrow, and contemplativeness of another time. A must for anyone who loves traditional music. *The Colour Of Amber* received a "Gem Of Canada Album" Porcupine Award in 1992.
See also Figgy Duff.

※※※※✓ **The Colour Of Amber**
1991 Amber Music (ACD 9008)

Súil A Grá; She's Like The Swallow; The Lowlands Of Holland; Le Vingt-Cing De Juillet; A Sailor's Trade Is A Weary Life; The Two Sisters; The Green Mossy Banks Of The Lee; John Barbour (Willy O'Winsbury); Brave Marin; The Maid On The Shore; Lowlands Low *48:24*

The Bird Sisters

FOLK; A CAPPELLA; SINGER-SONGWRITERS

The Bird Sisters of Guelph, Ontario began their career as an a cappella group, later branching into a mix of a cappella and instrument-backed numbers. By their second album, *Different Stories* (the first was never released on compact disc), they centred their vocal harmonies around original material written by the members of the group: Tannis Slimmon, Sue Smith, and Jude Vadala. The Bird Sisters, with their acoustic guitar work and excellent lyrics, provide melodic listening for anyone who loves tight, three-part harmony.

❋❋❋(❋)   **Different Stories**
[no date] The Bird Sisters (TBS 002)

Why Can't You Read My Mind; Slips Through The Crack; Skylark; Carley's Song; Gettin' Lots Of Sleep; Back To The Desert; Spirit House; To The Bone; Falling For You; The Dove Flies; Get Up And Fly; Different Stories *41:33*

Heather Bishop
FOLK/POP; SINGER-SONGWRITER

Manitoba singer-songwriter Heather Bishop is one of Canada's most independent artists, following a muse that doesn't follow any predictable musical styles or channels. Her fresh, intimate, lyrics are combined in arrangements that are more pop-like than folk, but there's a rootsiness to her work that springs from the Prairies. Folkies new to her work may want to try one of her earlier albums, *A Taste Of The Blues*, to test the waters.

❋❋❋(❋)   **A Taste Of The Blues**
1986 Mother of Pearl (MPCD006)†

Taking My Baby Up Town; A Taste Of The Blues; On The Run Again; You Don't Own Me; Seduced; Tell Me More And More; Daddy's Little Girl; Spirit Healer; Keeping On; If You Love Freedom *34:04*

❋❋❋(❋)   **Walk That Edge**
1989 Mother of Pearl (MPCD007)†

Coming For You; Let Them Talk; Walk That Edge; Blanket Of My Love; Given For Free; Break My Heart; It Calls You To Sail; I'm Not The One; Lay Me Down; Anna Mae *40:35*

❋❋❋(❋)   **Old New Borrowed Blue**
1994 Mother of Pearl (MPCD009)†

Yes To Life; Nothing Like The Freedom; Grandmother's Song; Waltz Me Around; Do I Move You; I'm Not The One; Spirit Healer; Our Silence; Les Moutons; Did Jesus Have A Baby Sister; Tell Me More And More; Yukon Rain; Prairie Wind; Sailing Away; Cry Me A River; Break My Heart; If You Love Freedom; Ancient Cry *73:08*

❋❋❋(❋)   **Daydream Me Home**
1994 Mother of Pearl (MPCD010)†

Let Me Make It Up To You Tonight; Sheik Shaboom; Daydream Me Home; Waitin' For You Mama; Born To Live; If You Leave Me Darlin'; The Galaxy/Lighten Up; Dream Line Special; Hymn To Her; Warrior *38:00*

Louis Blanchette
FRENCH CANADIAN

With harmonica accompanied by guitar and lively foot tapping, Quebec artist Louis Blanchette is highlighted on the historical recording, *Louis Blanchette*, in a delightful series of reels. Issued as part of the Héritage Québécois series, this MCA CD contains no liner notes.

❋❋❋(❋)   **Louis Blanchette**
[no date, reissued 1991] MCA (MCAD-10494)

Reel Blanchette; Reel Des Noces D'Argent; Reel Des Trois Rivières; Reel Como; Reel Des Fiançailles; Reel D'Argenteuil; Reel D'Or; Reel Yankee Doodle; Reel Des Jeunes Mariés; Reel Bastringue; Reel Bagot; Reel D'Union; Reel De Cap Rouge; Reel Des Noces De Diamants; Reel De Campbellton *42:44*

La Bolduc

FRENCH CANADIAN; SINGER-SONGWRITER

Mary Rose-Anna Travers (1894-1941), known by her stage name "La Bolduc," was born of an Irish father and a French-Canadian mother. From them she developed a love of folk music and "chant populaire." From an early age she played violin, bombarde, and concertina. Her family left the Gaspé and moved to Montreal when she was thirteen. She later married Edouard Bolduc and began performing on stage as Mme Edouard Bolduc. More of a "chanteuse" than a folksinger, La Bolduc wrote topical, satirical songs that were extremely popular. The CD, *La Bolduc*, from the MCA Héritage Québécois series, provides a good sampler of her work, but, alas, contains no liner notes. In contrast, the lovingly crafted four-CD box set, *L'Intégrale*, from Analekta contains liner notes (in French), lyrics, and lexicography that translates La Bolduc's colloquialisms and witticisms into everyday French. The discs from *L'Intégrale* are also available as individual CDs.

❋❋❋❋   **La Bolduc**
[no date, reissued 1991] MCA (MCAD-10486)

J'Ai Un Bouton Sur La Langue; Les Maringouins; Le Petit Sauvage Du Nord; La Bastringue; Ça Va Venir, Découragez-Vous Pas; La Lune De Miel; Je M'En Vais Au Marché; Les Policemen; Un Petit Bonhomme Avec Le Nez Pointu; Nos Braves Habitants; Si Vous Avez Une Fille Qui Veut Se Marier; Les Agents D'Assurance; Les Souffrances De Mon Accident; Johnny Monfarleau; La Pitoune *40:37*

❋❋❋❋   **L'Intégrale**
1993 Analekta (AN 2 7001-4)†

CD1: Je M'En Vais Au Marché; Les Souffrances De Mon Accident; Tout Le Monde À La Grippe; Le Voleur De Poule; Les Belles-Mères; Quand J'Ai Vingt Ans; Gédéon Amateur; Les Pompiers De St-Eloi; Arrête Donc, Mary; Les Médecins; Les Colons Canadiens; La Lune De Miel; Les Cinq Jumelles; La Gaspésienne Pure Laine; Les Vacances; Sans Travail; En Revenant Des Foins; Les Conducteurs De Chars; Les Policemen; Les Américains; L'Enfant Volé *60:01*

CD2: Si Les Saucisses Pouvaient Parler; Quand J'Étais Chez Mon Père; Les Femmes; J'Ai Un Bouton Sur La Langue; Rose Cherche À Se Marier; Bien Vite C'Est Le Jour De L'An; Voilà Le Père Noël Qui Nous Arrive; Danse En Souliers De Boeuf; R'Garde Donc C'Que T'As D'L'Air; Tit Noir A Le Mal Imaginaire; Chanson De La Bourgeoise; Ah! C'Qu'il Est Slow Tit Joe; Le Commerçant Des Rues; La Côte Nord; Aux Chauffeurs D'Automobile; C'Est La Fille Du Vieux Roupi; Il Va M'Faire Mourir C'Gars-Là; L'Ouvrage Aux Canadiens; La Chanson Du Bavard; Le Sauvage Du Nord; Jean Baptiste Beaufouette *59:47*

CD3: Les Filles De Campagne; No Braves Habitants; Fêtons Le Mardi-Gras; Un Vieux Garçon Gêné; La Grocerie Du Coin; Le Propriétaire; Le Jour De L'An; Le Bas De Noël; Les Agents D'Assurance; Rouge Carotte; La Bastringue; Mademoiselle,

Dites-Mois Donc; Ça Va Venir, Découragez-Vous Pas; Fin Fin Bigaouette; Toujours «L'R-100»; Les Maringouins; Un Petit Bonhomme Avec Un Nez Pointu; Chez Ma Tante Gervais; Mon Vieux Est Jaloux; La Pitoune; Reel Turluté; Valse Turlutée *62:25*

CD4: Fricassez Vous; La Morue; Gigue Des Commères; Fantaisie Écossaise; Le Joueur De Violon; Ton Amour, Ma Catherine; Reel Comique; Galop Des Pompiers; Le Bonhomme Et La Bonne Femme; Si Vous Avez Une Fille Qui Veut Se Marier; Arthimise Marie Le Bedeau; Tourne Ma Roulette; La Servante; Regardez Donc Mouman; La Cuisinère; Johnny Monfarleau; Valse Denise; Reel De La Goëlette; Gendre Et Belle-Mère; Quand On S'Est Vu; Y'A Longtemps Que Je Couche Par Terre; La Gaspésienne *59:36*

Bob Bossin
FOLK; SINGER-SONGWRITER

With the 1994 release of *Gabriola VOR1XO*, British Columbia folksinger Bob Bossin returned to recording after being away from the studio for fifteen years. With friends and guest musicians galore, Bossin, a founder of the earlier Toronto-based Stringband, starts off the album with "Sulphur Passage," a protest song about logging in Clayoquot Sound on the west coast of Vancouver Island. After this captivating start, the album meanders through a delightful set of original songs, some whimsical, some profound. Fans will be delighted to listen to Bossin once again. And for any non-Canadians who are grappling with the album's title, Gabriola is the name of the island on which Bossin lives, and V0R 1X0 is its Canadian postal code.

✳✳✳✳✓ **Gabriola VOR1XO**
1994 Nick (007-CD)

Sulphur Passage; Madelyn's Lullabye; La Chanson Francée; Love In Seven; Ya Wanna Marry Me?; Lying Here With Annie; Bill Miner; Cleaning Up The Oil; 1800-And-Froze-To-Death; Our Little Town; The Secret Life According To Satchel Paige; People Like You *42:09*

La Bottine Souriante
FRENCH CANADIAN;TRADITIONAL/CONTEMPORARY FOLK/JAZZ; SINGER-SONGWRITERS

Juno Award-winning La Bottine Souriante (the name translates as "smiling boot") may be the best known folk group from Quebec. La Bottine Souriante arose as part of the fresh and exciting atmosphere that accompanied the founding of the Parti Québécois and the rediscovery of Québec roots and traditions that gave its people a renewed sense of pride. In its relatively long performing career, the band has undergone several changes of personnel and direction, but what remains is always a lively, instrumentally-oriented sound that gets fans up and dancing. At press time, all but one of their albums (*Les Épousailles*, 1980) have been reissued on CD. *Y'A Ben Du Changement* (1978) and *Chic N' Swell* (1982) emphasize the traditional reels and the *chansons à répondre* (call-and-response singing) of Quebec folk music. The album features mouth music, step dancing, and fiddle pieces all played with delight, respect, and a strong underlying sense of humour. The personnel on this album are André Marchand, Daniel Roy, Martin Racine, Yves Lambert, and Mario Forest. *La Traversée De L'Atlantique* continues in the same vein, with what appears to be the same personnel (the cast was accidentally left off the CD liner notes). With *La Traversée*, the band began to add its own original compositions into the mix. By *Tout Comme Au Jour De L'An* (1987) and *Je Voudrais Changer D'Chapeau* (1988), the material was becoming increasingly eclectic. *Je Voudrais Changer* won a Juno in 1990 in the "Roots & Traditional" category. On these albums the personnel consist of Michel Bordeleau, Yves Lambert, André Marchand, Denis Fréchette, and Martin Racine.

With the release of *Jusq'aux P'tites Heures* in 1991, which won a 1993 Juno in the "Roots & Traditional" category, the band underwent a fundamental change in personnel and sound. Wildly eclectic by this point, the band added trumpets, trombones, and saxophones to the traditional base. The enlarged band now consists of Régent Archambault, Michel Bordeleau, Laflèche Doré, Robert Ellis, Denis Fréchette, Jean Fréchette, Yves Lambert, Martin Racine, and André Verreault. With the release of *La Mistrine*, La Bottine Souriante appears to have veered its brassy, energetic mix back towards its roots. *La Mistrine* received a Porcupine in the "Mme La Bolduc Award For Québécois Folklore" category in 1994.

❋❋❋❋ **Y'A Ben Du Changement**
1978 Mille Pattes (MMPCD-265)

Sur La Montagne Du Loup; Trinque L'Amourette; La Ronfleuse Gobeil; Pinci Pincette; Y A Ben Du Changement; Le Manifeste D'Un Vieux Chasseur D'Oies; La Banqueroute; Reel Des Ouvriers; L'Ivrogne; Sur La Grande Côte; La Tuque Rouge; Le Reel À Bouche Acadien *42:12*

❋❋❋❋✓ **Chic N' Swell**
1982, reissued 1987 Green Linnet (GLCD 3042)

Le Batteux/La Grande Gigue Simple; La Tapinie/Le Reel Des Voyageurs; Sure Le Chemin Du Mont; Le Rossignol Sauvage; Nos Braves Habitants; La Danse Des Foins; Le Bal Chez Ti-Guy; Les Robineux; Les Patins De Pauline/Le Petit Bu Cheux; La Ziguezon; Le Tablier Du Macon/Le Reel À Rémi; Les Trois Capitaines *38:29*

❋❋❋❋✓ **La Traversée De L'Atlantique**
1986, reiussed 1988 Green Linnet (GLCD 3043)

Sur Le Pont D'Avignon; Le Meunier Et La Jeune Fille; Le Reel Des Vieux/Le Reel À Jules Verret; J'Aurai Le Vin/Le Reel Du Petit Cheval De Bois; La Belle Ennuitée; La Traversée De L'Atlantique/Le Set Carré À Pitou Boudreault; Le Lac À Beauce/Le Reel St-Jean; Le Madelon; Le Reel Du Mal De Do; La Chanson Des Menteries; Hommage À Philippe Bruneau/La Valse D'Hiver; La Chanson Des Pompiers *40:19*

❋❋❋(❋) **Tout Comme Au Jour De L'An**
1987 Mille Pattes (MPCD-2035)

La Fille Engagère; Le Réveillon Du Jour De L'An; La Parenté; La Poule À Colin; Un Dimanche Au Matin; Oublions L'An Passé; Pot-pourri De L'Essouflé; Pot-pourri Surf and Turf; Valse Bernadette; Reel De Jos Cormier *38:56*

❋❋❋(❋) **Je Voudrais Changer D'Chapeau**
1988, reissued 1990 Rounder (CD 6041)

Le Festin De Campagne/Marie Sauce Ton Pain; La Gigue De M. Lasanté/La Gigue À Médée; C'Est Dans Paris; Le Reve Du Queteux Tremblay; La Brunette Est Là/Les

Quatre Fers En L'Air; Belle Virginie; Je Voudrais Changer D'Chapeau/Reel Béatrice; Les Filles De La Rochelle; La Valse Des Bélugas; Hommage À Edmond Parizeau/ Dedicado À Jos; La Contumace; Le Reve Du Queteux Tremblay 2 *40:21*

❋❋❋(❋) **Jusq'aux P'tites Heures**
1991 Mille Pattes (MPCD-2037)†

La Chanson Du Quéteux; Le Reel De Pointe-au-Pic; Un P'tit Coup Mesdames; Nuit Sauvage; Par Un Dimanche Au Soir (Ou Ninette); L'Acadienne; Émilien; Corps Mort/Fleur De Mandragore; Turlutte Des 33 Voleurs; Brandy Payette; Picoro; Dérap De La Guerre *49:46*

❋❋❋❋ **La Mistrine**
1994 Milles Pattes (MPCD-2038)†

Le Reel Des Soucoupes Volantes; Ici-Bas Sur Terre; Martin De La Chasse-Galerie; La Mistrine; Le Reel De La Main Blanche; La Tourtière; Le Reel Irlandais Ou Bees Wax, Skin Sheep; Christophe; La Complainte Du Folkloriste; Le Rap À Ti-Pétang; Reel De La Sauvagine; Dans Nos Vieilles Maisons *43:26*

Bourne & Johnson

FOLK/POP; SINGER-SONGWRITERS

After his collaboration with Allan MacLeod, Bill Bourne joined forces with Shannon Johnson to form the Alberta-based duo Bourne & Johnson. Bourne's syncopated lyrics continue to dominate the tracks, with Johnson's engaging voice in harmony and her subtle fiddle playing taking the place of MacLeod's bagpipes. The result is highly effective. Bourne has lost none of his bounce, and Johnson's voice adds a new dimension to the delivery. *Dear Madonna* also shows another side of Bourne—thoughtful, introspective songs that contrast sharply with his previous work.

❋❋❋(❋)✓ **Dear Madonna**
1994 Rynde (CD-1502)†

Dance The Night Away; Here Is A Heart; Dear Madonna; Carnal Minded Men; Red Moon; Shinin' Mary & The Bad News Bears; Beer Belly Billy And Mary Laydown; Wildwood Flower; The Hobo Sunny Blue; Baggins; The Road To Tokyo; Gone Fishin' *52:11*

Bourne & MacLeod

FOLK/POP; SINGER-SONGWRITERS

Alberta-based Bill Bourne and Alan MacLeod put together one of the most infectious, unique sounds to hit the festival circuit. Bourne's unforgettable voice and syncopated lyrics combine with MacLeod's inspired bagpipe accompaniment to create a fresh, joyous sound that sets you dancing in the aisles. *Dance & Celebrate* is aptly named— one of the most enduring and listenable albums released in 1991, it was awarded a 1991 Juno in the "Roots & Traditional" category. *Moonlight Dancers*, from 1992, is cut from the same mould and it, too, is an extremely danceable album. Both are highly recommended for those who don't mind their folk music blended with a dose of pop.

✳✳✳✳✓ **Dance & Celebrate**
1991 Attic (ACD 1314)

> Dance & Celebrate; The Turkey (Take Him Down); I Love Jeanie; Around The Horn; Ole Buffalo; Communicate; Lost On The Bayou; Trust In Love; Riding Mountain/Hare O' The Dug; The House; Tumblin' Down; Let The Children Rule *47:02*

✳✳✳(✳) **Moonlight Dancers**
1992 Attic (ACD 1343)†

> Oh Love; Home Sweet Home; The Circus Song; Back To The Island/The Clumsy Lover; Pitsberg; Ship Of Fortune; Solomon; Oblioh; Roll River Roll; Moonlight Dancers; Livin'; Long John Silver; The Riverboat Song; Raven's Song *55:16*

Mark Bracken
GUITAR COMPOSITIONS

If you love guitar music, *Revival* is a must buy. British Columbia guitarist Mark Bracken plays a lovely set of original compositions in open tunings that carry you into the simple, special essence of six- and twelve-string acoustic guitar. The sound is laid-back—this is the kind of album you should listen to while curled up in front of a fireplace.

✳✳✳(✳) **Revival**
1994 Mark Bracken (AMB 10943)

> Sun Rays; Reflections; Carolina; White Rose; Heaven's Angels; Sea Bird; Ancient Journeys; Fantasia; The Raven; Angelic Rose; Revival; Open Chords; Dawn *42:37*

Diana Braithwaite
FOLK/BLUES/POP; SINGER-SONGWRITER

On *In This Time* Diana Braithwaite sings compelling songs about the experiences of Black people. "Black Angel" is "dedicated to the thousands of Black women and men who sought freedom via the Underground Railroad during slavery." "Just The Way That I Planned It" is a song "dedicated to the Maroons—a proud group of Black people who refused to be enslaved. Upon arriving in Nova Scotia from Jamaica, many left to return to Africa." Braithwaite combines strong lyrics with sparse arrangements in projecting her full, excellent voice.

✳✳✳(✳) **In This Time**
1991 Aural Tradition (ATRCD 304)

> I Know That The Road Is Long; Black Angel; Good Blessings; Just The Way That I Planned It; Desperado Star; Every Step Of The Way; Carry My Name; In This Time; Pretty Brown Girl; Sister Sarah; Mrs. Jones & The Elephant/I Know That The Road Is Long (Reprise) *54:16*

Brakin' Tradition
MARITIME CELTIC; FOLK/COUNTRY; SINGER-SONGWRITERS

Brakin' Tradition is a Celtic-flavoured group based in Nova Scotia. Performing mainly original material, they combine traditional instrumentation with tight harmonies. *Music Man*, a 1992 release includes the countryish "Johnny Rye" and the bouncy "Kathaleen"—a song about a schooner. *Powerfolk* provides a continuation of Brakin' Tradition's commentary on life in the Maritimes. The album includes fresh versions of "Headin' for Halifax" and Stan Rogers' "The Bluenose," as well as original songs from various members of the band. The members of Brakin' Tradition include V. Roger Stone, the group's principal songwriter, Cyril MacPhee, Dave Forsey, Harold Davidson, and Louanne (Bona) Baker.

✳✳✳ **Music Man**
1992 Brakin' Tradition (CD-0903)†

Rollin' On The Sea; Music Man; Johnny Rye; Together; Old Schoolyard; The Kathaleen; Send Me A Picture; Charlie; Listen To Me People; Can't Get Enough Of You; Sleepy Head *35:22*

✳✳✳ **Powerfolk**
1993 Brakin' Tradition (CD-0904)†

Fait Do Do; Headin' For Halifax; Lonesome Driver; Breakaway; Age Old Memories; Salmon River Road Blues; The Bluenose; L'Acadie; Lovers' Prayer; Her Father Didn't Like Me; Life's A Beach; Lullabies *40:35*

Bonnie Brigant & Clare Adlam
OLD-TIME COUNTRY; SINGER-SONGWRITER

There's something refreshingly honest about old-time country music and it is remarkable to hear a recent album like *Bonnie Brigant & Clare Adlam* in an age when country is dominated by Nashville and "new country." Clare Adlam, the producer and songwriter of the album, is mostly known as a fiddler. A native of Grey County, Ontario, Adlam released many albums of fiddle music and was a regular performer on the Wingham, Ontario, *CKNX Barndance* with Earl Heywood in the 50's and 60's. Bonnie Brigant grew up in eastern Ontario, singing in church choirs. She gave up a potential career in country music to raise her family and is only now getting back into recording. This album of country vocals, broken up with a few fiddle tunes, is delightfully old fashioned.

✳✳✳ **Bonnie Brigant & Clare Adlam**
1992 Circle 'M' (CM 2931)

I'm Saving Today For Tomorrow; Lost In The Wilderness; Free And Easy; Silver River; I'll Always Be Your Buddy; Painting On The Wall; God's Home Above; Spring Valley Jig; Sweet Face Caress; The Old Fiddle Waltz; Prairie Sunset; Never; What's Gonna Happen To Me; The Day We Met; Is This World A Little Better *42:59*

Anne Beverly Brown

FOLK/NEW AGE; SINGER-SONGWRITER

In *Keyhole And The Eternal Kiss*, Alberta songwriter Anne Beverly Brown creates dream-like songs drawn from her immediate environment. The album has a meditative quality that will appeal to those who enjoy travelling the magical and mystical side of the folk road. Others may find the lyrics a bit obscure. Brown is joined, on various tracks, by many of the other artists in this guide: Jenny Allen, Mary Anderson, Ken Brown, Oscar Lopez, and Cathy Miller.

❊❊❊ **Keyhole And The Eternal Kiss**
1993 Akashic (AR2)†

> The Rivers Of Eden; The Old Road; The Man Who Planted Trees; Send Me Rachmaninoff; The Church Door; Keyhole And The Eternal Kiss; Never Thought I'd Sing The Blues; Indigo Blue; Chicago Joe; Quiet Heart *47:22*

Jacquelyn Brown

HARP AND VOCALS; SINGER-SONGWRITER

On *Awakening ... The Breath Of Life*, harpist and singer Jacquelyn Brown, from London, Ontario, credits Loreena McKennitt as the person "whose music first called my Celtic heart to ancient dreams of plucking harp strings." Brown has proven an apt student of the harp—her sensitive playing and songwriting explore the lyrical, poetic side of the Celtic spectrum. The album is meditative and gentle. Most of the songs are originals written by Brown, with the exception of the traditional "Bonny Love" and a Liona Boyd composition, "Days Of Love And Innocence."

❊❊❊ **Awakening ... The Breath Of Life**
1992 Bertina Celina (JBCD1292)

> Dreamscapes; Morning Breaking; Bed Of Roses; Deep Within My Soul; Bonny Love; Days Of Love And Innocence; Daughter Of The Moon; Mayfair; Come Little Children; Enter In; Water Gardens; Lovely Elora; Leslie's Isle; Sonja; River Of Gods (Thames); On The Shore Of Leamington; Can You Sense Mother Earth?; Elephants Of Kenya *69:34*

Edith Butler

FRENCH CANADIAN/ACADIAN; FOLK/POP; SINGER-SONGWRITER

Acadian chanteuse Edith Butler, from Caraquet, New Brunswick, began her career as a French-Canadian folksinger playing coffeehouses and festivals in the early 60's. Drawing upon a repertoire of Acadian folksongs, she played the Mariposa Folk Festival in 1970 and began doing television shows, including a regular spot on the CBC program, *Singalong Jubilee*. Her early, folk, albums are out of print, with the exception of *L'Acadie S'Marie*, which has been reissued on CD. Her popularity ultimately led her to abandon the folk genre as she began releasing popular material and disco-oriented party records. It is to be hoped that more of her forceful, traditional work will eventually be reissued.

❋❋❋(❋) **L'Acadie S'Marie**
1974?, reissued 1991 Sony (BUK 50076)

L'Acadie S'Marie; Le Dix D'Avril; Le Reve; Mon Ami; Je Voudrais Etre; Il M'Envoit A L'Ecole; Berceuse Pour Emmanuel; On Parlera De Nous, Some Day *24:46*

❋❋❋ **Édith Butler**
1990 Disques Kappa (KA-CD1990)†

Drôle D'Hiver; Un Million De Fois Je T'Aime; Certains Jours De Pluie; Matawila; Coeur Qui Danse; Cajuns De L'An 2000; Comme Un Béluga; Ne Pleure Pas; Super Happening *35:19*

❋❋❋ **Tout Un Party!**
1992 Disques Star (STR-CD-8042)

Le Reel Des Reels: Reels De Sherbrooke Et Du Cordonnier/La Danse À St-Dilon/ Poules Et Guenilles/Tout Le Monde Est Malheureux/Le Quadrille De Rivière-Du-Loup/Y Mouillera Pu Pan Toutte/Raspa; On N'A Pas Tous Les Jours Vingt Ans/ Voulez-Vous Danser Grand-Mere; Les Petits Coeurs; Hommage À Madame Bolduc: J'Ai Un Bouton Sur La Langue/Ça Va Venir, Découragez-Vous Pas/Le Petit Sauvage Du Nord; La Bastringue; Son Voile Qui Volait; Vot'Ti Chien Madame; Paquetville; Louisiane Jamboree: Jambalaya/Collinda/Aiko Aiko/L'Arbre Est Dans Ses Feuilles/ Diggy Diggy Lo; Rock And Roll, Rock And Roll: Rock Around The Clock/Blue Suede Shoes/Johnny B. Goode; Ma Mere Chantait Toujours; La Bamba; Samba Samba: Faut Rigoler/Si Tu Vas À Rio/Un Ti Bo/L'Incendie À Rio; Na Na Hey Hey Goodbye *63:22*

Liam Callaghan & The Water Of Life

CELTIC/FOLK/ROCK; SINGER-SONGWRITER

Liam Callaghan and The Water Of Life are an Irish-Celtic band from Montreal. Their CD, *Crooked Jack*, ranges from Pogues-like rockers to traditional-style reels like "Connaught Man's Ramble/Jenny's Chickens." The Water Of Life is David Gossage, Thom Gossage, Bob Cussen, Christophe Comte, Bill Gossage, and Jenny Gilbert. David Gossage is also a member of Orealis.

❋❋❋ **Crooked Jack**
1994 Allan Patrick (IWM-001)

Paddy's Green Shamrock Shore; Bangin' Away; Connaught Man's Ramble/Jenny's Chickens; Johnny All American; Married Molly; Kerry Reel; Drunk Again; Éamann An Chnoic; South Wind; Crooked Jack; Father O'Flynn/Morning Dew; Don't Let Me Be Misunderstood; Little Drummer; Christophe's G Tunes *49:35*

John Allan Cameron

TRADITIONAL/CONTEMPORARY FOLK

Maritimer John Allan Cameron is Canada's ambassador of folk music. A popular guest on Canadian and American television programs during the 1960's folk revival, and the host of his own television series during 1975-76, Cameron's friendly personality made him a household name among mainstream viewers. An interpreter of other people's songs, Cameron was among the first to to record the songs of John Pryne,

Eric Bogle, and Stan Rogers. Cameron received a "Lifetime Achievement Award" at the 1995 East Coast Music Awards. A popularizer of Cape Breton music, Cameron has always delivered honest, workmanlike performances, though the pace of his playing is too slow for many listeners. Those who enjoy Cameron's style will want both *Wind Willow* and *Classic John Allen Cameron*. Both are collections of old favourites, with a sprinkling of more contemporary pieces such as Gordon Lightfoot's "Sit Down Young Stranger," and Stan Rogers' "Mary Ellen Carter."

❋❋❋   **Wind Willow**
          [no date] Margaree Sound (MSCD 9128)

> The Ballad Of St. Anne's Reel; Wind Willow; The Four Marys; Calin' Mo Ruinsa; Banks Of Sicily; Flower Of Scotland; Mary Ellen Carter; Sit Down Young Stranger; Molly Bond; Liberty *39:02*

❋❋❋   **Classic John Allen Cameron, Vol. 1 & 2**
          [no date] Margaree Sound (MSCD 9231)

> Sound The Pibroch; Mingulay Boat Song; Butterfingers Medley; Fisherman's Song; Mary Mac; Free Born Man; Broom O'Cowdenknowes; Fiddle Medley; Gaelic Songs; Make And Break Harbour; And The Band Played Waltzing Matilda; The Lord Of The Dance; Mrs. Hamilton And The Dominion Reel; The Minstrel Of Cranberry Lane; Birds Of Joy; Banks Of Sicily; Trip To Mabou Ridge; I Can't Tell You; Please Don't Bury Me; Elizabeth Lindsey; Maggie Brown; The Four Marys *66:46*

Moira Cameron

TRADITIONAL FOLK

The liner notes to *One Evening As I Rambled ... A Collection Of Traditional Songs, Stories, And Tunes* provide very little information about Moira Cameron other than that she hails from Yellowknife in the Northwest Territories and that she specializes in traditional music. The album itself is riveting. Whether Cameron is playing recorder, bowed psaltery, Appalachian dulcimer, or singing traditional songs with or without accompaniment, this is a splendid album for those who love the traditional repertoire. Moira Cameron is the daughter of the late Stu Cameron, one of the founding members of Friends of Fiddler's Green.
   See also Ceilidh Friends.

❋❋❋❋✓   **One Evening As I Rambled**
          [no date] Moira Cameron (MKC3968)

> Ronde/Gavotte; Outlandish Knight; Banks Of Primroses; Shepherd's Song; Morgan Megan; Banks Of Airdire-O; Bransle De Champaigne; Johnny Be Fair; Drimindown; Reynardine/Mr. Fox; Gathering Peascods *42:59*

Bill Candy

FOLK/POP; SINGER-SONGWRITER

Ontario singer-songwriter and talented guitarist Bill Candy is a folk/pop artist with a James Taylor-like, laid-back delivery and mixed styles that range from folk to swing to pop. A well-produced album, *Closer To The Music* features Candy's smooth vocals on songs like "My Rainbow," "Closer To The Music," "Peace Of Mind," "Too Full To Boogie," and "The Fat Cat Blues."

✳✳✳ **Closer To The Music**
1994 Mill Street (BCCD-1)†

> My Rainbow; The Dough's On The Rise; Closer To The Music; Peace Of Mind; Too Full To Boogie; There's Magic Tonight; I'm On A Roll; I Can't Say That It's True; The Fat Cat Blues; Baby You Mean So Much; Darling You Can Talk To Me *39:55*

Cape Breton Chorale
CHORAL FOLK

The Cape Breton Chorale is a mixed chorus of fifty-five voices. Founded in Sydney, Nova Scotia, in 1973, it includes members from many communities in Cape Breton. Their album, *Songs Of Atlantic Canada*, is more tightly focused on music of the region than are the albums of similar Maritimes choral groups. In addition to two Rita MacNeil songs—"Home I'll Be" and "Working Man"—the Chorale performs a traditional song collected by folklorist Helen Creighton, "The Hills And Glens" and Kenzie MacNeil's "The Island." Those who enjoy choral performances of folk music will enjoy this album.

✳✳✳ **Songs Of Atlantic Canada**
1991 Cape Breton Chorale (D91-2)

> The Dashing White Sergeant; Cape Breton Lullaby; The Hills And Glens; She's Called Nova Scotia; The Road To The Isles; Song Of Cape Breton; Home I'll Be; Feller From Fortune; Away From The Roll Of The Sea; Working Man; A Great Big Sea; Song For The Mira; The Island *42:54*

Cape Breton Summertime Revue
MARITIMES CELTIC; TRADITIONAL FOLK

Each year since the early 1980's, the Summertime Productions Society has staged a concert in Halifax called the Cape Breton Summertime Revue. In a program of singing, instrumentals, and comedy, the revue features regulars plus a changing cast of invited artists. Fiddle fans, for instance, will find some wonderful tracks by Natalie MacMaster and the late, extremely talented Tara Lynne Tousenard. The mixed, eclectic albums are treasure chests waiting to be explored.

✳✳✳(✳) **Cape Breton Summertime Revue 1991**
1991 Summertime Productions (SPC-9101)

> Fiddle Medley: Spey In Spate/The Fourth Bridge/The Fox Hunter *(Natalie MacMaster)*; When Angels Brush Their Hair *(Max MacDonald)*; From Here To There *(Doris Mason)*; The Country's Got The Blues *(Matt Minglewood)*; Trust Fund *(Maynard Morrison)*; Strathlorne *(Doris Mason; Matt Minglewood)*; Fiddle Medley: Blackberry Blossom/The Red Haired Lady/Paddy O'Brien's/The Dawn *(Natalie MacMaster)*; Summer By The Sea *(Doris Mason)*; Ninja Tories *(Max MacDonald)*; From Father To Son *(Matt Minglewood)*; Wind Song *(Fred Lavery)*; Good Dear Good *(Bette MacDonald)*; Song For Peace; Fiddle Medley: Strathspey/Paddy On The Turnpike/ Neil's Reel *(Natalie MacMaster)*; Home In My Harbour *(Max MacDonald)* *55:59*

❋❋❋(❋) **Cape Breton Summertime Revue 1992**
1992 Summertime Productions (SPSCD-9201)

Let The Music Begin; Fiddle Medley: Christy Campbell/Wissahickon Drive/The
Springer *(Tara Lynne Tousenard)*; Bras D'Or *(Max MacDonald)*; Feed The Fire
(Doris Mason); Chet Frettin' *(Fred Lavery)*; Stop Knocking The Cape *(Max
MacDonald; Maynard Morrison)*; As Don Goes By *(Doris Mason)*; Piper's Lament
(Bette MacDonald); Four Marys; Remember The Miner *(Richard Burke)*; Fiddle
Medley: Ashokan Farewell/Sweep's Hornpipe/Molly Rankin's Reel/Donegal Reel/
Cape Breton Welcome To The Shetland Islands *(Tara Lynne Tousenard)*; 3000 Miles
(Doris Mason); Song For Cape Breton (Tic's Song); Fiddle Medley: Constitution
Breakdown/Big John MacNeil *(Tara Lynne Tousenard)*; Rural Dignity *(Richard
Burke)*; Said It With A Bongo *(Maynard Morrison)*; Fiddle Medley: Miss MacLeod's
Reel/Brenda Stubbert's Reel *(Tara Lynne Tousenard)*; You Never Get Away *(Max
MacDonald)*; Only Mulroney *(Bette MacDonald)*; Medley: Some Summer/Crossing
The Causeway/MacDonald's Reel/Sea People/Go Off On Your Way/Song For The
Mira/Along The Shores Of Cape Breton/St. Anne's Reel/As The Circle Continues
60:41

❋❋❋(❋) **Cape Breton Summertime Revue 1993**
1993 Summertime Productions (SPSCD-9301)

Fiddle Medley: Til Daylight Comes/The Marchioness Of Huntley/Miss Maules
Strathspey/Sandy MacIntyre's Trip To Boston/Andy Renwick's Ferret; Cheticamp
Sky *(Max MacDonald)*; Let's Bring Back The Railroad; Cruel One *(Richard Burke)*;
Brand New Day *(Doris Mason; Maynard Morrison)*; No Way Nanette *(Bette
MacDonald)*; Fiddler's Bow *(Bette MacDonald)*; Marcel Doucet Medley: Space
Available March/Cornelia's Reel; The Coal Tones; Rollin' On The Sea *(Richard
Burke)*; Owen's Clog Medley: Owen's Clog/Triplet Clog/Barra Falls Hornpipe/Mike
And Marlene's Reel; She Can't Help It *(Doris Mason)*; Placebo Dominion *(Richard
Burke)*; Tiny Boats *(Max MacDonald)*; Comedy Sketches: Decisions, Decisions/The
Way It Is?/Over The Fence/Mass Appeal *71:53*

❋❋❋(❋) **Cape Breton Summertime Revue 1994**
1994 Summertime Productions (SPSCD-9401)

Prelude: Lord And Lady/John MacCormick's Jig/Run In The Nylon Jig/William
Norbert's Reel/Sheehan's Reel/Mrs. MacLeod's Reel; Songs Of Home *(Richard
Burke)*; Come A Ki Yi Yippie Yippie Yea *(Max MacDonald)*; Oh Love *(Doris
Mason)*; The Skinner Medley *(Shawn MacDonald; Krista Tousenard)*; Driver
McIvor *(Maynard Morrison)*; Happy Birthday Rita; To Tara: Tara's Melody/Let's
Never Say Farewell/MacKinnon's March/Tara Lynne Tousenard's Reel/Swinging On
The Gaetz *(Krista Tousenard)*; The Coal Tones; Mood For Mira *(Richard Burke)*;
From A Rocking Chair *(Max MacDonald; Doris Mason)*; Underneath The Sun;
Hangman's Reel *(Shawn MacDonald)*; Make And Break Harbour; Comedy
Sketches: Toe The Line/You're On The Air/A Stitch In Time/John Who?/The Way It
Is *75:24*

Captain Tractor
CELTIC-FLAVOURED ROCK; SINGER-SONGWRITERS

Edmonton's Captain Tractor is an energetic Celtic-rock band reminiscent of early
Spirit Of The West. With rocked up arrangements, combined with a sprinkling of
mandolin, banjo, harmonica, penny whistle, and twelve-string guitar among the electric guitars and drums, the band could play any Celtic pub in the country. Two bouncy

folksongs, the traditional "Jug O' Punch" and Wade Hemsworth's "The Logdriver's Waltz" close out the group's slightly frenetic debut album, *Land*. Captain Tractor is Brock Armstrong, Aimée Hill, Jules Mounteer, Scott Peters, Jeff Smook, and Chris Wynters.

✳✳✳ **Land**
1994 Captain Tractor (RCD 219)†

Pitcairn Island; Not In This Town; This Is Not A Sad Song; Sound Strange; Give It Back, My Heart; Ghost Riders; Fish; Ministry; Mmm Donut; The Rose Bowl Song; The Road Ahead; Hold Me; 400X; Jug O' Punch; The Logdriver's Waltz *55:35*

Ceilidh Friends

FOLK; SINGER-SONGWRITERS

Ceilidh Friends, a folk group from Yellowknife, performs traditional, modern, and Northern songs on *Yellowknife Evening*. Combining voice with instruments like guitar, recorder, Appalachian dulcimer, hammered dulcimer, bohdran, spoons, and moose bones, the group consists of Moira Cameron, Steve Goff, Dawn Lacey, and Steve Lacey. This album is a treat for those who enjoy traditional music, instrumentation, and homespun vocals.
See also Moira Cameron.

✳✳✳ **Yellowknife Evening**
1994 Ceilidh Friends (MDS-2)

Calling-On Song/The Red-Haired Boy/The Battle Of Aughrim/The Great Orange Whale; Farewell To Tarwathie; Daddy Fox; Farewell To Canada; Yellowknife Evening; The Prairie Pagans; Catch Round The Table; The Female Drummer; She's Like The Swallow/Memory; The Cutty Wren; The World Turned Upside Down, Part 2; Mingulay Boat Song *40:37*

Don Chambers

FOLK; SINGER-SONGWRITER

Victoria singer-songwriter Don Chambers has put together a solid debut album with *Free Falling*, a collection featuring songs like "Sing River Sing," inspired by a canoe trip, "One By One," written for a peace rally, "Georgia," dedicated to a faltering pet dog, and "Free Falling," inspired by involvement in preserving old growth forest. Chambers' pleasant voice and uncluttered acoustic guitar arrangements make this a very enjoyable folk recording from an emerging songwriter. *Free Falling* was produced by Allen des Noyers.

✳✳✳ **Free Falling**
1993 Olive House [no catalogue number]†

Sing River Sing; One By One; God, Gold And Glory; Sound Of Waves; Georgia; Half Way Along; The Return; Free Falling; Curious Place Called Home *43:50*

Al Cherny
FIDDLE

A regular on the venerated *Don Messer Jubilee* and *Tommy Hunter* TV shows, Al Cherny, née Chernywech, born in Medicine Hat, Alberta in 1932, was a splendid fiddler who shifted from style to style with ease. In addition to winning most of the fiddle championships in Canada, he was also a highly-regarded studio musician who recorded for Sylvia Tyson, Jesse Winchester, and others in the 1970's. Cherny died in 1987. The PolyTel compact disc—*A Tribute To Al Cherny*—captures a fine sampling of the spectrum of Cherny's adroit playing. It's a pity the disc contains no liner notes to provide more information on this accomplished, polished musician.

❋❋❋❋ **A Tribute To Al Cherny**
1989 PolyTel (841215 2)

> Alabama Jubilee/Down Yonder/Turkey In The Straw; Old Joe Clark/Golden Slippers/Boil Them Cabbage Down; Rubber Dolly/Maple Sugar; Spanish Two-Step/Little Home In West Virginia; Orange Blossom Special; Maiden's Prayer/Faded Love/San Antonio Rose; Golden Wedding Waltz/Blue Skirt Waltz; Life In The Finland Woods/Westphalia Waltz; Cold, Cold Heart/Your Cheatin' Heart; Last Date/Sleep Walk; Perdido; In The Mood; Tennessee Waltz/Fascination/Anniversary Waltz; Melody Of Love; Anniversary Song; French Minuet; Al's Seven Step; Happy Hours Schottische; Shannon Waltz/Let Me Call You Sweetheart; Road To The Isles/Scotland The Brave; Irish Washerwoman/McNamara's Band; Beer Barrel Polka/Wedding Polka; Heel And Toe Polka; Clarinet Polka; Butterfly; Bird Dance; Cherry Pink And Apple Blossom White/Yellow Bird/Never On Sunday; Dark Eyes/Spanish Eyes; Autumn Leaves *73:38*

Cindy Church
COUNTRY/FOLK; SINGER-SONGWRITER

Alberta singer-songwriter Cindy Church, along with her husband and musical partner Nathan Tinkham, is best known for her vocal support for Ian Tyson and her membership in Quartette. Her solo album, *Love On The Range*, highlights her outstanding voice in a set of country/western songs that include some Church originals such as "Road To Home," "Cowgirl's Lullaby," and "Tonight He's Mine."

❋❋❋(❋) **Love On The Range**
1994 Stony Plain (SPCD 1194)

> Rockabilly Heart; Road To Home; Old Fashioned Love; My Wishing Room; Walking The Dog; Cowgirl's Lullaby; Love On The Range; This October Day; Tonight He's Mine; Maybe We Should Stay Strangers; I Thought We Were Falling In Love; Ride Cowboy Ride *35:57*

Bruce Cockburn
FOLK/BLUES/ROCK; SINGER-SONGWRITER

A diverse artist of international renown, Toronto singer-songwriter and exemplary musician Bruce Cockburn (pronounced *co-burn*) came to fame as the 1960's folk revival was drawing to a close. While the 60's were clearly among Cockburn's formative influences, Cockburn has never been stuck in any particular musical style. He has roamed freely, exploring the possibilities offered in both the acoustic and electric worlds. Cockburn begins his career as a folkie, moving into a precursor of New Age during the mid 70's with meditational kinds of albums. Later he catches fire with electric instruments and hard lyrics that propel him into a rock mode. Most recently he has synthesized his various periods into a new kind of folk/rock.

Most, but not all, of Cockburn's albums have been reissued on compact disc. It is his earliest albums that reflect the primary folk/acoustic period of his development. The earliest CD available is *High Winds White Sky*. The catchy ramble of the opening track—"Happy Good Morning Blues"—sets the tone. Dating from the same period is *Sunwheel Dance* which provides additional vintage Cockburn. The album's highlights include the bouncy opener, "My Lady And My Lord," the bluesy "Up On A Hillside", and the lengthy "Dialogue With The Devil." *Night Vision*, perhaps Cockburn's best-known early album, starts off with four classic tracks—the sprightly instrumental, "Foxglove," followed by "You Don't Have To Play The Horses," "The Blues Got The World...," and "Mama Just Wants to Barrelhouse All Night Long." *Salt, Sun And Time*, from 1974, is another Cockburn landmark. It opens with the classic "All The Diamonds In The World" followed by the elegant "Salt, Sun And Time." These early Cockburn albums rank among the finest contemporary Canadian folk recordings.

Beginning with *Joy Will Find A Way*, a 1975 release, Cockburn slips into a meditational genre reminiscent of today's New Age music. He continues in this vein on the 1976 album *In The Falling Dark*. The 1979 release, *Dancing In The Dragon's Jaws* moves Cockburn into a more electric mode. The album produced the hit single "Wondering Where The Lions Are." The 1980 *Humans* reveals a stronger political/ social-issue orientation. With *Inner City Front*, 1981, Cockburn's transition to electric instrumentation and folk/rock is fully complete.

As Cockburn works further into the 80's with his 1983 release, *The Trouble With Normal*, it becomes difficult to describe Cockburn's music as folk/rock. By this point he is a solid rocker except for occasional soft spots in his track listings where the introspective Cockburn peeks out from time to time. The 1984 *Stealing Fire* continues this trend, as does the 1985 *World Of Wonders*. The 1987 retrospective collection, *Waiting For A Miracle*, is a two-CD boxed set that covers Cockburn singles from 1970-1987. The two opening tracks, "Going To The Country" and "Musical Friends" are taken from Cockburn's 1980 *Bruce Cockburn* album, not available on CD at this time. The collection also features songs from other non-reissued albums—*Circles In The Stream* (1977), *Further Adventures Of* (1978), and *Mummy Dust* (1981). For anyone who enjoys both the acoustic and electric phases of Cockburn's work, this set is a particularly good buy. *Big Circumstance* (1988) continues the exploration of political/ social/environmental themes in a rock style. The high-energy 1990 *Live* recording presents Cockburn on stage. *Nothing But A Burning Light*, released in 1991, suggests another turn in Cockburn's music. The electric instrumentation is still present, but it's more subtle. There's a sense of return to folk/rock where the instrumentation enhances and emphasizes the lyrics rather than simply taking the lyrics for a ride.

Christmas, released in 1993, was unexpected. The selections are inspired and Cockburn, playing primarily acoustic instrumentation, does justice to all of them. If you enjoy Christmas music done in a folk style, this one is a must. *Dart To The Heart*, from 1994, picks up where *Nothing But A Burning Light* left off. It starts off with a rocker, "Listen For The Laugh," then settles into a mix of more personal and introspective material. There's a return to acoustic instrumentation on many of the tracks. The result is a highly satisfying album.

See also Anthologies: *Kick In The Darkness:Songs Of Bruce Cockburn*

❋❋❋(❋)✓ **High Winds White Sky**
1971 True North (WTNK 3)

Happy Good Morning Blues; Let Us Go Laughing; Love Song; One Day I Walk; Golden Serpent Blues; High Winds White Sky; You Point To The Sky; Life's Mistress; Ting—The Cauldron; Shining Mountain *38:41*

❋❋❋(❋)✓ **Sunwheel Dance**
1971 True North (WTNK 7)†

My Lady And My Lord; Feet Fall On The Road; Fall; Sunwheel Dance; Up On The Hillside; Life Will Open; It's Going Down Slow; When The Sun Falls; He Came From The Mountain; Dialogue With The Devil (Or "Why Don't We Celebrate"); For The Birds *34:48*

❋❋❋❋✓ **Night Vision**
1973 True North (TNK-11)

Foxglove; You Don't Have To Play The Horses; The Blues Got The World...; Mama Just Wants To Barrelhouse All Night Long; Islands In A Black Sky; Clocks Don't Bring Tomorrow—Knives Don't Bring Good News; When The Sun Goes Nova; Déjà Vu; Lightstorm; God Bless The Children *41:04*

❋❋❋(❋)✓ **Salt, Sun And Time**
1974 True North (WTNK 16)†

All The Diamonds In The World; Salt, Sun And Time; Don't Have To Tell You Why; Stained Glass; Rouler Sa Bosse; Never So Free; Seeds On The Wind; It Won't Be Long; Christmas Song *36:17*

❋❋❋ **Joy Will Find A Way**
1975 True North (WTNK 23)

Hand-Dancing; January In The Halifax Airport Lounge; Starwheel; Lament For The Last Days; Joy Will Find A Way (A Song About Dying); Burn; Skylarking; A Long-Time-Love Song; A Life Story; Arrows Of Light *43:16*

❋❋❋ **In The Falling Dark**
1976 True North (WTNK-26)

Lord Of The Starfields; Vagabondage; In The Falling Dark; Little Sea Horse; Water Into Wine; Silver Wheels; Giftbearer; Gavin's Woodpile; I'm Gonna Fly Someday; Festival Of Friends *49:02*

❋❋❋ **Dancing In The Dragon's Jaws**
1979 True North (WTNK 37)†

Creation Dream; Hills Of Morning; Badlands Flashback; Northern Lights; After The Rain; Wondering Where The Lions Are; Incandescent Blue; No Footprints *37:23*

❋❋❋ **Humans**
1980 True North (WTNK-42)†

Grim Travellers; Rumours Of Glory; More Not More; You Get Bigger As You Go; What About The Bond; How I Spent My Fall Vacation; Guerilla Betrayed; Tokyo; Fascist Architecture; The Rose Above The Sky *43:31*

❋❋❋ **Inner City Front**
1981 True North (TNK-47)†

You Pay Your Money And You Take Your Chances; The Strong One; All's Quiet On The Inner City Front; Radio Shoes; Wanna Go Walking; And We Dance; Justice; Broken Wheel; Loner *45:20*

❋❋❋ **The Trouble With Normal**
1983 True North (WTNK-53)†

The Trouble With Normal; Candy Man's Gone; Hoop Dancer; Waiting For The Moon; Tropic Moon; Going Up Against Chaos; Put Our Hearts Together; Civilization And Its Discontents; Planet Of The Clowns *42:04*

❋❋❋ **Stealing Fire**
1984 True North (VTNK 57)†

Lovers In A Dangerous Time; Maybe The Poet; Sahara Gold; Making Contact; Peggy's Kitchen Wall; To Raise The Morning Star; Nicaragua; If I Had A Rocket Launcher; Dust And Diesel *42:12*

❋❋❋ **World Of Wonders**
1985 True North (VTNK 66)

Call It Democracy; Lily Of The Midnight Sky; World Of Wonders; Berlin Tonight; People See Through You; See How I Miss You; Santiago Dawn; Dancing In Paradise; Down Here Tonight *44:09*

❋❋❋(❋) **Waiting For A Miracle: Singles 1970-1987**
1987 True North (TN2K-67)

CD1: Going To The Country; Musical Friends; One Day I Walk; It's Going Down Slow; Up On This Hillside; Feet Fall On The Road; Mama Just Wants To Barrelhouse All Night Long; All The Diamonds; Burn; Silver Wheels; I'm Gonna Fly Someday; Vagabondage; Free To Be; Laughter; Wondering Where The Lions Are; Tokyo; Fascist Architecture; The Trouble With Normal *65:41*

CD2: Rumours Of Glory; The Coldest Night Of The Year; Wanna Go Walking; You Pay Your Money And You Take Your Chance; Tropic Moon; Candy Man's Gone; Lovers In A Dangerous Time; If I Had A Rocket Launcher; Making Contact; Peggy's Kitchen Wall; People See Through You; Call It Democracy; See How I Miss You; Stolen Land; Waiting For A Miracle *63:28*

❋❋❋ **Big Circumstance**
1988 True North (TNK-70)†

If A Tree Falls; Shipwrecked At The Stable Door; Gospel Of Bondage; Don't Feel Your Touch; Tibetan Side Of Town; Understanding Nothing; Where The Death Squad Lives; Radium Rain; Pangs Of Love; The Gift; Anything Can Happen *61:17*

✳✳✳(✳) **Live**
1990 True North (TNK-73)†

Silver Wheels; World Of Wonders; Rumours Of Glory; See How I Miss You; After The Rain; Call It Democracy; Tibetan Side Of Town; Wondering Where The Lions Are; Nicaragua; Broken Wheel; Stolen Land; To Raise The Morning Star; Maybe The Poet; Always Look On The Bright Side Of Life *69:47*

✳✳✳(✳) **Nothing But A Burning Light**
1991 True North (TNK 77)†

A Dream Like Mine; Kit Carson; Mighty Trucks Of Midnight; Soul Of A Man; Great Big Love; One Of The Best Ones; Somebody Touched Me; Cry Of A Tiny Babe; Actions Speak Louder; Indian Wars; When It's Gone, It's Gone; Child Of The Wind *60:23*

✳✳✳(✳) **Christmas**
1993 True North (TNK 83)

Adeste Fidelis; Early On One Christmas Morn; O Little Town Of Bethlehem; Riu Riu Chiu; I Saw Three Ships; Down In Yon Forest; Les Anges Dans Nos Campagnes; Got Tell It On The Mountain; Shepherds; Silent Night; Iesus Ahatonnia (The Huron Carol); God Rest Ye Merry Gentlemen; It Came Upon The Midnight Clear; Mary Had A Baby; Joy To The World *57:31*

✳✳✳✳ **Dart To The Heart**
1994 True North (TNK 82)†

Listen For The Laugh; All The Ways I Want You; Bone In My Ear; Burden Of The Angel/Beast; Scanning These Crowds; Southland Of The Heart; Train In The Rain; Someone I Used To Love; Love Loves You Too; Sunrise On The Mississippi; Closer To The Light; Tie Me At The Crossroads *49:04*

Eddie Coffey
FOLK/COUNTRY; SINGER-SONGWRITER

Eddie Coffey, who now resides in Toronto, is an ex-Maritimer who has worked as a miner and a fisherman. As a performer who accompanies himself on accordion, his old-style country delivery has the ring of authority when he sings favourites from the East Coast repertoire. Coffey is also a songwriter, having penned tunes like "Where Have The Little Boats Gone?" "Cape St. Mary's Shore," "Spencil Hill," and "Shamrock Shore." Fans who like old-time country music will enjoy *Come Closer Eastcoaster*.

✳✳✳ **Come Closer Eastcoaster**
[no date] Heritage (HCD-4408)

Where Have The Little Boats Gone?; Cape St. Mary's Shore; Wild Mountain Thyme; Farewell To Nova Scotia; Spencil Hill; With Me Rubber Boots On; My Sweet Forget Me Not; Sonny's Dream; A Mother's Love Is A Blessing; Cec McEachern's Overture; Come Closer Eastcoaster; Nobody's Child; Shamrock Shore; Saltwater Cowboy; Fiddler's Green; Kelly's Mountain; Tiny Red Light; When We Were Sweet Sixteen; Black Velvet Band; Jack Delaney's Brew *63:56*

Leonard Cohen

FOLK/POP; SINGER/SONGWRITER

Montreal poet Leonard Cohen, a member of the Juno Hall of Fame, has maintained an amazingly durable and long career as a recording artist. Like Bob Dylan, Cohen is a cult figure and cultural icon. His early poetry and songs are indelibly linked to the 1960's folk revival where his "Suzanne," "Sisters Of Mercy," and "Bird On The Wire" became staples of the folk repertoire. Although Cohen defies easy classification, his early albums feature songs delivered in a folk style that relies on simple acoustic guitar, augmented at times with orchestral strings. Cohen is an original. His *épater les bourgeois* pose and seeming disregard for how he sounds is part of his attraction to his followers. In the main, however, it's Cohen's poetry that has made him so enduring. Cohen's early albums represent his freshest and most listenable work. His 1968 debut album, *Songs Of Leonard Cohen*, is a classic that should be on the shelf of every collection of Canadian folk music. It includes one excellent song after another, including "Suzanne," "Sisters Of Mercy," "So Long, Marianne," and "Hey, That's No Way To Say Goodbye." The 1969 *Songs From A Room* contains material such as "Bird On The Wire," "Story Of Isaac," and "The Partisan." *Songs Of Love And Hate*, 1970, features "Dress Rehearsal Rag," "Famous Blue Raincoat," and "Joan Of Arc."

New Skin For Old Ceremonies, released in 1974, marks a turn in Cohen's writing. He begins to rely on repetitious choruses, à la rock music, rather than the tight phrasing of his earlier work. He also begins to play on his public image rather than listening to the inner muse that made his earlier albums so special. *The Best Of Leonard Cohen*, a 1975 collection of many of the best songs, from his early albums is an excellent purchase. The 1977 *Death Of A Ladies' Man* continues the slide into indulgence that surfaced on *New Skin*. The 1979 release of *Recent Songs* shows a return to the kind of writing Cohen was doing on his early albums. With the exception of the bizarre "Lost Canadian," the album features Cohen back in strength. "The Guests," "Came So Far For Beauty," and "Ballad Of The Absent Mare" are among the album's highlights. The addition of Jennifer Warnes on backup vocals is another bonus. *Various Positions*, released in 1984, continues the successful merger of good lyrics and Jennifer Warnes backup vocals.

I'm Your Man, released in 1988, includes the well-known Cohen songs "First We Take Manhattan" and "Ain't No Cure For Love." The pop-music production suits the songs. This is Cohen gone into a rock-video phase. *The Futures*, 1992, continues in the same vein, but the songs are less interesting, with Cohen sounding like a parody of himself. It's his singing on this album that the Royal Canadian Air Farce (a popular Canadian comic troupe) loves to mimic. *Cohen Live: Leonard Cohen In Concert* is an album put together from live recordings from 1988 and 1993. The songs in these concerts represent his older work. His voice on the 1993 sections is the gravelly, uninflected intonation heard on his recent recordings. His 1988 voice sounds more like the Leonard Cohen most of us hear in our memories.

See also Jennifer Warnes.

✱✱✱✱✓ **Songs Of Leonard Cohen**
1968 Columbia (WCK 9533)

Suzanne; Master Song; Winter Lady; The Stranger Song; Sisters Of Mercy; So Long, Marianne; Hey, That's No Way To Say Goodbye; Stories Of The Street; Teachers; One Of Us Cannot Be Wrong *41:08*

✱✱✱(✱) **Songs From A Room**
1969 Columbia (WCK 9767)

Bird On The Wire; Story Of Isaac; A Bunch Of Lonesome Heros; The Partisan; Seems So Long Ago, Nancy; The Old Revolution; The Butcher; You Know Who I Am; Lady Midnight; Tonight Will Be Fine *35:36*

✱✱✱(✱) **Songs Of Love And Hate**
1970 Columbia (WCK 30103)

Avalanche; Last Year's Man; Dress Rehearsal Rag; Diamonds In The Mine; Love Calls You By Your Name; Famous Blue Raincoat; Sing Another Song, Boys; Joan Of Arc *45:05*

✱✱(✱) **New Skin For The Old Ceremony**
1974 Columbia (CD 32660)

Is This What You Wanted; Chelsea Hotel #2; Lover Lover Lover; Field Commander Cohen; Why Don't You Try; There Is A War; A Singer Must Die; I Tried To Leave You; Who By Fire; Take This Longing; Leaving Green Sleeves *37:11*

✱✱✱✱✓ **The Best Of Leonard Cohen**
1975 Columbia (WCK-34077)†

Suzanne; Sisters Of Mercy; So Long, Marianne; Bird On The Wire; Lady Midnight; The Partisan; Hey, That's No Way To Say Goodbye; Famous Blue Raincoat; Last Year's Man; Chelsea Hotel #2; Who By Fire; Take This Longing *46:51*

✱(✱) **Death Of A Ladies' Man**
1977 Columbia (CK 44286)†

True Love Leaves No Traces; Iodine; Paper Thin Hotel; Memories; I Left A Woman Waiting; Don't Go Home With Your Hard-On; Fingerprints; Death Of A Ladies' Man *42:34*

✱✱✱(✱) **Recent Songs**
1979 Columbia (WCK 36264)

The Guests; Humbled In Love; The Window; Came So Far For Beauty; The Lost Canadian (Un Canadien Errant); The Traitor; Our Lady Of Solitude; The Gypsy's Wife; The Smokey Life; Ballad Of The Absent Mare *53:06*

✱✱✱ **Various Positions**
1984 Columbia (WCK 90728)

Dance Me To The End Of Love; Coming Back To You; The Law; Night Comes On; Hallelujah; The Captain; Hunter's Lullaby; Heart With No Companion; If It Be Your Will *35:30*

❋❋❋ **I'm Your Man**
1988 Columbia (CK-44191)†

First We Take Manhattan; Ain't No Cure For Love; Everybody Knows; I'm Your Man; Take This Waltz; Jazz Police; I Can't Forget; Tower Of Song *40:58*

❋❋ **The Future**
1992 Columbia (CK 53226)†

The Future; Waiting For The Miracle; Be For Real; Closing Time; Anthem; Democracy; Light As The Breeze; Always; Tacoma Trailer *59:40*

❋❋❋ **Cohen Live: Leonard Cohen In Concert**
1994 Columbia (CK 80188)†

Dance Me To The End Of Love; Bird On The Wire; Everybody Knows; Joan Of Arc; There Is A War; Sisters Of Mercy; Hallelujah; I'm Your Man; Who By Fire; One Of Us Cannot Be Wrong; If It Be Your Will; Heart With No Companion; Suzanne *71:56*

Colcannon
MARITIMES CELTIC

Colcannon is a Celtic-oriented Maritimes group that, in the pub tradition, specializes in the interpretation of music by contemporary songwriters. With excellent voices and a sparkling banjo that adds an almost bluegrass touch to their arrangements, Colcannon works through well-known material such as "Portland Town," "The Leaving Of Nancy," and "Silver Sea." *Ode To Age* is a very lively, listenable album. Colcannon is John Curran, Wilf Curran, Dave Lush, and Art Payne.

❋❋❋❋ **Ode To Age**
1993 Colcannon (CLC001)

Portland Town; The Leaving Of Nancy; The Mason's Apron/The Devil's Dream; Silver Sea; Fox On The Run; Botany Bay; There Were Roses; The Leprechaun; The Boston Rose; The Mingulay Boat Song; Nancy Spain; Shuckin' The Corn/Foggy Mountain Breakdown; The Boys Of the Old Brigade; An Ode To Age *51:56*

The Cold Club
FOLK/JAZZ/OLD TIME

"The Cold Club is an eccentric group made up of Amos Garrett, Oscar Lopez, David Wilkie, Karl Roth, and Ron Casat...the musicianship is absolutely great"—*Festival Distribution Newsletter*. Calgary's Cold Club first recorded together for a CBC project and had such a good time they expanded the idea into a full CD recording—*The Cold Club*. The group plays old favourites, so the styles vary from show tunes to blues to swing. Here are some of the finest musicians in Canada all playing on the same album.

See also Karl Roth.

❋❋❋❋✓ **The Cold Club**
1994 Cold Club (CCR 001)

Nagasaki; Another French Waltz/Petite Waltz; Money Is King; The Dog Song; Say That You Were Teasin' Me; Monsoon; Nine Feathered Masks; Happy Talk; Jitterbug Waltz; Hey Buddy; One Minute Of Silence; Hey Buddy *45:48*

College Of Piping
CELTIC PIPING

The College of Piping and Celtic Performing Arts of Canada, located in Summerside, Prince Edward Island, has issued *Ancestral Voices* and *Ancestral Voices Across The Sea*, two collections dedicated to "keeping alive our Celtic heritage through voice and the sound of the great Highland bagpipe." These fine albums are hard to resist, though pipe lovers may find more vocals than they'd like.

❋❋❋(❋) **Ancestral Voices**
[no date] College of Piping [no catalogue number]

Island Sheiling Song; Green Hills; The Dark Island; Medley: Nan Ceadaicheadh An Tide Dhomh/The Ass In The Graveyard/Tommy Hunts Jig/The Cat And The Dog; Chi Mi Na Mor Bheanna (The Mist Covered Mountains); MacCrimmons Lament *(Scott MacAulay)*; March, Strathspey and Reel: Balmoral Highlanders/Captain Colin Campbell/The Ferryman; Come By The Hills; Solo Piping Medley: Carlabhagh/The Ferryman/Clean Pease Strae/The Barn Dance/The Maid Behind The Bar/The Congress Reel/The Piper's Bonnet *(Scott MacAulay)*; Tha Mi Sgith; Scotland The Brave; He Walked Through The Fair *(Shirley Williams)*; Margaret's Departure *(Scott MacAulay) 40:58*

❋❋❋(❋) **Ancestral Voices Across The Sea ...**
1994 College of Piping / Attic (ACD 1407)

My Youngest Son Came Home Today *(Patricia Murray)*; Reel Medley: Paddy O'Brien's/Josie McDermott's *(Sigrid Rolfe; Margie Carmichael-Scotto)*; Song For Ireland *(Patricia Murray)*; Scott MacAulay Pipe Solo: The Maiden From The Sea/ Karen Nuttall/David Ross *(Scott MacAulay)*; My Ain Country *(Jim Smith)*; The Water Is Wide *(Patricia Murray; Jim Smith)*; Medley—Guitars, Fiddle & Flute: Margaret Anne MacLeod/The Poisoned Dwarf/The Bush Reel/In And Out The Harbour/Kerry Fling/Calum And The Princess *(Kim Vincent; Margie Carmichael-Scotto; Sigrid Rolfe)*; Fair And Tender Ladies *(Patricia Murray)*; Flowers Of The Forest *(Scott MacAulay; Jim Smith)*; If Ever You Were Mine *(Kim Vincent; Sigrid Rolfe; Margie Carmichael-Scotto)*; Amazing Grace *(Patricia Murray) 44:02*

Connemara
MARITIMES CELTIC

Connemara, a Newfoundland Celtic group in the pub tradition, performs selections of contemporary material. *The River* includes songs from Stan Rogers, Sean McCarthy, Tommy Sands, Andy Stewart, and Bill Staines. Their middle-of-the-road approach to the material may not break any new ground, but the album is enjoyable. Connemara is Tom Nemec, Glenn Hiscock, and Jason Whelan.

❋❋❋ **The River**
1993 Piper Stock (PM 001)

The Hills Of Connemara; The Field Behind The Plow; Farewell To The Rhonda; Tickle Cove Pond; Quarry Road Jigs; Sam Hall; I Dream Of You; When The Boys Come Rollin' Home; The Queen Of Argyll; Sweet Sixteen; Alesis Reels; Sweet Forget Me Not; Trip To Jerusalem/Reel/The Wise Maid; The River *53:07*

Stompin' Tom Connors
FOLK/COUNTRY; SINGER-SONGWRITER

With a country-style delivery and folk-style lyrics, Stompin' Tom Connors, Porcupine Award Hall of Famer, is one of the most beloved of Canadian performers. Born in St. John, New Brunswick, Connors wrote his first song at age 11 and began playing guitar at age 15. Influenced by Wilf Carter and Hank Snow, Connors began playing professionally in 1964 at the Maple Leaf Hotel in Timmins, Ontario. He earned his nickname from his style of stomping the floor with his foot to establish the rhythm of his songs above the noise of the crowd. Connors, a fierce Canadian nationalist, dropped out of music altogether for a decade in protest over the lack of airplay of Canadian performers. Thankfully this black period of Canadian broadcasting is history and Connors has returned to his music.

Connors' songwriting ranges from clever, humourous ditties about Canadian life to Canadian tragedies. His obvious love for Canada expresses itself in the scope of his music, which includes songs about every region of the country. Many of his tunes have become Canadian classics: "Bud The Spud," "Sudbury Saturday Night," "Big Joe Mufferaw," "Roll On Saskatchewan," and "The Moon-Man Newfie," to name but a few. Connors has won many Juno awards and, in 1993, he was awarded an honourary doctorate, which prompted him to release a new album entitled *Dr. Stompin' Tom, Eh?*.

The problem, for the collector, is that Connors is such a prolific writer and recording artist that it's hard to know where to start. By 1979 he had released 29 LPs on Boot Records. Getting a sense of the sequence of the reissued albums is aggravated by Capitol's myopic decision not to put recording dates on the early CDs. Many of his albums are also quite short and frequently sold at full price in the record shops. For the casual fan, the best buy is *A Proud Canadian*, a collection of many of his best songs on one long-playing CD. From there you can branch out into Stompin' Tom's other recordings.

❋❋❋ **Bud The Spud**
1969 Capitol (C2 92974)

Bud The Spud; The Ketchup Song; Ben, In The Pen; Rubberhead; Luke's Guitar (Twang, Twang); My Brother Paul; The Old Atlantic Shore; My Little Eskimo; Reversing Falls Darling; She Don't Speak English; The Canadian Lumber Jack; Sudbury Saturday Night; T.T.C. Skidaddler; (I'll Be) Gone With The Wind *33:23*

❋❋❋ **Stompin' Tom Connors Meets Joe Mufferaw**
1970 Capitol (C2 93047)

Big Joe Mufferaw; Sable Island; Don't Overlove Your Baby; Log Train; Roll On

Saskatchewan; Jenny Donnelly; The Coal Boat Song; Algoma Central #69; The Night I Cremated Sam McGee; Poor, Poor Farmer; My Last Farewell; Rocky Mountain Love; Around The Bay And Back Again *31:55*

❊❊❊ ### My Stompin' Grounds
1971 Capitol (C2 92976)

My Stompin' Grounds; The Bridge Came Tumblin' Down; Snowmobile Song; "Wop" May; Cross Canada; Tillsonburg; Tribute To Wilf Carter; Song Of The Irish Moss; Song Of The Peddler; Bonnie Belinda; Name The Capital; Song Of The Cohoe *34:03*

❊❊❊ ### "Live" At The Horseshoe
1971 Capitol (C2 93048)

Happy Rovin' Cowboy; Big Joe Mufferaw; Come Where We're At; The Green, Green Grass Of Home No. 2; Spin, Spin; Muleskinner Blues; Horseshoe Hotel Song; I've Been Everywhere; Sudbury Saturday Night; Bus Tour To Nashville; Luke's Guitar; Bud The Spud *38:31*

❊❊❊ ### The North Atlantic Squadron
[no date] Capitol (C2 92977)

The North Atlantic Squadron; Red River Jane; High, Dry, And Blue; Blue Nose; Back Yardin'; Jack Of Many Trades; Unity; Fleur De Lis; I'll Love You All Over Again; (Too Late To Hurry) When Snow Flurries Fall; Take Me Down The River; Gypsy Chant *33:27*

❊❊❊ ### Stompin' Tom At The Gumboot Cloggeroo
[no date] Capitol (C2 92978)

Legend Of Marty And Joe; Jacqueline; The I Don't Know How To Fix The Damned Thing Blues (Handy Man Blues); Man From The Land; Farewell To Nova Scotia; Ripped Off Winkle; Gum-Boot Cloggeroo (Gumboot Cloggin); The Happy Hooker; We Doubt Each Others Love; Little Old Forgetful Me; The Singer (The Voice Of The People); Isle Of Newfoundland; Roses In The Snow; Home On The Island *40:11*

❊❊❊ ### On Tragedy Trail
[no date] Capitol (C2 93045)

Tragedy Trail; How The Mountain Came Down; Shanty Town Sharon; Fire In The Mine; Somewhere, There's Sorrow; Don Valley Jail; Benny The Bum; Black Donnelly's Massacre; Battle Of Despair; Reesor Crossing Tragedy; The Little Boy's Prayer; Around The Bay And Back Again *33:52*

❊❊❊ ### Stompin' Tom And The Hockey Song
[no date] Capitol (C2 93049)

The Consumer; The Last Fatal Duel; The Curse Of The Marc Guylaine; Blue Spell; Singin' Away My Blues; The Hockey Song; The Maritime Waltz; Gaspe Belle Faye; Where Would I Be?; True, True Love; The Piggy Back Race; Your Loving Smile; Mr. Engineer *33:08*

❊❊❊ ### To It And At It
1972 Capitol (C2 93050)

Prince Edward Island, Happy Birthday; To It And At It; Keepin' Nora Waitin';

Marten Hartwell Story; New Brunswick And Mary; Moonlight Lady; Muk Luk Shoo; Manitoba; Don Messer Story; Alcan Run; Pizza Pie Love; Golden Gone Bye; Cornflakes *34:43*

❈❈❈ Stompin' Tom Meets 'Muk Tuk' Annie
1974 Capitol (C2 93051)

Streaker's Dream; My Home By The Fraser; Bibles And Rifles; Paddlewheeler; Unfaithful Heart; Ballad Of Muk Tuk Annie; We're Trading Hearts; Oh Chihuahua; Zakuska Polka; I Saw The Teardrop; Wishful Hummin'; Renfrew Valley; My Old Canadian Home *37:03*

❈❈❈ The Unpopular Stompin' Tom
1976 Capitol (C2 93052)

Good Morning Mr. Sunshine; Where The Chinooks Blow; Zephyrs In The Maple; My Door's Always Open To You; Blue Misery; The Pole And The Hole (Money Pole); A Damn Good Song For A Miner (Muckin' Slushers); Cowboy, Johnny Ware; Ghost Of Bras D'Or; Don Valley Jail; Big And Friendly Waiter John; The Olympic Song *36:01*

❈❈❈ Fiddle & Song
1988 Capitol (C2-92921)†

Lady, K.D. Lang; Fiddler's Folly; It's All Over Now, Anyhow; The French Song; I Never Want To See The World Again; Hillside Hayride; Morning And Evening And Always; Return Of The Sea Queen; Canada Day, Up Canada Way; Jolly Joe MacFarland; Skinner's Pond Teapot; Teardrop Waltz; Entry Island Home; I Am The Wind; Wreck Of The Tammy Ann *41:24*

❈❈❈ Stompin' Tom And The Moon Man Newfie
[no date] Capitol (C2 92975)

Oh, Laura; The Isles Of Magdalen; Fire In The Mine; I Can Still Face The Moon; The Bug Song; The Moon-Man Newfie; Roving All Over The Land; Movin' In (From Montreal By Train); Benny The Bum; Twice As Blue; Little Wawa; Rubberhead *31:28*

❈❈❈❈✓ A Proud Canadian
1990 Capitol (7777-80010-2)

Bud The Spud; Snowmobile Song; Roll On Saskatchewan; Manitoba; Sudbury Saturday Night; Tillsonburg; Roving All Over The Land; New Brunswick And Mary; Big Joe Mufferaw; Gumboot Cloggeroo; The Old Atlantic Shore; Blue Nose; Fleur De Lis; The Moon-Man Newfie; The Ketchup Song; Lady, K.D. Lang; The Bridge Came Tumblin' Down; Marten Hartwell Story; I Am The Wind; The Singer (The Voice Of The People) *55:18*

❈❈❈ More Of The Stompin' Tom Phenomenon
1991 Capitol (C2-95897)†

Margo's Cargo; Flyin' C.P.R.; Rita MacNeil (A Tribute); Brown Eyes For The Blues; J.R.'s Bar; Loser's Island; St. Anne's Song And Reel; Made In The Shade; Love's Not The Only Thing; Land Of The Maple Tree; A Real Canadian Girl; Okanagan Okee; No Canadian Dream; Gone With The Wind (I'll Be) *41:59*

※※※ **Once Upon A Stompin' Tom**
1991 Capitol (C2 97103)

Canada Day, Up Canada Way; The Ketchup Song; Zephyrs In The Maple; The
Piggy-Back Race; The Hockey Song; Cornflakes; Song Of The Cohoe; C-a-n-a-d-a
(Cross Canada); Name The Capitals; Little Wawa; Moon-Man Newfie; The Olympic
Song; "Wop May"; Unity *38:06*

※※※ **Believe In Your Country**
1992 Capitol (C2 99599)†

Johnny Maple; My Home Cradled Out In The Waves; Prairie Moon; She Called
From Montreal; Lover's Lake; Lena Kathleen; Believe In Your Country; Alberta
Rose; Sunshine And Teardrops; My Sleeping Carmello; Lookin' For Someone To
Hold; Paper Smile; Smile Away Your Memory; The Ballinafad Ball *39:38*

※※※ **Dr. Stompin' Tom...Eh?**
1993 EMI (72438-27225-26)†

Football Song; Horse Called Farmer; Road To Thunder Bay; Your Someone
Lonesome; Just A Blue Moon Away; Old Flat-Top Guitar; Honeymoon Is Over,
Poochie Pie; Canada Day, Up Canada Way; Blue Berets; Let's Smile Again; Suzanne
De Lafayette (aka Girl From Lafayette); Gumboot Cloggeroo; Shakin' The Blues
41:28

Joe Cormier
ACADIAN FIDDLE MUSIC

Cape Breton French-Acadian Joe Cormier absorbed the local Scottish tradition of
fiddle playing during his youth. Directly influenced by Angus Chisholm and, especially, Winston Fitzgerald, Cormier developed a unique style with heavily empha-
sized triplet bowing. *Joseph Cormier And Friends* captures the sprightly energy of
Cormier's style. A must for collectors of Canadian fiddle music.

※※※※✓ **Joseph Cormier And Friends**
1992 Rounder (CD 7013)

The Bungalow Reel/Coire An Lochan/Traditional Pipe Reel; Culloden House/
Rothermurche's Rant/The Braes Of Auchertyre/The Braes Of Glencoe; The Drover's
Lad/Green Grass Of Gasque/Hills Of Glenorchy/Rosewood Jig; Flee As A Bird
Clog/East Neuk O' Fife/Lord Seaforth; Miss Minnie Foster's Clog/Fred Wilson's
Clog/Archie Menzie/The Perth Assembly; Annie Is My Darling Medley/The Red
Shoes; Ashokan Farewell; Forth Bridge/The Marquis Of Huntley's Highland Fling/
Largo's Fairy Dance/Cottonwood Reel; Old Time Wedding Reels/The Contradiction/
Magnetic Hornpipe; Margaret Chisholm/The Chanter/Thompson's Jig/Light And
Airy; Miss Hutton/The Marquis Of Huntly/Col. McBain/Strathbogie/The Old Reel;
Neil Gow's Lament For The Death Of His Second Wife/Stirling Castle/John
Howatt's Reel; Neil Gow's Lament For Dr. Moray/Don Side/Harness The Old Grey
Mare/Fiddler's Favorite; H. MacWorth/Newcastle Clog/The Arthur Seat *55:12*

Courage Of Lassie
FOLK/POP; SINGER-SONGWRITERS

The Toronto band Courage Of Lassie is a slightly Celtic-oriented group that blends an eclectic set of folkish lyrics with semi-acoustic instrumentation. Courage Of Lassie consists of several people who have been active in the Toronto folk scene for many years, including Ron Nelson, Mady Schenkel, Rod Booth, Rachel Melas, and Jason Fowler. Guest musicians include vocals by Molly Johnson and the late Karen Gamble, to whom the album is dedicated.

❋❋❋ **This Side Of Heaven**
1994 PolyGram (76974 2011-2)†

Urge For Going; City Of Tears; The Ballad Of Handsome Ned And John MacLeod; Pour Toi Mon Amour; In Montreal City; Kali Nichta (Good Night); Hey Hey Hey (Positively Queen Street); The Rainforest Falls; The Desert Song; This Side Of Heaven; Portland Isle; Kali Mera (Good Morning) *54:10*

Doug Cox
FOLK/BLUEGRASS/COUNTRY; ORIGINAL DOBRO COMPOSITIONS; SINGER-SONGWRITER

British Columbia dobro player Doug Cox, a member of the band Travels With Charley, puts a contemporary spin on this undervalued instrument. In the hands of Cox, the dobro takes stage centre with its unique, evocative sound. On *Canadian Borderline*, Cox joins forces with a tightly-knit group of musicians to create a mixed instrumental/vocal album of his compositions and songs. While Cox's workman-like vocals aren't quite as polished as his instrumentals, the harmonies from his colleagues help smooth over any rough patches. Although the album has many highlights, especially Cox's instrumental compositions, the dobro interpretation of Neil Young's "After The Gold Rush" lingers in the mind like a fondly-remembered dream.
See also Travels With Charley.

❋❋❋(❋) **Canadian Borderline**
1993 Malahat (MMM-CD-001)

Mary Greig; Let The Mystery Be; Garry Owen/Banish Misfortune; Canadian Borderline; My Father; Lenny; Don't Bring Me Water; Caravan; We're All The Way; Rain On; Fool's Paradise; Shuckin' The Corn; Take Back The Nation; After The Gold Rush *58:20*

Cravan Spirit
FOLK; SINGER-SONGWRITERS

Cravan Spirit is a folk duo consisting of Bill Crawford and Ed VandenDool who, along with Linda Crawford, have run the Caledonia Folk Club, in Caledonia, Ontario, since 1988. With soft voices and harmonies somewhat reminiscent of early Simon and Garfunkel, Cravan Spirit mixes a few original songs among covers of material by contemporary songwriters. Their debut album, *Singing The Spirit Home*, includes songs by Nick Kier, Dan Seals, Si Kahn, Dougie Maclean, Eric Bogle, and Dick Gaughan, as well as "Bill's Caledonia," by Crawford and "Rest Sweet Child," by VandenDool.

Guest artists on this recording include Allison Lupton, flute, Donald McGeoch, whistle, and Brian Morton on keyboards.

✳✳✳ **Singing The Spirit Home**
1995 Unity Arts (UA02 140)

Festival Lights; We Are One; Sound Song; Arragon Mill; If My Wheels Skid In The Rain; Caledonia; Singing The Spirit Home; Rest Sweet Child; Pleasant And Delightful; Both Sides The Tweed; Rolling Hill Of The Borders; If Wishes Were Fishes; Going Home; Bill's Caledonia *54:13*

Seamus Creagh
IRISH FIDDLE

For a short while Irish master fiddler Seamus Creagh immigrated to Canada and made his home in Newfoundland before returning to Ireland. While in Canada he recorded *Came The Dawn*—accompanied by Newfoundland musicians. Creagh's technique is light and restrained. Anyone who loves fiddle music will find this album immensely satisfying.

✳✳✳✳✓ **Came The Dawn**
[no date] Pigeon Inlet (PIPCD 7330)

Reels: Pete Cooper's/Cronin's; Jigs: Connie The Soldier/Paddy Fahy's; Hornpipes: Julia Clifford's/Sean Healy's; Reels: Cottage In The Grove/Star Of Munster; Air: Lament For Kinsale; Slides: Kiskeam/Aut O'Keefe's; Reels: Col. McBain/ O'Reilly's; Nfld. Reels: Bridgett's/Jim Hodder; Slides: Merrily Kiss The Quaker/ Dingle Regatta; Polkas: Connie In The Pool/The Gortnatubrid; Air: Táimse I M' Chodladh Is Na Dúistear Mé (I'm Asleep, Don't Wake Me); Reels: The Glen Road To Carrick/Gan Anam; Hornpipe: Johnny Cope; Reels: The Dawn 1-2 *45:24*

Crickle Wood
MARITIMES CELTIC

Cricklewood is the performing duo of David Craig and Paul DuJohn. Cricklewood plays traditional and contemporary Celtic-flavoured material. *Almost Tight* offers a middle-of-the-road delivery of old favourites such as "Fiddler's Green," "Moonshiner," and even the old Bob Shane, Kingston Trio classic "Scotch And Soda." *Barley Famous* continues in the same groove with songs such as "Banks Of The Roses," "The Dutchman," and "Lark In The Morning." The albums are pleasant, if unexceptional.

✳✳✳ **Almost Tight**
[no date] David Craig [no catalogue number]

Star Of The County Down; Fiddlers' Green; Moonshiner; Merrily Kissed The Quaker/Morrison's Reel; Flower Of Scotland; Why Don't Women Like Me?; Scotch And Soda; Ramblin' Rover; Right Alright; Fields Of Athenry; Sheehan's Reel; Shenandoah; Woman In The Bed; Song For The Mira; Sonny's Dream *53:45*

✳✳✳ **Barely Famous**
[no date] David Craig (RDRCD-663)

Banks Of The Roses; Dirty Old Town; Si Bheag Si Mhor; Prison Dance; Lady By

The Sea; The Dutchman; Take Her In Your Arms; Mairi's Wedding; Garden Song; Ringsend Rose; Wind, Wood and Sail; Skin; Tarbolten Lodge; Sea People; Lark In The Morning *49:17*

Crosby, Stills, Nash & Young
FOLK/ROCK; SINGER-SONGWRITERS

When Canadian folk/rock artist Neil Young joined Crosby, Stills & Nash, he galvanized the group with his lyrics and electric guitar, elevating them into another dimension. This classic 1970 album is one of the landmarks of the late 60's folk/rock movement.

See also Neil Young.

❋❋❋(❋)✓ **Déjà Vu**
　　1970　Atlantic (CD 19118)
　　　Carry On; Teach Your Children; Almost Cut My Hair; Helpless; Woodstock; Déjà Vu; Our House; 4 + 20; Whiskey Boot Hill/Down, Down, Down/Country Girl (I Think You're Pretty); Everybody I Love You *36:21*

Susan Crowe
FOLK/POP; SINGER-SONGWRITER

Halifax singer-songwriter Susan Crowe has returned to recording after a decade's absence. With the release of *This Far From Home*, fans can once again listen to her engaging alto voice and sure lyrics. Her quiet exploration of relationships, as heard on "Faithless" and "On Your Way To Mars," rank her among the strongest of contemporary lyricists. Highly recommended.

❋❋❋❋✓　**This Far From Home**
　　1994　River Records (RR 001CD)†
　　　The Step Of A Long Lost Love; Faithless; On Your Way To Mars; As I Come, As I Go; I Know; The Colour Of The Sky; My Mother's Girl; Let Me Stay; This Far From Home; They Used To Call This Sin *40:56*

Danko, Fjeld & Anderson
FOLK/COUNTRY/ROCKABILLY; SINGER-SONGWRITERS

"*Danko/Fjeld/Anderson* is as good a folk-rock recording as has been released in recent years"—*Dirty Linen*. A collaboration of Canadian Rick Danko (one of the founding members of The Band), Norwegian Jonas Fjeld, and American Eric Anderson, *Danko/Fjeld/Anderson* is a happy musical happening similar to two other successful collaborations: UHF and Quartette. Danko injects a sound similar to his lead-vocal work with The Band, Fjeld adds a Nashville sound, and Anderson provides the glue that binds it all together. Danko's version of Anderson's "Blue River" is one of the album's high points.

❋❋❋❋　　**Danko/Fjeld/Anderson**
　　1993　Rykodisc (RCD 10270)†
　　　Driftin' Away; Blue Hotel; One More Shot; Mary I'm Comin Back Home; Blue

River; Judgement Day (Slått); When Morning Comes To America; Wrong Side Of Town; Sick And Tired; Angels In The Snow; Blaze Of Glory; Last Thing On My Mind *45:34*

Tracy Dares

CELTIC PIANO

Crooked Lake, the long-awaited album from Cape Breton's Tracy Dares, will delight fans and newcomers alike. Dares is one of the most sought-after pianists by Celtic musicians. On this solo album, Dares emerges as a fine interpreter of the Cape Breton Celtic repertoire. You simply cannot sit still while her fingers dance on the ivories. Dares is accompanied by Dave MacIsaac, guitars, Natalie MacMaster, fiddle and viola, Lucy MacNeil, harp, Hamish Moore, small pipes and highland pipes, Bruce Jacobs, bass, and Tom Roach, drums, plus a chorus on "The Milling Song" that includes Rita Rankin and Rod MacNeil as soloists.

❋❋❋❋✓　**Crooked Lake**
　　　1995　Ground Swell (GSR 077)

A Group: Morag Ramsay/Betty Lou Beaton's/Miss Drummond Of Perth/ McKinnon's Rant/Miss Charlotte Alston Stewart/Senator's Reel; Castle Bay Scrap; Mustang Jig/Castle Bay Scrap; Black Mary; G Jigs: John Morris Jig/Irish Whiskey/ Mary Ann Kennedy Jig; F Group: Lord Moira/Miss Anne Amelia Stewart/Earl Marshall/Easter Elchies; Pipe Group: The Duke Of Kent's Lodge At Glentilt/Malts On The Optics/Farewell To Decorum; B-flat Group: Travels With Tracey/Miss Rose Of Dranie/Perth Assembly; Port Augusta; C Group: Lady Caroline Montague/Lady Lucy Ramsay/Mrs. Dundas Of Arniston/Miss Campbell Monzie/Marquis Of Queensberry; Old Grey Goose; Professor Blackie; Milling Song *47:26*

Daisy DeBolt

FOLK/BLUES/ROCK; SINGER-SONGWRITER

Half of the legendary 70's duo, Fraser & DeBolt, Daisy DeBolt has taken up accordion and produced an energetic, electric, accordion-laced solo album—*Souls Talking*. DeBolt has written or co-written all the selections on the recording, including "Come Hell Or High Water," "Eagle Hill," and "Dreams Cost Money." DeBolt has a unique, haunting voices that grabs you from track one and carries you through the entire album and then has you hitting the play button so you can listen all over again. Longtime DeBolt fans will revel in this recording and newcomers should check it out.

❋❋❋(❋)　**Souls Talking**
　　　1992　DeBolt (DCD 102)

Come Hell Or High Water; Eagle Hill; Epic Aire; Dreams Cost Money; Catalunya Sun; Sometimes; Monte Leuze Bleuze; Cage Monte; The Ballad Of Edouard Beaupré; Blue Jays Mocking Me *55:27*

Linda Dempster
PARLOUR FOLK

Every so often a singer in the arts community attempts to take folk music and turn it into parlour music. The results, from a folkie's perspective, are inevitably unsatisfying, despite the trained voices. Such is the case with Linda Dempster's *Folklore In Song*, recorded in a church in Toronto. Accompanied by Brahm Goldhamer on piano, Dempster sings her way through a folksong repertoire as if they were *lieder*. Her voice is professional, but you have to like the style to find the material interesting. The recording is muddy. Recommended only for completists.

❋❋ **Folklore In Song**
1991 Folklore In Song [no catalogue number]

Sweet William; Backwoodsman; La Lettre De Riel; She's Like The Swallow; J'Entends Le Moulin; The Huron Carol; Time To Be Made A Wife; The Fisher Who Died In His Bed; Là-Bas Sur Ces Montagnes; I'll Give My Love An Apple; Ah! Si Mon Moine Voulait Danser!; Pirate's Serenade; Ô Canada, Mon Pays, Mes Amours! *40:16*

Allen des Noyers
FOLK/POP; SINGER-SONGWRITER

British Columbia singer-songwriter Allen des Noyers has put together a solid debut album of original songs on *Sunset Theatre*. His engaging voice and sparkling acoustic guitar accompaniment are highlighted on songs like "Seasons Of Change," "Speak To Me In Spanish," "Savin' This Dance," "Not Such Badlands," and instrumentals like "Basement Suite" and "Brooks."

❋❋❋(❋) **Sunset Theatre**
1994 Azimuth (AZ-0002-2)†

Seasons Of Change; Speak To Me In Spanish; Savin' This Dance; Basement Suite; Lay Down Your Armour; Not Such Badlands; Brooks; Let It Go; Farewell To Erin; Bethlehem Light *36:15*

Alpha Yaya Diallo
TRADITIONAL AND ORIGINAL WEST AFRICAN MUSIC

Alpha Yaya Diallo was born and raised in Guinea, West Africa. In addition to performing original and traditional music on acoustic and electric guitar, balafon (wooden zylophone), djembé (vase-shaped hand drum), chekre (beaded calabash), and doum doum (bass drum), he sings in the Fulah, Malinke and Susu languages. On a North American tour Alpha Yaya fell in love with Canada where he now makes his home. His album *Nènè*, a gentle, infectious introduction to West African music, is highly recommended for those ready to embrace world music. *Nènè* was nomintated for a Juno in 1995.

❋❋❋❋ **Nènè**
1993 Alpha Yaya Diallo (SA93279CD)†

Yèkè Yèkè; Fatumata Diallo; Fierte; Djarabi; Yaadu; Afriki Djama; Mayimbo *35:19*

Djolé
FOLK/JAZZ; TRADITIONAL/CONTEMPORARY WORLD INSTRUMENTS

Djolé (pronounced *jo-lay*)—the word the Mandinka people of West Africa use to describe the joy of life—is also the name of a British Columbia ensemble formed in 1993. Djolé's musical instruments and styles come from West Africa, North India, Brazil, and North America. In the liner notes to *Indiscretion*, Djolé describes its music as an attempt to create a "timeless sound interwoven with jazz influences," using traditional melodies on the West Africa kora and ancient rhythm cycles on the North Indian tabla. *Indiscretion*, nominated for a Juno in the "Global Recordings" category in 1995, is a catchy, upbeat recording that is easy to listen to.

❋❋❋(❋)   **Indiscretion**
1994 Djole (DPM 101)

> Kema Bourema; Phox And Pheasant; Neuchâtel; Kossa Yambe; Indiscretion; Obvenge; Nossa Bossa; Jazzy Jig; Looking For You *59:46*

Melanie Doane
FOLK/POP; SINGER-SONGWRITER

A one-time member of both Tamarack and The Mamas And The Papas, Nova Scotia singer-songwriter Melanie Doane's flute-like soprano is featured on *Harvest Train*, a very short album with only six songs. The highlights of the album are James Gordon's "Harvest Train" and a modern interpretation of "She's Like A Swallow."

❋❋❋   **Harvest Train**
1993 Page (MRD 026)†

> She's Like The Swallow; Harvest Train; I Pray; Once He Was Mine; Sweet 16; The Zoo Is Closed *22:13*

Dobb & Dumela
FOLK/POP/ROCK; SINGER-SONGWRITERS

The Vancouver band Dobb & Dumela was formed in 1989 by Allen Dobb, who was raised on a farm near Beaverlodge, Alberta, and spent nearly three years in Lesotho, Africa, working in rangeland and livestock development. The band describes itself as a fusion that combines elements of reggae, R&B, folk, and South African township jive. Since 1992 the group has played some of the major folk festivals in Canada. Their first release, *One Drop*, features reggae-like lyrics presented in a mainly rock envelope. *Riverboat Free* shows a maturing in the songwriting with more diversity in the arrangements. Both albums will hold more appeal for campus-age rock fans than for folkies. Dobb & Dumela are Allen Dobb, Cameron Dobb, Scott Holder, Aggie Richichi, Shelley Campbell, plus former member Sherri Leigh.

❋❋❋   **One Drop**
1992 Resource (RESCD 1001)†

> Indigo; Get Down Low; Snake In The Grass; Like The Crow Flies; One Drop; Vertigo; The Same Heartbeat; Bus Stop; So Lonely; Feel Your Own Tears; Heartburn *46:47*

✳✳✳ **Riverboat Free**
1994 Resource (RESCD1003)†

Tin Town; Quicksand; Skipping Stones; Digging The Manhole; Machine Boy; Riverboat Free; Be Someone; The Picture's Perfect; Novelty Song; Whispers (Speak Up Your Mind) *45:39*

Dario Domingues
SOUTH AMERICAN-INFLUENCED COMPOSITIONS; COMPOSER

Born in the Patagonia region of Argentina, Ottawa-based Dario Domingues, flautist, singer, and percussionist began his musical career by mastering the kena, a seven-holed bamboo flute of ancient origins, played by the Quechuas, Aymaros, Incas, and other Indian cultures. After moving to Canada in 1977, he began work as a composer. Domingues' music, while inspired by traditional rhythms and melodies of South America, shows a progression towards a more contemporary sound. His live performances and concerts include a large variety of African, Asian and self-made instruments. Since 1980, Domingues has toured Europe annually, and has also performed in the United States and Japan. His music is recorded on the German Westpark label. *Sunset Over The Cordilleras* is an outstanding recording of innovative original music that lies somewhere between the traditional and modern ends of the musical spectrum. Two other Domingues Westpark CD's (not available in time to be highlighted in this guide) are *Under The Totems, Part One* (1993) and *Under The Totems, Part Two* (1994).

✳✳✳✳ **Sunset Over The Cordilleras: Improvisations**
1992 Westpark (WESTPARK 87027)

Sunset Over The Cordilleras; Lanin; Sunset II; Cerros Colorados *53:48*

Donnie & Buddy
MARITIMES CELTIC; SINGER-SONGWRITERS

The Cape Breton duo, singer-songwriter Buddy MacDonald and singer Donnie Campbell (former member of the 1970's folk group Miller's Jug), are frequent performers at the Summer Ceilidh Series at Gaelic College, St. Ann's, Cape Breton. Five of the ten songs on *At The Gaelic College* were written by MacDonald. The vocals, while not arresting, are delivered in a plain, honest, homespun style.

✳✳✳ **At The Gaelic College**
1990 Buddy MacDonald (ACD-9001)

Fisherman's Token; Autumn In A Rhyme; Retreat From Ross Ferry; Molly Bawn; Brew Of MacGillivray; Song For Peace; No Small Boats; The Garden Song; Song Not A Rifle; Thick O' Fog *37:01*

Teresa Doyle
MARITIMES FOLK; SINGER/SONGWRITER

"Doyle's versatile singing goes from sweet to soulfully hoarse but is always very expressive"—*Dirty Linen*. Teresa Doyle is based on Prince Edward Island. Her material, a combination of traditional Maritimes songs and her own, original compositions about historical events and people of the region, are sung in a distinctive, unusual voice that is totally confident. This is a singer who knows what she wants to sing and why she wants to sing it. The results, if you take to her voice, can be unusual and exciting. *Forerunner* takes its title, and its theme, from ghost tales and tales of the supernatural. *Stowaway*'s punchy musicianship lifts Doyle's material to a new plateau. Produced by Oliver Schroer, *Stowaway* is a saucy, satisfying album.

❋❋❋ **Forerunner**
1991 Bedlam Records (TD002)

Iridescent Blue; Maggie Daly; Salisbury Plain; She's Like The Swallow; The Shearing; The Slaugh "Swoogh"; Agincourt Carol; If I Was A Blackbird; Haul The Jib; Blue's Hollow; The Giant; Cape Breton Lullaby *47:55*

❋❋❋(❋)✓ **Stowaway**
1993 Bedlam Records (TDC 003)†

Land For The Tiller; Stowaway; Path Of Destiny; Isabeau; Belle Marie; Jock O'Hazeldean; Pretty Fair Maid; The Cuckoo; Paddy's Lamentation; The Wind That Shakes The Barley; Eilean An Aigh *45:02*

Teresa Doyle & Toshizo Tanaka
RENNAISSANCE MUSIC FOR LUTE AND VOICE

Toshizo Tanaka, who was born in Kyoto, Japan, studied guitar with Andres Segovia and later began playing Renaissance lute at the Schola Cantorum Basiliensis in Switzerland. On a trip to Canada he began searching for a singer interested in Renaissance lute songs. While in Prince Edward Island he met folksinger Teresa Doyle, who had become interested in the music of John Dowland while living in Montreal. The two teamed up to play, and later record, an album of John Dowland songs. *Songs For Lute And Voice* may be a bit off the beaten track for folkies. Doyle's voice lacks the purity at the top of her range that one associates with English singers who perform this music, and Tanaka's lute playing has not been balanced forward enough—it sounds distant. Nonetheless, this is an album worth listening to.

❋❋❋ **Songs For Lute And Voice**
1995 Bedlam (TDCD004)†

If My Complaints Could Passions Move; Awake, Sweet Love, Thou Art Returned; Dear, If You Change; Come Again: Sweet Love Doth Now Invite; Flow My Tears; Shall I Sue; Now Cease My Wand'ring Eyes; My Choice Is Made; Can She Excuse My Wrongs; All Ye, Whom Love Or Fortune; Behold A Wonder Here; Greensleeves *38:52*

Tommy Duchesne
FRENCH CANADIAN

Quebec accordionist and harmonica player Tommy Duchesne was a noted square-dance caller and all-around entertainer. A very popular and well-known performer in Quebec, Duchesne's music is preserved on *Tommy Duchesne*, a Héritage Québécois CD from MCA that features his upbeat playing and singing. It is unfortunate that MCA has provided no liner notes to accompany this historical recording.

✳✳✳✳ **Tommy Duchesne**
[no date, reissued 1991] MCA (MCAD-10493)

Reel Du Pendu; Chicken Reel; Reel De L'Oiseau; Valse Des Raquetteurs; Money Musk; Gigue De Duchesne; La Grande Gigue Simple; Reel De Tommy; Paul Jones Du Saguenay; Paul Jones De Chez-Nous (I); Musette Québécoise; Paul Jones De Chez-Nous (II); Valse Des Ouvriers; Le Quadrille De Charlevoix; Reel Des Patineurs *42:24*

Jack Duncan & Shangó Ashé
WORLD FOLK/JAZZ/PERCUSSION

Jack Duncan, Canadian percussionist and founder and artistic director of ShangóAshé, has travelled to Africa, Cuba, and South America to study drums and rhythms. The blend of these influences can be heard on *Shangó Ashé*, which features music ranging from ceremonial batá drumming to rhumba, mozambique and comparsa with a tinge of jazz. Percussion fans will want to add this lively album to their collection.

✳✳✳(✳) **Shangó Ashé**
[no date] Ashé (ASHE 3483)

Open For Eleggua; Kabiosilé; Orunla; Pello El Afrikan; Didilaaro; Conga Con Cinco Tumbas; Orishanlá; The Warriors; Rhumba Pa' Mis Orishas; Don't Kick The Hand That Feeds You; Close For Eleggua *54:15*

Donna Dunlop
FOLK/COUNTRY; SINGER-SONGWRITER

Donna Dunlop is an emerging Toronto-based country-folk singer-songwriter who has showcased in Nashville. On *She Used To Be A Dancer*, she performs some solid vocals on "The Prince In Disguise," "The Place Of No Return," and the title track, "She Used To Be A Dancer." Additional musicians on the album include Caitlin Hanford, Tony Quarrington, and Chris Whiteley.

✳✳✳ **She Used To Be A Dancer**
1994 Northern Dancer (NDM 103)

She Used To Be A Dancer; The Prince In Disguise; The Place Of No Return; The Night, The Angel Boy And Me; Accidentally On The Road; No Devil's Bargain; Where In The World; Closer To The Heart; Eagles; Only You; Jamaica, 1839; Oh Mama; A Little Light; The Ghostly Cowgirl; Buried In The Bone

Ken Dunn
FOLK; SINGER-SONGWRITER

Burlington, Ontario singer-songwriter Ken Dunn has released a soft, intimate collection of original songs on *Winds Of Emotion*. The quiet delivery, maintained with acoustic guitar, lends an introspective, poetic atmosphere to songs like "Pause And Reflection," "Muskoka," "Gone To Gaspé," and "The Rain And The Snow." The simple arrangements allow the lyrics to come front and centre.

❋❋❋   **Winds Of Emotion**
          1994 Snowrose (SRCD002)†

> Pause And Reflection; Muskoka #1; Gone To Gaspé; Burning Bridges; Somali Eyes; Nothing; Prison In The Sun; Honestly; Hard Yellow Light; Winds Of Emotion; The Rain And The Snow; Saskatoon *38:39*

Eagleheart Singers & Drummers
FIRST NATIONS MUSIC

"As children of Mother Earth, along with our relatives—the Birds, the Animals and Water Creatures, Thunder Beings and the Rain, Winds and Sky—we hope that everyone enjoys this unique blend of songs with the natural sounds of the forest"—liner notes from *Songs From Mother Earth*. Sung against a background of environmental sounds, these songs from Saskatchewan and Alberta take you as near as you can get to a pow-wow without actually being there. *Songs From Mother Earth* is nothing less than a celebration of life. While seeing the Eagleheart Singers and Drummers live, in their resplendent dress, is the best way to experience the music, this album is the next best thing.

❋❋❋❋✓   **Songs From Mother Earth**
          1993? Ashmore Audio Productions (AAPCD 004)

> Grand Entry Song; Intertribal Song; Round Dance Song (I); Fancy Dance Song; Come Out Fighting; Fred's Song; Round Dance Song (II); Grass Dance Song *49:00*

Fred J. Eaglesmith & The Flying Squirrels
FOLK/COUNTRY; SINGER-SONGWRITER

Fred J. Eaglesmith may be Ontario's best-kept secret. A long-time veteran of the folk-music circuit, and a former farmer from southern Ontario who was born and raised in a large farm family, Eaglesmith writes profound and often dark lyrics about country life. The deceptively simple lyrics are set against sparse, effective instrumental backups. Eaglesmith's voice is not one that will be universally admired, but its plain, countryish quality with its pronounced rural accent, is a perfect vehicle for his material. The earliest Eaglesmith album available on compact disc is *Things Is Changin'*, packaged in a neat wooden box guaranteed not to fit on your CD rack. Packaging aside, the album is a superb collection of Eaglesmith songs including "Things Is Changin'," "Harold Wilson," "Joe," and "Rodeo Rose." *From The Paradise Hotel* was recorded live at an Eaglesmith concert in Birmingham, Michigan. While there's some overlap in material between this album and *Things Is Changin'*, the tempo is faster on *Paradise* and there are vintage songs such as "Yellow Barley Straw" and "Thirty Years Of Farmin'" that have, until now, only been available on Eaglesmith's cassette and LP recordings. The Flying Squirrels on this album are Ralph Schipper and Willie P. Bennett, with Lynn Miles adding vocals on "Harold Wilson."

✻✻✻✻✓ **Things Is Changin'**
1993 Sweetwater Music [no catalogue number]†

Sharecroppin'; Things Is Changin'; Harold Wilson; White Ash And Black Ash; Joe; Carmelita; Summerlea; Rough Edges; Reprise; Brand New Boy; Cryin' Yet; Rodeo Rose *45:56*

✻✻✻(✻) **From The Paradise Motel**
1994 Barbed Wire (BWR2001)†

Yellow Barley Straw; Thirty Years Of Farmin'; The Highway Callin'; I'm Just Dreamin'; Sweaburg General Store; Sunflowers; Little Buffalo; Summerlea; My Last Six Dollars; Rough Edges; Sharecroppin'; The Mindless Side Of Town; Rodeo Rose; Go Out And Plough; Jericho; Harold Wilson *69:16*

Eco Andino
BOLIVIAN/ANDEAN MUSIC

Montreal-based Eco Andino is a sparkling musical troupe whose members originally came from Bolivia. Their melodic songs and haunting Andean instrumentation, including guitars, pipes, and percussion, are exotic, yet easy to listen to. On *Mensajeros*, the group consists of Efrain Gutierrez, Franz Villegas, Willy Rios, Ricardo Renteria, and Remy Lucas.

✻✻✻(✻) **Mensajeros**
1994 Eco Andino (ECOCD-1994)†

Mensajeros; Yuyaway; Saya Yungueña; Regreso; Morenita; Cancion Para Una Estrella Azul; El Picaflor; Mi Cholita; La Mariposa; Amigo *37:42*

Shirley Eikhard
FOLK/POP; SINGER-SONGWRITER

A songwriter at age eleven, Shirley Eikhard, born in Sackville, New Brunswick, is the daughter of fiddler June Eikhard, "Canada's First Lady Of Fiddle." Daughter Shirley made her first appearance at the Mariposa Folk Festival at age thirteen and sang on the CBC-TV *Singalong Jubilee* at age fourteen. A popular festival singer in the 70's, Eikhard's husky alto voice can be heard again on *Child Of The Present*, a retrospective collection from a career that spanned folk, country, and pop. Eikhard received Juno awards in 1972 and 1973 as "Female Country Singer."

✻✻✻ **Child Of The Present / Horizons**
1975/1977, reissued 1992 Attic (ACD 24120)

To Love; Sure Thing; Walk Away; I Wanna Know; Play A Little Bit Longer; Child Of The Present; It Doesn't Matter Anymore; Best Friend; Leave The Windows Open; I Just Wanted You To Know; Don't Let Me Down; Let Me Down Easy; I Still Believe

> In Love Songs; It All Comes Down To Caring; I Don't Want To Lose Your Love; Play A Little bit Longer; Strangers Now; Nothing To Lose; Any Way The Wind Blows; Some Day Soon *59:03*

Jimmy Ekho
FIRST NATIONS MUSIC; SINGER-SONGWRITER

Susan Aglukark has introduced Canada to the sound of music sung in Inuit. Those who wish to pursue this should check out Jimmy Ekho, a singer-songwriter from the Northwest Territories who sings all his original compositions in his native language, accompanied by acoustic guitar, traditional Inuit drum, and backup musicians on acoustic and electric instruments. The only non-Ekho song on the album, "Be Bop A-Lula," has been translated into Inuit. This is the pop music of the Far North.

❋❋❋ **Guti**
1993 Jimmy Ekho [no catalogue number]

> Guti, 1st Version; When I First Saw You; When I Was A Kid; Today's Teenagers; God's Words; I'm Crazy About You; Be Bob A-Lula; Nuka; Inuit; Guti, 2nd Version *36:52*

Kirk Elliott
CELTIC/FOLK; COMPOSER

Ontario musician Kirk Elliott has put together an unusual album with *Celtic Moon*— a recording that combines original compositions with traditional tunes and instruments, many of which Elliott plays himself through the magic of the recording studio. The diverse instrumentation on this all-instrumental album includes celtic harp, keyboards, tambourine, psaltery, accordion, cello, baroque flute, penny whistle, electric violin, uilleann pipes, mandolin, dobro, bass, drums, autoharp, and electric and acoustic guitars. The arrangements are tasteful, imaginative, and definitely non-traditional. Guest musicians include Don Ross on acoustic guitar and Loretto Reid on uillean pipes.

❋❋❋(❋) **Celtic Moon**
1993 Soundwright (KECMSW93-2)

> Druids At The Disco; The Red Haired Boy; Petty Harbour Theme; The Ancient Irish Blues; Carolan's Quarrel With The Landlady; St. Brigid's Ramble; Celtic Moon; Sheebeg Sheemore; Rain Forest Variations; The Jigs Are Up; The Enchanted Coracle *45:20*

David Essig
FOLK/BLUES/ROCK; SINGER-SONGWRITER/COMPOSER

Currently living in British Columbia, David Essig is one of the deans of Canadian folk/blues. A master guitarist and songwriter, who records his solo albums on an Italian label, Essig has backed up many of the best names in folk music. *In The Tradition*, a 1981 recording reissued in 1994, highlights Essig's experimental style. Based on an exploration of Jungian psyche and symbol, the music frequently veers into flights of imagination. The effect was extraordinary in 1981 and it can still tax today's listeners. *Rebel Flag*, recorded live at a concert in Cosenza, Italy, presents Essig alone on voice and guitar, beginning with the strong opening track "Rebel Flag," and continuing through a series of Essig songs and guitar compositions including "Woman In The Snow," "Jamieson's Farewell," and "Highland Clearances." Very few artists could make this much music all by themselves. This intense recording is highly rewarding. *State Of Origin* may be one of the finest Canadian-music recordings released in 1993. From the folk/rock opener, "State Of Origin," to the countryish "Long Sweet Ride," to the bluesy "Blue And Lonesome," to the electric guitar solo, "Ricordando," the album moves from one memorable moment to another.

❋❋❋ **In The Tradition**
1981, reissued 1994 Appaloosa (AP 113-2)

Far Away From Home; Looking Out The Window—Version 1; Super Falcon; Upper Paradise; I'se The Cucaracha...; Down In The Pines; Looking Out The Window—Version 2; Suite For Carter Stanley; Pulse Piece (1-5-6); Music From Calgary; John Hardy Suite; Jamison's Farewell; Variations On A Theme By Albert Price *74:59*

❋❋❋❋ **Rebel Flag**
1990 Appaloosa (AP072-2)†

Rebel Flag; Woman In The Snow; Jamieson's Farewell; Albert's Cove; Bourrasque; Highland Clearances; Great Wall Of China; Berkley Springs; In The Pines; Two Weeks Home; Anthem For The New Nations *62:01*

❋❋❋❋✓ **State Of Origin**
1993 Appaloosa (AP 093-2)†

State Of Origin; Long Sweet Ride; Blue And Lonesome; Ricordando Lowell George; Sisters Of Desmond Grew; Leaning On The Everlasting Arms; Quiet Money; That Was Before I Met You; Villa San Giovanni; Weight Of Experience; Hold Fast To The Right; The Cross And The Fountain *54:41*

Evans & Doherty

FOLK/CELTIC; SINGER-SONGWRITERS

Halifax performers Kevin Evans and Brian Doherty perform a mix of original material written by Evans and contemporary material from other songwriters. Their Celtic-oriented delivery tends toward middle-of-the-road, lyrical, material rather than the more upbeat dance-oriented parts of the Celtic repertoire. *Road Not Taken* features an easy-listening mix of material including Evans' "Road Not Taken," Joe MacDonald's "Save The Whales," Bill Staines' "Lady In Montana," Ralph McTell's "Streets Of London," plus traditional numbers such as "Carrickfergus" and "Wild Mountain Thyme." *Sailors On The Asphalt Sea* moves the duo up a notch in energy and delivery. The approach is still MOR, but the material is better recorded and Evans' engaging voice and guitar come through to advantage on song after song. The album includes a Stan Rogers song—"Acadian Saturday Night"—never released by Rogers, plus excellent songs from John Prine ("Sailin' Around"), Richard Thompson ("Galway To Graceland"), and Ron Angel ("The Chemical Workers Song"). The best track on the album may be Evans' "My Baby And My D-18."

❋❋❋ **Road Not Taken**
1991 Evans & Doherty (EVANDOH 1003)

Road Not Taken; A Drink For My Father; Christmas In The Trenches; Save The
Whales; Lady In Montana; Streets Of London; Carrickfergus; Wave To The Water/
The Day The Tall Ships Came; Dungarvan My Hometown; The Mermaid; Wild
Mountain Thyme *49:32*

❋❋❋(❋)✓ **Sailors On The Asphalt Sea**
1994 Evans & Doherty (EVANDOH 1004)

The Second Week Of Deer Camp; Acadian Saturday Night; Sailin' Around; My
Baby And My D-18; Hi For The Beggarman; Galway To Graceland; Brennan On
The Moor; Oh, No More; Winds Of Morning; The Chemical Workers Song; Whiskey
In The Jar; The Man With The Cap; The Galway Races *49:58*

Tammy Fassaert

COUNTRY/FOLK; SINGER-SONGWRITER

British Columbia singer-songwriter Tammy Fassaert produces a kind of roots-based
country music that lies about halfway between Nashville and traditional folk. Part of
the west coast progressive music scene since she graduated from university (with a
degree in agriculture), Faessert adds her fine voice to songs written by T-Bone Burnett,
Clive Gregson, Fred Koller, and Cyd Smith as well as several of her own on *Just
Passin' Through*, an album that mixes traditional country and bluegrass with touches
of calypso and rockabilly. This is a good album for folkies who also enjoy a touch of
country music.

❋❋❋(❋) **Just Passin' Through**
1994 Strictly Country (SCR-36)

Never See Your Face Again; Wish Me Well; I Remember; Everybody Cheats On
You; Winter's Night; You Never Said Goodbye; You Shouldn't Have Told Me That;
Just Passin' Through; Carry You Along; When The Sun Comes Up; Forest Belle
35:59

Fat Man Waving

FOLK/ROCK/POP; SINGER-SONGWRITERS

The Ottawa band Fat Man Waving is made up of musicians who are also part of Six
Mile Bridge and Three Sheets To The Wind. As Fat Man Waving they explore more
experimental material than they do in their other, more traditionally-oriented, groups.
Parade features up-tempo songs such as "Duped Again," "Blind No More," and "If I
Lived" written by band members plus a Lynn Miles song, "One By One." The musi-
cianship and Rebecca Campbell's lead vocals are solid, but this electric-oriented al-
bum may be too far from the centre of folk music traditions for some fans. *The Habit
Of Gravity* continues the experimental flavour with some excellent vocals and upbeat
and unusual new material like "Parallel Lines," "Stop The Car," and "Angel's Shoes."
The combined band members on the two albums are Rebecca Campbell, Fred Guigon,
Peter Kiesewalter, Ross Murray, James Stephens, and Ian Mackie.
See also Six Mile Bridge; Three Sheets To The Wind

❋❋❋ **Parade**
1992 Canal Records (258CD)†

(Ain't No More) Train To Ride; Duped Again; Blind No More; If I Lived (To Be One Hundred And Ten); In The Shadow; Flight Of Fancy; One By One; Reputation; Hide Your Eyes; Sons And Lovers *40:43*

❋❋❋ **The Habit Of Gravity**
1995 Aquarius (CD Q200576)†

Falling Down (Marathon Of Love); Parallel Lines; Only We Can; Stop The Car; Angel's Shoes; Eye For An Eye; Critter Time; Running Down The Days; It's Not The Heat; Toll The Bell; Feeling Better; Dreaming Heart; I Want To Talk With You *63:52*

Stephen Fearing

FOLK/POP; SINGER/SONGWRITER

"Fearing gets inside the heads of his characters but, unlike many songwriters who are just telling stories, he *becomes* his characters. That is perhaps the genius of this songwriter"—*Dirty Linen*. A vortex of energy and talent, Irish-born Stephen Fearing brings his special guitar work and probing lyrics to a set of albums that are among the most contemporary of any listed in this guide. Formerly based in British Columbia and recently settled in Ontario, Fearing, who combines elements of jazz, blues, and rock with his fine acoustic guitar work and arresting lyrics, is gaining a higher profile in the music industry with each album he releases. *Out To Sea*, originally released on another label and later acquired and reissued by True North, introduces Fearing's penetrating lyrics and captivating guitar. The songs are intense, personal, and, frequently, painful. *Blue Line* is an angry album, reflecting the sensibilities of an entire generation of younger Canadians born into a society they find hypocritical and frequently uncaring: "Our father of the golden rule / You can shape the lesson if you shape the school / Tradition is your biggest tool / When you ride the big wheel of fortune" ("Our Father And The Big Wheel Of Fortune"). *The Assassin's Apprentice* raises Fearing to a new dimension of musicianship and songwriting. Less angry than *Blue Line*, *Apprentice* seems to reflect a coming to terms with life. There may be more optimism, but it's tempered with reality, as in these lyrics from the title song: "I've been living in a country / where everyone's split in two / a state of limbo that divides us / what we feel from what we do / where silence is a virtue / emotion is a child that's seen / but never heard." *The Assassin's Apprentice* is one of the most striking Canadian folk albums on CD.

❋❋❋(❋) **Out To Sea**
1991 True North (WTNK 80)†

Out To Sea; Dublin Bay; Carsten; Welfare Wednesday; Cain's Blood; August 6th And 9th; Tryin' Times; The James Medley: St. Patrick's Breastplate/The Lights Of St. Louis/Barrelhouse Keys; Beguiling Eyes (Both Sides Now) *47:20*

❋❋❋(❋)   **Blue Line**
1991   True North (TNK 76)†

The Bells Of Morning; Our Father And The Big Wheel Of Fortune; Sarah's Song; Race Of Fractions; Little Child Eyes; Blind Horses; Blue Line; Born In A Story; Turn Out The Lights; Jesse Meets His Future Wife Zee Mimms *49:55*

❋❋❋❋✓   **The Assassin's Apprentice**
1993   True North (TNK 84)

The Assassin's Apprentice; Give It Up; The Longest Road; Expectations; The Station; Lark And Duke; Down The Wire; Echoes; (I Heard That) Lonesome Whistle; The Brilliance You Need; The Life; Martin's *54:54*

Salvador Ferreras
LATIN AMERICAN MUSIC

Based in Vancouver, with roots in Puerto Rico and Venezuela, percussionist Salvador Ferreras journeys through Latin music, exploring its rural and urban forms. On *Invisible Minority* he embraces a wide range of instruments, including the cuatro and guiro of Venezuela, rainsticks, bird whistles and maracas from Mexico, plus bells, gongs, shakers, and rattles from various parts of the world. He melds these, and North American instruments, into a fusion of world/roots/jazz that is imaginative and absorbing. This is an album you'll find yourself playing repeatedly.

❋❋❋(❋)   **Invisible Minority**
1992   Aural Tradition (ATRCD 121)

El Casorio De Los Compas; Caterete/Xote; The Tropic Of Casual; Danza Negra; Como Ilora Una Estrella; Gcina; Plena Santa María; Active Past; Olinda; Un Diálogo; Nè A Rory; East Of Eaton's *46:42*

Ferron
FOLK/POP; SINGER-SONGWRITER

"One day there will be a Canadian postage stamp with Ferron's image on it"—Festival Distribution *Catalogue*. One of Canada's most poetic songwriters, Ferron, a British Columbia native, currently resides in the state of Washington. Her influence on songwriting in Canada has been profound, and she has had a major impact on women's music throughout the world. Anyone new to her music should start out of sequence with the 1992 *Not A Still Life* live recording. Stripped of her usual backup band, the album features Ferron in a warm, intimate concert where she simply sings and accompanies herself on acoustic guitar. The lyrics come front and centre, limning themselves on the mind in vivid detail. The earliest Ferron recording available on compact disc is *Testimony*, a 1980 album presenting a young songwriter backed by a soft rock band. Anyone who has heard James Keelaghan's rendition of "Misty Mountain," will want to hear the original that inspired his tribute. Ferron continues to impress on the 1984 *Shadows On A Dime*. Among the highlights are "Snowin' In Brooklyn," "I Never Was To Africa," and "Shadows On A Dime." The songwriting is remarkable and haunting. *Phantom Center*, from 1990, is a richly produced album that includes Tori Amos, among others, on backup vocals. *Resting With The Question*, released in 1992, is a departure. This album features Ferron instrumental compositions, with no singing. The compositions are delicate, introspective keyboard pieces heavily synthesized. The 1994 release of *Driver* features a somewhat softer Ferron, but a Ferron who remains a forceful poet and songwriter. From the dreamy opener, "Breakpoint," the album shifts into the folkish "Girl On A Road" on track two and continues to present new Ferron material, including the incomparable "Cactus."

❋❋❋(❋) **Testimony**
1980 Cherrywood Station (CW 003)†

Almost Kissed; Rosalee; Our Purpose Here; Who Loses; Testimony; Bellybowl; Satin Blouse; O Baby; Misty Mountain; Ain't Life A Brook *39:06*

❋❋❋(❋) **Shadows On A Dime**
1984 Cherrywood Station (CW 004)†

Knot 53; Snowin' In Brooklyn; As Soon As I Find My Shoes I'm Gone; Proud Crowd/Pride Cried; I Never Was To Africa; Shadows On A Dime; Circle Round; The Return; It Won't Take Long *42:43*

❋❋❋ **Phantom Center**
1990 Cherrywood Station (D2-74830)†

Stand Up (Love In The Corners); The Cart; Harmless Love; Indian Dreams; Sunken City; White Wing Mercy; Heart Of Destruction; Inside Track; Phantom Center; Higher Wisdom *48:47*

❋❋❋ **Resting With The Question**
1992 Cherrywood Station (CW 006)

Anything We Want; High Head Sept. '90; Beacon; Forgiveness; In Your Eyes; Old Haunts; Cave At Montana De Oro; Just Leave; Resting With The Question; No Matter What Happens; Anything We Want *46:47*

❋❋❋❋✓ **Not A Still Life**
1992 Cherrywood Station (CW 007)†

Light Of My Light; Shadows On A Dime; Our Purpose Here; I Am Hungry; Ain't Life A Brook; I Know A Game; Call Me Friend; Snowin' In Brooklyn; I Never Was To Africa; Higher Wisdom; Dear Marly; The Cart; Shady Gate; Harmless Love; Testimony; The Wind's All A'Whisper *64:16*

❋❋❋(❋)✓ **Driver**
1994 Cherrywood Station (CW 008) / Earthbeat (EBCD42564)†

Breakpoint; Girl On A Road; Call Me; Cactus; Love Loves Me; Borderlines; Sunshine's Lament [Prologue]; Sunshine; Sunshine's Lament [Epilogue]; Independence Day; A Name For It; Maya *62:58*

Rick Fielding

FOLK; SINGER-SONGWRITER

Toronto singer-songwriter Rick Fielding fell under the spell of folk music early in life in his original home of Montreal when he first encountered Folkways recordings. Teaching himself guitar licks from blues and folk recordings, Fielding went on to become a first-rate guitarist and performer with several albums to his credit. In recent years he has retired from extensive touring, devoting his time to teaching guitar, playing for entertainment, creating leather crafts, and hosting the weekly folk-music show *Acoustic Workshop* on CIUT-FM, University of Toronto. His latest release, and first CD, *Lifeline*, is a dandy folk album that highlights Fielding's fine singing voice and excellent guitar, banjo, and mandolin playing. The album includes covers of tunes like Wade Hemsworth's "Wild Goose" and Grit Laskin's "Margins Of My Neighborhood" plus a number of Fielding originals, including "So Long, Charlie," "If Jesus Was A Picker," and "Obray's Fancy."

❋❋❋(❋)✓ **Lifeline**
  1995 Folk-Legacy (CD-123)

> So Long, Charlie/Jim's Polka; Pitman Blues; If Jesus Was A Picker; Alouette/La Bastringue; Bachelor's Hall; Obray's Fancy; Lifeline; Company Town; Docherty's Jig/Stairsteps; Wild Goose; Margins Of My Neighborhood; Hutchison's Ramble; Birth Of Robin Hood; Angus Fraser; Handful Of Songs; Rag, Eh?; Old -Time Riverman; Voices Of Struggle; Same Old Song *65:30*

Figgy Duff
FOLK/ROCK; SINGER-SONGWRITERS

Figgy Duff was a riveting, fresh Newfoundland band that instilled new life and energy into the traditional repertoire. Their debut album, *Figgy Duff*, released to wide acclaim in 1980, was reissued on compact disc in 1991. The founding members, Pamela Morgan, the late Noel Dinn, Dave Panting, and Geoff Butler, put a new spin on songs like "The Greenland Disaster," "Tinker Behind The Door," and "Rosy Banks Of Green." On the 1982 recording, *After The Tempest*, the band picks up the pace. With the addition of Derek Pelley to the group, Figgy Duff once more embraces the traditional repertoire, performing memorable instrumental versions of "Heel And Toe Polka," "Paddy's Jig," and "The Gypsy." The arrangements of "A Sailor Courted A Farmer's Daughter," "The Darby Ram," and "The Ten Commandments" feature Pamela Morgan on lead vocals. *Weather Out The Storm*, a 1990 recording, marks a change in the personnel, sound, and style of the band. Half the selections are traditional music and half are new songs written by Morgan and Dinn. With a decade's experience exploring traditional music, the new compositions have a "roots" flavour, but the increased use of electric instruments and drums shifts the sound into a more pronounced folk/rock style. "Woman Of Labrador," and "Henry Martin" are the album's highlights. New members of the enlarged band are Kelly Russell, Rob Laidlaw, Bruce Crummell, and Frank Maher. With *Downstream* Figgy Duff completes its transition from a "trad" band to a folk/rock band doing entirely original songs by Noel Dinn and Pamela Morgan. The sound and the songs are very good, but not as convincing as Figgy Duff doing traditional material.

Figgy Duff broke up after the death of Noel Dinn. Pamela Morgan joined forces with Anita Best and other members of the band have gone on to Rawlins Cross and the Plankerdown Band. For his seminal work in reviving the folk music of Maritimes, Noel Dinn has been inducted into the Porcupine Awards Hall of Fame.

See also Anita Best & Pamela Morgan; The Plankerdown Band; Rawlins Cross.

❋❋❋(❋) **Figgy Duff**
1980, reissued 1991 Hypnotic (71356-5000-2)

Half Door/Larry's Lancer/Mother On The Doorstep; Rabbits In A Basket; Now I'm
64; The Greenland Disaster (Sealing Song); Tinker Behind The Door; Fisher Who
Died In His Bed; 4-Stop Jigs; Quand J'Etais Fille A L'Age Quinze Ans; Kissing
Dance Medley; Rosy Banks Of Green; Geese In The Bog; Matt Eiley; Emile's Reels
43:31

❋❋❋❋✓ **After The Tempest**
1982, reissued 1991 Hypnotic (71356-5001-2)†

Honour, Riches (Song From The Tempest)/Breakwater Boys Breakdown; Heel And
Toe Polka/Paddy's Jig; A Sailor Courted A Farmer's Daughter; Centennial Highway
Reel/Cooley's Reel; The Darby Ram; Auntie Mary/Brother's Jig; The Gypsy; The
Ten Commandments; Lake St. John Reel/The Blackthorn Stick; Dans La Prison De
Londres; Thomas And Nancy; Jim Rumbolt's Tune *37:44*

❋❋❋ **Weather Out The Storm**
1990 Hypnotic (71356-1000-2)†

Weather Out The Storm; Heart Of A Gypsy; Jealous Lover/Wedding Waltz; Snowy
Night; Woman Of Labrador; Inside A Circle; Yankee Skipper; Rumbolt; Bad Blood;
Henry Martin *45:43*

❋❋❋ **Downstream**
1993 Hypnotic (71356-1009-2)†

Freedom; Sweet Temptation; Allanadh; Song For Paul; True Or False; Children Of
The Night; Crown Of Thorns; Pirates Of Pleasure; Twilight; Downstream *41:30*

Finjan
KLEZMER

Finjan, based in Winnipeg, is one of Canada's leading klezmer bands. *Crossing Selkirk Avenue* is Finjan's third recording, and the first available on compact disc. Selkirk
Avenue, the liner notes explain, "was the heart of Winnipeg's 'North End.' It was a
bustling avenue in this city-within-a-city where Eastern European immigrants, Ukrain-
ians, Poles and Jews bargained, discussed, bought, and sold...The bagels are still baked
fresh daily." Finjan freshens up the immediacy of these memories. Members of Finjan,
on this recording, are Shayla Fink, Eli Herscovitch, Daniel Koulack, Kinzey Posen,
Myron Schultz, and Victor Schultz.

❋❋❋(❋) **Crossing Selkirk Avenue**
1992 Fat Uncle (FUR 003)

Oy Tate, S'is Gut; Abi Gezunt; Bosphourous Freilach; Greenhorn Blues; I Wanna
Fellow; Second Avenue Freilach; Crossing Selkirk Avenue; A Brivele Der Mam'n;
Shpiel Klezmer, Shpiel; Freilach Fun Der Chupa; Odessa Bulgar *45:30*

Winston "Scotty" Fitzgerald
MARITIMES FIDDLE

Born in White Point, Cape Breton, in 1915, Winston "Scotty" Fitzgerald, dean of Cape Breton master fiddlers, profoundly influenced the young fiddlers of the island who still study his graceful phrasing and ornamention. A carpenter by profession, Fitzgerald was a frequent performer on radio stations in Nova Scotia and fiddling festivals in Canada. Joe Cormier is one of Fitzgerald's many protégés. *Classic Cuts* is a compact disc re-release of some of his LP recordings. For fiddle music fans, this album is a treasure beyond compare. Fitzgerald is a memorial member of the Porcupine Awards Hall of Fame.

❋❋❋❋✓ **Classic Cuts**
[no date] Breton Books & Music (BBMCD 001)

Welcome To Your Feet Again/The Bonny Lass Of Fisherrow/The Bird's Nest; Medley Of Highland Jigs: Traditional/I'm Off With The Good St. Nicholas Boat; Miss Ann MacCormack/Sleepy Maggie; Marchioness Of Huntley/Miss Maules/Lady Glen Orchy; McNab's Hornpipe/Farmer's Daughter; James F. Dickie's Delight/ James Scott Skinner/Mrs. E. MacLeod; The Mill Of Newe/Mrs. James Forbes; Jimmy MacKinnon Of Smelt Brook/Scotch Cove; Bonnie Isabell Robertson/John Howett; Mrs. Menzies Of Culdare/Welcome Whiskey Back Again/Captain Keeler; Gramin/Mr. R. Cato; The Haggis/Caber Feidh; The Iron Man/Riddrie/Mrs. Douglas Of Edman; Tom MacCormack/Capers; The Firefly/The Horn; Archie Menzies/ Fisher's Hornpipe; St. Kilda's Wedding/Trip To Windsor; Mist On The Loch/Bonnie Kate; Medley Of Antigonish Polkas; McDonaugh's Clog/Slievman's Hornpipe; Crossing To Ireland/Rights Of Man Reel; Stirling Militia March/The Green Fields Of White Point *65:37*

Flatland 6
ACOUSTIC BLUES; SINGER-SONGWRITERS

As the liner notes tell it, *At The Roadhouse* "is inspired by the rough and tumble players found in the smoky honky-tonks and roadhouses of the southern States. In the early part of this century these musicians carved out a lasting heritage of gritty and honest music. Names like Son House, Charlie Patton, Bo Carter and Jimmie Rodgers (The Singing Brakeman) have to be added to the more well known Robert Johnson, as players who have left us the hard-earned milestones of country-blues." The Vancouver group Flatland 6 uses this tradition as a cornerstone for the nine original songs in this collection. These excellent musicians turn out some highly satisfying tracks on *At The Roadhouse*. Blues fans will seriously enjoy this one. Flatland 6 are Gerry Siemens and Craig McKerron on guitars, Alan Mann on piano, Ed Goodine on drums, Chris Taylor on harmonica, Ken Wilson and Tammy Fassaert on bass.

❋❋❋(❋) **At The Roadhouse**
1994 Flatland 6 (FLS-2001)

Flatland Blues; Chauffeur Blues; Flim Flam Man; Same Old Way; Broken In Two; I Told You So; I Want You To Know; No Longer Mine; Goin' Down To Memphis; Dogline Blues; Downtime *39:06*

The Flying Bulgar Klezmer Band
KLEZMER

Klezmer music is, according to the liner notes to *Flying Bulgar Klezmer Band*, "Jewish roots/folk/dance and party music ... it's like nothing you've ever heard before yet it's immediately familiar: shades of the circus, the synagogue and the New Orleans street band—the sound of celebration." This bouncy album lives up to the definition. It's a fun, and delightfully rowdy, listen. The Toronto-based Flying Bulgar Klezmer Band takes klezmer styles and extends them into the present as a living tradition, with new compositions and innovations. *Agada* follows in the same vein. The combined musicians on the two albums (they don't all play on both) include David Buchbinder, Laura Cesar, Evelyne Datl, Anne Lederman, John Lennard, Allan Merovitz, Martin Van De Ven, and Allen Cole.

❋❋❋(❋) **Flying Bulgar Klezmer Band**
1990 Flying Bulgar (FBR CD001)

Ishai's Freylekh; Der Rebbe Elimelekh; Araber Tants; Fun Der Khuppe; Fishelekh In Vasser; On Sunday The Rabbi Stretched Out; Kandel's Hora; Dance Medley: Violin Doyne/Unser Toirele/Varshaver Freylekhs/Kolomeyke; Saposhkelekh; Der Yiddisher Soldat In Die Trenches; Alle Brider *53:16*

❋❋❋(❋) **Agada**
1993 Flying Bulgar (FBR CD002)†

Cooking Bulgar(s); Naftule Shpilt Far Dem Rebn; Aleyn In Veg; Bulgar Blues; Agadot; Feter Elye; High Noon In Volgograd; Spirits; Wiggle Town; Yam Lid; Sumkinda Hora; Bukoviner Freylekhs; Vus Vet Zayn *57:42*

Folk Of The Sea
FOLK; CHORAL

Folk Of The Sea is a singing group of fishermen and fisherwomen of Newfoundland and Labrador. Their album, *In Concert*, is an easy-listening collection of contemporary and traditional songs that alternate between choral singing, choral-backed soloists, and instrumentals. Unfortunately the scanty liner notes don't include a publisher's address. Watch for this one in the bins of your favourite record shop, or purchase a copy if you happen to catch them in concert.

❋❋❋ **In Concert**
1994 Folk Of The Sea [no catalogue number]

Let Me Fish Off Cape St. Mary's; Make And Break Harbour; I'se The B'y/Cock Of The North; Shenandoah; Amazing Grace; Boil Down The Cabbage; Fisherman's Son; Swiss Moonlight Lullaby; They Call Me A Wry Man; We're Folk Of The Sea; Petty Harbour Bait Skiff; Salt Water Joy; Waltz And Jig; Ah, The Sea; Come Home To Newfoundland; The Hand That Rocks The Cradle; Sea People; Sailor's Prayer; Who Is My Brother *68:59*

Roy Forbes

FOLK; COUNTRY; SINGER-SONGWRITER

British Columbia singer-songwriter Roy Forbes began his career as a folksinger, using the stage name "Bim." His unique voice, driving guitar, and strong songwriting brought him popularity at folk festivals. Later Forbes turned to his country roots and has since become a successful country music artist. In addition to his solo career, Forbes is part of the UHF project (*see* UHF), as well as being a record producer. *Love Turns To Ice* and *The Human Kind* present the high-energy and excellent songwriting of Forbes' country music. Both are fine recordings that will appeal to Forbes fans, but may be a bit too far removed from the folk mainstream to appeal to folkies in general. *Almost Overnight* is another matter. This 1994 recording has Forbes in the studio re-recording his Bim material. The result is electrifying. It's amazing how much music one voice, one guitar, and one tapping foot can create. Fans will find "Thistles," "Waitin' For You Mama," "Right After My Heart," "Woh Me," plus twelve more Bim classics on this disc. A must for Bim fans and recommended for folkies everywhere.

❋❋❋(❋) **Love Turns To Ice**
[no date] Flying Fish (FF 70499)

Love Turns To Ice; Wildman; Breaks My Heart; Tiny Island; And Now You Want My Love; This Feeling; Away From Me; For So Long; Lost On The River; Winterkill; Sweet Shameless Hours; The Damage That We Do *48:00*

❋❋❋(❋) **The Human Kind**
1992 AKA (AKA-CD 1002)

Still A Fool; Your Image Of Me; A Sweet Kind Of Love; Not Tonight; Alone And Forsaken; Let Me Make It Up To You Tonight; The Human Kind; Wondering; The Winding Stream; Saskatoon Moon; Just One Time; A Fool Such As I; Days Turn To Nights; Anna Marie *47:54*

❋❋❋❋✓ **Almost Overnight**
1994 AKA (AKA-CD 1003)

Thistles; Waitin' For You Mama; Right After My Heart; Woh Me; Headed The Wrong Way; Betsy And The Blue Boys; You Can't Expect Me To Change; So Close To Home; I'm So Lonesome I Could Cry; Peer Pressure; The Farmer Needs The Rain; Kid Full Of Dreams; Colder Than Ever; Tender Lullaby; So Afraid; Yellow Moon; Ironbelly; Talk Around Town *70:04*

Four The Moment

FOLK/BLUES/GOSPEL; A CAPPELLA; SINGER-SONGWRITERS

For over a decade Four The Moment, an a cappella vocal group from Halifax, has been creating original compositions that tell the story of African-Nova Scotian history, and women's and Third World struggles. Blending together elements of Black music—blues, soul, reggae, and gospel—they have performed their music from Nova Scotia to Vancouver. *Four The Moment—Live!*, released in late 1993, is a recording of their Tenth Anniversary Concert in Halifax. The soaring harmonies and deep-rooted lyrics are guaranteed to please fans of a cappella music. Four The Moment is Delvina Bernard, Kim Bernard, Andrea Currie, and Anne-Marie Woods.

✹✹✹(✹)　**Four The Moment—Live!**
1993　Jam (FTM101)†

I Love You Woman (Black Mother Black Daughter); Inkululeko Iyeza; Africville;
It's So Hard To Say Goodbye To Yesterday; Harriet Tubman; Buffalo Soldiers; Old
Pictures; Betty's Blues; Farther Along; In My Soul; Lullaby For Cole Harbour;
Freedom Has Beckoned *52:02*

J. Hubert Francis & Eagle Feather
FIRST NATIONS MUSIC; FOLK/ROCK; SINGER-SONGWRITER

J. Hubert Francis and Eagle Feather, based in New Brunswick, perform a mix of original songs written by Francis and covers of other songwriters. A smooth, tight-sound-
ing band that would sound at home on any radio station, Eagle Feather switches between blues and rock styles effortlessly. On *Reverence* Francis sings "Booglatamootj,"
which sounds like it might have been a direct influence on Kashtin. Other Francis
songs include "Grandfather," "Alone Again," "Only Love," and "The Dream." The
band also kicks in with numbers from the Stampeders, Redbone, Chuck Berry, and
Bob Dylan. Francis' laid-back vocals and the band's soft rock style make this a very
easy-listening album.

✹✹✹　**Reverence**
[no date]　Sunshine (SSCD 4190)

Grandfather; Booglatamootj (The Indian Song); Alone Again; Oh My Lady; Six
Days On The Road; Only Love; The Dream; Alcatraz; Maybelline; Knockin' On
Heavens Door *34:02*

Les Frères Labri
FRENCH CANADIAN

Les Frères Labri (a made-up name that doesn't stand for anything) was an outstanding
folk group from Quebec that performed traditional music. On *Quand L'Vent* Les Frères
Labri combined instrumentals, foot tapping, and mouth music into fine performances
that rivalled the best early recordings of La Bottine Souriante. Anchored by former La
Bottine Souriante member André Marchand, the group included Jean-Claude
Mirandette, Jean-Paul Loyer, and Normand Miron. *Quand L'Vent* received a "Gem of
Canada" album of the year Porcupine award in 1994. Unfortunately, the group has
since disbanded and there will likely be no further Les Frères Labri recordings.

✹✹✹✹✓　**Quand L'Vent Vire De Côté**
1993　Les Éditions Des Frères Labri (LAB-CD-060)†

À L'Âge De 16 Ans/La Marche Du Quêteux Pomerleau; Ah, Du Temps Que J'Étais
Jeune/Le Reel En Viole; La Poule À Colin; Pot-pourri D'Airs De Lucien Mirandette:
La Bonne Femme Noël/La Double Gigue; Par Derrière Chez Ma Tante/Le Reel Du
Coq "Boiteux"; La Chapelle De La Bonne Femme Giroux; Gédéon Amateur/Le Reel
De La Tuque Bleue; J'Aime Le Vin; Trois Brandy; Hommage À Durant *43:16*

Friends Of Fiddler's Green

FOLK

Ontario legends, Friends Of Fiddler's Green, have played and sung together for over twenty years. The liner notes to *Road To Mandalay* point out that throughout their time together, "one clear principle has remained constant: performances are social events first of all, and everything else after that." It comes as no surprise then that this group of comrades has not put a high priority on making recordings. In fact, *Road To Mandalay* is only their second, and the only one available on compact disc. The whole point of *Road To Mandalay* is that everyone is having a good time—the album is more hearty than heady. This is one to place on your CD player when you're feeling festive or sentimental. The Friends of Fiddler's Green, on *Road To Mandalay* are instrument-maker Grit Laskin, mandolin, guitar, Northumbrian pipes, concertina; Tam Kearney, guitar, mandolin, banjo, concertina; Ian Robb, concertina, baritone concertina; Laurence Stevenson, fiddle; David Parry, anglo concertina, melodeon, guitar, harmonica; Alistair Brown, melodeon, harmonica, jew's harp, concertina; and Geoff McClintock, keyboards.

See also David Parry; Ian Robb

✲✲✲(✲)   **Road To Mandalay**
1994 FOFG [no catalogue number]

> Blaydon Races/Off She Goes; We Are Three Jolly Fishermen; Mary Ann; The S.S. Shieldhall; Galopede/Petronella/The Green Cockade; Mandalay; Coats Off For Britain; Jamaica/Childgrove; My Old Man; Schoolday's Over; Sir Sydney Smith's March; One Of The Old School; Arthur Bignold Of Lochrosque/The Lark In The Morning; The Long, Long Trail *50:00*

Cate Friesen

FOLK/POP; SINGER-SONGWRITER

"Friesen's writing is consistently strong, with thoughtful lyrics and tunes"—*Dirty Linen*. Cate Friesen is a singer-songwriter based in Toronto, but the Prairies, where she was raised, still figure prominently in her lyrics, as in the opener on *Tightrope Waltz*: "Oh, when you think of me / Won't you remember me / As prairie grass rooted deep and strong." Friesen's lilting voice carries her engaging personality through varied material, including "Think Of Me," "Waltzing," and "Grandma's Song." She combines elements of folk, pop, klezmer, and jazz on her recordings, but it's her folkish material that highlights her lyrics to best advantage.

✲✲✲(✲)   **Tightrope Waltz**
1993 Wide-Eyed Music (WEM002)†

> Think Of Me; Waltzing; Tina; Desert; Wake Me Up; Baptized (Prodigal Daughter); Grandma's Song; Walking With The Wind; Passing; Whirlwind *40:17*

Bill Gallaher & Jake Galbraith

FOLK; SINGER-SONGWRITERS

"Bill Gallaher keeps folk music alive with his Stan Rogers-like narratives and fine writing... [and] Jake Galbraith really makes it sparkle"—*Victoria Times-Colonist*. The Victoria, British Columbia, folk duo Bill Gallaher and Jack Galbraith have been turning heads wherever they play, but until now their performances have been limited primarily to the Pacific Northwest and Alberta. Their first three albums, available only on cassette, have been featured regularly on CBC's Max Ferguson show and other CBC programs, as well as public radio in the United States. Gallaher, who writes the duo's material, began his performing career over ten years ago in Ireland. Galbraith is a seasoned musician who has performed at venues from California to Alberta. His harmonies and skill on a broad range of instruments have helped the duo earn their national reputation. With the release of *The Last Battle: The Best Of Bill Gallaher & Jake Galbraith* on CD, their music is available to a wider listening audience who will be spellbound by songs like "The Last Battle," "Newfoundland Sealers," "The Hold Up," "Mary And The Seal," and "The Ballad Of Ginger Goodwin." This is music that compares favourably with the historical songs of Stan Rogers and James Keelaghan.

✻✻✻(✻)✓ **The Last Battle: The Best Of Bill Gallaher & Jake Galbraith**
1995 Bill Gallaher / Theatre Erebus (BGM 1002)

> The Last Battle; Augustus And Catherine; Shadow Boats; 1914 (The Grand Illusion); Male Bonding Song; Newfoundland Sealers; The Hold Up; Mary And The Seal; Traveller's Song; The West In Her Eyes; Canadian BBQ; Three Dollar Dreams; The Chilkoot Pass; The Ballad Of Ginger Goodwin *72:08*

Lennie Gallant

FOLK/POP; SINGER-SONGWRITER

Lennie Gallant, from Prince Edward Island, has emerged as one of the strongest songwriters from the Maritimes. His fresh, varied lyrics span folk, pop, and country music. Gallant's soft, expressive voice and thoughtful arrangements make him the kind of singer-songwriter who will appeal to a broad range of listeners. The most folkish of Gallant's albums is *Breakwater*. Songs like "Tales Of The Phantom Ship," "Island Clay," and "Raise The Dead Of Wintertime" feature a Gallant who is comfortable working in a "roots" style. The more typical, contemporary, Gallant style emerges on tracks like "Breakwater," "Big City," and "La Tempête" where the instrumentation is decidedly more electric. The electric-oriented style carries through into *Believing In Better*. The strong lyrics of "Believing In Better," "Man Of Steel," "Crumbling Foundations" convey both anger and hope. Gallant also writes expressive love songs such as "The Stairs" and "Someone Like You." *The Open Window* takes Gallant to a new level. The arrangements are tighter and the backup musicians provide Gallant with a fuller, richer sound. From the strong contemporary opener, "Which Way Does The River Run," through the soft rocker, "The Open Window," to the folkish, introspective finale, "Northern Lights," this fine album, which was awarded "Album of the Year" at the 1995 East Coast Music Awards, places Gallant among Canada's leading folk/pop artists.

❊❊❊(❊) **Breakwater**
1988 Revenant (LGCD 101)†

Tales Of The Phantom Ship; Island Clay; Raise The Dead Of Wintertime; Back To Rustico; From A Distance; Marie And He; The Hope For Next Year; Breakwater; Big City; The Reconciliation Two-Step; La Tempête; Down On The Promenade; Destination *47:25*

❊❊❊(❊) **Believing In Better**
1991 Revenant (LGCD 102)†

Believing In Better; Man Of Steel; Martyn's Brook; Is It Love I Feel (Or Courage I Lack); The Hope For Next Year; How Many Bridges; The Cry For Love; Crumbling Foundations; The Stairs; Someone Like You; The Other Side *46:41*

❊❊❊❊✓ **The Open Window**
1994 Columbia (CK80196)†

Which Way Does The River Run; The Pearl (Would You Meet Me There); The Open Window; Peter's Dream; Embers; Mademoiselle (Voulez-Vous Danser); How Can I Trust The Captain; Fighting For Your Love; Three Words; Looking At The Moon (For The First Time); Year Of The Angel; Northern Lights *47:19*

Boying Geronimo
SALSA

With the arrival of new Canadians from Latin American countries, salsa bands have become a regular feature at Canadian folk festivals, spicing up the entertainment with their hot dance music. Vancouver-based Boying Geronimo is among Canada's leading proponents of salsa. His Cuban salsa jazz band is featured on *Rumba Calzada*, an album with pumping latin beats. The album contains the classic movie tune "The Continental" as well as tracks that feature a variety of percussion treats from band members like Poncho Sanchez, a noted conga drummer from Los Angeles. The tight arrangements and catchy rhythms are recommended for salsa lovers.

❊❊❊(❊) **Rumba Calzada**
[no date] Boying Geronimo (BGCD1000)

Mentirosa; Continental; Rumba Calzada; Southern Comfort; Bamboleate; Bajo Con Tumbao; Ran Kan Kan; Dahil Sa Iyo; Obatala, Cajita Y Rumba Con Mi Hijo; Have I Told You Lately; Oye Como Va *51:57*

Geoff Gibbons
FOLK/ROCK; SINGER-SONGWRITER

On *Geoff Gibbons*, British Columbia-based Gibbons' electric arrangements carry his folkish lyrics through an impressive set of original songs, including "Life On The Ball," "Just What I Am," "Ribbons And Chains," and "Can't Curse The Rain." Gibbons is a strong songwriter, though the thoroughly electric rock-flavoured style of the album may put him on the edge of the definition of folk for those who prefer a more acoustic-based sound.

✹✹✹ Geoff Gibbons
1991 Energy Discs (NRG CD 143)†

Forty Dollar Dove; Life On The Ball; Just What I Am; Love Makes No Rules;
Ribbons And Chains; Can't Curse The Rain; Nowhere Town; House Of Horrors;
You'll Remember Me; Sweet White Rose *43:28*

James Gordon
FOLK/POP; SINGER-SONGWRITER

James Gordon is a prolific singer-songwriter best known for his contributions as a
founding member of Tamarack. *Farther Along*, a solo album, features Gordon performing a wider range of songs than his Tamarack material. Songs like "We Work
Away," a reggae-influenced number, "Caledonia Street," a contemporary love song,
and "The Ozone Layer," a rock-flavoured environmental piece, display the non-folkish
side of Gordon's songwriting. Gordon's voice is most convincing when blended into
tight harmonies with other voices. The Tamarack-like arrangement of "Lonesome
Cowboy's Lament" with backup vocals from the Bird Sisters is the most successful
track on the album.

✹✹✹ Farther Along
1990 SGB Records (SGB CD 10)†

Head Me Home; We Work Away; Caledonia Street; Lonesome Cowboy's Lament;
The Ozone Layer; Farther Along; All The Other Dolphins; This Poor Old Village;
Essequibo River; The Golden Fleece; Without You; The Human Cannonball; These
Are The Nineties *54:46*

Myk Gordon
FOLK/POP; SINGER-SONGWRITER

British Columbia-based Myk Gordon writes contemporary material in the protest,
social-injustice tradition. His album *Seventh Candle* includes a song about his relationship with his father, "Bye Bye Papa," a lament for Canada, "Oh, Kanada," and a
song about race/religion, "I'm A Jew." Gordon weaves in acoustic guitar, fiddle, and
harmonica alongside drums and electric instruments. While Gordon is not gifted with
an extraordinary voice, his lyrics are worth exploring.

✹✹✹ Seventh Candle
1994 Blasphemy (MYK-102)†

Bye Bye Papa; Oh, Kanada; I'm A Jew; No One But Me; Adam And Eve; Bag Of
Bones; Who Will Remember; Tommy Evans; Before The River Runs Dry; Creation
Shining *46:12*

Great Big Sea
MARITIMES CELTIC; SINGER-SONGWRITERS

The Newfoundland group Great Big Sea combines traditional material with songs
written by members of the band. The result, on their debut album, *Great Big Sea*, is a
lively selection that includes traditional Celtic-flavoured numbers such as "Great Big

Sea," "I'se The B'y," and "Berry Picking Time" alongside original pieces like "Someday Soon," "What Are Ya' At?" and "Time Brings." On the whole the band is most successful on the traditional material. Great Big Sea is Bob Hallett, Alan Doyle, Darrell Power, and Sean McCann.

✱✱✱   **Great Big Sea**
1993   NRA (NRA3-1002)

> Great Big Sea/Gone By The Board; Someday Soon; Excursion Around The Bay; What Are Ya' At?; Fisherman's Lament; I'se The B'y; Drunken Sailor; Irish Paddy/ Festival Reel/Roger's Reel; Time Brings; Jigs: Eavesdropper's/Both Meat & Drink/ Off We Go; Berry Picking Time *38:51*

The Great Western Orchestra

FOLK/COUNTRY/WESTERN; SINGER-SONGWRITERS

The Great Western Orchestra is the smallest orchestra in the world—two Alberta musicians and singers: David Wilkie and Stewart MacDougall. Wilkie, who was born in California and moved to Canada at an early age, is known in Canadian country as "The Mandolin Kid." MacDougall, originally from Fredericton, New Brunswick, is a musician who has played for Laura Vinson and k.d. lang. Both musicians have at one time played for Ian Tyson. The original GWO also included Cindy Church and Nathan Tinkham, but the CD recording made by that foursome, *The Great Western Orchestra*, has been deleted from the catalogue and is not available for this guide. *Wind In The Wire*, the first album issued as a duo, with guest musicians, is an eclectic exploration of the West. "The Railroad Corral" chronicles the seemingly endless days of a trail drive. "Magdalena And The Jack Of Spades" is a Mary Robbins-like desperado/ outcast song. "The Cowboy Waltz" is a traditional fiddle tune turned into a mandolin masterpiece. Oscar Lopez adds some hot Latin guitar licks on several of the tracks. *Buffalo Ground* continues the direction started with *Wind In The Wire*. With saucy liner notes by Sid Marty and more accompaniment by Lopez, GWO focuses on more aspects of the West. While there are many good tracks, the haunting "Buffalo Ground" is the album's highlight.

    See also David Wilkie.

✱✱✱(✱)   **Wind In The Wire**
1991   Centerfire (CFA002)

> Great Western Overture; The Railroad Corral; Magdalena And The Jack Of Spades; Wrong Side Of The Hill; Cowboy Boogie; The Cowboy Waltz; Cactus Swing; Nowhere To Go; Buccaneer/Buckaroo; Wind In The Wire; Great Western Overture (Reprise) *38:04*

✱✱✱(✱)   **Buffalo Ground**
1993   Centerfire (CFA 005)†

> Joanne's Song/Prelude For Buffalo Ground; Buffalo Ground; Forest Fanfare/Warrior And The King/Swan With Two Necks; Out Of My Hands; Down Along The Livingstone; Doney Gal; Big Rock Candy Mountains; Monsoon; Dangerous Age; The Heart Of The Matador (El Corazon De Un Matador); Come Away; Buffalo Ground Revisited; Pets And Dinner *49:37*

Grievous Angels
FOLK/ROCK/COUNTRY; SINGER-SONGWRITERS

Grievous Angels, an Ontario-based electric folk band founded in 1987, combines a slightly country sound with soft rock and thoughtful, contemporary lyrics. Most of the songs are written by guitarist, vocalist, and band leader Chuck Angus, of Cobalt, Ontario. Angus remembers his grandmother listening to Stompin' Tom Connors when he was two or three years old and Stompin' Tom has been an influence on his writing ever since. Angus has won two Porcupines for his songwriting: the "New Canadian Songwriter" award in 1990 for the song "Sarah Gordon" and the "Mac Beattie Award for Ontario Songwriting" in 1993 for "The Ballad Of Red Dan." "Red Dan" was also selected by CBC radio host Peter Gzowski as one of his "favourite all-Canadian songs."

On Grievous Angels' second album, and first CD, *One Job Town*, lead vocalist Michelle Rumball cranks up her beautiful, plaintive voice on Angus classics like "Crossing The Causeway" and "When Love Came Around." A personnel change on *Watershed* finds the band without Rumball. Without her distinctive voice, the band loses some of the vocal edge, despite Angus' persistently good lyrics. Historically, the various members of Grievous Angels are Chuck Angus, Michelle Rumball, Peter Jellard, Tim Hadley, Peter Duffin, and Rick Conroy. Jellard, Hadley, and Conroy are also members of the Cajun Ramblers.

❋❋❋(❋)✓ **One Job Town**
   1990 Moose Records / Stony Plain (SPCD 1162)†

   Crossing The Causeway; When Love Came Around; The Ballad Of Leonard And
   Cecile; B.C. In The Winter Time; Sarah Gordon; Peter's Shuffle; Staying In On
   Weekends; Friday Night; The Kapuskasing Highway Song; Last Room On The Left
   (At The Ramore Hotel); Death's Dark Stream; Gordie And My Old Man *41:29*

❋❋❋(❋) **Watershed**
   1993 Jimmy Boyle Records (CD 181093)†

   Starting Over At Thirty; Pot Of Gold; A Mile Outside Of Kirkland; Parking The Cod;
   Saskatchewan; Maybe It's The Rye That's Talking; Salamanca; I Didn't Mean To
   Make You A Gypsy; The Pipeliners Song; North Of The Watershed; We Don't Seem
   Able To Love Anymore; La Bastrange; Sea Of Galilee; The Ballad Of Red Dan; Six
   Hundred Dollars; The Polkas; Grand Narrows Where I Belong *59:48*

Guignolée
FRENCH-CANADIAN; SINGER-SONGWRITERS

Guignolée is a band from the Lanaudière area of Quebec. They come from the same region of Quebec as Les Freres Labri and La Bottine Souriante—a region well known for its traditional musicians. The band includes the Laporte brothers, two exceptional fiddlers, and their CD, *Retour*, features songs as well as instrumental jigs and reels. If you're a fan of traditional Québécoise music, you should seek out this recording. Guignolée is Gilles Cantin, Pierre Laporte, Rémi Laporte, Jean Cantin, Luc "Pom-pon" Loyer, and Raynald "Doc" Dupras.

✳✳✳(✳)   **Retour**
1994 Guignolée (GUI CD 327)†

Les Plaisirs De Basile/Reel La Chicaneuse; L'Empêchement/6/8 De Joseph Allard;
Bonny Kate/Jenny's Chickens; Les Coucous; Medley De La 1ière Chaloupe; Les
Récollets/Pride Of Petravore; Marie-Calumet; Ma Mie; Haley's Favorite/Kitty Come
Over/Mullins Fancy/The Opera Reel; Les Draveurs De La Gatineau *45:12*

Rufus Guinchard
MARITIMES FIDDLE

Rufus Guinchard taught himself fiddle at the age of eleven and played until his death
on September 7, 1990, at the age of 91. The liner notes to *Humouring The Tunes*
indicate he was the "fiddler of choice" for decades of get-togethers in communities
along the Great Northern Peninsula of Newfoundland. Guinchard "possessed an extensive and unique repertoire of tunes, many learned from fiddlers who were old men
when he was a boy, and whose names they now bear." *Humouring The Tune*, recorded
when Guinchard was in his 90's, is a must purchase for any collection of historical
Canadian folk recordings. His infectious love of traditional tunes still carries through
in this recording project that he didn't quite finish before his death. The lovely tunes
are deftly accompanied by Jim Payne's unobtrusive guitar work. Payne was also the
album's producer.

✳✳✳(✳)✓ **Humouring The Tunes**
1990 SingSong (RDR-CD-178)

Lizzie's Jig; Jackson's Fancy; Stan Rogers; Sam's Jig; River Of Ponds; Country
Waltz; Jim Rumboldt's Tune #2; Torrent River Jig; The Wreck Of The Steamship
"Ethie"; Martin Keough's Tune; Father's Jig; My Loving Little Sailor Boy; Sydney
Pittman's Tune; Sally's Cove Reel; Free Payne's Tune Too; Lige Gould's Double;
Hunt The Squirrel; Hughie Wentzell's Tune/Israel Got A Rabbit; Prosper's Jig;
Arthur Perry's Jig *45:26*

The Gumboots
FOLK; SINGER-SONGWRITERS

The Gumboots, from Yellowknife, first formed in 1984 as a folk group that performed
traditional Canadian folk songs. Over the years the members of the group have changed
and the band began writing and performing original songs about the north. Founding
member Bill Gilday is still the group's musical leader and chief songwriter. Their first
CD, *Spirit Of The North*, is a diverse collection of songs about Canada. The styles
range from the a cappella opener, "The Mouth Of The Peel," about a Dene storyteller
with a gift of gab, to barbershop quartet-like songs like "The Flow'r Of Old Fort Rae,"
a love song. "Goin' Out In Style" is a song on an environmental theme; "Martha" is a
song in remembrance of Martha Oovayuk who died when she lost her way in a fierce
Arctic storm and wandered from the shelter of her home and the community. Their
second CD, *Northern Tracks* follows in a similar vein, with songs such as "Willy And
The Bandits," "Yellowknife Tonight," and "Nancy McKenzie's Lament." Gumboots,
on these two albums, include Bill Gilday, Bill Stephen, John Bunge, Bob MacQuarrie,
Dan Lee, Chris Philpotts, Rich Hintz, and Chic Callas.

✳✳✳ **Spirit Of The North**
1992 Gumboots [no catalogue number]†

The Mouth Of The Peel; The Bay Boys; The Flow'r Of Old Fort Rae; Martha; Goin'
Out In Style; Abadoo; Long Johns; The Resurrection Of Billy Adamache; The
Feelin' Is There; Spirit Of The North; Doctor John Rae; 1789—Journey To The Sea;
New Day Dawning *46:54*

✳✳✳ **Northern Tracks**
1994 Gumboots (GBTD 7002)†

Willy And The Bandits; The Voyagers; You're There; Clean Up The Mess; Hay River
Bombardier Run; Fly Like An Eagle; Nancy McKenzie's Lament; Yellowknife
Tonight; Wop May; Dance Grandfather; Song For The Sailors; Farewell *49:08*

Gypsalero
GYPSY-DERIVED INSTRUMENTALS

British Columbia instrumental band Gypsalero performs updated gypsy music. The
liner notes to *El Runway* explain it this way: "Gypsalero...The name conjures up images of Romance...of music born of passion, struggle and dreams...The music of the
original gypsy tribes has evolved and taken many forms. Ron Thompson's exuberant
and expressive interpretation shows this is music that must not be left behind in these
hi-tech times...This recording offers a colorful new vision of a timeless musical tradition." That may be so, but it might require some verbal jujitsu to explain how Del
Shannon's "Runaway" qualifies as part of the gypsy tradition. This recording by Ron
Thompson, Budge Schachte, and Brent Gubbels, plus guest musicians, is a pleasant
enough mix of styles, but it doesn't really capture the excitement and hard edge of
traditional gypsy music.

✳✳(✳) **El Runway**
[no date] Gypsalero [no catalogue number]

Natasha; Runaway; La Cumparsita; Café Django; Dance Of The Hand People;
Manoir De Mes Rêves; Señor Jeraldo; Esmeralda, Flower Of Egypt; Douce
Ambiance; Los Braseros; Gypsology; Queensland Stomp; Coeur D'Alene *54:15*

Mark Haines & The Zippers
FOLK/ROCK; TRADITIONAL

The Toronto band of Mark Haines and The Zippers have been playing concerts, folk
festivals, and pubs for years. Haines is a solid fiddler with a strong sense of humour
and wit. A bouncy, versatile band, the Zippers can switch effortlessly from rock and
roll to reel and jig. With Tom Leighton on accordion, Haines put out an earlier cassette
recording of traditional fiddle tunes. *Like It Is: Live!* captures the zest and versatility
of the band on numbers like "Mercury Blues" and "Honky Tonk Women." The Zippers are Tom Leighton, Glenn Anderson, Rick Ramsey, and Miles Raine.

✳✳✳ **Like It Is: Live!**
1993 Mark Haines (MHZL 93-2)

Mercury Blues; Honky Tonk Women; Does This Mean It's Over?; I'm Gonna Be A

DJ; I Can't Wait To Get Off Work; Jingle Jangle Jingle; Leopard Skin Pillbox Hat; Diggy Diggy Lo; Let's Dance; Farewell To Nova Scotia; Fishin' Blues; Southern Bells; Orange Blossom Special; Like A Rolling Stone *60:01*

Joe Hall
FOLK/SATIRE; SINGER-SONGWRITER

By any measure, Joe Hall, a resident of Mississauga, Ontario, writes unusual material. Off-the-wall and satirical songs form the tracks on *Rapture*. Hall's lyrics, at times, seem to be in an almost direct line of descent from The Fugs. While the musicianship is good and some of the tracks are infectious, this is not an album for the timid or unadventurous. The sometimes brilliant, often odd, dreamscape lyrics of songs like "Roadkill Barbeque" and "The Mutant Starlings" require a sympathetic listener. Nonetheless, it should be pointed out that Hall received a "Stan Rogers Golden Quill Award for Songwriting" Porcupine in 1993. Caveat Auris.

✳✳✳ **Rapture**
1993 Wingnut (1993)

The Man Who Has No Country; The Revolution And Sweet Gypsy Nose; Roadkill Barbeque; All The Mutant Starlings; Home Entertainment Suite: Watchin' TV/ Thanks For Sharing; Let's Get Stupid; Middle Aged Guys With Guitars; What A Wonderful World; Crack The Code; Dave Town; Pressure Drop; Moammar In Mississauga; Weary Of Perfection; Happy With My Hair *60:20*

Karen Leslie Hall
FOLK/POP; SINGER-SONGWRITER

Ontario-based Karen Leslie Hall is a singer-songwriter blessed with a gorgeous voice and an interesting turn of phrase. *On The Dream Road*, which takes its title from a line in the opener, "Walkabout," is a laid-back album that beckons you inside to travel the lyrics. This easy-listening CD includes the gentle "Sing Me To Sleep," the lyrical "Too Soon For Love Songs," the introspective "Uphill In The Snow," plus eight additional songs. The album was produced by Don Ross, who also plays guitar and piano. A very pleasant, low-key, recording.

✳✳✳(✳) **On The Dream Road**
1994 Seadance Music (SDM-694-2)†

Walkabout; Sing Me To Sleep; Too Soon For Love Songs; So What Else Is New?; Uphill In The Snow; This Is Our Last Goodbye; Look Me In The Eye; I Think Of You Always; Water Baby; Today I Danced With Angelfish; A Homecoming *45:17*

Ken Hamm
FOLK; GUITAR; SINGER-SONGWRITER

British Columbia singer-songwriter and outstanding guitarist Ken Hamm, originally from Thunder Bay, Ontario, has released a retrospective collection of his work from the past two decades on *Inter-Tidal Zone*. This fine folk collection of original material and covers features songs like "Intertidal Zone," "Water Lines," "Bad Luck Blues," "Fixing To Die," and "That House On Hornby."

米米米(米) **Inter-Tidal Zone**
1993 North Track (NTCD9301)

Dave Macon Rag; Intertidal Zone; Water Lines; Bad Luck Blues; Angel Eyes; Living In The Country; Evil; Ballad Of R And V; Last Fair Deal Gone Down; Strawberry Creek; Crosscut Saw; Burns Lake Bounce; Heart And Only; Maybellene; Redhaired Shake; Keys To The Hiway; So Long Mamalillaculla/Jorma's Song; Fixing To Die; Fire Eyes; That House On Hornby *70:36*

Marie-Lynn Hammond
FOLK; HUMOUR; SINGER-SONGWRITER

Ontario singer-songwriter Marie-Lynn Hammond, a former member of Stringband, brings her infectious voice and wit to *Black And White ... And Shades Of Grey*. "Not Another Benefit," a comic song, includes a cameo voice-track by Nancy White. "Mothers Teach Your Sons," like several of the women's-issue songs on the album, scores points with wit rather than sarcasm. The album has its serious moments, such as Hammond's haunting "Temagami Round," about one of Canada's infamous logging disputes.

米米米(米) **Black & White ... And Shades Of Grey**
1990 Aural Tradition (ATRCD 303)†

Not Another Benefit; Mothers Teach Your Sons; Science Is Wonderful; Why Do I Have This Thing (For Jewish Men); Eve Gave Adam The Apple; Temagami Round; Sisters And Friends; Pleine Lune; Shades Of Grey; Nobody Knows What's Happening To Love; Les Deux Amies; Still Not Over You Yet *48:11*

Slavek Hanzlik
BLUEGRASS INSTRUMENTALS; ORIGINAL COMPOSITIONS

"Slavek Hanzlik is one of the guys who proves just how much the guitar has become the international musical instrument. His story as a refugee from the old Communist world who found political asylum in Canada is well known. But that story is so dramatic that it is easy to overlook how amazing the rest is. The rest is that Slavek is a world-class guitar player who not only brought his art from Czechoslovakia to North America, but also brought his expertise in North American traditional music with him. It truly has become a small world, bridged by the guitar, and by great guitarists like Slavek Hanzlik"—Dan Crary, liner notes to *Summer Solstice*. Hanzlik's contemporary bluegrass-style instrumentals will delight those who love guitar. *Spring In The Old Country*, from 1991, and *Summer Solstice*, from 1993, both bring a fresh twist to guitar and guest instruments, including fiddle, mandolin, dobro, bass, and banjo.

米米米(米) **Spring In The Old Country**
1991 Flying Fish (FF70582)

So Long Jake; Paradise Found; High Level Hornpipe; Minority; Bonaparte Crossing The Rhine; Spring In The Old Country; Bill Cheatham; Big Strong Waldo; Great Season Waltz; Belame Fiddle; Gypsyland; Home Sweet Home *37:34*

✻✻✻(✻)   **Summer Solstice**
1993 Musa (MCD 93-2)

> Summer Solstice; Wind In The Heather; Latintude; Harvest Of Change; My Grandmother's Clock; Pauper's Cotillion; Cascades; Potzelbaum; Eventide; Sally Noggin; Bohemian Concerto; Spirit Of The South; Autumn Farewell *39:11*

Kyp Harness
FOLK; SINGER-SONGWRITER

A high-energy singer-songwriter, Toronto-based Kyp Harness may remind older folkies of an early Bob Dylan. *God's Footstool* features the same kind of off-beat, cadence-driven lyrics that uniquely identified Dylan. Harness joins his slightly off-key, rap-like delivery to acoustic and electric arrangements. The result is a half-chanted, half-sung poetry recital. *Welcome To The Revolution* continues in the same vein. Harness is not for those who like an easy-going sound.

✻✻✻   **God's Footstool**
1992 Amatish (SWO1921)

> God's Footstool; Won't Be Long Now; Take Me To The Limit Of Love; Thumbelina Farewell; Brunswick Avenue Blues; Don't Forget The Complicated Child; Butcher Shop; Dreams For Sale; Pot Full O' Money; Little Doggie; Allison; Hope I Don't Have To Tell Ya; Sing The Song *42:42*

✻✻✻   **Welcome To The Revolution**
1994 Amatish (SWO194)

> Welcome To The Revolution; Ballad Of Curtis Merton; Song For A Man; Chemical Valley; Jackson Homer; Moon Rider; Beneath The Sky; Captain; Ashes + Sand; Soldier Song; Wayward Son; Remember Love *62:27*

Tim Harrison
FOLK/POP; SINGER-SONGWRITER

Ontario singer-songwriter Tim Harrison has been artistic director of several folk festivals and other folk venues, as well as host of the radio show *Acoustic Espionage* on CKLN-FM, Ryerson Polytechnic University, Toronto. As a performer he has recorded two previous albums, *Train Going East* produced by the late Stan Rogers, and *In The Barroom Light*, produced by David Essig. On *The Stars Above*, his third album, and first CD, Harrison combines a strong voice with acoustic instrumentation and contemporary lyrics. Highlights include "Your Love Brings Me Around," "Maps Of Paris," "Looking At The Stars Above," "Wheatfield With Crows," "Elizabeth's Lament," and "Innocent Eyes." Guest musicians on *The Stars Above* include Willie P. Bennett on harmonica, Dennis Pedrith on bass, and Nick Naffin on guitar.

✻✻✻   **The Stars Above**
1995 Tim Harrison (TBA)

> Your Love Brings Me Around; Joy Alright; Maps Of Paris; Looking In The Stars Above; Hometown Reveries #6 And #10/We Believed; Wheatfield With Crows; Born In The Mirror; The Parting Letter To Ophelia; Elizabeth's Lament; Innocent Eyes

Paul Haslem
HAMMERED DULCIMER

Paul Haslem, who resides in Fordwich, Ontario, has been playing the hammered dulcimer for over fifteen years. He first saw a dulcimer—the world's oldest form of percussive stringed instrument—in a museum. Since building his first dulcimer and learning to play it, he has become internationally known as a dulcimer performer and craftsman. Haslem, who is also a story teller, performs at concerts, festivals, markets, and craft shows. He loves to have people try out the dulcimer and ask questions about the instrument, so if you happen to be where Haslem is performing, drop by for a chat. If you don't see him in person, you can listen to his fine playing on two CD's: *Step Out Of Time* and *Dulcimer Traditions*. These beautiful albums capture the special magic of hammered dulcimer—the warbly, chorus-like effect that comes from its paired strings that are not exactly the same length. Both albums wear well, though *Dulcimer Traditions* is the slightly more polished of the two. These could very quickly become two of the favourite albums in your collection. On *Step Out Of Time* Haslem is accompanied by Glenn Chatten, guitar and tablas; Kate Cushing, cello; Terri Burns, vocals; and Rob Geisler, beaded percussion. Additional musicians on *Dulcimer Traditions* are John Bigelow, arch guitar; Mary Anderson, Celtic harp; and Ken Brown, guitar, flute, keyboards, bass, mandolin, and accordion.

❋❋❋(❋)✓ **Step Out Of Time**
   1992 Dulcimer Traditions (RDRCD 372)

> Sandy's Fancy; The Ash Grove; First Snow; The Black Rogue; Bridgett O'Malley; Grace O'Malley; Miss Murphy; Lamentation For Owen Roe O'Neill; The King Of The Fairies/The Children's Lament; Sheebeg And Sheemore/Lord Inchiquin; Raincoat; Over The Waterfall/In The Barrel; Planxty Irwin/Fanny Power; Sweet Adare; Sliding Off The Roof; Squire Woods' Lamentation; Jivewalk; The Misty Morning Waltz; Blind Mary (I Will Love You When You're Old) *52:27*

❋❋❋❋✓ **Dulcimer Traditions**
   [no date] Dulcimer Traditions (DT-002)

> The Fordwich Jig; The Log Driver's Waltz; The Tailor's Dance; Blind Mary; Lady Athenry; The Londonderry Air (Danny Boy); The Wilderness Lament; Jesu Joy Of Man's Desiring; The Rabbit's Real; Greensleeves; The Merry Sherwood Rangers/ The Poor Old Woman; The Sally Gardens; Ave Maria; The Horse's Bransle *44:09*

The Henrys
GUITAR COMPOSITIONS

The Henrys are an Ontario group that performs original instrumental compositions featuring kona and dobro. According to the liner notes of *Puerto Angel* the kona "is an acoustic slide guitar made in Los Angeles in the 1920's and early 30's, when Hawaiian music was popular in North America. They were made out of koa wood and often had hollow necks." Whatever the history, the sound is gorgeous and the compositions on this album are outstanding, with decent vocals thrown in as a bonus. The Henrys are made up of Don Rooke on kona, dobro, and other guitars, Kim Ratcliffe, on acoustic guitar, Victor Bateman on acoustic bass, Howard Gaul on drums and percussion, and Paul Pasmore on electric bass, plus guest musicians and singers.

✳✳✳(✳) **Puerto Angel**
1994 Festival (TRAINREC 007)

Adobe Adobe; Get Out The Shovel; Bunt; The One Rose; Sea Of Tranquillity; Nunc Pro Tunc; Dark Dear Heart; Look So Good; Muscle Beach; Radio Girl; Coyote Basin; Riff Raff; Puerto Angel *49:23*

Paddy Hernon

FOLK

Based in Victoria, British Columbia, Paddy Hernon is a popular folksinger and story teller who has issued a delightful CD, *By Request*, that includes a collection of songs he has "picked up through the oral tradition over the years." Most of the songs are traditional and all are well sung. Among the highlights of this long-playing album are "Broom O' The Cowdenknowes," a fine version of Archie Fisher's "Dear Dark Eyes," (also known as "Dark Eyed Molly"), "The Brazos River," Tom Paxton's "Wild Flying Dove," and a fresh version of "Wild Mountain Thyme." And hobbit fans take note: the album closes with "The Fireside Song," a poem from J.R.R. Tolkien's *The Fellowship Of The Ring*, that Hernon has set to music.

✳✳✳(✳) **By Request**
1994 Scuttlebutt (CDC SBR 461)

Broom O' The Cowdenknowes; Loch Tay Boatsong; Dear Dark Eyes; The Brazos River; John O' Dreams; Wild Flying Dove; Leaving Shanty; Donegal Danny; The Mingulay Boatsong; Shallow Brown; The Jolly Beggar/Planxty Hewlett; Wild Mountain Thyme; The Fireside Song *60:36*

Jean Hewson

TRADITIONAL FOLK

"[Newfoundlander] Jean Hewson's *Early Spring* is a lovely collection of mostly traditional songs. She has a fine voice and has assembled a good group of backing musicians"—*Dirty Linen*. The group of backing musicians include Kathy Phippard, Esther Squires, and Vonnie Barron on vocals, with Wade Pinhorn on bass and Noel Dinn on bodhran. Their presence on "The Bonny Banks Of Virgie-O" turns the arrangement into a memorable event—easily the album's highlight. The rest of the album is enjoyable and is a very worthwhile purchase for those who love the traditional repertoire, but the album never again quite reaches the height set on the opening track.

✳✳✳ **Early Spring**
[no date] Pigeon Inlet (PIPCD-7328)

The Bonny Banks Of Virgie-O; Early Spring; The Straits Of Belle Isle/Mate's Reel; The Green Shores Of Fogo; Pat Murphy's Meadow; The Jolly Butcher; Where Once Stood A House; Wexford City; Oh No, Not I; Sweet Forget Me Not; The Gallant Ship *42:06*

Veda Hille

FOLK/POP; SINGER-SONGWRITER

Vancouver singer-songwriter Veda Hille takes you on a musical roller-coaster with quick drops and sharp turns. *Path Of A Body* is an avant garde recording that is extremely rewarding if you accept it on its own terms. The opener, "Driven," sets the tone with a collage of musical sounds that include Hille's rich, fruity voice set against quick changes of pace driven by piano. This is followed by the somewhat slower "Precious Heart," which is also driven by dynamic underlying piano rhythms. If you're still listening by this point, you'll love the rest of the tracks. Hille is an exciting singer-songwriter/musician who can stretch your vision of folk/pop music, introducing you to key changes you've never heard before.

❋❋❋(❋) **Path Of A Body**
1994 Ball Of Flames (VH-112-2)†

(Driven Into); Driven; Precious Heart; Three; The Same; Small Weight; With No Caring; Corridor; Rhapsody; Old Song; And Birds *51:50*

Jim Hiscott

BUTTON ACCORDION; FOLK VARIATIONS

Winnipeg-based accordionist Jim Hiscott has a special interest in folk and popular music from around the world, especially modal scales, repetition, and rhythms. His album *Spirit Reel* is composed of three major sections. "Spirit Reel" is a set of variations on a reel tune partially inspired by the rhythms of Cree and Metis fiddling. "Lesotho" was inspired by the accordion-based pop music of the tiny, mountainous African state of the same name. "Metis Dance Variations" was commissioned by the Metis Arts of Manitoba to commemorate the centenary of the death of Louis Riel. The piece is a set of variations on "The Red River Jig," the best-known Metis tune. The album is more "academic" and less danceable than the Celtic accordion and fiddle music of the Maritimes, but it provides deep pleasure for those willing to listen their way inside the structure.

❋❋❋(❋) **Spirit Reel**
1991 Blue Ocean (OCCD-9071)

Spirit Reel, For Violin And Button Accordion (5 Parts); Lesotho, For Solo Button Accordion (2 Parts); Metis Dance Variations, For Violin, Button Accordion, Piano, and Percussion *54:42*

Jerry Holland

MARITIMES FIDDLE

One of the joys of compact disc technology is that it has rescued many fine out-of-print recordings from obscurity. A case in point is Jerry Holland's *Fiddlesticks Collection*, a CD reissue of material from five earlier LP's: *A Session With Jerry Holland, Cape Breton Fiddler, Collection Of Fiddle Tunes, Lively Steps,* and *Fathers & Sons.* A slightly more strident and livelier fiddler than fellow Cape Bretoner Buddy MacMaster, Jerry Holland energizes fiddle tunes with a driving melody that will have you dancing instantly and will keep you that way until you fall, exhausted. He's also a prolific writer of new fiddle tunes. A wonderful collection.

✳✳✳✳✳✓ **The Fiddlesticks Collection**
1992 Fiddlesticks Music (CD1)

Reichswall Forest/Easter Elchies/Winston In The 50's/Mrs. Gordon Of Knockespoch; Andy De Jarlis' Jig/Ingonish Jig/Mrs. McGhee; Cutting Ferns/Alex Dan MacIsaac's/Brenda Stubbert's/Mutt's Favorite/ Bernadette's/Lady Gordan's Of Gordanstown's; Jenny's Wedding/Dowsy Maggie/The Shaskeen Reel; The Hearty Boys Of Ballymote/Dan Collin's Father's Jig; Cranking Out/Lively Steps/Garmont Smiddy's Reel; Reel For Carl; Beautiful Lake Ainslie/Miss Grace Menzies/Mr. Bernard; Arthur Muise/Buddy In Big Pond/Mary Cotter's; Souter Johnny/Irvine Steeple/O'Corse; Alex Menzies/ Lad O'Byrne's/Dublin Porter; Ashokan; The MacDonald's Of Hamilton/Danny Big Alec MacDonald/ Big Alec's Jig; The Old Boar/My Old Fiddle/Fiddle On Fire; Fr. John Angus Rankin/Trip To Dublin/Aoife's/ Harry Bradshaw's/Johnny Muise's; Sweet Journeys; Mrs. Crawford/Over The Moor Among The Heather/Kiss The Lass Ye Like The Best/Uist Lasses/Sir David Davidson Of Cantry/Celtic Ceilidh; Memories Of Elmer Briand/Hughie Johnny Angus Of West Mabou/An Old Inverness County Reel/The Cross Of Inverness; Drummond Castle/What Will Be King But Charlie/Jerry's Pipe Jig; Sheehan's Reel/ The Fowers Of Edinburgh/Mrs. MacLeod's Reel *71:06*

Ron Hynes
FOLK/COUNTRY/POP; SINGER-SONGWRITER

Nova Scotia's Ron Hynes is a leading songwriter whose work is appreciated and sung by both folk and country performers. Hynes is also an excellent performer who delivers most of his material in a Martimes-flavoured country style. *Cryer's Paradise* is another strong collection of Hynes songs. The most folkish tracks on the album are "No Kathleen," "Maybe She Went Crazy," "River Of No Return," and "Atlantic Blue."

✳✳✳(✳) **Cryer's Paradise**
1993 Atlantica (E2 07777 89466 2 5)†

Cryer's Paradise; Man Of A Thousand Songs; No Kathleen; If I Left You Alone With My Heart; Story Of My Life; Maybe She Went Crazy; River Of No Return; False Hearted Love; Where Do You Get Off; Picture To Hollywood; Roy Orbison Came On; Atlantic Blue *43:51*

Ian & Sylvia
FOLK/COUNTRY/WESTERN; SINGER-SONGWRITERS

For many older folkies the distinctive voices of Ian & Sylvia Tyson define the essence of the 1960's folk music sound. These Juno Award Hall of Famers became popular in the United States at the start of the 60's folk revival, paved the way for other Canadian performers at a time when there were limited recording opportunities for musicians in Canada. One of the top acts of the folk scene, Ian & Sylvia helped boost the careers of Gordon Lightfoot and Joni Mitchell with their recordings of "Early Morning Rain," "For Lovin' Me," and "The Circle Game," and they introduced outstanding songs of their own, including Sylvia's "You Were On My Mind" and Ian's "Someday Soon" and "Four Strong Winds." Photographs of Sylvia playing autoharp while Ian plays guitar are among the most romantic evocations of the coffeehouse era.

"Their early Vanguard albums were an eclectic mix of traditional and contemporary folksongs, sung with a purity and clarity that was unusual, even in the stripped-down days of folk music"—Mary Katherine Aldin, liner notes to *Long Long Time*. Those albums include *Four Strong Winds*, *Northern Journey*, and *Early Morning Rain*. *Play One More*, marks a change in direction to new material and electric and orchestral arrangements. *Nashville*, a countryish album, sounds surprisingly modern. Along the way they formed a backup band called Great Speckled Bird, featuring Amos Garrett and Buddy Cage. *Great Specked Bird*, released in 1970, became a collector's item when the company that originally released it pulled out of the record business. Rare vinyl copies of the album have exchanged hands for as much as $150. With no master tapes to work from, Stony Plain rescued this album from oblivion by remastering and re-engineering from high-quality vinyl. Because of the eclectic nature of Ian & Sylvia's material, their *Greatest Hits* collection makes an outstanding purchase. It shaves off some of their less successful efforts and includes many of their best songs. The collection covers the entire range of their early Vanguard period. Similarly, *Long Long Time* captures some great tracks from out-of-print albums from their post-Vanguard period, including *Lovin' Sound* (MGM 1967), *Full Circle* (MGM 1968), *Great Speckled Bird* (Ampex 1969), *Ian & Sylvia...With David Wilcox* (Columbia 1971).

See also Ian Tyson; Sylvia Tyson; Quartette.

❊❊❊(❊)   **Four Strong Winds**
1963 Vanguard (VMD 2149)

Jesus Met The Woman At The Well; Tomorrow Is A Long Time; Katy Dear; Poor Lazarus; Four Strong Winds; Ella Speed; Long Lonesome Road; V'La L'Bon Vent; Royal Canal; Lady of Carlisle; Spanish Is A Loving Tongue; The Greenwood Sidie (The Cruel Mother); Every Night When The Sun Goes Down; Every Time I Feel The Spirit *41:55*

❊❊❊(❊)   **Northern Journey**
1964 Vanguard (VMD 79154)

You Were On My Mind; Moonshine Can; The Jealous Lover; Four Rode By; Brave Wolfe; Nova Scotia Farewell; Some Day Soon; Little Beggarman; Texas Rangers; The Ghost Lover; Captain Woodstock's Courtship; Green Valley; Swing Down, Chariot *39:00*

❊❊❊❊   **Early Morning Rain**
1965 Vanguard (VMD 79175)

Come In, Stranger; Early Morning Rain; Nancy Whiskey; Awake Ye Drowsy Sleepers; Marlborough Street Blues; Darcy Farrow; Travelling Drummer; Maude's Blues; Red Velvet; I'll Bid My Heart Be Still; For Lovin' Me; Song For Canada *35:54*

❊❊❊   **Play One More**
1966 Vanguard (79215-2)

Short Grass; The French Girl; When I Was A Cowboy; Changes; Gifts Are For Giving; Molly And Tenbrooks; Hey, What About Me; Lonely Girls; Satisfied Mind; Twenty Four Hours From Tulsa; Friends Of Mine; Play One More *38:39*

❄❄❄ **Nashville**
1968 Vanguard (79284-2)

The Mighty Quinn; Wheels On Fire; Farewell To The North; Taking Care Of Business; Southern Comfort; Ballad Of The Ugly Man; 90° X 90°; She'll Be Gone; London Life; The Renegade; House Of Cards *37:09*

❄❄❄(❄) **Great Speckled Bird**
1969, reissued 1994 Stony Plain (SPCD 1200)

Love What You're Doing Child; Calgary; Trucker's Cafe; Long Long Time To Get Old; Flies In The Bottle; Bloodshot Beholder; Crazy Arms; This Dream; Smiling Wine; Rio Grande; Disappearing Woman; We Sail; New Trucker's Cafe (Live Version) *43:37*

❄❄❄❄✓ **Long Long Time**
1967-70, reissued 1994 Vanguard (79478-2)

Hang On To A Dream; You Were On My Mind; Summer Wages; Lovin' Sound; Stories He'd Tell; Trucker's Cafe; Here's To You; Reason To Believe; Joshua; Long Long Time To Get Old; Big River; Salmon In The Sea; Last Lonely Eagle; Crazy Arms; Windy Weather; Tears Of Rage *50:58*

❄❄❄❄✓ **Greatest Hits**
1970, 1987 Vanguard (VCD-5/6)

Early Morning Rain; Tomorrow Is A Long Time; Little Beggarman; The Mighty Quinn; Nancy Whiskey; Catfish Blues; Come In Stranger; The French Girl; The Renegade; Mary Anne; You Were On My Mind; Four Strong Winds; Short Grass; Southern Comfort; Some Day Soon; Ella Speed; The Circle Game; 90° X 90°; Cutty Wren; Un Canadien Errant; Lonely Girls; Spanish Is A Loving Tongue; This Wheel's On Fire *70:21*

Inconnu

FOLK/POP; SINGER-SONGWRITERS

A band from the Yukon, Inconnu sings an eclectic mix of original material. The songs on their debut album, *Inconnu*, range from soft, introspective numbers like "Icebound" and "Seventh Day" to up-tempo pieces like "Henry's Claim" and "When My Breath Comes Back." The French "Jigi Dou" is an accordion-driven folkish piece that would not sound out of place on a Maritimes album. Because the album is so diverse, you're not left with any "signature" sound. A pleasant, if somewhat undefined, album. *Inconnu* is Lucie Desaulniers, lead vocal; Jay Burr, tuba; Nick de Graff, guitar, vocals; Andrea McColeman, piano, organ, accordion, vocals; Len Osland, drums, vocals.

❄❄❄ **Inconnu**
1994 Inconnu (IP1-1994)†

Icebound; Henry's Claim; Jigi Dou; Oh No; When My Breath Came Back; Seventh Day; Water; My Old Ford; Kenny; Cold Feet; Tagish; Balance *47:23*

May Ip
FOLK; SINGER-SONGWRITER

May Ip recently moved to Toronto from Hong Kong where she was living on Lama Island. While in Hong Kong she was moved by the music of Patsy Cline and American folk music. For a short time she was in a Cajun band called Asian Cajun, and she has played at folk festivals in the UK. Her second album, and first CD, *Very Personal*, is mainly sold at open mike sessions where she performs. It is a remarkable work, honest and simple, with songs mostly in English plus one, "Ngy Pang Yao," in Cantonese. Abandoning conventional packaging, Ip's CD comes in a hand-folded cover, hand printed on cardboard and recycled unbleached paper that includes her own art work. This very interesting and enjoyable album is bound to become a very rare CD.

✳✳✳ **Very Personal**
1994 May Ip [no catalogue number]

> Lyin' Naked (Beside You); Silent Game; Home Home; A Love Song; Love Is Always A State Of Confusion; Free Spirits Lonesome Souls; No Heartbreakin' Situation; Give Us A Smile; Can We Believe; Ngy Pang Yao; Wayfarin' Stranger *47:05*

The Irish Descendants
TRADITIONAL/CONTEMPORARY CANADIAN-IRISH FOLK

The Newfoundland-based Irish Descendants combine full harmonies with excellent musicianship, mixing together a repertoire of traditional Irish tunes and contemporary lyrics. Their first album, *Misty Morning Shore*, was once issued on compact disc, but due to a dispute over distribution rights, it is no longer available. Their second album, *Look To The Sea*, is a noteworthy album that provides enjoyment play after play. Highlights include an upbeat arrangement of "Rocky Road To Dublin," "Last Of The Great Whales," and "Oh No Not I." The band excels at instrumental sets, such as "Dancin' Dick/Lough Geil/Fisherman's Widow." On their third album, *Gypsies & Lovers*, the Descendants re-recorded some of the material from *Misty Morning Shore* along with new material. Descendants fans can once again listen to "Rattlin' Bog," the band's tour de force. The album also includes a successful version of Stan Rogers' "Barrett's Privateers," a somewhat less successful version of Donovan's "Catch The Wind," and a dubious, if heartfelt, version of "Let Me Fish Off Cape St. Mary's." The Irish Descendants are D'Arcy Broderick, Con O'Brien, Ronnie Power, Larry Martin, Gerard Broderick, and Kathy Phippard. The Irish Descendants received an "Entertainer of the Year" East Coast Music Award in 1995.

✳✳✳✳✓ **Look To The Sea**
1993 Warner (CD 94017)

> Rollin' Of The Sea; Useta Love Her; Rocky Road To Dublin; Days Of Yore; Dancin' Dick/Lough Geil/Fisherman's Widow; Peter Street; Go To Sea No More; Last Of The Great Whales; Thousand Tall Ships/The Scholar/Miss McCloud's Reel; Oh No, Not I; Lark In The Morning; Fisherman's Song *44:03*

❋❋❋(❋) **Gypsies & Lovers**
1994 WEA (CD 98237)†

> Raggle Taggle Gypsy; Catch The Wind; Barrett's Privateers; Merry Blacksmith/
> Swallow's Tale/Banshee; Let Me Fish Off Cape St. Mary's; Rattlin' Bog; Will They
> Lie There Evermore; My Lagan Love/Drowsy Maggie/Dionne Reel; A Walk In The
> Irish Rain; Lovers *43:31*

The Irish Rovers
FOLK/POP

The Irish Rovers, who first formed in 1964 in Calgary, are Jimmy Ferguson, Will
Millar, George Millar, Wilcil McDowell, and Joe Millar. Canada's most enduring pub
band, the Rovers were catapulted to fame with their hit single, Shel Silverstein's "The
Unicorn," in 1968. They also had solid commercial success with "The Biplane Evermore," "Lily The Pink," and "Wasn't That A Party." From 1971-74 they hosted a
weekly variety show on CBC TV. Fans from the 60's and 70's will find plenty of CD's
to choose from—the Rovers were nothing if not prolific—but their commercially cute
sound has not aged particularly well. For many of today's fans, the Rovers don't have
the substance and resonance of contemporary Canadian Celtic groups.

See also Will Millar.

❋❋❋ **Greatest Hits**
1974 MCA (MCAD 4066)

> The Unicorn; The Biplane Evermore; Rhymes And Reasons; Years May Come,
> Years May Go; The Orange And The Green; Black Velvet Band; Goodbye Mrs.
> Durkin; Donald Where's Your Trousers; Farewell To Nova Scotia; Lily The Pink;
> Mrs. Crandall's Boarding House; The Minstrel Of Cranberry Lane; The Puppet Song
> (Whiskey On A Sunday); The Wind That Shakes The Corn; Bonnie Kellswater; My
> Old Man's A Dustman; Nancy Whiskey; Goodnight Irene; Liverpool Lou; Winken,
> Blinken, And Nod *61:44*

❋❋❋ **No More Bread And Butter / The Rovers**
1980-81, reissued 1992 Attic (ACD 24109)

> What's A Nice Guy Like Me (Doin' In A Place Like This); No More Bread And
> Butter; Roly Poly Ladies; Class Of '69; Chattanoogie Shoe Shine Boy; Pain In My
> Past; The Other Side Of The Sun; Me And Millie; Willie McBride; One Sunday
> Morning; Mexican Girl; Yo Yo Man; Tara; Matchstick Men; Pheasant Plucker's Son;
> Wasn't That A Party; Fireflyte; Movie Cowboys/Happy Trails To You; Victory
> Chimes; Here's To The Horses *68:21*

❋❋❋ **It Was A Night Like This**
1982 Attic (ACD 1149)

> Grandma Got Run Over By A Reindeer; The Christmas Wish; The Christmas
> Traveller; Christmas Eve; Merry Bloody Xmas; Honky Tonk Christmas; Scarlet
> Ribbons; It's Christmas; Rock Along Christmas; The Peace Carol; It Was A Night
> Like This *39:16*

❋❋❋ **Years May Come, Years May Go**
1985, reissued 1993 MCA (MCBBD 20307)

The Unicorn; Lily The Pink; Whiskey On A Sunday; Years May Come, Years May Go; Fifi O'Toole; Goodnight Irene; Sam Hall; The Life Of The Rover; Bonnie Kellswater; Liverpool Lou *30:15*

❋❋❋ **Party With The Rovers**
1985 Attic (ACDM 1205)

Everybody's Making It But Me; Lonesome Traveller/This Train; Mama Was A Moonshine Man; Down In The Devil's Den; Swallow's Tail; Rollin' River; The Boys Are Going Drinking Tonight; Bottle Of Wine; Dig A Little Deeper In The Well; Frail Tho' My Spirit May Be; Does Your Chewing Gum Lose Its Flavour; Wasn't That A Party *32:13*

❋❋❋ **Hardstuff**
1989 Attic (ACD 1253)†

All Sing Together; Paddy On The Turnpike; Belfast; Buy Us A Drink; First Day On The Somme; Mama's Got A Squeezebox; Don't Fly Away; Down By The Sally Gardens; Finnegan's Wake; The Other Side Of The Evening *38:19*

❋❋❋ **Silver Anniversary**
1989 Attic (ACD 1303)

What Wid Ye Do; Mick Maguire; McDonalds' Raiders; Reels: Pigeon On The Gate/ The Teetotaller; Castle Of Dromore; Rare Old Mountain Dew; Maggie Mae; Mama Was A Moonshine Man; New York Gals; The Unicorn; Come And Dance To Paddy's Reels; Song Of The Antrim Coast; Jigs: The Frost Is All Over/The Rakes Of Kildare/ I Will If I Can; The Flower Of Sweet Strabane; The Shores Of Americay; Maid Of Fife-O; Summertime Is Coming; Sweet Jazz Babies; Come By The Hills; Wasn't That A Party *49:5948:49*

❋❋❋ **The Boys Come Rollin' Home**
1992 Attic (ACD 1381)

When The Boys Come Rollin' Home; The Spanish Lady; Lorena; Killiburn Brae; Music In The Glen; The Sand And The Foam; The Bonnie Lady; Las Vegas In The Hills Of Donegal; The Shadow Of O'Casey; The Irish Rover; Travellin' Man; Isle Of Innisfree; Bold O'Donahue; Bonnie Kellswater; Farmer's Song

❋❋❋ **Celebrate! The First Thirty Years**
1994 Rover Records (ROV 30-2)

Ryan's Reel; The Irish Rover; What Wid Ye Do; When The Boys Come Rollin' Home; The Summer Time Is Coming; The Galway Races; The Black Velvet Band; The Isle Of Innisfree; Valapariso; Marie's Wedding; The Moonshiner; The Spanish Lady; New York Gals; Molly Malone; Star Of The County Down; The Unicorn; The Drunken Sailor; Wasn't That A Party *51:18*

Jackson Delta

FOLK/BLUES; SINGER-SONGWRITERS

Perennial festival favourites, Jackson Delta is an acoustic blues trio from Peterborough, Ontario, consisting of Alan Black, Rick Fines and Gary Peeples. *Acoustic Blues*, recorded with no overdubbing, introduces the musical tightness they developed through years of playing together. In addition to traditional numbers like "C.C. Rider" and "John Hardy" the band plays original compositions such as "Back Up From Zero," "Path To The Liquor Store," and "Bad News Blues." A sparse, excellent recording. *Lookin' Back* picks up the pace with the addition of guest musicians on some of the tracks, including vocals by Colleen Peterson on "Little Sister's Gonna Be Alright" and piano by Gene Taylor on "The Feel Of Uncertainty." A live album recorded at Toronto's Ultrasound, *Jackson Delta Live With Gene Taylor* continues the collaboration of Jackson Delta with Gene Taylor on piano. The performances are gutsy and the audience rapport is excellent.

❋❋❋❋ **Acoustic Blues**
[no date] Jackson Delta (0012384)†

Statesborough Blues; I Need You By My Side; Back Up From Zero; Path To The Liquor Store; Sugar Bee; Baby Please Don't Go; I Ain't Got No Baby Now; Bad News Blues; Sink Or Swim; Talk To Your Mama; C.C. Rider; John Hardy *43:38*

❋❋❋❋✓ **Lookin' Back**
[no date] Jackson Delta (0012385)†

Lookin' Back; Fool In Love; Goin' Back To Memphis; My Mistake; Honey, What's Wrong With You; My Ears Keep Hearing Voices; Little Sister's Gonna Be Alright; The Feel Of Uncertainty; Silly Rules; Unpaid Bills Blues; I Sleep With A Ghost; Crazy (About You); Worried Life *47:51*

❋❋❋❋ **Jackson Delta Live With Gene Taylor**
[no date] Jackson Delta (0012386)

Bad News Blues; Liquor Store Blues; Howlin' For My Darlin'; T.V. Mama; Ain't No Tellin'; All By Myself; Statesborough Blues; Fanny Mae; Same Old Blues; Ain't Got No Baby Now; Mojo Boogie; Saved *48:50*

Tom Jackson
FIRST NATIONS MUSIC; FOLK/COUNTRY/POP; SINGER-SONGWRITER

Winnipeg-based Tom Jackson, actor and star of the Canadian TV series *North Of 60*, is also a singer-songwriter. His first CD, *The Huron Carole* is a collection of Christmas songs with the net proceeds of album sales going to the Salvation Army. The album shows him to have a decent, if not especially powerful, voice. His second CD, *No Regrets*, is a middle-of-the-road folkish, countryish pop album. Songs like "No Regrets," "Humble Me," and "Song For A Lady" are interesting compositions well played by his backup musicians. This album doesn't shake up anything on the musical Richter scale, but it's a good workmanlike set of tunes. Jackson fans will enjoy this one.

❋❋❋ **The Huron Carole**
1994 PEG (PMK 077)

Soulin'; Midnight Clear; Friendly Beasts; Silent Night; Huron Carole; Christmas Wish; O Holy Night; Drummer Boy; Medley; Passage; What Child Is This; Passage; First Noel; Passage; A Star In The East; Huron Carole *29:39*

❋❋❋ **No Regrets**
1994 PEG (PMK 078)

No Regrets; Hooker; Humble Me; Few And Far Between; Can't Take That Away
(The Vampire); Song For A Lady; Love Turning Blue; Do Me Right; Move On
Down The Line; Out Of Control *39:51*

Jar O' Comfort
MARITIMES CELTIC

Jar O' Comfort, a Celtic-flavoured band from Prince Edward Island, performs a mix
of traditional and contemporary material. *Preserved* is a compilation of selections
from two of the band's previous albums, *Surrounded By Water* and *Scatter The Mud!*
From the opener, Lennie Gallant's "Nellie J. Banks," through Celtic-style instrumental medleys like "Sailor's Hornpipe/Big John MacNeil/Devil's Dream" to the traditional "Four Marys," Jar O' Comfort provides entertaining performances with excellent musicianship and decent, if occasionally rough, vocals. Jar O' Comfort is Gordon
Belsher, Charlene Belsher, and Stephen Sharratt.

❋❋❋ **Preserved**
1993 Guernsey Cove Parlour (GCP 013)

Nellie J. Banks; Sailor's Hornpipe/Big John MacNeill/Devil's Dream; The Nightin-
gale; Thank God We're Surrounded By Water; All The Way To Cardigan; Rough
Pavement; Twelve Weeks Of Workin'; Ballad Of The St. Ann's Reel; Four Marys;
Jigs: Paddy O'Brien's/Scatter The Mud/Arthur Darley's; Mud, Beautiful Mud; Song
Of The Irish Moss; The Sea & The Soil; Stand To Your Glass *50:22*

Larry Jensen
FOLK/BLUES/POP; SINGER-SONGWRITER

Larry Jensen, a singer-songwriter based in Owen Sound, Ontario, has released *Song
House*, a long-playing compact disc containing a re-release of material from his earlier albums plus some new tunes. Highlights of the album include "How Does She Do
It?" "Pluggin' In Pluggin' On," "Illusions," "Desert Rain," and "Carolyna." Jensen is
a solid performer who writes catchy, contemporary lyrics.

❋❋❋ **Song House**
1994 Larry Jensen [no catalogue number]

Peculiar; How Does She Do It?; Pluggin' In Pluggin' On; The Day My Baby Said
Goodbye; Illusions; She Don't Live Here; Business; Desert Rain; I'm Your Boy;
Five Weeks; Show Me Where It Hurts; Do You Know Where Your Children Are?;
Daddy's Back In Town; Face On A Billboard; Agent Of The Road; Big Money;
Home To Die; Carolyna; Wave It Goodbye *73:03*

Jerusalem Ridge
BLUEGRASS

Jerusalem Ridge is an Edmonton bluegrass group with zing, dash, and variety. Their
debut CD, *Looking Back*—a compilation of two earlier albums, *Jerasulem Ridge* and
North Wind—is a long, lively album filled with delights such as a banjo-driven ver-

sion of Gordon Lightfoot's "Early Morning Rain," plus a pair of a cappella southern gospel numbers: "I'm Willing To Try" and "I'll Wear A White Robe." With good voices and excellent bluegrass instrumentation, Jerusalem Ridge works its way through traditional numbers such as "Little Maggie" with enthusiasm. This eclectic album is a delight—a must purchase for bluegrass fans. Their success with gospel numbers convinced Jerusalem Ridge to record an entire gospel album, *Make A Joyful Noise*. Individually, many of the songs on this album are well delivered, but there can be too much of a good thing. In comparison to the varied material on *Looking Back*, this album gets tedious. The instrumental work also lacks the customary sparkle and bright edge. Gospel enthusiasts will want this one, but others will be satisfied with the touch of gospel on *Looking Back*. Jerusalem Ridge consists of Craig Korth, Bill Lopushinsky, Dave Wright, and Keith Burgess.

❋❋❋❋✓ **Looking Back**
1993 JR Records (JR-030-493)

> Early Morning Rain; North Wind; Cora's Gone; White Water; I'm Willing To Try; 32 Acres; Spring Flowers; Little Girl Of Mine In Tennessee; On Down The Line; Too Late To Cry; Roving Gambler; I'll Wear A White Robe; Can't You Hear Me Calling?; Lost And I'll Never Find A Way; Brand New Tennessee Waltz; Ghost Riders In The Sky/House Of The Rising Sun; On The Sea Of Life; Just A Little Talk With Jesus; Little Maggie *56:58*

❋❋❋ **Make A Joyful Noise**
1994 JR Records (JR-040-494)

> Climbin' Up The Mountain; Hallelujah, I'm Ready; March Around The Throne; Satan's Jewel Crown; Leaning On The Everlasting Arms; Rank Strangers; Paul And Silas; Consider The Lillies; Cryin' Holy; A Beautiful Life; Goodnight, The Lord's Comin'; Green Pastures *33:42*

Jimmy George
CELTIC FOLK/ROCK; SINGER-SONGWRITERS

Those who want unabashed folk/rock will be pleased to encounter Jimmy George, an Ottawa band that lights a fire under its songs. *A Month Of Sundays* provides Celtic banjo, accordion, and mandolin laced with a strong dose of electric guitar and drums. The alt-rock-style lyrics lean towards youthful irreverence (the Jimmy George credo is "if you are not completely satisfied with this product, you should lower your expectations.") There are elements of Spirit of the West and Grievous Angels on the album and the driving energy of the band compensates somewhat for the absence of outstanding singing voices. Jimmy George is Eric Altman, Joel Carlson, Steve Donnelly, Michael Eady, Jeff Kerr, Mike Lawson, J. Todd, and Mickey Vallee.

❋❋❋ **A Month Of Sundays**
1994 Waxy Skin (WSCD-001)

> My Final Days With You; Barnstorming; Breakfast With St. Swithin; Parading; Four Feet From Shore; Under Study; Things I Did Wrong; Frontiers; Prophet Of Doom; Suicide; Owen; The Recuperative Powers Of The Soul; Slept All Afternoon; What I Should Do *46:45*

Juba!
SOUTH AFRICAN-INSPIRED MUSIC

Juba! is an Edmonton group that came together to perform South African freedom songs. Over time the group has evolved its drumming and improvisation based on a continuing study of South African music. All the songs on *Mafaro* (which means "I'm happy" in the Shona language of Zimbabwe) are sung in South African languages, with English liner-note translations. Despite the language hurdle, it's easy to enjoy this album just by listening to the pleasing harmonies, choruses, and percussion. Juba! is Warren Albers, Cleve Alexander, Arthur Bollo-Kamara, Lark Clark, Kelly Collins, Beth Portman, and Scott Rollans.

✹✹✹(✹)　**Mafaro**
　　　　1993　Juba! [no catalogue number]

> Juba Lethu; Tichano Imba; Tichano Imba; Vakuru Vanoti; Umam'uyajabula; Freedom Is Coming; Mafaro; Siyaya eJerusalema; Masambe; Langa More; Doumbé; Chogugudza Two; Mockingbird; New Siyahamba; Mambo Jesu; Ngeke Ngiye; Meva; Demba; Zulu Seliyaduma *52:22*

Jughead
JUGBAND/BLUEGRASS; SINGER-SONGWRITERS

Jughead is a Toronto jug band that likes to have a good time. They are known for their Saturday afternoon matinées at Toronto's Horseshoe Tavern where they fit ten or more musicians on stage and let rip on jug, washboard, kazoo, washtub, fiddle, banjo, mandolin, and accordion. Their lighthearted lyrics, such as "Bury Me In My Shades," are captured on *Uncorked!*. Jughead, on this album, is Michael "Lopez" Phillips, John Mets, Michael Smith, Dan Ouellette, Andrew Queen, Doug Queen, Christopher Quinn, Nik Tjelios, Brian Morgan, and Michael F. Jursic

✹✹✹　**Uncorked!**
　　　　1993　On Tap (SUDS 002)

> Slewfoot; Barn Song; Bury Me In My Shades; Wabash Cannonball; Ace Of Spades; Pirates Of Paradise; Hockey Song; San Francisco Bay Blues; I Know You Rider; G.S.T.; Monkey And The Hammer; Hush; Ain't Got The Time; Stumblin Drunk; Been Away Too Long *44:36*

Connie Kaldor
FOLK/POP; SINGER/SONGWRITER

"An artist who has rightly earned a reputation for being one of the most beloved performers on the Canadian folk scene"—*Sing Out!* A regular at folk festivals for many years, Saskatchewan singer-songwriter Connie Kaldor has been entertaining audiences with her very contemporary brand of folk/pop material. *Moonlight Grocery* features pop-oriented songs like "Wanderlust," "Caught In A Crossfire," and "Moonlight Grocery." The slower "Calais Maine" and "Wood River" are the rootsiest songs on the album. *Gentle Of Heart*, a more introspective album than *Moonlight Grocery* is a more successful effort in part because the arrangements don't obscure Kaldor's expressive voice and lyrics. The strong songwriting is evidenced on nearly every song, including the opener, "Gentle Of Heart": "Some are born on second base / And think they've hit a double." *Wood River: Home Is Where The Heart Is ...*, much of it recorded live, begins with "Wood River" and continues through Kaldor's "prairie song" repertoire. This album, produced by Roy Forbes, is likely to be the Kaldor album of choice for folkies. Its countryish, down-home flavour dispenses, for the most part, with pop arrangements and gets to the heart of the lyrics. Recommended. *Out Of The Blue*, also produced by Roy Forbes, presents excellent new Kaldor material in a variety of styles from the pop/rock opener "Relax" to the rootsier "Singer Of The Sacred Heart" and "Mother's Prayer." Kaldor, like Joni Mitchell, has too many facets to her songwriting to confine herself to one musical style. If you don't mind a strong layering of pop, you'll find *Out Of The Blue* highly rewarding.

❋❋❋   **Moonlight Grocery**
1984 Coyote (CEGCD 1002)†

> Wanderlust; Caught In The Crossfire; Danger Danger; Calais Maine; Get Back The Night; Talk Without Speaking; Love Or Something; Moonlight Grocery; Wood River; Bird On A Wing; Maria's Place/Batoche *44:20*

❋❋❋(❋)   **Gentle Of Heart**
1989 Coyote (CEGCD 1009)†

> Gentle Of Heart; Love Letters; Rage Inside; If You Leave Me Now; River Song; Thin Thread; Heart For The Boy; Warm Yourself; Passion; One Hit; I Go Out Walking *45:17*

❋❋❋❋✓   **Wood River: Home Is Where The Heart Is ...**
1992 Coyote (CEGCD 1010)†

> Wood River; Outlaw; Sleepy Little Town; Can't Go Back; Modern Lullaby; Canoe Song; Bird On A Wing; Harsh And Unforgiving; Just A Little Dream; Hymn For Pincher Creek; Spring On The Prairies; Margaret's Waltz; Grandmother's Song; Saskatoon Moon *42:21*

❋❋❋(❋)   **Out Of The Blue**
1994 Coyote (CEGCD 1015)†

> Relax; I Don't Love Easy; I'll Take Good Care; Singer Of The Sacred Heart; Mother's Prayer; Why Aren't You Here?; What A Mess Love Is; Hope In My Heart; I Am A Believer; Bigger Than Anywhere Else *37:09*

Kanatan Aski
FIRST NATIONS MUSIC; SINGER-SONGWRITERS

Kanatan Aski (Cree for "Clean Land") is a First Nations group whose goal is bringing together contemporary native musicians and styles from across the Americas, North and South. On *The Condor Meets The Eagle*, Kanatan Aski is joined by Pura Fe (Tuscarora) and Monique Mojica (Cuna). The combination is a creative mix of pan-pipe sounds of the Andes, drums, guitars, and the contemporary and traditional singing styles of Pura Fe and Monique Mojica.

❋❋❋ **Condor Meets The Eagle**
[no date] Black Jaguar [no catalogue number]

Navajo Song; Acapana; Round Dance; Muskuy; Imaginacion; Tres Virtudes; The Condor Meets The Eagle; Yacu; Nishin; Mamatow; El Amor; Takile *48:41*

Kashtin
FIRST NATIONS MUSIC; SINGER-SONGWRITERS

Florent Vollant and Claude McKenzie, who perform under the name "Kashtin", offer a bridge to the music of Canada's native peoples. You don't need to understand the words of their songs—written in the Montagnais language (Innu Aionun)—to enjoy their music. The liner notes provide you with a background for each song and you can listen your way into the rhythms and instrumentation that accompany their work. Their debut album, *Kashtin,* introduces the duo's folk/rock style with catchy melodies and warm arrangements that continue on their second release, *Innu*. Compared with other First Nations music, however, you begin to wonder, as did a reviewer in *Dirty Linen*, "when is music by an indigenous people part of its roots music continuum, and when is it merely indistinguishable pop/rock music sung in the people's language?" There seems to be nothing particularly unique about these albums other than their language. Kashtin has responded to this question with *Akua Tuta*, their third and easily most successful album to date. The musicianship is tighter and richer and, for the first time, you start to get an underlying sense of First Nations rhythms and chants as an integral part of the music. This convincing album provides a good reason to introduce yourself to Kashtin.

❋❋❋ **Kashtin**
1989 Groupe Concept Musique (PPFL AC-2009)†

E Uassiuian (My Childhood); Kashtin (Tornado); E Peikussian (Solitude); Pakuakumit (Pointe-Bleue); Shashish (A Long Time Ago); Apu Tshekuan (It Doesn't Matter); Tshinanu (What We Are); Tipatshimun (The Devil's Song); Uitshi (Help Me); Ashtam Nituapam (Come Find Me); Shteteian (Departure); Nitanish (N'Teish/My Daughter) *47:05*

❋❋❋ **Innu**
1991 Groupe Concept Musique (PPFLC 2011)†

Ouverture; Nikanish (Les Miens/My People); Nekashtuamani (Surprise: Angoisse/Anguish); Nte Tshitshuat (Chez Vous/Your Place); Apu Tshekuan Nikan'Kuian (Rien Pour M'Arrêter/Nothing Can Stop Me); Harricana (Longue Route/Long Road); Son Of The Sun (Fils Du Soleil); Tshinuau (Vous Autres/All Of You); Apu Min'Tan (Fiche-moi La Paix/Leave Me Alone); Uishama (Version Kashtin); Ishkuess (Fille/Girl) *38:07*

❋❋❋(❋) **Akua Tuta**
1994 Columbia (CK80209)†

Akua Tuta (Take Care/Fais Attention); Uasset (All The Children/Tous Les Enfants); Ashtam Nashue (Come Follow Me/Viens Suis-Mois); Nuitsheuan (My Friend/Mon Ami); Miam Uapukun (Like A Flower/Comme Un Fleur); Ne Puamun (My Dreams/Mes Rêves); Tapue Shtutune (You Really Make Me/Vraiment Tu Me Fais); Apu

Shapentaman (Without Interest/Sans Intérêt); Uauitemu (Tell Me/Dis-Moi);
Tshekuanu Mak (Why/Pourquoi); Utei Teu Etaian (Here With Me/Ici Avec Moi);
Iame (Good Bye/Au Revoir) *47:08*

Katari Taiko
PERCUSSION; TAIKO DRUMS

Commotion is a live recording from Katari Taiko's 15th anniversary concert on June 28th and 29th, 1994 in Vancouver. The title of the album comes from the opening number, "Ja Sawago" which is a Japanese phrase for "let's create a commotion!" or "let's raise hell!" Katari Taiko performs percussion compositions based on folk themes. Of "Oedo" the liner notes state that the piece was composed "using rhythms that originate in the festivals of Tokyo, or *Edo*, as it was once called." If you enjoy percussion, you'll find this album fascinating.

✺✺✺✺ **Commotion**
1994 Katari Taiko (KT1000-2)

Ja Sawago; Interlude; Oedo; Talking Drums; Elephants And Tools; Been Down So Long; Mountain Moving Day *46:52*

James Keelaghan
FOLK; SINGER-SONGWRITER

One of Canada's outstanding singer-songwriters, James Keelaghan's fine baritone voice and strong twelve- and six-string acoustic guitar arrangements accompany some of the most captivating lyrics written north of the 49th Parallel. A native of Calgary, Keelaghan studied history at the University of Calgary where he began playing in local folk venues during the mid-1980's. Keelaghan's interest in history is borne out strongly in his debut album, *Timelines*. The opening song, "Fires Of Calais," relates the fictional account of a participant rescuing British soldiers across the English Channel in the retreat from Dunkirk. "Boom Gone To Bust," recounts the hard times of Canadians in the 1930's, crossing the country to find work. The haunting "Jenny Bryce" was written after a conversation with his mother about conditions for women under the reign of Peter the Great. By his second album, *Small Rebellions,* Keelaghan achieves a high level of consistency and maturity. The songs continue to reflect historical themes. The opening song, "Hillcrest Mine," documents Canada's worst mining disaster. "Red River Rising" is set during the Riel Rebellion. "Rebecca's Lament," chronicles the ill-fated love between Tecumseh and Rebecca Galloway. "Small Rebellion," about the Bienfait Massacre, relates an attempt to organize miners in the coal field. In addition to these historically-based compositions, Keelaghan pays respects to other songwriters, notably Tony Kaduck and Ferron, with "Princes Of The Clouds" and "Misty Mountain," respectively.

With his third album, *My Skies*, Keelaghan began recording for the American Green Linnet label. Winner of a Juno award in the "Roots & Traditional" category in 1994, *My Skies* reflects a turn from the explicit, historical songwriting of his earlier works to more introspective, indirect lyrics. The result is some of the strongest material Keelaghan has yet created. Highlights include the title song, "My Skies," "Hold Your Ground," "River Run," "Kiri's Piano," and "Orion." Keelaghan's fourth album, *A*

Recent Future, is different enough from his previous releases that it may catch a few fans off-guard on first listen. The opener, "Sweetgrass Moon," with its moody intro and haunting melody tells you this album's going to be unique. This is followed by a bouncy Colleen Eccleston song, "Dance As You Go." "Turn Of The Wheel," "Get To You," and "A Recent Future" are similar in feel to material on *My Skies*. Keelaghan has not abandoned historical writing altogether. The highlights of the album are its two historical songs, "Cold Missouri Waters," about the survivor of a forest-fire-fighting team at the Man Gulch fire in 1949, and "Lament For The Passing Of Honoré Jaxon," Riel's English secretary during the 1885 Rebellion. The album's overall unity is weakened by the inclusion of "Sweet Lorraine," a song strangely out of character with the rest of the tracks.

❋❋❋(❋) **Timelines**
1987, 1992 Tranquilla Music / Dirty Linen (CDL103)†

Fires Of Calais; Boom Gone To Bust; Railway Tune; Jenny Bryce; Follow Me Up To Carlow/Morison's Jig; Refugee; Roll Down; Lost; Snap The Line Tight; Sea For The Shore/Stephen Behind The Eight Ball *44:24*

❋❋❋❋✓ **Small Rebellions**
1990 Tranquilla Music (TMCD-002)

Hillcrest Mine; Princes Of The Clouds; Red River Rising; The Ones Who Made Home; Rebecca's Lament; Timeless Love; Small Rebellion; Misty Mountain; Somewhere Ahead; Country Faire; Departure Bay; Gladys Ridge *44:56*

❋❋❋❋✓ **My Skies**
1993 Green Linnet (CLCD 2112)†

My Skies; Hold Your Ground; I Would I Were; River Run; Big Picture; Glory Bound; Kiri's Piano; Hope Princeton Road; Orion; Abraham; Tomorrow Is Another Day *40:29*

❋❋❋(❋) **A Recent Future**
1995 Green Linnet (TBA)†

Sweetgrass Moon; Dance As You Go; Hero On The Straightaway; Get To You; Turn Of The Wheel; Cold Missouri Waters; Sweet Lorraine; A Recent Future; Lament For The Passing Of Honoré Jaxon; Lazarus; Never Gonna Stop That Train

Faye Kellerstein
YIDDISH THEATRE AND FOLKSONGS

"They say you don't have to understand opera to love it. The same goes for Yiddish music...Kellerstein has a vocal warmth that ignites the senses to the sad and not-so-sad subject matter of the lyrics"—Walt Grealis, *RPM Magazine*. Toronto's Faye Kellerstein, born in a refugee camp in postwar Germany to Polish-born Jewish survivors of the Holocaust, has collected and performed Yiddish music for years. *A Feygele Zingt* (A Little Bird Sings) captures the traditional flavour of the songs that have been collected from the Yiddish folksong repertoire and from Yiddish theatre. This album is an important preservation of historical material for a new, young audience.

✳✳✳ **A Feygele Zingt**
1994 Feygele (YIDDISH-1)

Abi Gezunt; Oy, Mame, Bin Icht Farliebt; Oyfn Veg Shteyt A Boim; Yankele; Unter Boimer; Oygn; Un A Malach Zingt; A Brivele Der Mamen; Farges Mich Nit; Tif Vi Di Nacht; Oy, S'lz Gut; Der Nayer Sher; Abi Gezunt (Reprisal) *39:38*

Terry Kelly
FOLK/POP; SINGER-SONGWRITER

Upbeat rocker and Halifax singer-songwriter Terry Kelly delivers a mix of original songs and covers in a folk/rock style. *Face To Face*, from 1988 features material like "Mama Likes To Rock 'N' Roll," Ron Hynes' "How Far Can A Little Girl Fall," and Jamie Snider's "Evangeline." Highlights from *Divided Highway* include "The Girl Is On A Roll Tonight," "River Of No Return," and "You Can't Stop Rock N' Roll." Kelly's high-spirited vocals add punch to his folk/rock material.

✳✳✳ **Face To Face**
1988 Attic (ACD 1248)†

Mama Likes To Rock 'N' Roll; California Night; How Far Can A Little Girl Fall; Evangeline; You Can't Hide From Love; You Really Did It; Greater Than Love; Inspiration; Full Time Lovers; Sorry Lori *36:44*

✳✳✳ **Divided Highway**
1992 Gun Records (TKCD92)†

The Girl Is On A Roll Tonight; River Of No Return; There Goes The Fire; We Can Do Anything; Your Backyard; In My Father's House; I Ain't Got No Money; Heart Set On You; Roy Orbison Came On; You Can't Stop Rock N' Roll *37:40*

Kathy Kidd
SALSA

Vancouver pianist and composer Kathy Kidd is a jazz artist who fell in love with Latin and African rhythms and has turned her hand toward original salsa compositions. *Serious Fun*, by the Kathy Kidd Afro Latin Jazz Septet provides a contemporary "world/ jazz/salsa" sound that can enliven a folk festival or an evening commute. The infectious rhythms and catchy compositions keep you listening from track one and will likely have you hitting the restart button when it's over. *Do What You Love*, by Kathy Kidd & Kongo Mambo, follows in the same vein. When you've hit a saturation point with guitar and fiddle, these are good albums for changing the pace.

✳✳✳(✳) **Serious Fun**
[no date] Lowrider (LOW-0041)

Care To Dance; Serious Fun; Kondo Mondo; Sambaku; Betty; Secret Talking; Follow Me; San Juan Freeway; Where's The One; Strong Earth *49:41*

❈❈❈(❈)   **Do What You Love**
[no date] Lowrider (LOW-0043)

El Conguero; Drive Me Home; Manzanita; Do What You Love; Ropa Vieja; When I'm At Home; Arturo Goes To Nueva York; Terapia; Love Your Neighbour; Straight Forward *52:10*

Kilgore Trout

FOLK/CELTIC; SINGER-SONGWRITERS

The Calgary musical troupe Kilgore Trout describe themselves as being composed of "working stiffs and students." Lori Hogg is a general practitioner studying to be a psychiatrist, Bob Brennan is an engineer working on a Ph.D., Gail Korchinski is a systems analyst, Kari Strutt and Jackie Bell are writer/editors. They are joined by their passion for music. The material on their debut album, *One Voice Starts...*, is drawn from a variety of sources from traditional ballads to the Trout's own brand of "folk and roll." The soaring vocals, frequently joining in two-, three-, and four-part harmony, highlight the group's solid songwriting. If you like the Bird Sisters, Quartette, and the Wyrd Sisters, you'll enjoy Kilgore Trout.

❈❈❈   **One Voice Starts...**
1994 Kilgore Trout (KT01)†

Faerie Gold; About The Weather; The Bitter Sea; To A Lover Leaving; Rockfall; Northern Skies; Mother May I?; Saturday Girl; Kensington; Widow's Lament *31:12*

Killiecrankie

TRADITIONAL SCOTTISH

The Southern Ontario Scottish group Killiecrankie is one of the most engaging Celtic bands currently playing folk festivals. With an inspired choice of material and confident, sure playing, Killiecrankie belongs in every CD collection. *The Haggis Egg*, their second release, and the first available on compact disc, features their gentle, effective vocals mixed with satisfying instrumental medleys. Highlights include "Bonnie George Campbell," "Rantin Rovin Robin," and "The Bonnie Earl Of Moray." *Haggis Egg* is a disc that sneaks up on you. At first you like it, then you begin to like it very much, and soon it becomes one of your most played recordings. Highly recommended. Killiecrankie is Andrea Barstad, Bill Aitken, Allison Lupton, and Martin Smit.

❈❈❈❈✓   **The Haggis Egg**
1994 Killiecrankie (CD464693)

Bonnie George Campbell; Mist Covered Mountains Of Home/The Osprey/Blair Athole; Rantin Rovin Robin; The Haggis Egg/The Marquis Of Huntly; The Lowlands Of Holland; David Glenn's/Duncan's Bones; The Bonnie Ship The Diamond; The Bonnie Earl Of Moray; The Piper's Hut/The Ale Is Dear/The Torn Kilt; Far Frae Your Hame; Coilsfield House; Live Not Where I Love; Leezie Lindsay/Believe Me If All Those Endearing Young Charms/The Loch Tay Boat Song *46:14*

The Kitchen Boys
FOLK/COUNTRY; SINGER-SONGWRITERS

"[Their songs present] images of open prairies, abandoned farmhouses, rusty forgotten plows, dusty farmers and their families, railroad yards, hobos, sun and sky"—Bill Bourne, liner notes to *Passion Town*. An Edmonton duo formed in 1992, The Kitchen Boys are Steve Coffey and Jay Bigam. Coffey, the principal songwriter, writes regional material that explores the roots of prairie existence. With influences ranging from country to blues, roots, and alternative, the duo came up with the term "kitchen music" to describe their raw, aggressive approach. After a successful cassette release, The Kitchen Boys released *Passion Town*, a CD featuring Coffey's rough-sung lyrics amid some sparkling musicianship. Some of the album's highlights are "The Crop," "Mrs. Shire," and "Fifty Thousand Doorways," plus a tribute to Stompin' Tom Conners, "Stompin' Tom." Guest musicians and vocalists include Bill Bourne, Shannon Johnson, Stan Stewart, Jake Peters, and Elvin Berthiaume. *Passion Town* was produced by Bill Bourne.

✳✳✳(✳) **Passion Town**
1994 Backburner (BRI CD1201)†

The Crop; Thirty Acres; You Say You're Frightened; Mrs. Shire; Boxcar; Gave You A Name; Passion Town; Saved; Not A Love Song; Stompin' Tom; Fifty Thousand Doorways; Young Son *51:11*

Lorraine Klaasen
SOUTH AFRICAN MUSIC; SINGER-SONGWRITER

Montreal-based performer Lorraine Klaasen, originally from South Africa, has recorded an infectious mix of songs and styles on *Free At Last*, an upbeat album that features Klassen singing in English, Xhosa, Zulu, and Swahili. Raised in a musical family that counted Miriam Makiba among its frequent guests, Klaasen's fine, expressive voice, backed up by a fairly large band, is a pleasure to listen to.

✳✳✳(✳) **Free At Last**
1994 Klaasen Connexion (KLAA1474)

No Turning Back; Mbathi Yekelu Mama; Soweto Groove II; Kudala Ndikulindile; Jolinkomo; Sabadubula; Comon Comon; Helele; Wake Up Mama; Yiza Izi *40:44*

Richard Knechtel
FOLK/POP; SINGER-SONGWRITER

Veteran songwriter Richard Knechtel (pronounced *neck-tle*) is a regular at Ontario folk festivals. Based in Walkerton, Ontario, Knechtel is a versatile performer who, in addition to solo appearances, also fronts the folk-based Richard Knechtel Quartet, the traditional country trio Northern Lights, and a dance band, The Cabin Cruisers. He's also a children's entertainer under the name "Dickie Bird." Knechtel's first compact disc release, *Drifting Dreams*, presents a solid collection of original songs, backed by guest musicians including David Essig on mandolin. Highlights include "Lone Wolf Howling," "Lakeshore Road," and "Sand And Sea." *Like An Old Friend*, featuring the

Richard Knechtel Quartet, is a collection of tunes supported with acoustic guitar, electric guitar, drums, a bit of fiddle and a touch of harmonica. The simple and relatively sparse arrangements include "Wait," "Like An Old Friend," and the poignant closer, "If I Only Knew." Other members of the Richard Knechtel Quartet are Bill McWaters, David Zdriluk, and Peter Robertson.

❋❋❋ **Drifting Dreams**
[no date] Greentree Music (GT-CD656)

Lone Wolf Howling; People; September Waltz; Lakeshore Road; Song After Midnight; Travel On; Happy Lad; After The Fall; Somebody Like Her; Sand And Sea *42:29*

❋❋❋ **Like An Old Friend**
[no date] Greentree Music (GT-CD658)

Carry A Song; Wait; Like An Old Friend; Scugogin'; Zócalo; This; The Wrong Way; What I Should Do; On The Beach; Cheap Imitation; 1969; How'd We Ever...; If I Only Knew *55:19*

Mary Knickle
FOLK; SINGER/SONGWRITER

Nova Scotia singer-songwriter Mary Knickle (pronounced *k-nickle*) brings an exciting, versatile voice to original and traditional folk material. Her second album, and first compact disc, *Who Will Take The Throne?*, features contemporary songs written by Knickle, such as "Who Will Take The Throne?" "Whispering Muse," and "If You Return." Her striking "Female Sailor" sounds like an old ballad from the traditional repertoire. She also performs two traditional numbers, "Mic Mac Song," and "Barbara Allen," plus a sung version of John Masefield's "Sea Fever." Knickle's fine voice makes this a very good album, but it may be a trifle eclectic for some tastes. The traditional and contemporary pieces don't always fit together seamlessly.

❋❋❋(❋) **Who Will Take The Throne?**
1992 Windward (WPP CD-02)†

Who Will Take The Throne?; Whispering Muse; Female Sailor; If You Return; Daughters Of The Land; Mic Mac Song; The Dream; The Wish; Sea Fever; Barbara Allen *45:38*

Daniel Koulack
BANJO

Clawhammer Your Way To The Top—"its brilliant title notwithstanding, this is not exclusively a clawhammer recording ... rather, this release takes the banjo into a more introspective terrain"—*Dirty Linen*. Winnipeg musician Daniel Koulack, who is also a member of the Klezmer band Finjan, introduces banjo pieces backed with a touch of Klezmer/Country on *Clawhammer Your Way To The Top*. The result, if different, is also pleasant. Koulack does not exclusively play clawhammer style, nor is he a banjo virtuoso, but the album features a range of compositions that are upbeat and frequently charming.

❊❊❊ **Clawhammer Your Way To The Top**
1991 Little Giant (DK-1CD)

Bakan Up The Car; Joshua's Tune; The Waltz That Never Was; Puddle Jumping;
Wounded River; Wardlaw Polka; The Insomniac's Song; Sunrise Tune; Echo; Tom
Cat; Lullaby *33:37*

Susan Kuelken
FOLK/POP; SINGER-SONGWRITER

British Columbia singer-songwriter Susan Kuelken has issued a solid album, *Wischt
Ida*, featuring songs such as "Far Side Of The Wall," "Before The Earthquake," and
"Never Met A Soldier." Backed by acoustic, electric, and slide guitars, hammered
dulcimer, banjo, and accordion backup, Kuelken delivers lyrical punch with a good
folk/pop voice. Unfortunately the album is difficult to obtain. There is no address on
the CD and it isn't available through the usual channels, so watch for a Kuelken
concert and pick one up at a live show. Musicians on the album include Marilyn
MacDonald, James Oldenburg, Lawrence Potapoff, Keith Walker, and Ian Smith.

❊❊❊ **Wischt Ida**
1992 Lookout [no catalogue number]

Far Side Of The Wall; Before The Earthquake; Not A Little Girl; Logically; Never
Met A Soldier; Something Strange; The Other Song; Faces; Fly On The Wall; It Ain't
Easy; Power Of The Land; When I Grow Old; To The Moon *44:59*

Gérard Lajoie
FRENCH CANADIAN; ACCORDION; FIDDLE

Quebec accordionist and champion fiddler Gérard Lajoie is featured on *Gérard Lajoie*,
a lively set of Lajoie historical recordings issued on the Héritage Québécois series by
MCA. There are no liner notes to accompany this delightful album.

❊❊❊❊ **Gérard Lajoie**
[no date, reissued 1991] MCA (MCAD-10491)

Reel De L'Oiseau Moqueur; Reel Du Nouveau Brunswick; Les Variétés Lajoie (II);
Breakdown De Neufchatel; Paul Jones De Québec (I); Le Reel De La Tourtière;
Samba Du Baiser; Reel St Sauveur; Les Variétés Lajoie (I); Samba Canadienne;
Valse De Montréal; Polka Du Lac St Jean; Reel Du Carnaval De Québec; Quadrille
De St-Cyr; Paul Jones De Québec (II) *40:59*

Chris Lakerdas
ACOUSTIC GUITAR INSTRUMENTALS; COMPOSER; SINGER-SONGWRITER

Toronto guitarist Chris Lakerdas' debut album, *Chris Lakerdas*, displays his talents
as a composer and performer. The liner notes provide background notes to each of his
compositions and you can't help but identify with someone who admits to having
avoided homework to play guitar. The notes for "La Petite Montagne" state that "in
the spring of my first year of university, a friend and I would avoid our homework by
carrying our guitars up a drumlin and playing some music. It was those windy, warm

afternoons on that small mountain that originally inspired this piece." Lakerdas' playing is warm and intricate—the only distraction is an appreciable amount of squeak on the strings. The instrumental compositions are lively and infectious. The last two cuts on the album are songs written and sung by Lakerdas. Songwriting is not yet Lakerdas' forte.

❋❋❋ **Chris Lakerdas**
1991, reissed 1995 AVA (AVA CD952)

Romantic Rag; La Petite Montagne; The Kottke Concerto (In D Maj); Jesu, Joy Of Man's Desiring/On The Shoulders Of Giants; Playground; Something Blue; Spanish Dance; Crickets; Behind The Veil; L'Harpe Ancienne; A Gig In The Patch; Liar's Lament; Sing To Me *56:17*

Mary Jane Lamond
CANADIAN GAELIC

Nova Scotian Mary Jane Lamond performs her entire repertoire in the Gaelic language. The result is enchanting. *Bho Thir Nan Craobh* which means "from the land of the trees" is taken from references from the Gaelic bards who were deeply impressed by the thick forests of Canada when they first arrived here. Some of the songs on this album originated in Ireland or Scotland and some were written by Gaelic-speaking Canadian settlers. The liner notes provide Gaelic lyrics, English translations, and background information on each song. Lamond sings in a voice so sweet you'd listen if she were singing restaurant menus. A cameo appearance by Ashley MacIsaac playing fiddle on "Dan Do Sean Ford" is another of the album's treats. Highly recommended.

❋❋❋❋✓ **Bho Thir Nan Craobh / From The Land Of The Trees**
1994? B&R Heritage (BRCD 0001)†

O Tha Mise Fo Ghruaimean (O, I Am Unhappy); Air Faillirinn Iu (Lovable Little Darling); Cagaran Gaolach (Loveable Little Darling); Domhnall Antaidh (Donald "Antaidh"); A Chuachag Nam Beann (Cuckoo Of The Mountains); He Mo Leannan (He My Love); Bodach Beag A Loinean (The Little Old Man Of The Pond); Ho Ro's Toigh Leam-Fhìn Thu (O I Do Love You); Cha Bhi Mi Buan (I Will Not Survive); Ba, Ba, Ba Mo Leanabh (Hush, Hush, Hush My Little Baby); Piuirt-a-Beul (Mouthmusic Medley); Dh'Olainn Deoch A Laimh Mo Ruin (I Would Take A Drink From My Love's Hands); Oran Gillean Alasdair Mhòir (Lament To The Sons Of Alasdair Mòr); Dan Do Shean Ford (Song To An Old Ford)/The Model T Jig *41:39*

Ned Landry
COUNTRY FIDDLE

Master fiddler Ned Landry was born in Saint John, New Brunswick, in 1921. He played harmonica, in 1934, on Don Messer's radio show *Backwoods Breakdown*. Having taught himself fiddle when he was a boy, Landry became the first oldtime fiddler to perform on TV (in Boston, Massachusetts, 1939). He was also the first Canadian to record for RCA Victor, in the 1940's. The winner of many fiddling contests, Landry was a regular guest on *Don Messer's Jubilee* and other TV shows in the 60's. He has also played at the Grand Ol' Opry and toured with Johnny Cash. *International Fiddling Champion* presents Landry's smooth fiddle and mandolin playing. He is joined by Aubrey Hanson on guitar, Robert McKenny on piano, Lloyd Hanson on bass, Balf Bailey on drums, and Mike Doherty on congas and percussion.

✻✻✻✻ **International Fiddling Champion**
1994 Atlantica (NL-00102)

> Cajun Two Step; Governor General's Waltz; Ontario Swing; Abbie Andrew's Calypso; Stompin' Tom Connors; Hillbilly Calypso; Maple Leaf Special; Lumberjack Special; After The Rain; Waltzing In The Garden; Ripple Rock Jig; Celina; United Way Special; Believing; Roy Acuff's Special; Happy Times; Gary Murphy's Special; Yvon Durelle's Shuffle; Terry Parson's Special; Lord Beaverbrook Special; Vivian And Ivan Hicks Waltz; Kaye's Jig; Cajun Fiddling On The Bayou; Bowing The Strings; Operetta Square Dance *62:11*

Penny Lang
FOLK/BLUES; SINGER-SONGWRITER

"Lang's stage presence is a letter from home, a sunny kitchen table, a crickety summer evening on the back porch"—Festival of Friends *Program Guide, 1994*. Montreal performer Penny Lang, who has been labelled "first lady of Canadian folk music," is an entertainer who delights audiences with her wonderful mix of strong original compositions and personalized versions of gospel, blues, and country songs. *Ain't Life Sweet* is like a return to the best of the 1960's folk revival—the songs are evocative, simple, and connected, carried by a slightly husky, totally real and infectious voice. The instrumentation is a fine statement in simplicity.

✻✻✻✻✓ **Ain't Life Sweet**
1993 Silverwolf Records (SWPL-9302)

> Open Up Our Hearts To See; Senses Of Your Leave; On Again, Off Again; Stomp, Bop, Bop; Ain't Life Sweet; Sometimes; Plumb Tuckered Out; Spanish Moss; Firewater; Laundromat Song; Happiness Is; Family Reunion; I Can't Stand Up Alone *36:37*

Daniel Lapp
FOLK/FIDDLE; SINGER-SONGWRITER

Vancouver artist Daniel Lapp, a one-time member of Spirit of the West, has put together a highly unusual album—*Daniel Lapp*—that may remind 60's folkies of the English group The Incredible String Band. This recording of Lapp singing and accompanying himself in a church chapel is not for traditionalists. But those who enjoy experimental music will find it challenging and adventurous. "Holy Water," "Beauty," and "Survival Poem" are chant-like and plaintive. The album does not work as background music—you have to listen carefully.

✻✻✻ **Daniel Lapp**
1994 Lappland (CD-00194)†

> Holy Water; Beauty; Survival Poem; Certain Love *(with Linda McRae)*; Silver Birch/ Canada Geese Reel; Lisa; Red Bud; This Moment; Someway, Someday; Let The Rhythm Sing; Lonesome Warrior; Puppet's Yell; The Thread; Certain Love (Solo Reprise) *56:49*

Sam Larkin
FOLK; SINGER-SONGWRITER

On *Ransom*, Sam Larkin delivers a set of original songs that seem to have stepped straight out of 60's open-mike sessions. The acoustic guitar and harmonica-driven lyrics are delivered in the simple, Dylanesque style that once dominated the folk scene. While Larkin's voice is undistinguished and the arrangements are frequently rough-edged, the lyrics sustain the songs. This is an album that will interest those who enjoy the poetic core of folk music and don't mind dispensing with some of the usual wrappings.

✳✳✳ **Ransom**
1994 Amatish (SWO294)†

Mirabeau Bridge; Sally On; Marie; Murmurings; Close; Somehow; Fascination; Children At Play; Highway One; Laughin Tears; Play With You; We Will Be Birds; Golden Albatross; Who Would We Be?; Oh *67:50*

Grey Larsen & André Marchand
FRENCH CANADIAN; IRISH; FOLK

The Orange Tree is "a marvellous album, both instrumentally and vocally"—*Dirty Linen*. In one of the most delightful musical collaborations of recent years, Grey Larsen, Irish master of wooden flute, has combined with André Marchand, Quebec co-founder of La Bottine Souriante, to explore the roots in common between the music of Ireland and French Canada. The music that emerges on *The Orange Tree* is simply some of the best traditional music you'll have the pleasure of hearing. Larsen's flute playing is agile and haunting and Marchand is a fine guitarist and singer.

✳✳✳✳✓ **The Orange Tree: Irish And French Canadian Roots**
1993 Sugar Hill (SH-CD-1136)†

Acadian Mouth Music (Reel À Bouche Acadien)/Horses, Geese, And One Old Man/Acadian Mouth Music (Reprise); Mornings At Bonny Doon (Les Matins De Bonny Doon)/Palm Sunday; Who Will Help Me Through The Woods? (Qui Me Passera Le Bois?); Brandy From Kedgwick (Le Brandy De Kedgwick); The Orange Tree (L'Oranger); The Waltz Of Time Passing (La Valse Du Temps Qui Va)/Plum Creek; The Road To Cashel/The Bunch Of Green Rushes/The Queen Of May; The Wife Of A Drunken Soldier (L'Ivrogne Pilier Du Cabaret); First Snow; A Pack Of Lies (Les Menteries)/Crossing The Saguenay (La Traversée De La Saguenay) *43:43*

Francis J. Leahy
FIDDLE; ORIGINAL COMPOSITIONS

For an upbeat, contemporary, non-Celtic fiddle album, it would be hard to beat Ontario fiddler Francis J. Leahy's *Bending The Bow*. Accompanied by a set of musicians playing guitars, banjo, bass, bagpipes, drums, harmonica, and piano, this is a swinging album that features a mix of Leahy compositions like "Teeswater," "Wally's Jig," and "Graduation Waltz" mixed with traditional pieces like "The Blue Bells Of Scotland," "Maple Sugar," and "The Orange Blossom Special." Fiddle lovers take note!

✱✱✱✱ **Bending The Bow**
[no date] Hapi (HCD 01)

Teeswater; Dewdrops On The Roses; The Blue Bells Of Scotland; Maple Sugar; MacPherson's Lament; Wally's Jig; Graduation Waltz; Karley's Edge; The Kindly Old Gentleman; The Orange Blossom Special *34:35*

Roland Lebrun
FRENCH CANADIAN; FOLK/COUNTRY

Country-style singer Roland Lebrun, born in Amqui, Québec in 1919, enjoyed widespread popularity during the years of World War II. Simple songs, delivered in an uninflected voice, were the trademark of this singer dubbed "le soldat Lebrun," who sang for other soldiers like himself who were separated from family and friends. "Some considered him the male counterpart of La Bolduc. Like her, he reached ordinary folk grappling with the difficulties of everyday life"—Benoît L'Herbier, *La Chanson québécoise*. Lebrun retired in 1966. He spent the last year of his life as a school crossing guard. He died in Quebec City in 1980. A collection of Lebrun's recordings, mostly remastered from 45's and 78's, have been reissued on the MCA CD, *Roland Lebrun*, as part of the Héritage Québécois series. The CD contains no liner notes.

✱✱✱✱ **Roland Lebrun**
[no date, reissued 1991] MCA (MCAD-10487)

L'Adieu Du Soldat; Un Baiser Puis Bonsoir; La Prière D'Une Maman; N'Oublie Pas Ta Prière; La Destinée; Courageux Canadiens; Grand'Maman; Ne Pleure Plus; Reviens Petit Papa; La Lettre D'Un Soldat Canadien; La Complainte D'Une Mère; Retour Du Printemps; Adieu Chérie; Amour, Victoire, Liberté; Prière Exaucée *37:53*

Félix Leclerc
FRENCH-CANADIAN CHANSONNIER; SINGER-SONGWRITER

Félix Leclerc may be thought of as the founding father of the *chansonnier* tradition in Quebec. A singer-songwriter, poet, novelist, playwright, and actor, Leclerc rose from being a labourer and farmhand to becoming an international superstar by the 1940's and 50's. Billed in France as "le Canadien," Leclerc revitalized the chanson in France, providing a catalyst for the careers of such artists as Georges Brassens, Guy Béart, and Jacques Brel. Leclerc's songs recall elements of the traditional songs of France, folk forms from France and Canada, and even medieval influences. The recordings listed below represent a comprehensive, retrospective set of Leclerc recordings put together by Philips. There are no liner notes on the individual CD's. Volume numbers on the discs suggest that these might albums might also be packaged as a boxed set.

✱✱✱✱ **Le P'tit Bonheur**
1950-51, 1953, 1959 Philips (838 072-2)

Moi, Mes Souliers; Contumace; Elle N'Est Pas Jolie; Bozo; Echo; Francis; Lettre De Mon Frère; Demain Si La Mer; La Danse La Moins Jolie; Le P'tit Bonheur; Le Train Du Nord; Petit Pierre; La Complainte Du Pêcheur; L'Hymne Au Printemps; La Mer N'Est Pas La Mer; Présence; Comme Abraham; Attends-Moi Ti-Gars; La Drave; La Chanson Du Pharmacien; Prière Bohémienne; Le Roi Et Le Laboureur; Un Petit

Soulier Rose; J'Ai Deux Montagnes; À Pierrot; Le Québécois; Le Dialogue Des Amoureux; Le Roi Viendra Demain; Chanson Des Colons; Les Perdrix; Ce Matin-Là; Sensation *72:20*

❋❋❋❋ La Vie, L'Amour, La Mort
1959, 1964 Philips (838 073-2)

L'Héritage; Tirelou; Tour De Riens; L'Abeille; L'Agite; Sur Le Bouleau; Je Cherche Un Abri Pour L'Hiver; L'Imbécile; Litanies Du Petit Homme; La Chanson Du Vieux Polisson; Les Dimanches; Si Tu Crois; Les Cinq Millionnaires; Le Testament; Mouillures; L'Eau De L'Hiver; Le Roi Heureux; Le Loup; La Gigue; Le Chant De La Création; Le Bal; Elle Pleure; Les Soirs D'Hiver; Perdu Gagne; Ton Visage; Complot D'Enfants; Notre Sentier; Tu Te Leveras Tôt; Au Même Clou; Mac Pherson; La Fille De L'Île; Le Jour Qui S'Appelle Aujourd'hui; Y'A Des Amours; Chanson En Russe; La Fête; La Vie, L'Amour, La Mort *71:55*

❋❋❋❋ La Gaspésie
1964, 1966, 1967 Philips (838 074-2)

Les Nouveaux-Nes; Le Roi Chasseur; La Valse À Joseph; Douleur; Les Soupirs; Premier Amour; Les Algues; Le Traversier; Sur La Corde À Linge; Ailleurs; Bon Voyage Dans La Lune; Nuage Noir; Noces D'Or; En Muet; Mes Longs Voyages; Oh! Mon Maître; Qu'Ont Vu Tes Yeux?; Manic 5; Chanson De Nuit; Le Bonhomme Et La Jeune Fille; Dieu Qui Dort; La Gaspésie; Passage De L'Outarde; L'Écharpe; Une Valse; Les Moutons Sur La Rivière; La Vie; Errances; Do Re Mi Fa Sol La Si; Blues Pour Pinky *70:07*

❋❋❋❋ L'Alouette En Colère
1967, 1969, 1973 Philips (838 075-2)

Variations Sur Le Verbe Donner; Tzigane; La Mort De L'Ours; Les Escaliers Devant; J'Inviterai L'Enfance; Le Père; Richesses; Grand Papa Pan Pan; Naissance; En Attendant L'Enfant; Les Mauvais Conseils; Le Veuve; L'Alouette En Colère; Viendra-T-Elle Aujourd'hui?; My Neighbour Is Rich; La Légende Du Petit Ours Gris; Un Soir De Février; Batelier Batelier; Les 100 000 Façons De Tuer Un Homme; Races De Monde; La Mouche À Feu; Pour Bâtir Une Maison; Tu T'En Iras Demain *58:11*

❋❋❋❋ La Complainte Du Phoque En Alaska
1974 Philips (838 076-2)

L'Encan; Chant D'Un Patriote; Comme Une Bête; La Complainte Du Phoque En Alaska; L'Ancêtre; Les Poteaux; Le Dernier Point; Sors-Moi Donc Albert; Fatalité; Un An Déjà; Le Tour De L'Île *31:29*

❋❋❋❋ L'Encan: Le Tour De L'Île
1951, 1953, 1971, 1975, 1976 Philips (838 077-2)

La Vie; J'Inviterai L'Enfance/Les Mauvais Conseils; L'Encan/Chant D'Un Patriote; Les 100 000 Façons De Tuer Un Homme; Notre Sentier; Les Poteaux; Moi, Mes Souliers; L'Ancêtre; La Complainte Du Phoque En Alaska; Races De Monde; L'Alouette En Colère; Le Tour De L'Île; Le Boiteux Amoureux; Épousailles (Matin De Noces); Le Galérien; L'Homme Au Vélo; Tu Allumes Ma Nuit; Le Procès D'Une Chenille *62:20*

Anne Lederman
FOLK

On *Not A Mark In This World* Toronto singer and musician Anne Lederman has compiled a fascinating selection of historical Canadian folksongs most of which have never before been recorded. Accompanying herself on a variety of instruments, including the five-string fiddle, Lederman is backed by a noteworthy set of musicians, including Grit Laskin, Oliver Schroer, Ian Bell, and members of the Flying Bulgar Klezmer Band. The musicians join in on the choruses of the songs. This is traditional folk music as it was meant to be sung. *Not A Mark In This World* received a "Heritage Preservation" Porcupine Award in 1991.

❊❊❊❊✓　**Not A Mark In This World**
1991　Aural Tradition (ATRCD 119)†

> Rattle On The Stovepipe; Banks Of Newfoundland; The Freebooter/New Scotland; Teist Dhomhnaill Air Manitoba; Les Draveurs De La Gatineau; Toronto Volunteers; Indian's Lament [An Indian Sat In His Little Bark Canoe]; Ukrainian Song; Schmulik Gavrulik; Auction Block Medley: Auction Block/The Free Slave; Jones Boys; Toper's Lament; I Wandered Today To The School, Maggie; Pauper's Last Ride; When I Went Up To Rosedale; Hard Times *59:03*

Lee Pui Ming Ensemble
TRADITIONAL CHINESE INSTRUMENTS; ORIGINAL COMPOSITIONS

Creating original compositions that express ancient themes on traditional Chinese instruments plus piano, Toronto artist and composer Lee Pui Ming has produced an arresting album: *Nine-Fold Heart*. Nominated for a Juno in the 1995 "Global Recordings" category, this album is complex, sophisticated, and unusual. While not an easy listen, it is a very rewarding one. Additional members of the ensemble are Qiu Li Rong, Yu Zhi Min, Huang Ji Rong, Pan Jian Ming, Salvador Ferreras, and Sun Yong.

❊❊❊❊　**Nine-Fold Heart**
1993　Pochee (PR CD002)

> Danse Extravaganza; Tale Of Three Snakes; Three Kingdoms; Nine-Fold Heart; The Monkey King Suite: March Of The Monkeys; The Monkey King Suite: The Monkey King; The Monkey King Suite: Monkey King Charges The High Heavens; The Monkey King Suite: Monkey King Triumphs; Why Don't We Eat Noodles?; The Grande Love Song *63:10*

Légende
FRENCH CANADIAN; FOLK

En Revenant Des Grands Chantiers by the Quebec group Légende provides over fifty minutes of traditional French-Canadian music. Similar to early albums of La Bottine Souriante, the album features vocals, accordion, fiddle, guitar, and foot tapping. If you happen to see it in a music bin, snap it up for your collection—the vocals and musicianship are first rate. Members of Légende are François Marion, Jacques Larochelle, Yves Marion, Christian Thériault, and Benoit Marion.

❋❋❋❋ **En Revenant Des Grands Chaniers**
[no date] Musicor (CDLCD-1802)

> Le Reel Des Voyageurs; Hut St-Nazaire; En Revenant Des Grands Chantiers; La Cantinée; La Palette; Les Buveurs; Margot; Reel Fisher Hornpipe; Allons-Y Donc S'Y Promener; Commandement De Guerre; Le Mississippi; Fonsine; Videz Le Rye; Vive L'Amour; Le Reel Ste-Anne; Le Gro Bélier *57:04*

Emory Lester
BLUEGRASS; ORIGINAL COMPOSITIONS

Emory Lester, Ontario mandolin master, has gathered a strong group of musicians to join him on *Pale Rider*. Working their way through original Lester pieces like "Pale Rider," "Cactus Pass," and "Neon Street," this ensemble takes bluegrass out of its traditional mould and into a new dimension. The other musicians on this upbeat compact disc include Tony Trischka on banjo, Slavek Hanzlik on guitar, Ray Legere on violin, Kene Hyatt on acoustic bass, and Andy Thompson on piano and keyboards. *The Emory Lester Set* features compositions by other members of the ensemble, including "Massanoga" by Linton, "Mexican Moon" by Hyatt, "Nighthawk" by Gorman, plus more pieces by Lester. This is another excellent album. The Emory Lester Set consists of Emory Lester, Marion Linton, Allan Gorman, Kene Hyatt, and Andy Thompson.

❋❋❋(❋) **Pale Rider**
1993 Northumberland (NRCD-002)

> Pale Rider; Rattlesnake; Forked Deer; At Dusk; Mandograss Medley; Cactus Pass; Neon Street; Alone; Lady Be Good; Front Royal; Little France *44:11*

❋❋❋(❋) **The Emory Lester Set**
1994 Northumberland (NRCD-025)

> Headin' South; Massanoga; Mexican Moon; Forever True; Smell The Coffee; 3 In The Side; Waltz For C.C.; Gingerbread Boy; Even Steven; Greetings; Nighthawk; Firm Roots; Waltz For C.C. (Reprise) *61:14*

Lewis, Pint & Dale
SEA SHANTIES; SINGER-SONGWRITERS

British Columbia-based Tom Lewis teamed up with old friends William Pint and Felicia Dale from Seattle for an album of sea shanties—*Making Waves*. This highly entertaining recording consists of a few traditional numbers mixed mainly with songs collected from Rudyard Kipling, Peter Bellamy, and others. Their strong vocals and harmonies are presented with minimal instrumentation on songs like "Rolling Down To Rio," "The Anchor Song," and "Swallow The Anchor." This is a must purchase for Tom Lewis fans.

See also Tom Lewis.

✱✱✱(✱)   **Making Waves**
1992 Self-Propelled Music (ASM103D)

Rolling Down To Rio; The Anchor Song; Sou' Spain; March Of The King Of Laois;
Herzogin Cecile; Congo River; The African Trade; The Whale; Ex-Sailor's Life;
Catherine; La Paimpolaise; Swallow The Anchor; Pull Down Lads *47:37*

Tom Lewis
SEA SONGS AND SHANTIES; SINGER/SONGWRITER

British-born Tom Lewis may be one of Canada's most unusual folk artists. An ex-
sailor, Lewis writes and sings sea songs and shanties. These infectious creations, sung
a cappella in the traditional style, are a throwback to an earlier tradition. *Surfacing*
delivers over 40 minutes of mostly unaccompanied shanties. These are bread-and-
butter songs that charm you and set your foot tapping. On *Sea-Dog, See Dog!* Lewis
alters course slightly, singing other people's songs and adding more instrumentation
and voices. Teaming up with American folksingers William Pint and Felicia Dale on
choruses, the songs are less stark and the harmonies are smoother. The album includes a Richard Thompson song, "Down Where The Drunkards Roll," and one by
Stan Rogers, "Down At The Sailor's Rest." If you liked *Surfacing*, you'll like this one
even better.

✱✱✱   **Surfacing**
1987 Self Propelled Music (ASM101D)†

A Sailor Ain't A Sailor (Last Shanty); Recall; Inside Every Sailor (Deceptions);
Sailorman's Port In A Storm; Watches; The Hunter Home From The Hill; Land-
locked Sailor; Marching Inland (Legend); Away; Bread And Butter To Me; Diesel
And Shale; Cyril Said It All Before; Sailor's Prayer *42:23*

✱✱✱(✱)   **Sea-Dog, See Dog!**
[no date] Flying Fish (FF70547)†

The Captain's Lady; Chicken On A Raft; A Whaler's Tale; The Big Fella'; Safe
Harbour (For A Storm Tossed Heart); Doc "Lemon"; Snap The Line Tight; Down
Where The Drunkards Roll; North To Calleo; Down At The Sailor's Rest; A
Seaman's Hymn; BUNTS! *57:56*

Gordon Lightfoot
FOLK/POP; SINGER-SONGWRITER

Orillia, Ontario native Gordon Lightfoot, Canada's troubadour laureate and Juno Hall
of Famer, has sustained a long, productive songwriting career that took flight in the
early 1960's. His songs are among the most durable and memorable of any Canadian
songwriter. Every 60's folk act, large and small, covered "For Lovin' Me" and "Early
Mornin' Rain." Ian Tyson has referred to the northernness of Lightfoot's music as his
"Group of Seven" sound (after a group of Ontario artists famous for their paintings of
northern Ontario). His voice echoes the birches, blue skies, and solitary lakes of the
North.

Many long-time fans feel that Lightfoot's best work was for United Artists, his
first record label, during the Riverboat years. His original five albums have been re-

issued on CD as a boxed set: *The Original Lightfoot*. From "For Lovin' Me" to "The Canadian Railroad Trilogy" to "Mountains And Maryann" to "Pussy Willows, Cattails," the freshness of an emerging artist leaps out at you on track after track. A must purchase.

Lightfoot later switched labels to Reprise/Warner Brothers where he achieved his greatest commercial success. He became so popular that many of the songs of this "golden" period have suffered from overplay—only now, after some years have passed, can we begin to hear them anew. As Lightfoot faded from the radio charts, many of his classic albums from the Warner period went out of print. Warner began reissuing original Lightfoot albums as Reprise/Warner Archives compact discs in 1994. For Lightfoot fans, this has been a godsend—an opportunity to replace those worn-out vinyls and listen to one of Canada's master songwriters all over again.

For those who prefer a sampler, Lightfoot has been issued, piecemeal, in several collections. Two successful collections are the two volumes of *Gord's Gold*, which include many of the better-known songs from his Warner period, plus earlier United Artist material he re-recorded for this collection. One caution: Lightfoot has a disconcerting tendency to tamper with his older recordings. If you have a strong aural memory of some of his work, the "new" versions often sound wrong. "The Wreck of the Edmund Fitzgerald," on *Gord's Gold II*, for instance, is lower in pitch and slightly different in its arrangement than the original on *Summertime Dream*. If these differences don't bother you, the *Gold* CD sets offer good value. Other samplers include *The Best Of Gordon Lightfoot, Over 60 Minutes with Lightfoot* and *Early Morning Rain*. None of the samplers are as satisfying as the original albums.

If You Could Read My Mind, released in 1970, was Lightfoot's first album for Warner. With Red Shea on guitar and Rick Haynes on bass, plus a generous dollop of strings, this was the album that brought Lightfoot out of folk circles and into the North American mainstream. Highlights include "Minstrel Of The Dawn," "Me And Bobby McGee," "Approaching Lavender," "Sit Down Young Stranger," and "If You Could Read My Mind." *Summer Side Of Life*, dating from 1971, continues the sound with Red Shea and Rick Haynes as sidemen. The album includes "10 Degrees And Getting Colder," as well as Lightfoot classics "Miguel," "Summer Side Of Life," "Cotton Jenny," and "Love And Maple Syrup." *Don Quixote*, from 1972, and reissued in 1994, is one of the most sought-after Lightfoot albums. Backed by Red Shea, Rick Haynes, and Terry Clements, Lightfoot delivers what many consider to be his best overall album. From the opener, "Don Quixote," to "Christian Island," "Alberta Bound" (with Ry Cooder on Mandolin), "Ode To Big Blue," and "Beautiful," this is one of the most cohesive Lightfoot albums you'll find. *Sundown*, released in 1974, is a close contender to *Don Quixote* in popularity. Featuring the usual bevy of excellent musicians, it includes songs like "High And Dry," "Circle Of Steel," the incomparable "Sundown," "Carefree Highway," and "Too Late For Prayin'."

Cold On The Shoulder, from 1975, includes the lovely "Rainy Day People" and the pungent "Cold On The Shoulder." The unusual, piano-backed "Bells Of The Evening" provides excellent contrast. There are no weak tracks—every song is well written. A fine album from Lightfoot's middle period. The 1976 album *Summertime Dream* contains one of the most powerful, haunting songs ever written: "The Wreck Of The Edmund Fitzgerald." Unfortunately it eclipses everything else on the album. While there's still some good songwriting on "Race Among The Ruins" and "Summertime Dream," there's a sense that Lightfoot had started to repeat himself. *Endless Wire* dates from 1978. Although it's a decent pop album—and second-rate Lightfoot is better than most songwriters ever achieve—compared with his earlier albums, it's a disappointment. It's an overproduced work that hides Lightfoot's voice behind a mesh of pop sound. An intimate studio album, *East Of Midnight*, from 1986, contains some solid songwriting, including "Stay Loose," "Morning Glory," "East Of Midnight," and "A Lesson In Love." *Waiting For You*, from 1993, while not vintage Lightfoot, still contains some archetypal Lightfoot guitar picking and some strong songwriting. Highlights include "Restless," "Ring Them Bells," (a Bob Dylan song), "Fading Away," and "Drink Yer Glasses Empty."

❋❋❋❋✓ **The Original Lightfoot: The United Artists Years**
1965-1969, reissued 1992 EMI Records (S2 80748; S2 80749; S2 80750)

> **CD1: Lightfoot / The Way I Feel** Rich Man's Spiritual; Long River; The Way I Feel; For Lovin' Me; The First Time Ever I Saw Your Face; Changes; Early Mornin' Rain; Steel Rail Blues; Sixteen Miles; I'm Not Sayin'; Pride Of Man; Ribbon Of Darkness; Oh, Linda; Peaceful Waters; Walls; If You Got It; Softly; Crossroads; A Minor Ballad; Go-Go Round; Rosana; Home From The Forest; I'll Be Alright; Song For A Winter's Night; Canadian Railroad Trilogy; The Way I Feel *77:30*

> **CD2: Did She Mention My Name / Back Here On Earth** Wherefore And Why; The Last Time I Saw Her; Black Day In July; May I; Magnificent Outpouring; Does Your Mother Know; Mountains And Maryann; Pussy Willows, Cat-tails; I Want To Hear It From You; Something Very Special; Boss Man; Did She Mention My Name; Long Way Back Home; Unsettled Ways; Long Thin Dawn; Bitter Green; The Circle Is Small; Marie Christine; Cold Hands From New York; Affair On 8th Avenue; Don't Beat Me Down; The Gypsy; If I Could *73:51*

> **CD3: Sunday Concert** In A WindowPane; The Lost Children; Leaves Of Grass; I'm Not Sayin'/Ribbon Of Darkness; Apology; Bitter Green; Ballad Of Yarmouth Castle; Softly; Boss Man; Pussy Willows, Cat-tails; Canadian Railroad Trilogy *40:12*

❋❋❋❋✓ **If You Could Read My Mind**
1970 Reprise (6392-2)

> Minstrel Of The Dawn; Me And Bobby McGee; Approaching Lavender; Saturday Clothes; Cobwebs And Dust; Poor Little Allison; Sit Down Young Stranger; If You Could Read My Mind; Baby It's Allright; Your Love's Return (Song For Stephen Foster); The Pony Man *37:15*

❋❋❋ **Summer Side Of Life**
1971, reissued 1994 Reprise / Warner Archives (CDW 45686)

> 10 Degrees And Getting Colder; Miguel; Go My Way; Summer Side Of Life; Cotton Jenny; Talking In Your Sleep; Nous Vivons Ensemble; Same Old Loverman; Redwood Hill; Love And Maple Syrup; Cabaret *38:52*

❋❋❋(❋)✓ **Don Quixote**
1972, reissued 1994 Reprise / Warner Archives (CDW 45687)

> Don Quixote; Christian Island (Georgian Bay); Alberta Bound; Looking At The Rain; Ordinary Man; Brave Mountaineers; Ode To Big Blue; Second Cup Of Coffee; Beautiful; On Susan's Floor; The Patriot's Dream *41:46*

※※※(※)✓ **Sundown**
1974 Reprise / Warner Bros. (CD 2177)

Somewhere U.S.A.; High And Dry; Seven Island Suite; Circle Of Steel; Is There Anyone Home; The Watchman's Gone; Sundown; Carefree Highway; The List; Too Late For Prayin' *36:30*

※※※※ **Cold On The Shoulder**
1975, reissued 1994 Reprise / Warner Archives (CDW 45688)

Bend In The Water; Rainy Day People; Cold On The Shoulder; The Soul Is The Rock; Bells Of The Evening; Rainbow Trout; A Tree Too Weak To Stand; All The Lovely Ladies; Fine As Fine Can Be; Cherokee Bend; Now And Then; Slide On Over *43:39*

※※※ **Gord's Gold**
1975 Reprise / Warner Bros. (CD 2237)

I'm Not Sayin'/Ribbon Of Darkness; Song For A Winter's Night; Canadian Railroad Trilogy; Softly; For Lovin' Me/Did She Mention My Name; Steel Rail Blues; Wherefore And Why; Bitter Green; Early Mornin' Rain; Minstrel Of The Dawn; Sundown; Beautiful; Summer Side Of Life; Rainy Day People; Cotton Jenny; Don Quixote; Circle Of Steel; Old Dan's Records; If You Could Read My Mind; Cold On The Shoulder; Carefree Highway *72:00*

※※※ **Summertime Dream**
1976 Warner Bros. (CD 2246)†

Race Among The Ruins; The Wreck Of The Edmund Fitzgerald; I'm Not Supposed To Care; I'd Do It Again; Never Too Close; Protocol; The House You Live In; Summertime Dream; Spanish Moss; Too Many Clues In This Room *37:51*

※※※ **Endless Wire**
1978, reissued 1994 Reprise / Warner Archives (CDW 45685)†

Daylight Katy; Sweet Guinevere; Hangdog Hotel Room; If There's A Reason; Endless Wire; Dreamland; Songs The Minstrel Sang; Sometimes I Don't Mind; If Children Had Wings; The Circle Is Small *36:02*

※※※ **The Best Of Gordon Lightfoot**
1980 Capitol [EMI] (E2 48396)

Go-Go Round; Softly; The Way I Feel; For Lovin' Me; Early Mornin' Rain; I'm Not Sayin'; Black Day In July; Did She Mention My Name; Bitter Green; Pussywillows, Cat-tails; Canadian Railroad Trilogy *36:38*

※※※ **East Of Midnight**
1986 Warner Bros. (CD 25482)†

Stay Loose; Morning Glory; East Of Midnight; A Lesson In Love; Anything For Love; Let It Ride; Ecstasy Made Easy; You Just Gotta Be; A Passing Ship; I'll Tag Along *38:20*

※※※ **Over 60 Minutes With ... Lightfoot**
1987 Capitol [EMI] (CDP 7 48844 2)

For Lovin' Me; Steel Rail Blues; I'm Not Sayin'; Go Go Round; Early Mornin' Rain; Changes; Black Day In July; Bitter Green; Pussywillows, Cat-tails; Canadian Railroad Trilogy; Softly; Boss Man; The Way I Feel; Did She Mention My Name;

The Last Time I Saw Her; Mountains And Marian; The First Time Ever I Saw Your Face; Song For A Winter's Night; Ribbon Of Darkness; Home From The Forest *64:42*

✳✳✳   **Gord's Gold Volume II**
1988 Warner Bros. (CD 25784)

If It Should Please You; Endless Wire; Hangdog Hotel Room; I'm Not Supposed To Care; High And Dry; The Wreck Of The Edmund Fitzgerald; The Pony Man; Race Among The Ruins; Christian Island; All The Lovely Ladies; Alberta Bound; Cherokee Bend; Triangle; Shadows; Make Way (For The Lady); Ghosts Of Cape Horn; Baby Step Back; It's Worth Believin' *65:45*

✳✳✳   **Early Morning Rain: The Best Of Gordon Lightfoot**
1990 Capitol (CDLL-57275)

Early Mornin' Rain; Wherefore And Why; The Last Time I Saw Her; Ribbon Of Darkness; I Want To Hear It From You; The First Time Ever I Saw Your Face; Did She Mention My Name; The Way I Feel; Mountains And Maryann; I'm Not Saying; Does Your Mother Know; For Lovin' Me *38:03*

✳✳✳   **Waiting For You**
1993 Warner / Reprise (CDW 45208)†

Restless; Ring Them Bells; Fading Away; Only Love Would Know; Welcome To Try; I'll Prove My Love; Waiting For You; Wild Strawberries; I'd Rather Press On; Drink Yer Glasses Empty *36:16*

Su-Chong Lim

FOLKISH SHOW-TUNES; SINGER-SONGWRITER

Golden Mountain contains selections from the stage show of the same name, performed by Su-Chong Lim and the Golden Mountain Ensemble. In the show the hero, "reminiscing on his origins in Asia, describes his travels in this mysterious land of Golden Mountain [Canada], of the strange inhabitants there, and their even stranger customs." There are a number of very folkish and interesting songs on this compact disc, including some humourous take-off's such as "Dis Land Is Your Land?" Delightfully different.

✳✳✳(✳)   **Golden Mountain**
1992 Aural Tradition (ATCRD 306)†

Jasmine And The Bell; Muscle-Car Mike; Suriram; Shiro, Mariko And Me; Basic Two Bit Song; The Demon Fire-Carriage Road; Twelve-Foot Davis; Old Wive's Lake; Boat Song; Dis Land Is Your Land? *43:57*

Oscar Lopez

CANADIAN-LATIN FUSION; SINGER-SONGWRITER; COMPOSER

Guitarist Oscar Lopez, originally from Chile, has become a prominent artist on the Canadian folk circuit. In addition to his solo albums, he has played backup guitar for many performers, including James Keelaghan. *Sueños*, a 1991 release, features Lopez on original vocal and guitar compositions. Highlights of this upbeat album include "Vientos De Alberta," the title song, "Sueños," "Mudos," and "Soledad." The guitar work on this soft, laid-back album is customary Lopez: excellent. On *Dancing On The Moon Contigo*, Lopez revs it up a notch, instilling the album with additional energy, tension and excitement. From the opener, "Roots," to the closer, "Dancing On The Moon," Lopez is captivating. Recommended for all who love guitar music.

✻✻✻ **Sueños (Dreams)**
1991 Fantasy Of Latin Strings (FLS1)

Cuculina; Vientos De Alberta; Sueños; Santiago Charleston; Mundos; Soledad; Perfume Lluviero; Primera Vez; Hacia Ti; Quedate; La Española; Canta Y Baila
45:56

✻✻✻✻ **Dancing On The Moon Contigo**
1994 Fantasy Of Latin Strings (FLS2)

Roots; No Barricade; Bolero Amor; Crying For Carmen; Mi Tierra; Simple Moments; Nobody's Perfect; Guitarras From Heaven; Mr. Melody; Lucia; Bailando Rumba; Dancing On The Moon *40:43*

Howie MacDonald
MARITIMES FIDDLE

A fine young fiddler from Cape Breton, Howie MacDonald is featured engagingly on *The Ceilidh Trail*, a 75-minute compact disc drawn from earlier recordings. The album presents a great-listening anthology of traditional and contemporary reels, strathspeys, hornpipes and jigs—including a memorable version of "Skye Boat Song." A fiddle lover's delight!

✻✻✻(✻) **The Ceilidh Trail**
1993 Atlantica (ATLD0193)

Willow Tree/Sutherland's/Donegal; Kenmure's Awa/Murray River Bridge/Jerry Holland's; Lady Doune/Lennox To Blantyre/Dan Galbey's/Sister Dolena Beaton's; Gramin/Jabe Meadow/Compliments To Doug MacPhee; A Memory Of Angus/ Charlie MacCuspic's/The Piper's Whim; Loch Na Gar; Clark Road/The Bag O'Gight/The Witch/Biodagair MacThomas; Betty Matheson's/Mike Saunder's/ Swinging On Home/The Silver Spear/The White Leaf; Skye Boat Song; Cheticamp/ Dave MacNeil's/Miss Smyth Of Methevans; Locharber Gathering/The Kames Lassies/Hayfield House/Joe Moroze's; The Cape Breton Symphony/The Jolly Beggar Man/Irish Reel; Irish Reel/John Howat's; Lady Montgomery/Gandy Dancers/Uncle Victor's; Miss Ann Campbell/The Green Tree/The "Buddy" Jig; A Dan R. Favorite/Portland Fancy/Cronin's Favorite; Far From Home/The Ale Is Dear/ The High Reel; Happy To Meet, Sorry To Part/The Devil In The Kitchen/King George IV Strathspey/King George IV Reel/The Old King's/The Reconciliation/ Lady Glen Orchy/The Magnetic Reel/Sean Maguire's Reel; Compliments To Sean Maguire/Swiss Cheese/Compliments To Doug MacPhee/Celtic Cousins; Harvey Beaton's/Miss Lyle/The Old Man And The Old Woman/The Cavity Investigators/The Fashion Which The Lassies Have; Lots Of Pretty Girls/Ciaren Tourish/Brennan MacDonald's *75:29*

Laurel MacDonald
AVANT GARDE FOLK/CELTIC; SINGER-SONGWRITER

Toronto singer-songwriter Laurel MacDonald, cousin of Gaelic singer Mary Jane Lamond, approaches music from a theatrical point of view. The selections on *Kiss Closed My Eyes* are experimental, unusual arrangements that create a montage of sound cemented with Gaelic and Greek lyrics. MacDonald's music is studio-created material, evocative and moody. This album will probably be appreciated more by the New Age crowd than by folkies.

✻✻✻ **Kiss Closed My Eyes**
1994 Improbable Music (IMACD-01)†

Kyrie; Òran Na H-Eala (The Songs Of The Swan); Mo Chùbhrachan (My Fragrant Little One); Yet So Beautiful; Kiss Closed My Eyes; Aslumber; An Ribhinn Àlainn *46:33*

Celso Machado
BRAZILIAN GUITAR AND VOCALS; SINGER-SONGWRITER

Vancouver-based Celso Machado, who came to Canada from Brazil, performs music rooted in contemporary Brazilian expression. On *Bagagem* he combines an innate sense of rhythm with his smooth voice and delicate guitar arrangements. Highlights of the album include "Terra Dos Sonhadores," "Fuga," "Bagagem," and "Arandeia." This soothing, poetic album is recommended for those who would like a quiet break from step dancing.

✻✻✻ **Bagagem**
1994 Surucua [no catalogue number]†

Esconde, Esconde; Terra Dos Sonhadores; Fuga; India Sorriu; Chama Dor E Calor; Bagagem; Diagonais; Amor Divergente; Arandeia; Amendoeira; Sonho De Moleque; Guararapes; Canto De Fé; Solidão; Amor De Bêbado *69:24*

Jamie MacInnis & Paul MacNeil
BAGPIPE

Jamie MacInnis & Paul MacNeil form one of the more unusual Canadian folk collaborations. Playing duets, these pipers express a deep love for the Celtic music heritage and tradition of Cape Breton. With an ear for great tunes, MacInnis and MacNeil have put together inspired bagpipe arrangements of traditional and contemporary tunes on *Fosgail An Dorus*. The piping is augmented by the excellent guitar work of Dave MacIsaac and John Ferguson. The two are further accompanied by Sheumas, Kyle, and Lucy MacNeil of the Barra MacNeils. Produced by fiddler Jerry Holland, who sits in as a guest musician, this is an album that warms the heart.

✻✻✻✻✓ **Fosgail An Dorus (Open The Door)**
1992 Gigs & Reels (GRIP 101)

Thig A Staigh: The Feet Washing/The Irishmen's Heart To The Ladies/The Price Of A Pig; D.N.A.: Paul K.'s Strathspey/Lady Carmichael Of Castle Craig/A'Chuachag/ The Reel Of Bervie/The Black Hair'd Lad; Newmarket House; Paul's Solo: Do Mo

Chara Maith Blair Murphy/Coppermill Studio/Charms Of Whiskey/ A Deanadh Im/
Mary Gray; Rothesay: Donald MacLellan Of Rothesay/Miss Scott/Culdar's Rant/
Glenlyon's Piper/Largo Law; Milling Set: Do Lamh A Chriosda/Bal Na H-Aibhne
Deas/Te A Chuailein Bhuidhe/Oran Do'N Bhal Chatriona Iain; Cape Breton Set:
Malcolm Deleskie/The Village Music Teacher/Alex MacEachern's/Castle Bay/Mr.
Colin J. Boyd/Jack Daniel's Reel; Eireann's: Miss Eireann MacInnis/John Johnny
Mick's/Roddy C.'s; Gun Oran Binn, No Canain Grinn; Jamie's Solo: Memories Of
Paddy LeBlanc/N.J. Cardenden/The Firth O'Forth/The Black Shepherdess/Taighean
Geala Sheildag/The Pigtown Fling; Iain Ruadh: The Seagull/Walking The Floor/
Scatter The Mud; Electric Set: Lexy MacAskill/Roddy MacDonald's Fancy *44:04*

Ashley MacIsaac
MARITIMES FIDDLE

Fiddle phenomenon Ashley MacIsaac is becoming known to many Canadians as a
featured guest on televised music specials. A virtuoso fiddler in the Cape Breton style,
MacIsaac combines youthful energy (often stepdancing while he plays) with an aggressive "let's dance" attitude that brooks no denial. *Close To The Floor* is an aptly
named album whose enthusiasm is contagious. If you like fiddle music, this one is a
must. MacIsaac received the "Instrumental Artist of the Year" East Coast Music Award
in 1995.

❋❋❋❋✓　**Close To The Floor**
　　　　 1992, reissued 1994　A&M (79602 2000-2)

The Little House Around The Corner/Traditional Winston/The Wandering Minstrel;
74th Highlanders'/Roderick MacDonald/Sandy Cameron/Creignish Hills/A Pipe
Tune/Mary MacDonald; Hills Of Lorne/Sir Archibald Dunbar/Traditional/Pat
Carney's/Scourdiness/Mrs. Duff; The New Fiddle/Scotty's Favourite/3 Mile Bridge/
Champion; Miss Lyall's/Miss Lyall's/Sandy Cameron's/Carigoim Broach;
Livingstone Pond/Long Point/Campion; Lament For Prophet/Moxham Castle/
Children's Reel/Dublin Reel; Miss Elanor Stewart/Glen Grant/Miss Robertson/
Donalbane; Blue Bonnets Over The Boarder; Irish Lasses/Cambridge/Aubry
Foley's; Bonnie Anne Anderson/Headlight/Believe It Or Not/Mist Over The Loch
46:43

Dave MacIsaac & Scott Macmillan
GUITAR INSTRUMENTALS

Cape Bretoner Dave MacIsaac, who grew up accompanying his father, a fiddler, is
one of the most sought-after Celtic guitarists for session work. Because of this association he may not be as well known as a gifted blues/rock guitarist. Scott Macmillan,
who loves jazz and blues, is a guitarist/composer who has arranged music for many
Cape Breton groups. For over twenty years Dave and Scott have been jamming together whenever their schedules permitted. *Guitar Souls* has given them a chance to
spread their wings and take flight. These performances, recorded live, provide an
excellent album for those who love electric blues with a touch of Celtic thrown in for
seasoning.

❊❊❊(❊) **Guitar Souls**
1993 Atlantica (ATL CD 8835)

Country Crunch; Sad Night Owl; Hydrostone Rock; Lament For Albert King; Jig Medley: Rocks In My Tea/Curly Haired Mule/Keji Clay/Reg The Red/Lisa's Jig; March, Strathspey And 3 Reels: Cluny Castle March/Athole Brose Strathspey/ General Stewart Reel/Jenny Dang The Weaver/The Randy Wife Of Greenlaw; Halifax Shuffle; Mayall Bag; All Blues; The Stumble; Blue Bag; Hometown Polka *64:24*

Wendy MacIsaac
MARITIMES FIDDLE

Wendy MacIsaac, a popular young Cape Breton fiddler, pianist, and step dancer based in Port Hastings, Nova Scotia, has appeared at dances and ceilidhs throughout the Maritimes, Ontario, and parts of the northeastern United States. A cousin of Ashley MacIsaac, she plays in a traditional Cape Breton style influenced by two fiddlers in particular: John Morris Rankin and Willie Kennedy. Her sure, fast-paced touch will have you on your feet dancing the whole way her CD, *The "Reel" Thing*.

❊❊❊(❊) **The "Reel" Thing**
1994 Wendy MacIsaac (WMR002)

Pipe Major George Ross' Welcome To The Black Watch/William Lawrie; Traditional Strathspey; The Highlanders Farewell To Ireland Strathspey; Creignish Hills Reel/ Rev. Hugh A. MacDonald; Traditional Reel; Donalbane/Traditional Reel; Idle Road Jig; The Lame Duck Jig; The Old Dutch Churn Jig; The Dundee Clog; Foresters Clog; Master McDermot Reel; Lively Steps Reel/Jerry Holland; The Fairy Dance Reel; Amelia's Jig; The Murray River Jig/Graham Townsend; Traditional Jig; Lochnagar Slow Air; Traditional Strathspey; Athole Brose Strathspey; Traditional Reel; Jenny Bowser Reel; King Of The Fairies March; Bacon And Eggs Strathspey/ Wendy MacIsaac; Cooleys Reel; Drowsey Maggie Reel; Tarbolton Lodge Reel; Larry Down's Reel; Neil Gow's Lament For The Death Of His Second Wife; Miss Jessie Smith Strathspey; Glen MacIsaac's Reel/Wendy MacIsaac; Nicole Fakoory's Jig/John Morris Rankin; Traditional Jig; The Baddeck Gathering Jig; Da Peerie Hoose March Traditional; Arthur Muise's Traditional Strathspey; Duke Of Gorden's Birthday Strathspey; Heather Hill Reel/Dan R. MacDonald; The Mourne Mountains Reel; Miss Drummond Of Perth Strathspey; Muileann Dubh Reel; Pretty Marion Reel *40:22*

Buddy MacMaster
MARITIMES FIDDLE

Cape Breton master fiddler Buddy MacMaster, of Judique, Nova Scotia, has been ranked alongside fiddle legend Neil Gow as one of the greatest Scottish fiddlers ever to have lived. The intricate, flowing, and flawless passages he makes across the spectrum of traditional fiddle music on *Judique On The Floor* warms the heart and sets the foot into another realm. A gorgeous album. MacMaster received a "Winston 'Scotty' Fitzgerald Award for East Coast Fiddling" Porcupine in 1994.

❋❋❋❋✓ **Judique On The Floor**
1989 Sea-Cape (ACD-9020)

Golden Rod Jig/The New Stove Jig/Irene's Jig; Da Slockit Light/Glen Caladh Castle/ The Lasses Of Stewarton; Memories Of Paddy LeBlanc/Lord Alexander Gordon/The Marquis Of Huntly/Haud Er Guan; Kenloch Jig/The Strathlorne Jig/Spin N' Glow; King George The Fourth/Old King George/ Old King's Reel/ King's Reel/ Old Traditional Reel; Oban And Lorne Society/The Devil In The Kitchen/Miss Drummond Of Perth/ Traditional Reel/Traditional Reel; Don't Be Teasing Jig/ Richard Brennan's Jig/Bonny Lea Rig; P.M. Jim Christie of Wick/Miss Catrina Gillies/Coire An Lochan/ Andy Renwick's Ferret; Jackson's Trip To Augrim/ Tripping Up Stairs/Tar Road To Sligo/Swinging On Home; R.P. Cummings March/ Christie Campbell/Traditional Strathspey/Traditional Reel/Traditional Reel/The MacKentosh Of MacKentosh *40:35*

Natalie MacMaster

MARITIME FIDDLER

Young virtuoso fiddler and niece of legendary Buddy MacMaster, Natalie MacMaster is another in a long line of Cape Breton Island fiddlers who have kept the fiddle tradition alive and vibrant. Natalie brings a light, seemingly effortless, touch to the fiddle that sends the jigs, reels, strathspeys, and waltzes into overtime. Her third album, and first CD, *Fit As A Fiddle* is a must purchase for any fan of Maritime fiddling. "This album is a thoroughly joyful experience"—*Dirty Linen*. Additional musicians include Dave MacIsaac, guitars; Howie MacDonald, piano; Tracy Dares, piano, synth; Tom Roach, drums; MacInnis, Jamie, highland pipes; and Sandy Moore, Celtic harp. Natalie received a "Winston 'Scotty' Fitzgerald Award for East Coast Fiddling" Porcupine in 1993.

❋❋❋❋✓ **Fit As A Fiddle**
1993 Natalie MacMaster (NMAS-CD 1972)

John Campbell's/Miss Ann Moirs Birthday/Lady Georgina Campbell/Angus On The Turnpike/Sheehan's Reel; My Dungannon Sweetheart/Scaffies Cairet/Juniper Jig; Carnival March/Miller Of Drone/MacKinnon's Brook/ Lucy Campbell/Annie Is My Darling/Gordon Cote/Bird's Nest/Maid Behind The Bar; Nancy's Waltz; Compliments To Sean Maguire/President Garfield/Miss Watt/Casa Loma Castle; O'r The Moor Among The Heather/Traditional/Lady Mary Ramsay/Jenny Dang The Weaver/ The Lassies Of Stewarton/Garfield Vale; Jean's Reel; I'll Always Remember You; The Girls Of Martinfield/Bennett's Favorite/The Green Fields Of Glentown; Counselor's/The Rakes Of Kildare/The Lark In The Morning; The Lass Of Carrie Mills/Lennox's Love To Blantyre/Archie Menzies/Reichwall Forest; If Ever You Were Mine; The MacNeils Of Ugadale/MacLaine Of Loch Buie/Colville's Rant/ Pibroch O'Donal Dhu *54:12*

Scott Macmillan

LITURGICAL MUSIC; COMPOSER

Celtic Mass For The Sea, composed by Nova Scotia's Scott Macmillan was commissioned by the CBC in 1988. The text was researched, adapted and edited by Jennyfer Brickenden. The world premier of the work was on February 15, 1991 in Halifax. *Celtic Mass For The Sea* "celebrates the reverence of the ancient peoples for the sea's majesty, ferocity and vitality. More than at any other time in human history we need to learn from this long ago vision. Our oceans are depleted, our planet is in crisis. It is Scott and Jennyfer's belief that only through empowerment of the human spirit will we find the collective will to make the sacrifices that will restore balance and harmony to our global home"—liner notes. The music consists of voice, string orchestra, and a Celtic ensemble of fiddle, mandolin, Celtic harp, pipes, flute, whistle, and guitar.

❋❋❋   **Celtic Mass For The Sea**
        1993 Atlantica (ERAD149)

> Introit; Kyrie; Gloria; First Reading; Second Reading; Credo; Sanctus; Benedictus; Agnus Dei And Dismissal *56:31*

Rita MacNeil
"Rootsy" Pop; Singer-Songwriter

Although Rita MacNeil has evolved into a fine pop singer-songwriter with one of the most recognizable voices in Canada, she started her career playing folk festivals and small venues and her lyrics are still rooted in Big Pond, Cape Breton. A champion of Canadian music, her CBC television show *Rita & Friends* has showcased more Canadian talent, including many of the folk performers in this guide, than any recent entertainment show. MacNeil's first three albums, *Born A Woman* (1975), *Part Of The Mystery* (1981), and *I'm Not What I Seem* (1983) have not been issued on compact disc. The first CD available is her fourth album, *Flying On Your Own*, dating from 1987 when she signed with a major label. For folkies, the introspective "She's Called Nova Scotia" is the highlight of the album. It makes you wish MacNeil would, for one album at least, ditch her ubiquitous background orchestra and do an "unplugged" recording, letting her wonderful voice stand out in a more traditional context as it did on her earliest recordings. Alas, this is not likely to happen. We must content ourselves to listen to her very fine pop albums and just dream about what might have been. MacNeil received Junos as "Songwriter of the Year" in 1989 and "Female Vocalist of the Year" in 1990, and the "Country Artist of the Year" East Coast Music Award in 1995.

❋❋❋(❋)   **Flying On Your Own**
            1987 Lupins (RMCD 1001)†

> Flying On Your Own; Neon City; She's Called Nova Scotia; Baby Baby; Leave Her Memory; Fast Train To Tokyo; Everybody; Used To You; Loser (When It Comes To Love); Realized Your Dreams; I Believe In You *42:26*

❋❋❋(❋)   **Reason To Believe**
            1988 Lupins (RMCD 2001)†

> Walk On Through; Two Steps From Broken; City Child; Doors Of The Cemetery; Reason To Believe; When The Loving Is Through; Causing The Fall; The Music's Going Round Again; Sound Your Own Horn; Working Man; Good Friends *49:19*

❋❋❋(❋)   **Rita**
            1989 Lupins (RMCD 4001)†

> Crazy Love; Anna I.O.U.; I'll Accept The Rose; You've Known Love; Moonlight

And Clover; When Love Surrounded You And I; Black Rock; Part Of The Mystery; Why Do I Think Of You Today; The Other One; In The Spirit; We'll Reach The Sky Tonight *52:02*

❄❄❄(❄) **Home I'll Be**
1990 Lupins (RMCD 5001)†

You Taught Me Well; Call Me And I'll Be There; Watch Love Grow Strong; This Thing Called Love; Home I'll Be; How Many Hearts; Southeast Wind; The Hurtin' Kind; Old Flames Never Die; Does It Ever Change *45:53*

❄❄❄(❄) **Thinking Of You**
[no date] Lupins (RMCD06001)†

Old Man; Shining Strong; Moment In Time; Lupins; Bring It To Me; Broken Heartstrings; The Crossing; Thinking Of You; I Need To Feel Close Again; Bring It On Home To Me *38:40*

❄❄❄(❄) **Songs From The Collection, Volume One**
1994 Lupins (RMCD 68001)

Reason To Believe; We'll Reach The Sky Tonight; Home I'll Be; Shining Strong; Flying On Your Own; This Thing Called Love; Working Man; I'll Accept The Rose; Moment In Time; She's Called Nova Scotia; Leave Her Memory; Fast Train To Tokyo; The Crossing; Good Friends; Higher Power *65:47*

Mad Love
CELTIC FOLK; SINGER-SONGWRITERS

Mad Love was founded by a Toronto-based trio of sisters who previously operated under the name The Celtic Gales. Of *Knockin' The Myth* a *Dirty Linen* reviewer remarks that "the context of the lyrics is a fascinating mix of contemporary topics with a trad feel ... an excellent disc." The highlights of this acoustic, traditional-sounding album include "Rains Come Down," "A Woman Alone," "Tumblin' Down," and "Dance Dance." Mad Love's vocalists are Audrey, Wanda, and Linda Vanderstoop with Scott Rogers on guitar and banjo, Allan Beardsell on guitar and mandolin, and Tim Hadley on acoustic bass.

❄❄❄(❄) **Knockin' The Myth**
1991 Moose (CD007)†

Rains Come Down; Rose On The Briar; Mercy Mercy Me/Irish Spring; London Town; A Woman Alone; What Have We Done?; Not Our Own; Weather The Storm; Tumblin' Down; Dance Dance *38:33*

Mad Pudding
CELTIC FOLK; SINGER-SONGWRITERS

"It sounds like a musician's gag: what do you get when you put together two choral conductors immersed in Celtic music, a classical violinist who plays fiddle tunes, and a rhythm section consisting of a jazz-funk bassist and a rock drummer? Answer: a Vancouver band called Mad Pudding"—Tony Montague, *Georgia Straight*. The eclectic mix of backgrounds adds to the fun as you listen to Mad Pudding work its way through the tracks of their debut album, *Bruce's Vegetable Garden*. The underlying sense of humour, evidenced in both the band's name and the title of the album, never intrudes where it shouldn't. The playing is confident and sure and the vocals carry the material well. Highlights include "Lately By," "Grandma Groats," "Canadian Old Time Set," and "Johnny And The Devil." Listening to this album is like opening the window and letting in fresh air. Mad Pudding includes Andy Hillhouse, guitar, vocals; Amy Stephen, accordion, vocals, penny whistle, harp, guitar, piano, recorder; Cam Wilson, fiddle, vocals; Richard Ernst, bass, vocals; John Hildebrand, drums, percussion.

✻✻✻✻✓ **Bruce's Vegetable Garden**
1994 Fiendish (FR 101)†

Funk Reels/Boys Of The Lough/The Bob Of Fettercairn; As I Walked Out; Bruce's Vegetable Garden; Lately By; Grandma Groats/Mouth Music/Pretty Peg/Sweeping The Bees; Reptile Song; Canadian Old Time Set; Shores Of Brittany; Difficult Women; Johnny And The Devil/Johnny On The Woodpile/Devil's Dream; Burkeville Beach; Kitimat Mall/Mozart The Canary/The Creel Of Turf; Curragh Of Kildare *46:17*

Aimé Major
FRENCH CANADIAN

The fine baritone voice of Aimé Major has been captured on the historical recording, *Aimé Major*—part of MCA's Héritage Québécois series. The CD contains no liner notes.

✻✻✻(✻) **Aimé Major**
[no date, reissued 1991] MCA (MCAD-10490)

Tango Mystérieux; Tu M'As Donné; Passant Par Paris; Un Train Bleu Dans La Nuit; Un Souvenir; Tu Te Souviens; Chevaliers De La Table Ronde; Les Mirettes; Maman; La Prière; Ne Me Quittes Pas; Cythère; Chacun Son Bonheur; Comme L'Amour; Partons La Mer Est Belle *38:39*

Eval Manigat
CARIBBEAN FUSION; SINGER-SONGWRITER; COMPOSER

Montreal-based Eval Manigat came to Canada by way of his native Haiti, with extended stays in Martinique and St. Martin, where he became more and more impressed with the versatility of Caribbean-African musical culture and the new forms that emerge when it is fused with European classical and folk traditions. In Quebec, Manigat experimented with fusions that drew on jazz, funk, and salsa. His second album, and first CD, *Africa+* won a Juno in 1995 for best "Global Recording." On this upbeat recording, Manigat's band is joined by guest singers Emeline Michel, Karen Young, Vivianne Rangon, Juan Fernandez, and Lazaro René.

✻✻✻✻ **Africa +**
[no date] Tchaka (TRBC-9940)†

Africa +; Anna Maria; Salsa Sun; Élan-Yé; Afro-Cab; Salade Musicale; Somos; Con Sentimiento Latino; De Costa A Costa *35:13*

Mariposa In The Schools
FOLKSONGS FOR CHILDREN

Circle Of Friends is a very special album—a compilation celebrating twenty years of the Mariposa In The Schools project. Ken Whiteley, producer, explains the album this way: "We began a series of 'sing-arounds,' where those present go around a circle taking turns leading everyone in a song, story, tune, game, dance, etc. I realized this was how we should make the recording and so our sing-arounds became recording sessions. Most of this collection was recorded 'live off the living room floor.' I think it captures the spirit of people sharing with each other something that they love very much. It is our pleasure to now share with you what is but a portion of those moments."

※※※(※)✓ **Circle Of Friends**
  1990 Mariposa In The Schools (MITS2 0090)†

Donkey Riding *(Andrea Haddad; Chris Rawlings)*; Stomp Stomp *(Caitlin Hanford; Chris Whiteley)*; Talk About Peace *(Joe Hampson; Ted Roberts)*; A Tale *(Sally Jaeger)*; Saturday Night Up The Gatineau *(Ian Bell)*; La Laine Des Moutons *(Judith Cohen; Andrea Haddad)*; Diddle De Dum *(Sandra Beech)*; Same Boat Now *(Ken Whiteley)*; Oh Santa *(Jim MacMillan)*; My Candles *(Bluma Schonbrun)*; Jump Josie/ Skip To My Loo *(Sharon, Lois & Bram)*; Happy Birthday Round *(All)*; 10 Bright Candles *(Caroline Parry)*; Les Gens Du Pays *(Judith Cohen; Andrea Haddad)*; Red River Valley *(Shelley Gordon)*; Meet In The Circle *(Jerry Brodey; Kim Brodey)*; Nova Scotia Farewell *(Beverlie Robertson)*; Flee Fly Flow *(Deborah Dunleavy)*; The Bear Missed The Train *(Sandy Byer; Judy Greenhill; Kathy Reid-Naiman)*; St. Joe's Reel *(Ian Bell; Anne Lederman)*; My Band *(Chick Roberts)*; Puce Est Morte *(Marylyn Peringer)*; The Rain *(Jim MacMillan)* 55:42

Marcel Martel
FRENCH CANADIAN; FOLK/COUNTRY

Born in Drummondville, Québec, in 1925, Marcel Martel began singing and playing accordion by age ten. Deeply influenced by Roland Lebrun, he began performing the folkish songs of Lebrun in the 1940's, accompanying himself on guitar. A highly popular recording artist who began writing his own songs in a simple, country style, Martel toured with his wife Noëlla Therrien and his daughter Renée in the 1950's. He was also the star of a highly popular TV show, *Marcel Martel*, on CHLT, Sherbrooke, Québec, from 1962-65. According to the *Encyclopedia of Music in Canada* he had recorded 130 singles and 40 LP's for Compo, London, and Bonanza by 1979. The historical recording, *Marcel Martel*, provides a sampling of his work. Issued by MCA as part of its Héritage Québécois series, there are no liner notes to identify the fine female voice that accompanies Martel on several of the songs. It might be his wife, Noëlla Therrien.

※※※※ **Marcel Martel**
  [no date, reissued 1991] MCA (MCAD-10488)

Quand Le Soleil Dit Bonjour Aux Montagnes; Adieu Mauvaises Rêveries; Ton Coeur Est Froid; Les Trois Cloches; Allo Ma Patrie; Lettre Et Souvenir; Mon Coeur

Est Comme Un Train; Dans Mes Bras Ce Soir; Tu Dis Que Tu M'Aimes; Mon
Amour A Grandi; Fleurs Du Bon Dieu; En Prison Maintenant; Un Coin Du Ciel;
Amenez-Moi Là-Bas À Panama; Il Faudra M'Oublier *42:11*

Harry Martin
FOLK/COUNTRY; SINGER-SONGWRITER

On *Visions Of This Land*, Harry Martin, a singer-songwriter from Labrador, has put
together a solid album that will appeal to those who enjoy simple, dignified songs
delivered in an early country-music style. Martin's sensitive songs and easy-listening
voice highlight life in Labrador. "This Is My Home," is a song about an old trapper
who, having lived the life of a free man, wishes to die in the country. "Halfway Up
The Mountain" is about a person who "having reached middle age, reflects upon the
promise of the past and all of the plans that came to nothing." "Only In My Dreams"
is about "an old man longs to return to the coast where he spent his life as a fisherman.
His thoughts are of the beautiful spring days as the ice melts and the birds return to
nest on the islands." The album succeeds in expressing heartfelt sentiments without
becoming maudlin.

❋❋❋　　**Visions Of This Land**
[no date]　Piper Stock (PM 002)

This Is My Home; Raven Hair; Somewhere Beyond The Hills; Visions Of This Land;
Another Day Of Waiting; The Harbour Is Empty; Don't Think I Could Live Here;
Halfway Up The Mountain; Race To The Grave; This Old River; Eagles Got To Fly;
Dream Forever; Forgotten Soldiers; Only In My Dreams *50:41*

Lawrence Martin
FIRST NATIONS MUSIC; SINGER/SONGWRITER

Born of a Cree mother and an Irish father, Lawrence Martin (stage name Wapistan) is
an executive of the Wawatay Native Communications Society which provides radio,
television, and newspaper communications to nearly fifty reserves throughout northern Ontario. He has also served as mayor of Sioux Lookout, Ontario—the first native
to be elected mayor in Ontario history. According to the liner notes on *Wapistan Is
Lawrence Martin*, Martin was taught guitar by an aunt, and he became a songwriter
and performer to convey "the joy, heritage, wisdom, and new optimism of his people,
as well as the anger and bitterness that stems from five centuries of abuse, neglect and
ignorance."

　　Wapistan Is Lawrence Martin, which received a Juno in the "Best Music of Aboriginal Canada" category in 1994, explores many moods. The opening track, "Elders"
expresses a fundamental optimism: "The elders say there will come a day / When the
young will be strong like the eagle." The very next track, "Like A Bad Dream," presents
the uprooted sentiment "This world I'm living in feels like a real bad dream / I lost my
religion to Christianity / I lost my language and my dignity." The moods swing from
happy, in "Wache Ay," which means "hello" and "goodbye," to bitter and wistful in
"Betty Jean" and "What's Gonna Happen To The Indian?"

❋❋❋❋ **Wapistan Is Lawrence Martin**
1993 First Nations Music (Y2 10014)

> Elders; Like A Real Bad Dream; Wache Ay; The Polar Bear (Is Taking Me Home); Ashtum; Celtic Nemowin; Wawatay; Betty Jean; What's Gonna Happen To The Indian?; Canada O'Daskey; Red Road Of Life; Meegwetch Nashville *41:47*

Danielle Martineau
FRENCH CANADIAN; FOLK/POP/ZYDECO; SINGER-SONGWRITER

Quebec folklorist and performer Danielle Martineau ably blends a mix of musical genres that feature her excellent voice and accordion playing. Backed up by fine, if very electric, musicians, her music includes touches of zydeco, rock, and traditional. If you like latter-day La Bottine Souriante, you are sure to like her upbeat albums.

❋❋❋(❋) **Rockabayou**
1992 Les Disques Bros (BROS 2001-2)†

> Le Duc; Loupgarou; Belle; La Porte D'En Arrière; La Fête À Montréal; J'Pense Ringue À Toi; Zarico Charivari; Laisse Faire; Revenue Pour Rester; Dans L'Détour; Le Temps D'Une Valse *39:28*

❋❋❋(❋) **Autrement**
1994 Les Disques Bros (BROS 4002-2)†

> Téléguides; Zydeco Musico; Toi T'es Pas Là; L'Eau Et Le Vent (Valse D'Hiver); Chou Chou (Y'A Que Toi); Montréal Cotton Blues; En Silence; La Table Des Veuves; La Montagne Coupée; Nouveau Gouvernement; Dure Lutte; Suite Pierre-Antoine *45:13*

Barb Mattiacci
FOLK/POP; SINGER-SONGWRITER

Peterborough, Ontario singer-songwriter Barb Mattiacci has one of those voices, like Buffy Sainte-Marie's, that quickly grabs your attention and carries you into the lyrics. *Inside My Dream* shows Mattiacci to be a talented songwriter who concentrates on mood rather than visual images or clever twists of phrase. Songs like "Inside My Dream," "Fly With The Wind," and "Solid Ground" are gently evocative. This is introspective territory nicely done.

❋❋❋(❋) **Inside My Dream**
1992 Barb Mattiacci (AVACD 931)†

> Inside My Dream; Fly With The Wind; Long Time Ago; Solid Ground; Where Do We Go?; Walking Down The River; See To Believe; Fragile Facts; Dream Tonight; Angels *43:39*

Zeke Mazurek
VARIOUS FIDDLE TRADITIONS

Belleville, Ontario, fiddler Zeke Mazurek plays a fine collection of tunes on *I Ain't Dead... Yet*, subtitled "a choice and authentic collection of traditional and contemporary melody specially adapted for the violin, being gems culled from life in Canada."

The selections come from far and wide: examples are "Lament For Owen Christy," a Jim Stewart composition from New Brunswick, "Cinquantaine," a French tune learned from Vancouver street musicians, "Szla Dzieweczka Do Laseczka," a Polish tune Mazurek learned from his father, and "Si Pa Bi," a Laotian melody learned from Sneezy Waters. The melodies tend to be dark and mournful—this is introspective territory that tugs at the heart with sweet, lovely playing. Mazurek is accompanied by Danny Greenspoon, guitar, Rob Hollett, bodhran, Sneezy Waters, guitar, and Rick Bauer, guitar.

✵✵✵(✵)   **I Ain't Dead... Yet**
1995 Iady [no catalogue number]

> Lament For Owen Christy; A Brisk Young Man's Jig Medley: Teufelpferde (The Black Nag)/Colleraine/Miss Shepperd; Cinquantaine; Back To The Hills; Szla Dzieweczka Do Laseczka; The Battle Of Glencoe; Si Pa Bi; Medley: Rodney's Glory/Dust In The Lane/Sally Gooding/Billy Cheatem; Blind Mary; Variation On Sandor Lakatos' Verbunk In A; A Mira Melody; Captain O'Kane; Lament For Owen Christy *35:03*

Doug McArthur

FOLK; SINGER-SONGWRITER

Known for his excellent and unusual songwriting, Ontario performer Doug McArthur has been a festival favourite since the 1970's. The gentle lyrics and slightly husky voice of his two mid-70's albums have been reissued as a single compact disc: *Letters From The Coast / Sisteron*. This delightful reissue brings back such fine songs as "Dreams And Visions," "Hero," "Lord Douglas," "Sisteron," "Skyway," "1911," "Cowboy Bob," "Ain't Goin' Home," and "Almost Midnight." "[*Sisteron* is] one of the best Canadian folk records of the 1970's"—Craig MacInnis, *Toronto Star. Doug McArthur With Garnet Rogers* features thirteen of McArthur's later compositions, including "Break The Law" which was covered by Garnet Rogers on his debut album. Rogers fills in instrumentally on this album (along with David Essig) but the singing is strictly McArthur. From the haunting "Merlin" to the lyrical "Black Eyed Susan," McArthur sings memorable song after song. His voice is perhaps a trifle more husky than it was in the 70's, but like the taste of scotch whiskey, that adds to the ambiance.

✵✵✵(✵)   **Letters From The Coast / Sisteron**
1974, 1976, reissued 1991 Snow Goose (SGS-1119/10)†

> Dreams And Visions; Hero; Glory Road; Lord Douglas; The Painter's Song; I Do; One-Eyed Walden; Don't You Believe; The Devil's Pony; Skye Song; Sisteron; Whip Me; The Lights Of Town; Skyway; 1911; Cowboy Bob; Restless; The Way I Ride; The Lunenburg Shift; Ain't Goin' Home; Gentle People; Almost Midnight *71:38*

✵✵✵(✵)✓ **Doug McArthur With Garnet Rogers**
1989 Snow Goose (SGS-1116D)†

> Merlin; Break The Law; Isle Madelaine; The Siege Of Toronto; Bullwhip Jack And The Silver Bell; There Is A River; Bank The Fire; Thief In The Night; Ships At Sea; Black Eyed Susan; Wino Breath; Chella; The Un-named City *50:28*

John McDermott
FOLK

A graduate of St. Michael's Choir School in Toronto, McDermott sings "old favour-ites" in a voice that, while pleasant, is probably too stagey for most folkies. *Danny Boy* is a perfectly good album, in small doses, but the material is too sentimental to take in one sitting. McDermott's second album, *Old Friends*, continues in the same vein. The heartfelt delivery seems a bit overwrought if you're accustomed to bouncier Celtic bands that handle this material with a lighter touch. If you like McDermott's interpretations you'll undoubtedly like *Christmas Memories*. If not, you'll find it diffi-cult to enjoy.

✳✳✳ **Danny Boy**
1992 EMI (CDM 54772)

The Green Fields Of France; By Yon Bonnie Banks; Danny Boy; The Last Rose Of Summer; And The Band Played Waltzing Matilda; The Old House; The Faded Coat Of Blue; The Rose Of Tralee; The Sun Is Burning; Christmas In The Trenches; The Minstrel Boy; Auld Lang Syne; Danny Boy (A Cappella) *62:20*

✳✳✳ **Old Friends**
1994 EMI (E2 27467)

Ye Banks And Braes Of Bonnie Doon; One Last Cold Kiss; She Moved Thro' The Fair; The Bard Of Armagh; The Meeting Of The Waters; The Old Man; Mother Machree; Amazing Grace; Farewell To Pripchat; The Skye Boat Song; Lachin Y Gair (Dark Loch Nagar); My Love Is Like A Red, Red Rose; Massacre Of Glencoe; The Dutchman; The Parting Glass *62:53*

✳✳ **Christmas Memories**
1994 EMI (E2 27468/7243 827468 2 9)†

Instrumental Medley: Away In A Manger/Angels From The Realms Of Glory/Good King Wenceslas/In Dulci Jubilo; Gesu Bambino; Panis Angelicus; Ave Maria; What Child Is This; Lo How A Rose E'er Blooming; O Holy Night; Suo Gan; Instrumental Medley: Deck The Halls/Noel Nouvelet/Patapan/The Angels And The Shepherds/We Wish You A Merry Christmas; O Little Town Of Bethlehem; The Holly And The Ivy; Silent Night *(with Allison Girvan)*; Somewhere A Child Is Sleeping *(with Judith Durham)*; Old Tin Star; Christmas Memories; The Secret Of Christmas *60:05*

Eileen McGann
FOLK; SINGER-SONGWRITER

"Irish melodies are reason enough for anyone to become a singer"—Eileen McGann. Calgary resident Eileen McGann started as a singer of traditional Celtic songs and gradually inserted her own material into her repertoire. The daughter of Irish parents, McGann fell in love with traditional Irish music, especially the a cappella melodies. During her university years she did guest sets at the Fiddler's Green Folk Club in Toronto and later at festivals. Once folkies heard her beautiful, lilting voice and her perceptive, intelligent lyrics, it was only a matter of time before McGann became a fan favourite. McGann's first album, *Elements*, is a mix of traditional material and original songs. The supporting musicians and singers on the album read like a who's who of Canadian folk music: Grit Laskin, Garnet Rogers, Cathy Miller, and Ken

Whiteley, who also produced the album. A beautiful debut album. Her second album, *Turn It Around*, features a growing, maturing songwriter. Her original songs include "Turn It Around," about a street person in Toronto, "Requiem (For The Giants)," a protest and lament about proposed clearcutting of the old pines of Temagami, and "Westminster Bridge," inspired by a "cardboard city" in London. The strong supporting cast is continued, with the likes of Grit Laskin, Garnet Rogers, Mary Anderson, Ken Brown, Anne Lederman, and Cathy Miller. This is an extraordinarily good folk album. "Requiem (For The Giants)" received an "Environmental Song Award" Porcupine in 1991.

McGann's third album, *Journeys*, puts McGann more directly on her own personal journey as a songwriter. There are only three traditional songs on the album: "Bonny Portmore," "Braw Sailin' On The Sea," and "Jock O'Hazeldean." As usual, McGann injects magic into these numbers. But what's most impressive about the album is McGann's increasing confidence as a songwriter. Songs like "I See My Journey," "Reservations," "In The Silence," "Rolling Home Canadian," "Windigo's Coming," and "Too Stupid For Democracy" are fine contemporary folksongs. Once again McGann is surrounded by some of the industry's best—a partial list includes Mary Anderson, Ken Brown, Stephen Fearing, David Knutson, Anne Lederman, Cathy Miller, Oliver Schroer, and David Woodhead.

❋❋❋(❋)　**Elements**
　　　　　1987 Dragonwing (DRGN 111CD)†

> Live Not Where I Love; Isabella Gunn; My Lagan Love; Temagami; Sands; Man's Job; The Power And The Need; The Riddle Song; Here's To The Men; Canoe Song At Twilight *41:47*

❋❋❋❋✓　**Turn It Around**
　　　　　1991 Dragonwing (DRGN 112CD)†

> Turn It Around; The Fair Flower Of Northumberland; Requiem (For The Giants); Tiree Love Song; Leaving This Nation; Westminster Bridge; The Parting; The Dancers Of Stanton Drew; The Knight Of The Rose; Whitewater; Thyme *50:03*

❋❋❋❋✓　**Journeys**
　　　　　1995 Dragonwing (DRGN 113—CD)†

> I See My Journey; Bonny Portmore; Reservations; In The Silence; Braw Sailin' On The Sea; Rolling Home Canadian; Windigo's Coming; Reach For The Light; Too Stupid For Democracy; Jock O'Hazeldean; Kassandra; Another Train *54:59*

Kate & Anna McGarrigle

FOLK/POP; SINGER-SONGWRITERS

Daughters of French-Canadian and Irish parents, the immensely talented sisters Kate & Anna McGarrigle sing in English and French and each plays piano, guitar, banjo, and accordion. They began playing Montreal coffeehouses in the early 1960's and became internationally known as songwriters by the 70's. In a curious career that never quite catapulted them to major fame, they nonetheless generated a cult following that persists to this day. There's something unusual, almost vinegary, about their material that, when it gets under your skin, you're never the same again—once you're hooked on the McGarrigles it's hard to hear enough of them. Fortunately for McGarrigle junkies, only their third album, *Pronto Monto*, has not yet been reissued on compact disc. Their debut album, *Kate & Anna McGarrigle*, features the McGarrigle classics "Kiss And Say Goodbye," "Heart Like A Wheel," "Swimming Song," "Travellin' On For Jesus," and the incomparable "Talk To Me Of Mendocino." The loose and occasionally rough-edged arrangements are all over the map, sometimes folksy, sometimes jazzy, sometimes popish. Somehow it all works. Essential.

The McGarrigles' second album, *Dancer With Bruised Knees*, continues with the half-zany, half-serious mix of styles with lyrics that keep you guessing, line by line. Not quite as magical as their debut album, but highly recommended. Their fourth album, entirely in French, was originally titled *Entre La Jeunesse Et La Sagresse*. Deciding that this was perhaps a bit too challenging for anglophones, PolyGram reissued the album as *The French Record*. An excellent album, but a working knowledge of French helps. The CD liner notes include translations of all the songs, but not the French lyrics. *Love Over And Over* takes up where *Dancers* left off. The landscape is skewed by unusual, engaging lyrics and unexpected, entertaining arrangements. *Heartbeats Accelerating*, from 1990, is a departure from the carefree arrangements of the earlier works. The sound is tighter, more commercially acceptable. The songwriting is still insightful and quirky—as evidenced in "I Eat Dinner," "Rainbow Ride," "D.J. Serenade," and "I'm Losing You." Unfortunately, nothing on this album leaps out at you. The special quality of their voices is obscured by the production—the signature sound is missing.

✳✳✳✳✓ **Kate & Anna McGarrigle**
1975 Rykodisc / Hannibal (HNCD 4401)†

Kiss And Say Goodbye; My Town; Blues In D; Heart Like A Wheel; Foolish You; Talk To Me Of Mendocino; Complainte Pour Ste Catherine; Tell My Sister; Swimming Song; Jigsaw Puzzle Of Life; Go Leave; Travellin' On For Jesus *35:45*

✳✳✳(✳) **Dancer With Bruised Knees**
1977 Rykodisc / Hannibal (HNCD 4402)†

Dancer With Bruised Knees; Southern Boys; No Biscuit Blues; First Born; Blanche Comme La Neige; Perrine Etait Servante; Be My Baby; Walking Song; Naufragée Du Tendre (Shipwrecked); Hommage À Grungie; Kitty Come Home; Come A Long Way *41:13*

✳✳✳(✳) **French Record**
1980, reissued 1992 Polydor (314 513 554-2)†

Entre Lajeunesse Et La Sagesse; Complainte Pour Ste Catherine; Mais Quand Tu Danses; Cheminant À La Ville; Excursion A Venise; En Filant Ma Quenouille; La Belle S'Est Etourdie; Naufragée Du Tendre; Avant La Guerre; À Boire; Prends Ton Manteau *37:02*

✳✳✳(✳) **Love Over And Over**
1982 Polydor (422 841 101-2)†

Move Over Moon; Sun, Son (Shining On The Water); I Cried For Us; Love Over And Over; Star Cab Company; Tu Vas M'Accompagner; On My Way To Town; Jesus Lifeline; The Work Song; St. Valentine's Day; Midnight Flight; A Place In Your Heart *43:24*

❋❋❋ **Heartbeats Accelerating**
1990 Private Inc. (2070-2-P)†

Heartbeats Accelerating; I Eat Dinner; Rainbow Ride; Mother Mother; Love Is; D.J. Serenade; I'm Losing You; Hit And Run Love; Leave Me Be; St. James Hospital *42:50*

Donald McGeoch
CELTIC FOLK; SINGER-SONGWRITER

One of the founders of Ontario's Brantford Folk Club, Donald McGeoch, like Bobby Watt, is a native Scotsman who emigrated to Canada and has graced the Canadian folk scene with his fine arrangements of traditional Scottish folk material and original compositions. On *Land Of The Western Sky*, McGeoch's strong voice is highlighted on original songs like "Land Of The Western Sky," "Just Another State," "The Porcelain Waltz," and "Homeland." McGeoch is backed by a fine cast of musicians, including Stephen Fuller, fiddle; Allison Lupton, flute, whistle; Harry Jongerden, bass; Steve Didemus, guitar and dobro; Jeff Daw, mandolin; Ruth Sutherland, harp; and backup vocalists Sharon Fitzsimon, Gerry Dion, and Martin Zimber.

❋❋❋ **Land Of The Western Sky**
1994 Donald McGeoch (DMCD 11:11)

Lancashire Lads; Dumbarton's Drums; Land Of The Western Sky; Number Two Top Seam; Scot's Wha Hae; Leaving Nancy; Just Another State; Homeland; Come By The Hills; Sound The Pibroch; The Porcelain Waltz; Keep The Fiddle Playing; Jamie Raeburn's Farewell; Cadgwith Anthem *49:59*

McGinty
MARITIMES CELTIC

McGinty is a popular Celtic pub band from Nova Scotia that has played to audiences for over fifteen years. They perform traditional Irish tunes alongside material from contemporary songwriters. McGinty's *Live* album was recorded at their 15th Anniversary Concert in Halifax. The disc begins with the bouncy Irish medley "Rocky Road To Dublin/Morrison's Jig/Paddy On The Railroad" and proceeds through a selection of crowd pleasers, including two Stan Rogers tunes, "Forty-Five Years" and "Mary Ellen Carter," a Rita MacNeil song, "Working Man," and Roch Voisine's "A Fishing Day." The concert closes with a "Farewell To Nova Scotia/This Land Is Your Land" medley. The disc makes you wish you could have been there. *Atlantic Favourites* is a studio album that brings out the excellent musicianship of the group. The sparkly, upbeat arrangements of songs and medleys like "The Ballad Of St. Anne's Reel," "Inverness Ceilidh/Robert Hannigan's Reel," and "Farewell To Nova Scotia" put you in a ceilidh mood. The album also features material by several Canadian songwriters including Tom Lewis' "Last Shanty," Ron Hynes' "Sonny's Dream," Stan Rogers' "Barrett's Privateers," and Kenzie MacNeil's "The Island." *Ballads & Bar Tunes*, from 1994, is McGinty's most polished album to date. They do justice to all the old favourites on the recording, including "Roseville Fair," "Fiddler's Green," "Mary Mack," "Streets Of London," "Willie McBride," "Brennan On The Moor," and "Nancy Whiskey." McGinty is John Ferguson, vocals, guitar, fiddle, mandolin, bouzouki, tin whistle; Don Moore, vocals, guitar, mandolin, bodhran; and Dave Hickey, vocals, bass, banjo, twelve-string. McGinty received a "Rendition Of A Canadian Classic" Porcupine Award in 1990 for "Sonny's Dream."

✳✳✳ **Live**
1992 Rocky Coast (RCMI-CD 4)

Rocky Road To Dublin/Morrison's Jig/Paddy On The Railway; Sagely Wisdom; Forty-Five Years; Rollin' Down To Old Maui; The Mary Ellen Carter; New South Wales; The Musical Priest/Lucy Campbell/The Banshee; Working Man; The Man In The Moon; He's Nobody's Moggy Now; A Fishing Day; Farewell To Nova Scotia/ This Land *47:39*

✳✳✳(✳) **Atlantic Favorites**
[no date] Rocky Coast (RCMI-CD 5)

The Ballad Of St. Anne's Reel; The Bluenose Song; Last Shanty; Inverness Ceilidh/ Robert Hannigan's Reel; Sonny's Dream; Home In My Harbour; Barrett's Privateers; The Island; The Legend Of Kelly's Mountain; Song For The Mira; As Long As There Is Sail; Farewell To Nova Scotia *40:03*

✳✳✳(✳) **Ballads & Bar Tunes**
1994 Rocky Coast (RCMI-CD 6)

Roseville Fair; Fiddler's Green; Danny Boy; Mary Mack; Santiano/Sally Brown; Streets Of London; Jigs: Swallow's Tail/Kesh/Trippin' Up The Stairs; Willie McBride; Brennan On The Moor; Dirty Old Town; Nancy Whiskey; Ballads And Bar Tunes/Ashokan Farewell *48:45*

Loreena McKennitt
FOLK; CELTIC

"Anyone who can get an ancient Celtic ballad like 'The Bonny Swans' onto American pop radio must be doing something right"—*Dirty Linen*. Stratford, Ontario singer Loreena McKennitt began her career as a busker, driving to Toronto's St. Lawrence market where she would set up her fifty-pound harp just after dawn and play Celtic music to what must have been a very intrigued group of early morning shoppers. With flowing red hair and Elizabethan dress, her striking, theatrical appearance and unusual music soon created a substantial following. McKennitt's first independent recording, *Elemental*, is the best introduction to her work. Simpler and plainer than her later albums, it's the folksiest of McKennitt's albums. *To Drive The Cold Winter Away* is an album of traditional Christmas songs that will please anyone who appreciates an alternative to the standard Christmas fare. The album title comes from the lyrics of the eighteenth century English song, "In Praise Of Christmas." Other English, Scottish, and Irish songs include "The Seasons," "The King," "Balulalow," and "The Wexford Carol."

On *Parallel Dreams*, McKennitt begins a musical exploration that has led her to a more ensemble approach to her music. Mixing rich tapestries of sound into her original compositions, she is joined by a larger group of musicians. The intent is to delve into the mysterious side of Celtic music and McKennitt succeeds admirably on tracks like "Samian Night," "Moon Cradle," Standing Stones," "Breaking The Silence," and "Ancient Pines." There's also "Dickens' Dublin," based on a passage from Charles

Dickens, and one of the loveliest versions of "Annachie Gordon" on record. Quite different from her earlier material, but delightful if you have an ear for it. Beginning with *The Visit*, which won a Juno award in the "Roots & Traditional" category in 1992, McKennitt's recordings have been distributed by Warner Brothers. The album continues the trend towards musical tapestry started on *Parallel Dreams* but with more confidence and attack. From the stunning opener, "All Souls Night," to arranged poems by Tennyson and Shakespeare, "The Lady Of Shalott" and "Cymbeline," respectively, to the traditional "Greensleeves," this an exciting and varied album. On *The Mask And Mirror* McKennitt branches further afield from the British Isles and Brittany to the Celtic remnants found in the Galicia region of Spain. Fascinated by the crosscurrents of Judaism, Islam, and Christianity in this early material, McKennitt delves into mystical themes underscored with exotic arrangements. Compositions like "The Mystics Dream" and "The Dark Night Of The Soul" are darker in hue than her preceding work. She is analogous to a serious author who explores her themes more deeply with each successive novel. *The Mask And The Mirror* received a Juno in the "Roots & Traditional" category in 1995.

❋❋❋(❋)✓ **Elemental**
   1985 Quinlan Road (QR CD101)†

   Blacksmith; She Moved Through The Fair; Stolen Child; The Lark In The Clear Air; Carrighfergus *(with Cedric Smith)*; Kellswater; Banks Of The Claudy; Come By The Hills; Lullaby *36:34*

❋❋❋(❋) **To Drive The Cold Winter Away**
   1987 Quinlan Road (QRCD 102)†

   In Praise of Christmas; The Seasons; The King; Banquet Hall; Snow; Balulalow; Let Us The Infant Greet; The Wexford Carol; The Stockford Carol; Let All That Are To Mirth Inclined *45:48*

❋❋❋(❋) **Parallel Dreams**
   1989 Quinlan Road (QRCD 103)†

   Samain Night; Moon Cradle; Huron 'Beltane' Fire Dance; Annachie Gordon; Standing Stones; Dickens' Dublin (The Palace); Breaking The Silence; Ancient Pines *43:33*

❋❋❋❋✓ **The Visit**
   1991 Quinlan Road (WEA CD75151)†

   All Souls Night; Bonny Portmore; Between The Shadows; The Lady Of Shalott; Greensleeves; Tango To Evora; Courtyard Lullaby; The Old Ways; Cymbeline *49:08*

❋❋❋❋ **The Mask And Mirror**
   1994 Quinlan Road (WEA CD 95296)†

   The Mystic's Dream; The Bonny Swans; The Dark Night Of The Soul; Marrakesh Night Market; Full Circle; Santiago; Cé Hé Mise Le Ulaingt?/The Two Trees; Prospero's Speech *52:47*

John McLachlan
FOLK/POP; SINGER-SONGWRITER

Vancouver singer-songwriter John McLachlan brings a soft, gentle voice and laid-back sound to *Stepping Out*. The tracks range from a ramblin' song, "Railroad Town" to a song about mining, "Cumberland Coal," a song about a towboat captain, "Towboat Captain," to the lyrical "There Is A Star." The arrangements blend folk, pop, and rock.

✳✳✳ **Stepping Out**
1990 John McLachlan (JM 10001)†

Railroad Town; Rough Water; Cumberland Coal; Hard To Believe; Out Of Step; Towboat Man; There Is A Star; Bogota; Though Time Goes On; Wouldn't Say No *40:33*

Sarah McLachlan
POP; SINGER-SONGWRITER

Sarah McLachlan, who was raised in Nova Scotia and later moved to British Columbia, is a popular singer-songwriter who numbers many folkies among her fans. Perhaps it's the deft acoustic guitar playing she does occasionally in concert that creates the bond. McLachlan's albums are musically textured in a manner somewhat reminiscent of Loreena McKennitt's later work, but with a pop, rather than a Celtic, bias. She is a master of mood, creating impressive effects through a combination of her lyrics, her expressive voice, and an interlocked, interwoven sound. McLachlan has gained a very large following among college and university students. The sequence of her work is *Touch* (1989), *Solace* (1991), *Fumbling Towards Ecstasy* (1993), and *The Freedom Sessions* (1994). The first three show the normal maturing and progression you would expect from a growing pop/rock artist. *The Freedom Sessions* is an album of many of the cuts on *Fumbling Towards Ecstasy*, but in acoustic versions that captured the songs at an earlier stage of development before the heavy layering process began. The result is a folkish album that brings McLachlan's voice front and centre. From the perspective of this guide, it is her most successful album.

✳✳✳ **Touch**
1989 Nettwerk (W2-045)

Out Of The Shadows; Vox; Strange World; Trust; Touch; Steaming; Sad Clown; Uphill Battle; Ben's Song; Vox (Extended) *47:48*

✳✳✳ **Solace**
1991 Nettwerk (W2-30055)†

Drawn To The Rhythm; Into The Fire; The Path Of Thorns (Terms); I Will Not Forget You; Lost; Back Door Man; Shelter; Black; Home; Mercy *44:52*

✳✳✳ **Fumbling Towards Ecstasy**
1993 Nettwerk (W2-30081)

Possession; Wait; Plenty; Good Enough; Mary; Elsewhere; Circle; Ice; Hold On; Ice Cream; Fear; Fumbling Towards Ecstasy *54:59*

✳✳✳(✳)   **The Freedom Sessions**
1994 Nettwerk (W2-6321)

Elsewhere; Plenty; Mary; Good Enough; Hold On; Ice Cream; Ice; Ol '55 *38:04*

Murray McLauchlan
FOLK/ROCK/COUNTRY; SINGER-SONGWRITER

Born in Paisley, Scotland, in 1948, Murray McLauchlan was brought to Canada at age five. He began performing folk music in Toronto's Yorkville coffeehouses at seventeen and made his first appearance at the Mariposa Folk Festival in 1966. Musically his styles have ranged from folk to country to rock and, most recently, back to country. The durable McLauchlan has won nearly every Juno award Canada has to offer to folk/country performers. In 1973 McLauchlan won Juno awards for "Best Folk Single," "Best Country Single," and "Composer of the Year." He has won at least six Junos as "Country Male Vocalist," between 1976 and 1986. His instantly recognizable voice is embedded inextricably into the memory of folk music fans who listened their way through the 1970's. During the 80's and early 90's McLauchlan became a radio host for the CBC, first with his *Timberline* series and then with *Swingin' On A Star*.

Unfortunately most of his solo albums from the 70's are out of print and have not yet been reissued as compact discs. Fortunately *Greatest Hits* brings back some of the memories. Once again you can listen to "The Farmer's Song," "On The Boulevard," "Down By The Henry Moore," "Little Dreamer," and "Honky Red." McLauchlan has continued to grow as a songwriter since the 70's. *The Modern Age*, released in 1990 displays his writing talents on such powerful numbers as "The Modern Age" and "The Berlin Wall." The arrangements are more electrified and McLauchlan's singing has matured.

✳✳✳✳✓   **Greatest Hits**
1972-78 True North (WTNK-35)

Honky Red; Farmer's Song; On The Boulevard; Do You Dream Of Being Somebody; Hard Rock Town; Little Dreamer; Exiles; Child's Song; Shoeshine Workin' Song; Maybe Tonight; Down By The Henry Moore *44:57*

✳✳✳✳   **The Modern Age**
1990 Capitol (C2 95523)†

The Modern Age; Berlin Wall; Woman In A Checkout Line; So I Lost Your Love; Elvis Will Save The World; The Last Great War; Let The Good Guys Win; Back With You Tonight; When I Was Down; I'll Stand By You; Women Like That; Brownstone Streets *54:21*

Les Méchants Maquereaux
ACADIAN; FRENCH CANADIAN; SINGER-SONGWRITERS

Les Méchants Maquereaux, an electric-trad Acadian band from New Brunswick, has turned out a fine album with its initial release, *Les Méchants Maquereaux*. Winner of the East Coast Music Award "Acadian Recording Artist of the Year" in 1995, the album bounces with dance-oriented music laced with accordion, fiddle, acoustic instruments, electric guitar, and drums. The upbeat songs and tunes "Bayou Têche," "Stomp Du Lac Arthur," and "Acadie De Nos Coeurs" are written by band members. French lyrics are included. Les Méchants Maquereaux consists of Roland Gauvin, Johnny Comeau, Clarence Deveau, Jac Gautreau, Martin Melanson, and Charles Goguen.

✻✻✻(✻)   **Les Méchants Maquereaux**
1994 Hued (MM CD 940801)†

Bayou Têche; Stomp Du Lac Arthur; Le Départ Du Soldat; Danse Avec Moi; Acadie De Nos Coeurs; Oh Bébé; La Femme De L'Ivrogne; La Maquereel; Je M'Ennuie De Mon Pays; Ode À Marcel *34:20*

The Men Of The Deeps
MEN'S CHORUS; COAL-MINING SONGS

The Men Of The Deeps, Cape Breton's coal miners' chorus was founded in 1966. *Diamonds In The Rough* is a collection of some of the most popular arrangements recorded and performed by the chorus during its first twenty-five years. As you might expect, many of the songs have a mining theme, such as "Thirty-Inch Coal," "Dark As A Dungeon," "Coal Tattoo," "Sixteen Tons," and "Dust In The Air." A lovely, honest work that will please anyone who enjoys choral music.

✻✻✻(✻)   **Diamonds In The Rough**
[no date] Men Of The Deeps (MDCD-1025)

Thirty-Inch Coal; Dark As A Dungeon; Coal Tattoo; Sixteen Tons; I Went To Norman's; Man With A Torch In His Cap; Coal Is King Again; Working Man; Coal By The Sea; Mary Ann; Are You From Bevan?; Dust In The Air; Plain Ole Miner Boy; No. 26 Mine Disaster; Farewell To The Rhonda; Rise Again *50:04*

Scott Merritt
FOLK/ROCK; SINGER-SONGWRITER

"Scott Merritt is a masterful songwriter whose songs are clever, quirky and insightful"—Festival of Friends *Program Guide, 1994*. Ontario singer-songwriter and Juno nominee Scott Merritt has been a part of the folk scene for many years, frequently performing as part of groups such as Fred J. Eaglesmith's Flying Squirrels. On his solo album, *Violet And Black*, he presents his electric-folk music through a collection of original material. He has been labelled "a songwriter for the nineties," "one of Canada's finest exports," and "an original." Audiences enjoy the honesty and perception behind Merritt's lyrics.

✻✻✻   **Violet And Black**
1989 Duke Street (X2 13017)†

Burning Train; Bell To Bell; Sweet Accident; Are You Sending; Violet And Black; Radio Home; Copetown; Wild Kingdom; Blue Field *46:24*

Don Messer
FIDDLE; COUNTRY

Born in Tweedside, Prince Edward Island, in 1909, Don Messer became one of the most popular and influential performers in Canadian history. From early radio shows, featuring Don Messer and the New Brunswick Lumberjacks to the extraordinarily successful CBC-TV show *Don Messer's Jubilee*, featuring Don Messer and His Islanders, Messer influenced over three generations of Canadian musicians. Messer's excellent fiddling, which was broadcast across Canada and was made widely available on phonograph recordings, is said to have eliminated many pockets of traditional fiddling. Young fiddlers all wanted to sound like Don Messer and they copied his quick, steady rhythms and techniques, often abandoning local traditions. A more positive aspect of Messer's popularity was that he introduced thousands of listeners and viewers to traditional music and to talented performers like Catherine MacKinnon, Stompin' Tom Connors, and Graham Townsend, to name but a few. Messer insisted that his music was "not Western or cowboy music. Our tunes have been around for two or three hundred years. They're folk tunes passed from generation to generation"—*Encyclopedia of Music in Canada*. Among the many tributes to Don Messer, one of his fiddles resides in the Country Music Hall of Fame in Nashville, and Messer has been inducted into the Porcupine Awards Hall of Fame.

No serious collection of Canadian folk music can exist without a Don Messer CD or two. *Don Messer And His Islanders* and *The Very Best Of Don Messer* are both readily available. *The Very Best*, which features nearly 60 minutes of music, is a particularly good buy.

✳✳✳✳ **Don Messer And His Islanders**
[no date] Rodeo (SBSCD 5266)

Anniversary Schottische; Poor Girls Waltz; Plaza Polka; Westphalia Waltz; Lamplighter Hornpipe; Buckwheat Batter; Hannigans Hornpipe; Interlake Waltz; Riley's Favourite Reel; Pilot Mound Waltz; Grant Lambs Breakdown; The Girl I Left Behind *32:33*

✳✳✳✳✓ **The Very Best Of Don Messer**
[no date, reissued 1994] MCA (MCAD 4037)

The Great Atlantic Breakdown; Maple Leaf 2 Step; Blue Mountain Rag; Red River Waltz; Road To The Isles; Red Wing; Bowing The Strings; Woodchopper's Breakdown; Lamplighter's Hornpipe; Backwoodsman Reel; The Centennial Waltz; The Shannon Waltz; Atlantic Polka (1-4); Highland Hornpipe; Hill Lilly; Big John MacNeil/The Dusty Miller's Reel; Rustic Rig; Flop Eared Mule; Mother's Reel; The Dawn Waltz *58:34*

Lynn Miles
FOLK/POP; SINGER-SONGWRITER

"A singer with a fabulous voice who should be heard often and in large helpings"—*Dirty Linen*. Ottawa-based singer-songwriter Lynn Miles has been performing throughout Canada, the United States, and Europe for over a decade, appearing at most of Canada's festivals, including Winnipeg, Edmonton, Mariposa, and Summerfolk. Her lyrics probe themes from a distinctly northern point of view. Lynn says of her songwriting: "I often curse the winter, and lately have been leaving it as often as I can, but it's an indelible fact of Canadian life, and it does make us different. The things I write about—beauty, heartbreak, humour and survival—I approach quite differently from the way a southern songwriter would." *Chalk This One Up To The Moon*, from 1991, features these themes on songs like "All I Ever Wanted," "It's Hockey Night In Canada," "Whisky," "Nobody's Angel," and "The Venus Hotel." *Slightly Haunted* continues these themes with "The Ghost Of Deadlock," "This Heart That Lived In Winter," and "Loneliness." Miles' expressive, soaring vocals and deft guitar work are a treat.

❋❋❋(❋)   **Chalk This One Up To The Moon**
1991 Snowy River (SRR-S30-CD)†

All I Ever Wanted; It's Gone; It's Hockey Night In Canada; I Can't Tell You Why; Whiskey; Roses And Intentions; Nobody's Angel; A Little Rain; It'll Be Here; The Venus Motel; Never Again; A Bell Will Ring *46:35*

❋❋❋(❋)✓ **Slightly Haunted**
1995 [TBA]

You Don't Love Me Anymore; The Ghost Of Deadlock; I Always Told You The Truth; Loneliness; This Heart That Lives In Winter; I Loved A Cowboy; Long Time Coming; Last Night; I Know It Was Love; Big Brown City; I'm Still Here

Will Millar
CELTIC FOLK

Co-founder of the Irish Rovers, Vancouver Island resident Will Millar has gone on to a solo career that embraces children's music and Celtic instrumental music. Every folk collection should have a few children's albums and Millar's *The Keeper* fills this need well. With classics like "Waltzing With Bears," "The Tree Planting Song," and the inevitable Rovers hits, "The Unicorn" and "Biplane Evermore," this is an enjoyable collection of kid's songs that doesn't slick them up beyond decency. *The Lark In The Clear Aire*, a collection of instrumental Celtic tunes, is something of a surprise. It's an easy-listening, New Agey kind of album that features well-known pieces like "Carrickfergus," "Ashokan Farewell," and "Farewell To Tarwathie."
    See also The Irish Rovers

❋❋❋✓   **The Keeper**
1994 Attic (KACD 1400)

Just A Little Bitty Ball; The Tree Planting Song; The Keeper; Waltzing With Bears; Windy Old Weather; Hey Li Le Li Le Lo; The Unicorn; If We Try; A Place In The Choir; Sailing On The Bay; Bog Down In The Valley-O; The Biplane 'Evermore; Reel In The Flickering Light *38:56*

❋❋❋   **The Lark In The Clear Aire**
1994 Chacra (CHACD 042)

The Lark In The Clear Aire/My Singing Bird; Slieve Gallon Braes/Sally Gardens; The Irish Brigade-1864: Bold Fenian Men/Hills Of Shiloh/Skibereen/Ashokan Farewell; Carickfergus/Mary Of Dungloe; The Lark In The Clear Aire (Reprise);

Bonnie Kellswater; Factory Girls: Mo Mhuirnin Ban/By The Banks Of The Bann/
Factory Girls; Flower Of Sweet Straban; Islands: Dark Island/Mist Covered
Mountains/Rhumm/Farewell To Tarwathie *48:45*

Cathy Miller

FOLK/POP; SINGER-SONGWRITER

Calgary-based Cathy Miller, originally from Ottawa, is a singer, songwriter, and children's entertainer. Miller's music, which started out as folk with a twist ("I've never been able to write a three-chord wonder," she says) was heavily influenced by artists such as Connie Kaldor, Ian Tamblyn, and Bonnie Raitt and evolved to include blues and jazz influences. A popular festival performer and songwriting workshop leader, Miller has released two previous albums available on cassette: *Superwoman: Cathy Goes Camping* and *Footprints On The Moon*. Her third album, and first CD, *Dance Beneath The Moon* is a jazz-flavoured album that demonstrates Miller's new western influences with an acoustic approach that dominates the sound. Highlights include the title track, "Dance Beneath The Moon," "Ride The Wind," "Living In The Martinique," and "In A Perfect World." This is an album you keep coming back to, listen after listen.

❊❊❊(❊)　**Dance Beneath The Moon**
　　　　1991　Sealed With A Kiss Records (SWAK CD03)†

Dance Beneath The Moon; Ride The Wind; Smith Boys; Living In The Martinique; I Had A House; Desert Dancing; Empty In The Sunrise; No Point Of View; Two People; Indian Summer; In A Perfect World *44:40*

Joni Mitchell

FOLK/POP/JAZZ; SINGER-SONGWRITER

Brilliantly-gifted singer-songwriter and Juno Hall of Famer Joni Mitchell began her musical career playing Toronto's chief folk venues—The Riverboat and the Mariposa Folk Festival—in the mid 1960's. From the start it was obvious that she was unique and unusually talented. With her exotic open guitar tunings and her intensely personal, highly-charged lyrics, Mitchell acquired a huge following on the folk circuit before she became an international star. Her music quickly grew beyond what anyone would call folk music. Never afraid to experiment, Mitchell ranges widely between folk, folk/rock, jazz, and fusions of all three. From an audience point of view, some of her explorations have been more successful than others.

Mitchell's early period is the one most universally loved by her many fans, for it was this period that introduced her indelible sound and style and many of her best, if youthful, lyrics. Mitchell's early recordings became part of the fabric of the "flower-power" era. *Joni Mitchell*, from 1968, was originally divided into two sides, "I Came To The City," and "Out Of The City And Down To The Seaside"—a distinction lost on CD. *Clouds*, reveals a more confident Mitchell who has found her sound. The entire album is a gallery of Mitchell classics, including "Chelsea Morning," "Songs To Aging Children Come," "Both Sides Now," and the haunting "Tin Angel." The 1970 *Ladies Of The Canyon* is archetypal early Mitchell. From "Morning Morgantown," through songs like "For Free," "Ladies Of The Canyon," "The Arrangement," "Big

Yellow Taxi," to the closer, "The Circle Game," this is the album to purchase for those who want to revel in nostalgia.

Blue, released in 1971, is widely acclaimed as one of the finest albums Mitchell has ever done. Darker, more intimate, and more mature than her previous work, it includes masterful creations such as "All I Want," "Carey," "Blue," "California," "River," "A Case Of You," and "The Last Time I Saw Richard." Essential. *For The Roses*, 1972, features songs like "Banquet," "Cold Blue Steel And Sweet Fire," "For The Roses," and "You Turn Me On I'm A Radio." The 1974 album *Court And Spark* may be Mitchell's best-known and best-loved recording. Backed by outstanding jazz and rock musicians, the album represents the high-water mark of Mitchell's early career. From "Court And Spark" to the jazz classic "Twisted," this durable album wears well, still sounding fabulous over the years. The live album, *Miles Of Aisles*, another 1974 release, may be one of Mitchell's more underrated works. Backed by a good folk/rock band, the L.A. Express, Mitchell is in fine voice as she puts a new spin on her work.

With the 1975 release, *Hissing Of Summer Lawns*, Mitchell began to change direction into the experimental music that characterizes her "middle" period. The change between *Court And Spark* and *Hissing* was too abrupt for some fans. Songs like "The Jungle Line," "Don't Interrupt The Sorrow," "The Hissing Of Summer Lawns," and "Shadows And Light" are fascinating, but more demanding than her earlier work. The songs don't latch onto your psyche the way her earlier ones do. Sounding as if it could have been recorded in the 90's, *Hejira*, from 1976, is the most successful of Mitchell's mid-period work. It includes memorable songs like "Coyote," "Amelia," "Hejira," and "Refuge Of The Roads." The album features Mitchell exploring the textures and tapestries available on the electric guitar. *Don Juan's Reckless Daughter*, an album "which was very unpopular in the white community, was understood by the black community," according to Mitchell. This 1977 release left a lot of early fans behind. The distance between *Don Juan* and *For The Roses* was too great. *Don Juan* continues the exploration of rhythms and sounds that characterize her middle period. If *Don Juan* bothered fans, it was nothing compared to *Mingus*, Mitchell's 1979 album that carried her further into her avant garde explorations. Most fans, as well as critics, remain convinced that Mitchell's voice and lyrics were not meant for jazz. The 1980 *Shadows And Light* release is another live recording. A perhaps defiant Mitchell selected material almost exclusively from her middle period, as if turning her back on her early and more popular work.

Wild Things Run Fast, from 1982, is Mitchell's first album for Geffen and her first collaboration with Larry Klein. It takes Mitchell into her "contemporary" period, away from the jazz-based experimentalism of her middle period and back to a concentration on lyrics. Unlike her early albums, the instrumentation is very modern, with electric instruments and synthesized sounds. The 1985 *Dog Eat Dog* is a work that Mitchell describes this way: "*Dog Eat Dog* was a synthetic keyboard album, but I'm playing most of it. People think somebody has smeared all of this over me, but it is me, playing with a wider palette" (Interview in *Impact*, December 1994). For most fans, one of her least successful experiments. *Chalk Mark In A Rain Storm*, 1988, reunites Mitchell with Larry Klein as co-producers. The emphasis is back on lyrics (set among highly complex musical tapestries).

The 1991 album *Night Ride Home* is the first Mitchell album in years that is an unqualified success. This Mitchell/Klein recording features some of the best lyrics Mitchell has written in over a decade and although her voice is a ghost of its former self, the mature, penetrating songwriting is a joy to listen to. Highlights include "Night Ride Home," the stunning "Cherokee Louise," "Slouching Towards Bethlehem," and "The Only Joy In Town." The rich sound of Mitchell's acoustic, open-chord tunings is a pleasant relief from the instrumentation of her middle period. *Turbulent Indigo*, a 1994 recording, takes up from where *Night Ride* leaves off and does it one better. Her reduced vocal range notwithstanding, this might be the best Mitchell album ever. While not as prettily lyrical as her early work, the biting lyrics form a powerful album that grows on you play after play. Highlights include "Sunny Sunday," "Turbulent Indigo," "The Magdalene Laundries," and "Borderline."

❋❋❋ **Joni Mitchell**
1968 Reprise (CD 6293)

I Had A King; Michael From Mountains; Night In The City; Marcie; Nathan La Franeer; Sisotowbell Lane; The Dawntreader; The Pirate Of Penance; Song To A Seagull; Cactus Tree *38:03*

❋❋❋❋ **Clouds**
1969 Reprise (CD 6341)†

Tin Angel; Chelsea Morning; I Don't Know Where I Stand; That Song About The Midway; Roses Blue; The Gallery; I Think I Understand; Songs To Aging Children Come; The Fiddle And The Drum; Both Sides, Now *37:44*

❋❋❋❋ **Ladies Of The Canyon**
1970 Reprise (CD 6376)†

Morning Morgantown; For Free; Conversation; Ladies Of The Canyon; Willy; The Arrangement; Rainy Night House; The Priest; Blue Boy; Big Yellow Taxi; Woodstock; The Circle Game *44:58*

❋❋❋❋✓ **Blue**
1971 Reprise (CD 2038)†

All I Want; My Old Man; Little Green; Carey; Blue; California; This Flight Tonight; River; A Case Of You; The Last Time I Saw Richard *36:13*

❋❋❋(❋) **For The Roses**
1972 Asylum (5057-2)†

Banquet; Cold Blue Steel And Sweet Fire; Barangrill; Lesson In Survival; Let The Wind Carry Me; For The Roses; See You Sometime; Electricity; You Turn Me On I'm A Radio; Blonde In The Bleachers; Woman Of Heart And Mind; Judgement Of The Moon And Stars (Ludwig's Tune) *40:25*

❋❋❋❋✓ **Court And Spark**
1973 Elektra / Asylum (CD 1001)†

Court And Spark; Help Me; Free Man In Paris; People's Parties; Same Situation; Car On A Hill; Down To You; Just Like This Train; Raised On Robbery; Trouble Child; Twisted *36:58*

❋❋❋(❋) **Miles Of Aisles**
1974 Elektra / Asylum (202-2)

You Turn Me On I'm A Radio; Big Yellow Taxi; Rainy Night House; Woodstock; Cactus Tree; Cold Blue Steel And Sweet Fire; Woman Of Heart And Mind; A Case Of You; Blue; Circle Game; People's Parties; All I Want; Real Good For Free; Both Sides Now; Carey; The Last Time I Saw Richard; Jericho; Love Or Money *74:05*

❋❋❋ **The Hissing Of Summer Lawns**
1975 Elektra / Asylum (1051-2)†

In France They Kiss On Main Street; The Jungle Line; Edith And The Kingpin; Don't Interrupt The Sorrow; Shades Of Scarlett Conquering; The Hissing Of Summer Lawns; The Boho Dance; Harry's House/Centerpiece; Sweet Bird; Shadows And Light *42:37*

❋❋❋❋✓ **Hejira**
1976 Elektra / Asylum (CD 1087)†

Coyote; Amelia; Furry Sings The Blues; A Strange Boy; Hejira; Song For Sharon; Black Crow; Blue Motel Room; Refuge Of The Roads *51:55*

❋❋❋ **Don Juan's Reckless Daughter**
1977 Elektra / Asylum (701-2)†

Overture—Cotton Avenue; Talk To Me; Jericho; Paprika Plains; Otis And Marlena; The Tenth World; Dreamland; Don Juan's Reckless Daughter; Off Night Backstreet; The Silky Veils Of Ardor *59:41*

❋❋(❋) **Mingus**
1979 Elektra / Asylum (505-2)

Happy Birthday 1975 (RAP); God Must Be A Boogie Man; Funeral (RAP); A Chair In The Sky; The Wolf That Lives In Lindsey; I's A Muggin' (RAP); Sweet Sucker Dance; Coin In The Pocket (RAP); The Dry Cleaner From Des Moines; Lucky (RAP); Goodbye Pork Pie Hat *37:24*

❋❋❋ **Shadows And Light**
1980 Elektra / Asylum (704-2)

Introduction; In France They Kiss On Main Street; Edith And The Kingpin; Coyote; Goodbye Pork Pie Hat; The Dry Cleaner From Des Moines; Amelia; Pat's Solo; Hejira; Dreamland; Band Introduction; Furry Sings The Blues; Why Do Fools Fall In Love; Shadows And Light; God Must Be A Boogie Man; Woodstock *72:24*

❋❋❋ **Wild Things Run Fast**
1982 Geffen (GEFMD 2019)†

Chinese Cafe/Unchained Melody; Wild Things Run Fast; Ladies' Man; Moon At The Window; Solid Love; Be Cool; (You're So Square) Baby, I Don't Care; You Dream Flat Tires; Man To Man; Underneath The Streetlight; Love *36:44*

❋❋(❋) **Dog Eat Dog**
1985 Geffen (GEFD-24074)†

Good Friends; Fiction; The Three Great Stimulants; Tax Free; Smokin' (Empty, Try Another); Dog Eat Dog; Shiny Toys; Ethiopia; Impossible Dreamer; Lucky Girl *43:30*

❀❀❀ **Chalk Mark In A Rain Storm**
1988 Geffen (CD 24172)†

My Secret Place; Number One; Lakota; The Tea Leaf Prophecy (Lay Down Your Arms); Dancin' Clown; Cool Water; The Beat Of Black Wings; Snakes And Ladders; The Reoccurring Dream; A Bird That Whistles (Corrina, Corrina) *46:24*

❀❀❀(❀) **Night Ride Home**
1991 Geffen (GEFSD 24302)†

Night Ride Home; Passion Play (When All The Slaves Are Free); Cherokee Louise; The Windfall (Everything For Nothing); Slouching Towards Bethlehem; Come In From The Cold; Nothing Can Be Done; The Only Joy In Town; Ray's Dad's Cadillac; Two Grey Rooms *51:42*

❀❀❀❀✓ **Turbulent Indigo**
1994 Reprise (9 45786-2)†

Sunny Sunday; Sex Kills; How Do You Stop; Turbulent Indigo; Last Chance Lost; The Magdalene Laundries; Not To Blame; Borderline; Yvette In English; The Sire Of Sorrow (Job's Sad Song) *43:05*

Michael Mitchell

TRADITIONAL FOLK

Ottawa troubadour Michael Mitchell has led a dual career, as an officer in the Canadian Armed Forces, and as an entertainer who sings Scottish, Irish, and Canadian folksongs at clubs and in schools. Among his accomplishments, he is also the author of the book *Ducimus—The Regiments Of The Canadian Infantry*. Mitchell's albums are theme based. *Lest We Forget* is a collection of songs "dedicated to the men and women who have defended the peace and freedom of our nation on the field of honour." Mitchell's delivery of Bogle's "The Band Played Waltzing Matilda" and "No Man's Land," Whittaker's "The Last Farewell," and the traditional "Arthur McBride" stand up well. *Pub Night, Volume 1* is an uptempo set of songs recorded live. Highlights include "The Hills Of Connemara," "Silver Sea," "Streets Of London," and "Farewell To Nova Scotia." *Canada Is ...* is a collection of songs about Canada including "Log Drivers Waltz," "Sonny's Dream," "Canadian Railroad Trilogy," and "Canada Is." The similarly titled *Canada Is For Kids* is an album of songs about Canada aimed at schools. There's a separate book of lyrics and music that can be purchased to be used with singalongs.

❀❀❀ **Lest We Forget**
[no date] MKM (SA94201)†

Banks Of Sicily; The Last Farewell; Bonnie Dundee; Heaven Help The Devil; The Band Played Waltzing Matilda; Fare Thee Well Enniskillen; A Scottish Soldier; Arthur McBride; The Peat Bog Soldier; No Man's Land *38:01*

❀❀❀ **Pub Night, Volume 1**
[no date] MKM (SA94202)†

The Hills Of Connemara; Waltzing Matilda; Gypsy Rover; The Orange And The

Green; Song For The Mira; Silver Sea; Streets Of London; Bold O'Donoghue; Farewell To Nova Scotia; Skye Boat Song; Black Velvet Band; Working Man; Lord Of The Dance; Danny Boy; Scotland The Brave *56:40*

❋❋❋ **Canada Is ...**
[no date] MKM (SA94246CD)†

Log Drivers Waltz; Sonny's Dream; Canadian Railroad Trilogy; Nous Vivons Ensemble; The Island; The York Boat Brigade; Rolling Down To Old Maui; Roseville Fair; Canada Is ... *38:04*

❋❋❋(❋) **Canada Is For Kids**
[no date] MKM (MKMC 1004)

Something To Sing About; Little Trees; I'se The B'y; The Island; Farewell To Nova Scotia; V'La L'Bon Vent; Canada In My Pocket; This Land Is Your Land; Log Driver's Waltz; Lady Franklin's Lament; Alberta Bound; The Bluenose; Fly High; Canada Is ... *42:42*

Ann Mortifee
FOLK/NEW AGE; SINGER-SONGWRITER

Loosely associated with the folk circuit, British Columbia singer-songwriter Ann Mortifee brings her full, theatrical voice to original songs that lean towards the New Age side of the musical spectrum. Mortifee's fifth album, and her first CD, *Serenade At The Doorway*, is described as "songs to support and inspire a healing journey." The liner notes preface the lyrics with this passage: "We are forever at a doorway, going through endings and beginnings; being born or dying to a relationship, a dream, a way of being or to life itself. Those who have gone before us through the doorway, must yearn to send word to those of us who linger awhile." This theme is carried forward to her sixth album and second CD, *Healing Journey*. There are elements of the music that may remind some fans of the work of Irish singer-songwriter Enya. Highlights include "Healing Journey," "Baptism," "Oriental Breeze," "Shankarananda," and "When The Rains Come." Mortifee's voice is undeniably beautiful throughout, but the delivery may not be rootsy enough for some fans.

❋❋❋ **Serenade At The Doorway**
1990 Jabula (JR 043)†

Come With Me; I Always Thought I'd Have Tomorrow; Healing Journey; How Can I Say Good-Bye; Anger is A Fever; I Won't Stay Silent Any Longer; As Each Moment Goes By; Alone; The Garden Gate/Lead Me On *50:57*

❋❋❋ **Healing Journey**
1994 Jabula (JR 046)†

Healing Journey; Baptism; Gypsy Born; Oriental Breeze; Tyger! Tyger!; Shankarananda; Streets Of Banaras; Are You Lonely; Goodbye My Love; Born To Live; Take Me Back; Just One Voice; I Won't Stay Silent; Zulu Fairy Tale; When The Rains Come *67:02*

Brian Morton
FOLK; SINGER-SONGWRITER

Hamilton, Ontario singer-songwriter Brian Morton has been deeply inspired by Stan Rogers, as evidenced from the title of his first album, *A Lonely Cairn Of Stones*, a phrase from "Northwest Passage." Morton writes songs about incidents from Canadian history such as the sinking of the Canadian Pacific liner "The Empress Of Ireland," and "She's Gone Boys, She's Gone," about the fishing moratorium and its effects on Newfoundland. Morton also includes songs by other songwriters, including Scott Smith's "Green Town," Bill Gallaher's "The Last Battle," and Grit Laskin's "Where Does Love Come From." With great guest musicians, such as fiddlers Steve Fuller and Oliver Schroer, this is a solid debut album. Internet users may recognize Morton as the genial co-host of the "Northwest Passage" listserve *cdnfolk@io.org*.

❊❊❊   **A Lonely Cairn Of Stones**
1994 Theatre Erebus (BGM CD 1001)

The Empress Of Ireland; Green Town; Three Fishers; She's Gone Boys; The Nancy's Pride; U-Boat 534; The Maple Leaf Forever; The Last Battle; Friends Ain't Supposed To Die; Where Does Love Come From?; Young Jimmy In Flanders; Blind Dancers; The Franklin Trilogy: Lady Franklin's Lament/A Lonely Cairn Of Stones/Northwest Passage *73:45*

Moxy Früvous
HUMOUR/SATIRE/POLITICAL COMMENTARY

As Monty Python says, "And now for something completely different." Toronto-based Moxy Früvous sound like the Beach Boys doing Tom Lehrer. The sweet boyish harmonies (part of the comic effect) are laced with barbs, satire, political commentary, nonsense, and just plain fun. They began as an a cappella busker act working the Toronto subway system. The group, consisting of Mike Ford, Murray Foster, Jean Ghomeshi, and David Matheson write fresh, vibrantly fun material that is a counterpoint to the serious-mindedness that occasionally affects folksinger/songwriters. *Bargainville* presents the zany and highly original work that has made Moxy Früvous a catchy act on the folk circuit. Perhaps the funniest track is "King of Spain," a calypso-style ditty with quips like "Once I was the King of Spain / An' now I vacuum the turf at Skydome." Recommended for anyone who needs to shed some seriousness.

❊❊❊   **Bargainville**
1993 Warner (WEA CD 93134)

River Valley; Stuck In The 90's; B.J. Don't Cry; Video Bargainville; Fell In Love; The Lazy Boy; My Baby Loves A Bunch Of Authors; The Drinking Song; Morphée; King Of Spain; Darlington Darling; Bittersweet; Laika; Spiderman; Gulf War Song *52:07*

The Nationals
BLUES; SINGER-SONGWRITERS

The Nationals, a Toronto blues trio, are Brian Cober, Paul McNamara, and Nick Kent. Fronted by Cober, who uses a unique method of double slide playing (using slides on the fourth finger and thumb), *Piece Of Wood*, their first CD, features good instrumentals mixed with hard, raw blues songs.

❋❋❋ **Piece Of Wood**
1994 Chester (CHESTER02)†

> Walk The Line; I Can't Fight; I Long; Trouble Looks For Me; In Among The Trees; Statesboro Blues; I'm Over Here, She's Over There; Poor Boy; Piece Of Wood; Fifth Column Theme; Reds R Blues; Live-a This Life *40:18*

Nazka
LATIN-AMERICAN; SINGER-SONGWRITERS

Nazka, a Toronto-based group originally from Chile, expresses its engaging Latin-American rhythms, instrumentation, and vocals on *Latino American Music*. Nazka's blend of percussion, strings, and Andean winds is accompanied by vocals and, here and there, a touch of soft trumpet. This easy-listening album provides a gentle starting point for those interested in exploring world music. Nazka is Rodrigo Chávez, Lisa Lindo, Edgardo Moreno, José Sanhueza, and Miguel Vásquez.

❋❋❋ **Latino American Music**
1993 Nazka (N002-93)

> A La Orilla De La Cuidad; Silencio En Lima; Me Gusta Elena; Conversacion; Asi Suavecito; Coplas De Cantaclaro; La Vida Simple; Que Se Quema El Zango; San Pedro De Cayambe; Sikuriada Del Alba; Cueca De Dos Lugares; Los Matarifes/Yo Soy Dueño Del Baron *49:17*

New Earth
FOLK/NEW AGE/JAZZ INSTRUMENTALS

New Earth is a musical collaborative in Victoria, British Columbia consisting of Scott Sheerin, Niel Golden, and Dan Rubin. Playing instruments as varied as bouzouki, tabla, flute, sax, piano, guitar, tamboura, cekow, Chinese balls, violin, bansuri, tongue drum, and tabla tarang, their album *Music From Canada's West Coast*, with its unusual rhythms and exotic tapestry of sounds, is a listener's delight.

❋❋❋(❋) **Music From Canada's West Coast**
1991 New Earth (NSD111CD)

> Papardom; Flows Like A Wave; Chio; Solstice; Cherimoya; Chinese Balls; Bethlehem; Limahuli Lullaby; Passing The Verandah; Elephant Morning; Little One; Bing Bang Bong; Angular Chicken *51:58*

Ngoma
SALSA-FLAVOURED ECLECTIC WORLD MIX

Perhaps it's due to the long winters and the historical absence of exotic music, but Canadian music fans have increasingly been drawn to Latin music as more performers from Latin and Caribbean countries have entered the Canadian mainstream. Ngoma, a salsa-flavoured band with a mixed makeup, puts together a good salsa sound on *Culturally Modified Stone*. From the opener, "Everybody's Got Some Culture" to "Tout Est Possible" to "Ivory And Gold," there's plenty of listening here for salsa fans. Ngoma is Marcos X, Dan Cook, Vicki Rae, Karine Zamor, Wendie dB, Allain Allain, Tia Real, and Mike Eby.

✻✻✻(✻)   **Culturally Modified Stone**
1994 Ngoma (NCD 09406)

> Everybody's Got Some Culture; Solution; Tout Est Possible; Ivory And Gold; Agitator; Do Me A Favour; Directions; Breakfast; Need; Batucada IV *38:28*

Night Sun
FOLK/POP; SINGER-SONGWRITERS

Night Sun, a folk/pop band from Iqualuit in the Northwestern Territories, brings a strong sense of the Far North to their music. With lyrics and lead vocals by Ellen Hamilton, *Calling* starts off with "Damn This Wind," a song that, according to the liner notes, conveys "how the North is a constant nag at my heart whenever I flirt with going south." "You're Not Bad" deals with the problem of how so many northern, native boys, "despite their beauty and potential, have a better chance of going to jail than graduating from high school." "8 Months Of Snow" is a song Hamilton wrote as a teenager in Holman, an Inuvialuit community on the Beaufort Sea. Hamilton's soft, earthy vocals are backed up by Paul Meggs, Chris Coleman, Bob Longworth, and Erik Coleman.

✻✻✻   **Calling**
1993 Night Sun (NSCD 002)†

> Damn This Wind; You're Not Bad; Alone; Figure It Out; Different Kinda Love; Your Heart Calls; Kisses And Sighs; Midnight Sun; 8 Months Of Snow; Make It Right; Ride *47:26*

Faith Nolan
FOLK/BLUES/ROCK; SINGER-SONGWRITER

"Growing up in Halifax, Nova Scotia, and, later Toronto's working class Cabbagetown, deepened her commitment to representing the lives of Black and working class peoples in her songs. Her life experiences, and those of the women she grew up with, fill her songs. Her music is her political work. A politic firmly rooted in her Black working-class womanhood"—Dionne Brand, liner notes to *Freedom To Love*. Sometimes politically-oriented songs sacrifice musical excellence to statement, but such is not the case on *Freedom To Love*. This fine album will captivate you with its powerful mix of folk and blues. From the "Shake Sugaree" tribute to Elizabeth Cotten, to "Anna

Mae Aquash," who gave her life in the battle of First Nations peoples to retain their land and culture, this album succeeds lyrically *and* musically. *Freedom To Love* received the "Canadian Folk Blues" Porcupine Award in 1990.

❋❋❋(❋)✓ **Freedom To Love**
1989 Aural Tradition (ATRCD 302)†

Shake Sugaree; Freedom To Love; Where Does The Torturer Live?; Prove It On Me Blues; Anna Mae Aquash; Beloved Comrade; White, Brown, Black Blues; Aleticia; Jellyroll; Poor Glory; Strange Fruit; I Black Woman *33:57*

Chris Norman

WOODEN FLUTE; FOLK

A native of Halifax, Chris Norman began classical studies on flute at age ten with the aim of pursing an orchestral career. The lure of traditional music, however, drew him back to his roots when he was reintroduced to the folk tunes of Nova Scotia. An immensely talented flautist, his impeccable performances of dance tunes may seem, as one reviewer noted, just a bit too polite, but the overall effect is lovely. Both of his lengthy albums, *Man With The Wooden Flute* and *Beauty Of The North*, provide a relaxing way to enjoy the inner beauties of traditional music.

❋❋❋(❋)   **Man With The Wooden Flute**
1992 Dorian (DOR-90166)

Lament For James Moray Of Abercarney; Father Dollard's Favorite; The Flail; Guzzle Together; Isle Of Madeleine; Point Au Pic; Jacques Cartier; Bovaglie's Plaid; The Cradle Song; I Won't Do The Work; Thousand Pipers; The Road To Skye; Man Of Constant Sorrow; Chinkapin Hunting; King Of Naples; The Belle Of The Stage; The Fairy Queen; Hugh O'Donnell; Dry N' Dusty; Rochester Schottische; Frosty Morning; Shuffle About; The Wounded Hussar; Prince Charles'; The Prague; Mozart's Favorite; Northern March; Richard Dwyer's; High Road To Linton; Sleepy Waltz; An Irish Lullaby; Suo Gam *73:48*

❋❋❋(❋)✓ **The Beauty Of The North**
1994 Dorian (DOR-90190)

Highland Set: North Highland Country Dance/North Highland Country Dance/ Atlantic Polka/The Parry Sound/Nova Scotia; La Have River Set: La Have River Waltz/Quand Je Suis Près De Troi; Reel Montréal Set: Reel Montréal/Reel Amos/ Reel Rimouski/Reel St. Siméon; Valse Frontenac; Beauty Of The North Set: The Beauty Of The North/Rocky Brook/Castle Bay/Cape Wrath/Banks Of Newfoundland/Scotch Cove/Gigue De Joliette; Valse Parisienne; Chicoutimi Set: Reel De Chicoutimi/Reel St. Jean/ Reel Éboulement; Mull Set: Dirge Of Mull/Mull Rant/The Way To Mull River/Sound Of Mull/Mull River *60:07*

Bertha Norwegian

FIRST NATIONS MUSIC; SINGER-SONGWRITER

Bertha Norwegian, based in the Northwest Territories, has been a consultant on the CBC television show *North Of 60* as well as being a recording artist who performs striking original songs written by herself and her sister Bernadette Norwegian. Her album *Spearmaidens* contains songs that spread into your consciousness like snow sifting onto the landscape. Haunting, beautiful tracks like "Anthem Of The North," "The Swan Song," and "Spearmaidens" are among the album's highlights. Unusual and rewarding.

❊❊❊(❊)   **Spearmaidens**
1992 Bertha Norwegian [no catalogue number]†

Anthem Of The North; The Swan Song; Often I'm A Young Tree; Nomad; Early Fall; Two Agonies; Winter Hills; Spearmaidens *39:16*

Gary William O'Hart
FOLK; SINGER-SONGWRITER

Kitchener, Ontario singer-songwriter Gary William O'Hart has released a Celtic-oriented album, *Ninth Night Beyond Tara*, tinged with an alt-rock vocal delivery. The more successful cuts on the album are the traditional numbers, "An Gréasaí Bróg," "As I Roved Out," "À La Claire Fontaine," and "The Four Marys." Even these will stretch your ears if you're accustomed to a more melodic approach to singing.

❊❊(❊)   **Ninth Night Beyond Tara**
1993 Sound On Sound (SOS 193)†

Mysterious; An Gréasaí Bróg; Good Mornin' New Orleans; Sea Song; Wait For You; As I Roved Out; À La Claire Fontaine; Surreal Killer; The Four Marys; Moira; Cnoc Ná Sláine *52:36*

Tom O'Keefe
FOLK/POP; SINGER-SONGWRITER

Nova Scotia singer-songwriter Tom O'Keefe writes contemporary songs in a Maritimes Celtic/country style. Highlights from *Beyond The Dawn* include "Fly Away," "The Gift," "The Kitchen Racket," and "Beyond The Dawn." His pleasant voice and downhome lyrics create an easy-listening album that is great for relaxing to at the end of a busy day.

❊❊❊   **Beyond The Dawn**
1991 Overtom (OPCD004)

Fly Away; Girls Of Neil's Harbour; The Gift; The Kitchen Racket; Home Of My Heart; Nightwind; Sweet City Lady; Rosetown's Garden Girl; Sons Of Steel; Better Days Ahead; Beyond The Dawn *38:47*

The Octet
MARITIME FIDDLE TUNES

The Octet was a collaboration between a quartet of Atlantic Symphony musicians and some well-known Maritime traditional musicians. They created one album—*Songs Of The Cape*—before disbanding. The album, recorded in 1986 and recently reissued on CD, includes traditional tunes plus original reels and jigs written by Cape Breton musicians. "The group successfully blends classical sophistication and Celtic energy without exposing any of the seams that hold the whole project together so cohesively"—

Dirty Linen. The Octet is Scott Macmillan, guitar, bass; Andrew Russell, guitar, banjo; Dave MacIsaac, guitar, fiddle; Louis Benoit, mandolin; Karen Langille, first violin; Jim Danson, second violin; Yvonne De Roller, Viola; and Joan Danson, cello.

✳✳✳ **Songs Of The Cape**
1986, reissued 1992 Atlantica (ATL 8888)

Songs Of The Cape (A Suite In Four Movements), Jigs: You're Only As Good As Your Last Gig Jig/Ronnie Rankin's Jig/Whitehorse Jig/Nicole Fakoory's Jig/Charles MacCuspic's Jig/Little Black Dog Jig/John Alphonse's Jig/Angela Cameron's Jig/Angus Chisholm's Jig; Mr. Winston Fitzgerald (Strathspey And Reel); Song For The Cape; Reels: My Friend's Reel/Joey Beaton's Reel/Jeannie And Bruz's 25th Wedding Anniversary Reel/John Allan Cameron's Reel; Tribute To Angus Chisholm: Glengarry's Dirk/The Bonnie Lass Of Fisherrow/The Bird's Nest/The Argyle Bowling Green; Atlantic Polka; Eflat-C Medley: The Banks Of Hornpipe/The Earl Of Hyndford/Sticky Buns; MacPherson's Medley: MacPherson's Blade/MacPherson's Rant *37:37*

Terry Odette
FOLK/ROCK; SINGER-SONGWRITER

Kitchener, Ontario singer-songwriter Terry Odette has released the CD *Without Wings* that features a collection of original material in a mix of styles. Highlights include "Through The Silence," "Without Wings," "All In Motion," and "Bigger Than It Was." Odette's bluesy voice carries the material well on this solid folk/rock album.

✳✳✳ **Without Wings**
1990 WART (CD1001)†

Through The Silence; God Loves A Racist Too; Without Wings; All In Motion; Help Along The Way; Theo; Bigger Than It Was; Up The Gate; Will You Wait For Me; Sweet Caress; Once In A Life *49:44*

Lowry Olafson
FOLK/POP/COUNTRY; SINGER-SONGWRITER

British Columbia singer-songwriter Lowry Olafson writes contemporary songs that blend folk, pop, and country elements. *Wind And Rain* features Olafson's strong, expressive voice on songs like "Sweet And Strong," "Someone To Love," "Nova Scotia," and "Wind And Rain." *Good Intentions* shows a maturing songwriter on cuts like "When The Time Is Right," "I Wish You Were Mine," "Desperate Wind," and "After The Rain." In addition to Olafson's excellent backup musicians, there's a guest appearance by Amos Garrett on "Journey" and "Time To Grow." Olafson is an emerging songwriter to watch.

✳✳✳ **Wind And Rain**
1992 Festival (LO 9201 CD)†

Sweet And Strong; Words; Someone To Love; Living In The Country; Nova Scotia; Blues Out On The Road; Prodigal Son; Who Will Be The Ones?; Wind And Rain; Just Call *30:32*

✳✳✳(✳) **Good Intentions**
1994 River (RR9402CD)†

> When The Time Is Right; I Wish You Were Here; Change Your Mind; Journey; Ring
> Telephone; Hiding Behind Your Pride; Good Intentions; One Last Goodnight; Time
> To Grow; Desperate Wind; After The Rain *43:45*

Open Mind
FOLK; SINGER-SONGWRITERS

Open Mind, a folk duo from Hamilton, Ontario, are a throwback to the sound of the
60's. Chantal Chamberland sings lead vocal and plays twelve-string guitar. Cynthia
Kerr, who sings and plays six-string, is the duo's songwriter. Accompanying themselves with strong guitar rhythms, their fresh material brightens up the stages at folk
festivals. *The Stones We Carry*, their first CD, includes songs like "Lion's Den,"
"Strange Places," "The Mystic," "Wishful Thinking," and what has become the duo's
trademark song, "Kent State And Kennedy," always sung with gusto. This is a good
album for those who enjoy strong lyrics performed simply—two guitars and a bass.
On *Suspect Terrain* there's additional instrumentation, giving Open Mind a fuller sound.
Highlights include "One More Night," "Jagged Edge," "The Wall," "All The Love,"
and "Frustration." *Live At Luna*, recorded live at La Luna in Hamilton, Ontario, captures the sound of Open Mind in concert. Supported solely by their own guitar work,
they provide the driving rhythms and infectious sound that makes them so much fun
at festivals. The album includes new songs, including "Fed Up," "Space In My Heart,"
and the lovely "Mississippi River." The recording quality is a bit rough.

✳✳✳ **The Stones We Carry**
1991 Open Mind (DTMS-001)

> Lion's Den; Strange Places; The Mystic; Kent State And Kennedy; Desperate Eyes;
> Wishful Thinking; Nina's Circle; Things I Know How To Do; Deadly Sins;
> Aphrodisiac *42:10*

✳✳✳(✳) **Suspect Terrain**
1993 Open Mind (DTMS-002)

> One More Night; Jagged Edge; The Wall; All The Love; Blue Box; Touch The Water;
> What Are We To Do; King Of Vague; Frustration; Heartbeat *39:54*

✳✳✳ **Live At La Luna**
1993, 1994 Open Mind (DTMS-003)

> Fed Up; Space In My Heart; Blue Box; Frustration; Insomnia; I Just Want You To
> Want Me; Mississippi River; Sociable!; All You Need; Undone (A.K.A. The Orgasm
> Song); Don't Let Me Down *42:43*

Orealis
CELTIC FOLK

Orealis, an English-singing group from Quebec, performs Celtic music with arrangements that include hammered dulcimer, bouzouki, tin whistle, keyboards, guitar, and
percussion. *Celtic Music* features songs like "Spencer The Rover," "The Trooper And

The Maid," "Highland Way," and "Rob Roy," intermixing instrumentals with vocal arrangements. The sound is captivating, though traditionalists may find the arrangements a bit heavy on keyboard which sometimes overpowers the more delicate sound of the dulcimer. Orealis is Kirk MacGeachy, vocals, guitar; Jim Stephens, hammered dulcimer, bouzouki, tin whistle; and Renee Morin, keyboards. Guest musicians on *Celtic Music* include Kate and Anna McGarrigle.

❋❋❋ **Celtic Music / Musique Celtique**
1990 Green Linnet (GLCD 1106)†

L'Hiver Sur Richelieu/Miss B's Dreams; Spencer The Rover; The Trooper And The Maid; Dream Angus/Elgol; Highland Ways; Rob Roy; Jannie Walker; Plaisir De La Table/Eibhli Gheal Chiuin *38:34*

Orquesta BC Salsa

SALSA

Vancouver may be on its way to becoming Canada's Salsa capital. Orquesta BC Salsa, another fine salsa band from British Columbia, has released *Fiesta Caliente*, a good dance album that includes numbers like "Niños De America Latina," "Mi Condena," "Falsaria," and the English-language track, "I Lost The Key." The brassy delivery and strong vocals make this another good album for those who enjoy Latin rhythms.

❋❋❋(❋) **Fiesta Caliente**
1994 Orquesta BC Salsa [no catalogue number]

Niños De America Latina; El Rico Vacilon; Mi Condena; Nenita Linda; Humo; Falsaria; Simplemente Amigos; Colombia Rock; I Lost The Key *41:51*

Walter Ostanek

POLKA

Latin-oriented salsa bands aren't the only dance bands to be found at folk festivals. Polka bands are also represented, from time to time, and St. Catharines, Ontario accordionist Walter Ostanek, "Canada's Polka King," is just the person to provide this time-honoured form of dance music. Ostanek, who fell in love with the accordion while watching a button accordionist at a house party when he was four, has gone on to become Canada's leading proponent of polka music. Host of *Polka Time/i>, CKCO-TV, Kitchener, Ontario, Ostanek was inducted into the Porcupine Awards Hall of Fame in 1992, and was awarded three consecutive Grammy awards for his music in 1993, 1994, and 1995. If you enjoy accordion and polkas, you'll delight in the recordings of Walter Ostanek and his band.*

❋❋❋(❋) ***35th Anniversary***
[no date] Walter Ostanek (WACD 10015)

The Old Time Band Polka; Three Little Wishes Waltz; Sandra's Polka; Sweetheart's Polka; Tomsick's Waltz; So Many Times Polka; CB's Polka; Polka Nova Polka; Platt's Polka; Come Away With Me Waltz; Roseann Polka; CJ's Polka; Dance With Me This Polka; I Lied To You Polka 38:31

✼✼✼(✼) **Accordionally Yours**
[no date] Walter Ostanek (WACD 10016)

Whoop Polka; Singers And Players Polka; Pretty Polly Polka; I Never Knew Polka; Emily's Polka; My Mariea Polka; You Are My Sunshine Polka; I Knew From The Start Polka; Clarinet Polka; Please Leave Me Alone Waltz; That Is Why Polka; La Dee Da Oberek; Kenny's Polka; Lulubelle Polka *36:52*

✼✼✼(✼) **Music & Friends**
[no date] Walter Ostanek (WACD 10017)

Broken Heart Polka; Chipper's Polka; First Love Waltz; Anne T. Polka; Bye Bye My Baby Polka; Little Theme Polka; Smiling Eyes Waltz; Slovenian Gold Polka; My Shoes Keep Walking Back To You Polka; I Love To Polka; Pecon Medley Polka; It Thrills Me So Waltz; Don's Polka; Button Box Beat Polka; Over Three Hills Waltz; Wooden Heart Polka; Donnie's Polka; Polka Medley: Take Me Baby Polka/Tic Tock Polka *51:08*

✼✼✼(✼) **Music Music Music**
1989 Quality (RSPD-185-2)

It's A Small World; Julie's Polka; Red River Valley Polka; Button Accordion Polka; Rose Of Old Monterey; Wilkinson's Polka; It's Happy Polka Time; All In My Love For You; Stillman's Polka; Learning To Smile All Over Again; Gay Ranchero Polka; Tennessee Polka; Sailboat Polka; Polka Dots And Polka Dreams; Go Man Go; Highways Are Happy Ways; Jo Ann Polka; Beer Barrel Polka; Loretta's Polka; My Favourite Polka; Polka Ivories; Merry Maiden Polka; Wagon Wheels Polka; Thanks For A Wonderful Evening; String-A-Ling Polka *66:27*

Paris To Kiev
SLAVIC-CANADIAN FOLK

What makes Winnipeg's Paris To Kiev unique is its slavic focus, reflecting the origins of its musicians. Alexander Boychouk and Petro Lurashchuk both grew up in the Carpathian Mountains. Alexis Kochan and Nestor Budyk were born and raised on the Canadian prairies. This meeting of two cultural worlds has led to the recording of the captivating, Ukrainian-oriented folk album, *Paris To Kiev*.

✼✼✼(✼)✓ **Paris To Kiev**
1994 Olesia (AKBCD 02)

Pavochka (A Carol); Quiet Water; Bukovynshka Polka; Triyka (Three); Tylyn Kolomeyka; Dream; Lemko; Panflute Concerto; Alone; Wedding March; Kant; Kolomeyka *38:12*

David Parry
FOLK

Ontario performer David Parry, a member of Friends of Fiddlers Green, has put together one of the book's most unusual albums with *The Man From Eldorado: Songs And Stories Of Robert W. Service*. Parry had been introducing stories and poems of Robert W. Service into his concert and festival performances for years before it occurred to him that they could be set to music. Given that Service played penny whistle, piano, flute, piccolo, banjo, and guitar, this work is true to the inner feeling of

Service's work. Parry includes spoken passages and songs on the album. If you've ever succumbed to the charms of "The Cremation Of Sam McGee," this CD is for you.

See also Friends of Fiddler's Green.

❋❋❋(❋) **The Man From Eldorado: Songs And Stories Of Robert W. Service**

1993 Bonanza Creek (BCR 101)

We Are A People Few And Far Away; Heart Of The Sourdough; Athabaska Dick; In Praise Of Alcohol; The Atavist; The Man From Eldorado; Laziness; L'Escargot D'Or; There! My Pipe Is Out; Accordion; And Now I Fear I Must Write; The Volunteer; A Song Of Winter Weather; I Have Been At It For Over Six Months; A Pot Of Tea; The Petit Vieux; We Are A People Few And Far Away—Reprise *50:28*

Jim Payne
MARITIMES FOLK; SINGER-SONGWRITER

Based in St. John's, Jim Payne is one of the Newfoundland's most active producers and supporters of folk music. In addition to producing albums for Minnie White and Rufus Guinchard, working with the local folk festivals, and giving step dancing classes, Payne is a singer-songwriter. On *Empty Nets*, Payne brings home the reality of Maritimes life in songs like "Empty Nets," about the crisis in the fishing industry and "Two Fisherman Missing," about the sinking of the Andrea Denis. The medley "On The Passing Of Rufus" is a tribute to Rufus Guinchard. Payne's voice is occasionally rough edged, but the lyrics ring true. The liner notes on *State Of The Nation* indicate that Payne wrote the songs on this album for shows at the Rising Tide Theatre, with the exception of the traditional "Lukey's Boat" and "The Stampin' Ground," based on "The Squid-Jiggin' Ground." As befits show tunes, the arrangements are varied. The themes reflect contemporary conditions in Newfoundland.

❋❋❋ **Empty Nets**
1992 SingSong (SS-9192)

Work Work Work; Empty Nets; Two Fishermen Missing; Jack Hinks; The West Side Of Notre Dame Bay; A Crowd Of Bold Sharemen; On The Passing Of Rufus: Father's Jig/Esau Payne's Tune/The Bluebird; Always The Best Man; I've Been A Gay Roving Young Fellow/Rufus' Cordeen Tune/The Final Jig *42:11*

❋❋❋(❋) **State Of The Nation**
1992 SingSong (SS-9293)

State Of The Nation; Billion Dollar Baby; Ode To The Boys Of Mt. Cashel; The Windy Waltz; Christmas In The City; Lukey's Boat; Owed To Newfoundland; Dancing In Dreamland; Toronto Or Bust; A Ship Is Sinking; Much Darker Standing; The Stampin' Ground; I Watch Them Go; When The Dole Stops Coming From Up Yonder *43:15*

Mark Perry
FOLK/POP; SINGER-SONGWRITER

British Columbia singer-songwriter Mark Perry mixes elements of folk, pop, and touches of country into his work. His 1990 CD, *Dreams Of The Highway* contains some catchy singing, songwriting, and musicianship, including "These Days," "Secrets," "Dreams Of The Highway," and "Under Northern Skies." Produced by Roy Forbes, who also sits in as a guest musician, this is a thoughtful folk/pop album from a talented songwriter. *Still Around* is more decidedly electric and pop-oriented. Highlights include "My Year," "Still Around," "Sam," "I'm With You," and "Late Night Radio." By folkie standards, this one is overproduced.

❋❋❋ **Dreams Of The Highway**
1990 Northern Sky (MP 1001)†

These Days; I Don't Need Your Love Any More; Secrets; Dreams Of The Highway; Higher Place To Stand (Jane's Song); Crazy If You Let Her; Hard Girl; (Used To Be) A Rocker; Under Northern Skies; Ten Year Reunion *37:16*

❋❋❋ **Still Around**
1993 Coyote Entertainment (CEGCD 2010)†

My Year; Still Around; On Your Way Back; Sam; I'm With You; Growin' Up; If You Really Want To; Standin' Here Today; Another Chance; Leap Of Faith; Late Night Radio *36:19*

Colleen Peterson
FOLK/COUNTRY; SINGER-SONGWRITER

Ontario singer-songwriter Colleen Peterson began her career as a folkie and, after several years in country music, has become an integral part of Quartette. *Beginning To Feel Like Home*, from 1976, features Peterson's engaging voice on songs like Willie P. Bennett's "Music In Your Eyes," and Jesse Winchester's "Brand New Tennessee Waltz." The album includes two Peterson originals, "Souvenirs" and "You're Not The Only One." *Let Me Down Easy*, from 1991, is a more mature album. Most of the songs are by Peterson, often in collaboration with other songwriters, including Sylvia Tyson. Highlights include "What A Fool I'd Be," "If You Let Me Down Easy," "Deeper Waters," "Love Scares Me," and "Ghost Of Maggie's Sailor."

See also Quartette.

❋❋❋ **Beginning To Feel Like Home**
1976, reissued 1994 Capitol (S2 30656)

Don't It Make You Wanna Dance; Who Will The Next Fool Be; Richland Woman Blues; Sad Songs And Waltzes; Music In Your Eyes; Six Days On The Road; Brand New Tennessee Waltz; Souvenirs; Chattanooga Night; You're Not The Only One; Denver Hotel; It Takes A Lot To Laugh (It Takes A Freight Train To Cry) *38:46*

❋❋❋(❋) **Let Me Down Easy**
1991 Intersound (CDI 9102)

No Pain, No Gain; What A Fool I'd Be; If You Let Me Down Easy; Basic Fact Of Love; Deeper Waters; Hearts Still In Love; Love Scares Me; I'm Not Just Another April Fool; Mr. Conductor; Ghost Of Maggie's Sailor *34:16*

The Plankerdown Band
MARITIMES CELTIC; SINGER-SONGWRITERS

After the breakup of Figgy Duff, Newfoundlanders Kelly Russell and Frank Maher formed a new band—The Plankerdown Band—that has returned to the traditional/ roots approach of the original Figgy Duff material. "The music on *The Jig Is Up* is all instrumental, mostly traditional, and quite impressive ... unlike Figgy Duff, Plankerdown maintains an essentially acoustic melodic core"—*Dirty Linen*. The Plankerdown Band is Kelly Russell, Don Walsh, Frank Maher, Wade Pinhorn, and George Morgan.
　　See also Figgy Duff.

✽✽✽✽✓　**The Jig Is Up**
　　　　1993　Pigeon Inlet (PIPCD-7331)

　　　　The Jig Is Up; Clyde Wells' Dream And The Meech Lake Breakdown; How Swede It Is; El Carite; Skipper Sydney's Pussycat; Father's Jig; Waiting For Supper; Bridget And The Breton; Velvet In The Wind; Free Payne; The Ships Are Sailing *43:03*

Murray Porter
FIRST NATIONS MUSIC; FOLK/BLUES; SINGER-SONGWRITER

Blues artist Murray Porter, who grew up on the Six Nations Reserve near Brantford, Ontario, describes himself as "a red man who sings a black man's blues in a white man's world." *1492 Who Found Who* is an energetic blues album that features songs like "T.V. Repairman," "1492 Who Found Who," "Cryin' In My Sleep," and "Heart Of The Eagle." The songs have bite, and wit. Porter, who plays piano and sings in a rich bar-room voice, is one of Canada's emerging blues talents.

✽✽✽✽　**1492 Who Found Who**
　　　　[no date]　First Nations Music (Y2-10015)†

　　　　T.V. Repairman; 1492 Who Found Who; Cryin' In My Sleep; Tears Are Gonna Fall; Last Stand; 500 Years; Colours; Heart Of The Eagle; Baby You're My Good Thing; White Man's Card; Drinkin' Again; How Sweet It Is *49:11*

John Prince & A Piece Of The Rock
CELTIC FOLK; SINGER-SONGWRITER

John Prince & A Piece Of The Rock is a Toronto band that successfully blends a Celtic sound with pop/rock arrangements and a touch of bluegrass. Behind Prince's rich voice and strong songwriting, the band adds acoustic guitar, harmonica, accordion, mandolin, and tight harmonies. *Take Me Back* highlights Prince's songwriting, including "Take Me Back," "Vagabond," "The Schooner Song," "It's Good To Be A Canadian," and "Where Do Old Boats Go." A Piece Of The Rock includes ex-Maritimer John Prince, Bruce McDaniel, Joe Sexton, and Paul McKeracher.

✽✽✽(✽)　**Take Me Back**
　　　　1994　Rattle Falls (JP-001)†

　　　　Take Me Back (To The Good Kind Of Livin'); Vagabond; Superman (Ain't What He

Used To Be); The Schooner Song (Sail Away); It's Good To Be Canadian; Where Do
Old Boats Go; The Ballad Of Belfast; Newfoundland Blessing; Let's All Pull
Together; Blue Collar Blues; Smokin' In The Kitchen *42:13*

Quartette
FOLK/COUNTRY; SINGER-SONGWRITERS

Like a similar collaboration project, UHF, Quartette was formed by four independent
artists who enjoyed performing together: Sylvia Tyson, Cindy Church, Colleen
Peterson, and Caitlin Hanford. On their debut album *Quartette*, the vocals are gorgeous and the songs are perfectly selected—one or two by each singer. Each of the
members of the group is a formidable songwriter and their voices blend spectacularly.
The collaboration is an outstanding success—a must purchase for every Canadian
folk collection.

See also Cindy Church; Colleen Peterson; Sylvia Tyson.

❋❋❋❋✓ **Quartette**
1994 Denon Canada (CAN 9016)

The Circle; Denim Blue Eyes; Unabashedly Blue; Soul To The Bone; Neon
Cowboy; It Never Rains On Me; Hard Times; Cowboys And Rodeos; Lost Between
The Barren Shores; Papere's Mill; Hobo Girl; When God Dips His Pen Of Love In
My Heart; Red Hot Blues; King Of The Cowboys *44:42*

Quigley Ensemble
FOLK/JAZZ; SINGER-SONGWRITERS

Barbara Ann Quigley is well known for her folk presentations, but the Quigley Ensemble goes beyond folk. *Renovations*, which includes a mix of styles, is biased towards jazz-oriented arrangements and perky versions of folkish material. Highlights
include "I Went To Market," "Antique Eyes," "J'Ai Peur Des Loups," and "High
Germany." The Quigley Ensemble is Barbara Ann Quigley, Johanne Landry, Laura
Huffaker, and Monica Lang.

❋❋❋(❋) **Renovations**
1992 Moka (MMQE 001)†

I Went To Market; Je Ne L'Ose Dire; The Nursery; L'Amour De Moy; Antique Eyes;
Isabeau; Willie-O; J'Ai Peur Des Loups; High Germany; La Belle Françoise; All
Around My Hat; Russell In The Wind/À La Claire Fontaine; The Croppy Boy;
L'Hirondelle; The Ten Commandments *51:09*

Bob Quinn & The Quincept Project
MARITIMES FOLK/POP

Bob Quinn is a musician from Nova Scotia who has brought together some of Nova
Scotia's best as part of The Quincept Project. The liner notes tell little, but *Coast Of
Difference* is clearly a collaboration with different singer-songwriters. The opener,
"Nova Scotia, Nature's Song," is performed by its author, Kevin Evans, joined by
Quinn, members of the Symphony Nova Scotia, and pipers Ian MacKinnon, Jamie
MacInnis, and Paul MacNeil. The rest of the album follows suit, with the following

members of the collaboration singing lead vocal: Bobby Arvon, Jennifer Whalen, John Gracie, Brian Doherty, and Helen Bezanson. This is a beautiful album, though a trifle overproduced.

✳✳✳(✳)   **Coast Of Difference**
        1993? Bob Quinn (BAQ-1-93)†

> Nova Scotia, Nature's Song; Always There; Grand Bank Ladies; Eastern Wind; Forever Young; My Love, Cape Breton And Me; Night Train; Love Chant; A Drink For My Father; Coast Of Difference; Song For Canada *40:04*

Lester Quitzau
FOLK/BLUES; SINGER-SONGWRITER

Lester Quitzau (pronounced *quit-saw*) has been playing guitar and studying blues since his early teens. For the past ten years he has been a well-respected and recognized figure on the Canadian festival circuit and blues scene. His 1994 CD, *Keep On Walking*, lays down one excellent acoustic blues track after another. As the liner notes attest, the album "was recorded 'au natural' with no additives or artificial flavours. All tracks were recorded live to DAT (no over-dubs) with the exception of 'Keep On Walking'."

✳✳✳(✳)   **Keep On Walking**
        1994 L.Q. Productions (LQ-003)

> Intro; I've Got To Go; Rich Land Women Blues; Road; Someday Baby; Feel The Way I Do; Close To You; Turkish Theme; Rats In My Kitchen; Your Heart; Valhalla; Room Full Of Mirrors; Saddle Up My Pony; Keep On Walking; Lookin' For My Baby; Alone...But Not Lonely *53:24*

The Rankin Family
CELTIC FOLK/COUNTRY; SINGER-SONGWRITERS

A Canadian success story writ large, the Rankin Family's soaring harmonies and Gaelic-flavoured material have caught the fancy of fans in Canada and abroad. Their debut album, *The Rankin Family*, captures the freshness that captivated festival audiences before the Rankins attracted widespread attention. The sound is slightly tentative—the group had not yet attained full confidence in themselves—but the material is wonderful. Highlights include the Gaelic "Mo Rùn Geal, Dileas," "Chì Mi Na Mórbheanna," and the "Jigging Medley." *Fare Thee Well* is a leap forward for the Rankins. They sing confidently and totally convincingly on numbers such as "Orangedale Whistle," "An T-Each Ruadh," "Fare Thee Well Love," and "Gillis Mountain." Their harmonies are in total accord with their material. *North Country* is disappointing. The material is not as convincing and the group seems intent on trying to step into country music—a genre that does not particularly suit their voices or style. As usual, the Gaelic songs are the highlights: "Oich U Agus H-Iùraibh Éile," "Ho Ro Mo Nighean Donn Bhòidheach," and "Leis An Lurgainn." *Grey Dusk Of Eve* is a limited edition, five-song CD that represents a less-than-outstanding purchase. The music is not as inspired as earlier recordings and the packaging is questionable. The Rankins should have waited until they had enough material to master a full album.

The Rankin Family is Cookie Rankin, Heather Rankin, Raylene Rankin, and Jimmy Rankin. The Rankin Family received Juno awards in 1994 in the "Canadian Entertainer of the Year" and "Group of the Year" categories.

✳✳✳(✳) **The Rankin Family**
1989 Capitol (C2 99995)

Mo Rùn Geal, Dileas (My Faithful Fair One); Lonely Island; Loving Arms; Piano Medley: Memories of Bishop MacDonald/The Tweeddale Club/MacFarlane's Rant/ Lively Steps; Mairi's Wedding/Michael Rankin's Reel; Roving Gypsy Boy; Chì Mi Na Mórbheanna (Mist Covered Mountains); Fiddle Medley: The Warlock's Strathspey/Bog-an-Lochan/Nine Pint Coggie/Mr. J. Forbes/Hull's Reel; Lament Of The Irish Immigrant; Jigging Medley: Whiskey In A Cup/King George/Old King's Reel/King's Reel/Bodachan A'Mhìrein *42:29*

✳✳✳✳✓ **Fare Thee Well Love**
1990 Capitol (C2 99996)

Orangedale Whistle; An T-Each Ruadh (The Red Horse); Fair And Tender Ladies; Fiddle Medley: Lime Hill/Keep The Country Bonnie Lassie/Jack Daniel's Reel/Little Donald In The Pig Pen; Fisherman's Son; Tell My Ma; You Left A Flower; Fare Thee Well Love; Gillis Mountain; Gaelic Medley: Mo Shuil Ad' Dheidh/Buain A' Rainich/ He Mo Leannan/Fail 'Il O; Tripper's Jig *36:06*

✳✳✳(✳) **North Country**
1993 EMI (E2 80683)†

North Country; Oich U Agus H-Iùraibh Éile (Love Song); Borders And Time; Mull River Shuffle; Lisa Brown; Ho Ro Mo Nighean Donn Bhòidheach (Ho Ro My Nut Brown Maiden); Tramp Miner; Rise Again; Leis An Lurgainn (Boat Song); Christy Campbell Medley; Saved In The Arms; Johnny Tulloch; Turn That Boat Around *47:53*

✳✳(✳) **Grey Dusk Of Eve**
1995 EMI (E25Q 7243 8 82013 2 2)

Grey Dusk Of Eve (Portobello); The Ballad Of Malcolm Murray; An Teid Thu Leam A Mhairi (Will You Go With Me Mary); Twin Fiddle Medley; Sir James Baird *18:04*

Rita & Mary Rankin

CELTIC FOLK

Nova Scotia singers Rita and Mary Rankin plumb the Celtic repertoire in a different way than the Rankin Family, to whom they think they may be distantly related. These Rankins embrace a more traditional, less commercial, approach to the music. Their style works admirably, proving once again that there's no single method of interpretation. *Lantern Burn* is a traditionalist's delight. Backed by some of Nova Scotia's best musicians, including Dave MacIsaac on guitar, Tracy Dares on piano, and Jerry Holland on fiddle, Rita and Mary Rankin each sing solo numbers and occasionally combine on duets. Their soft, lyrical voices provide intimate interpretations of songs like "Hi Horò 'S Na Hòro Éile," "Long For The Sea," "Darkest Winter," "Lantern Burn," and the haunting "Greenwood Side."

✱✱✱✱✓ **Lantern Burn**
1994 Ingold / CBC Maritimes (2001-2)†

Three Love Songs; Hi Horò 'S Na Hòro Éile; Western Highway; Chi Mi'N
Geamhradh (I See The Winter); Eilidh; Cawdon Fair Strathspey/ Mairi Alasdair/
Raonuill Reel/Miss Charlotte Alston/Stewart's Reel/Traditional Reel; Gràdh Geal Mo
Chrìdh' (Fair Love Of My Heart); Long For The Sea; Oran Luathaidh (A Traditional
Walking Song)/Rannie MacLellan's Jig/McInerney's Fany Jig; Greenwood Side;
Nighean Donn À Chùil Réidh (Brown-Haired Maiden Of The Smooth Tresses);
Darkest Winter; Fear A' Bhàta (The Boatman); Sarah; Lantern Burn *59:05*

Rare Air

CELTIC ROCK/JAZZ; SINGER-SONGWRITERS

If you like your rock/jazz laced with bagpipe, Rare Air will interest you. This Toronto-
based group wrote and performed uptempo music infused with a touch of Celtic.
Hard To Beat, from 1987, is the most traditional sounding of the Rare Air recordings.
The bagpipes are front and centre on tunes like "Tribal Rites," "Taxi Suite," and
"Marvin's March." Other tracks, such as "Inside Out," "Small As Life," and "The
Waiting Room" are more avant garde. *Primeval* is more experimental with less bag-
pipe. The tracks range from fairly heavy rock, "Fourth World Reel," to a flute piece,
"Jungle," to a mixed bagpipe, jazz-like piece, "Volunteer Slavery." *Space Piper* con-
tinues the jazz influence. By this point, the Celtic bits have mostly disappeared, with
the exception of some cameo performances by bagpipe. Still, there are some interesting tracks, such as "Treebranch," "Mammoth No Arms," "Astral Jig," and "Death Of
A Space Piper." The various personnel of Rare Air included Patrick O'Gorman, Grier
Coppins, Dick Murai, Trevor Ferrier, Christian Frappier, and Richard Greenspoon.
Oliver Schroer put in a guest appearance on *Space Piper*. The group disbanded in
1991.

✱✱✱(✱) **Hard To Beat**
1987 Green Linnet (GLCD 1073)

Tribal Rites; Taxi Suite; Inside Out; Small As Life; Marvin's March; The Waiting
Room; Dee Dee Diddley Bop; Onward Blindly Onward; Beam Me Up *42:29*

✱✱✱(✱) **Primeval**
1989 Green Linnet (GLCD 1104)

Fourth World Reel; Jungle; Volunteer Slavery; New Swing Reel; O'Grady's Little
Italy; Chicago Shopping Mall; Behind The Garage; Hipbone; Highland Life;
Dreaming Of The Other Side *44:14*

✱✱✱ **Space Piper**
1991 Green Linnet (GLCD 1115)

Treebranch; Mammoth No Arms; Astral Jig; Snake MacMurray; La Marche De
Tintin To India; C'Est Fou, C'Est Toi, C'Est Tout; Madhouse; Death Of A Space
Piper *49:42*

Rawlins Cross

CELTIC FOLK/ROCK; SINGER-SONGWRITERS

No ethereal harps and dulcimers here. Rawlins Cross is a Newfoundland Celtic band that mixes bagpipe, tin whistle, bodhran, bouzouki, mandolin, banjo, drums, acoustic and electric guitar in a fusion that really rocks. Co-founded by one of the members of the original Figgy Duff, Dave Panting, Rawlins Cross is widely considered to be one of Canada's most entertaining folk/rock bands. Their first CD, *A Turn Of The Wheel*, is a driving album that includes a number of Panting brothers songs, including "Wild Rose," "A Turn Of The Wheel," "Mountainside," "Shaken Up," and "Ghost Of Love," plus some traditional reels and jigs such as "Farmer's Daughter/High Reel" and "Sleepy Maggie/Gavel Walk/Little Beggarman." The band's trademark, Ian McKinnon's soaring piping, is featured effectively on nearly every track. *Crossing The Border*, the band's second album, falls a little off the pace. It includes more excellent Panting material, but some of the rivetting instrumental blends lose their edge as the band centres more on vocals. The singing doesn't quite match the driving quality of the instrumentals.

On the brilliant *Reel 'N' Roll*, the band solved the vocal dilemma by bringing aboard Joey Kitson, whose powerful David Clayton Thomas-like voice is a perfect match for the electric/Celtic instruments. Between Kitson's voice and McKinnon's bagpipe, the band soars through track after track. Highlights include the opener "Reel 'N' Roll," "Don't You Be The One," "It'll Have To Wait," and a re-recording of "Turn Of The Wheel." The album also contains the powerful lament, "The Long Night," dedicated to the memory of Emile Benoit and Noel Dinn. Rawlins Cross is Dave Panting on guitars, mandolin, bouzouki, and tenor banjo; Geoff Panting on piano accordion with midi interface; Ian McKinnon playing highland bagpipe, tin whistles, trumpet, and bodhran; Brian Bourne on bass and Chapman Stick; Howie Southwood on drums; and Joey Kitson singing lead vocals and playing harmonica. Rawlins Cross received "Recording Group of the Year" and "Pop/Rock Artist of the Year" East Coast Music Awards in 1995.

✻✻✻(✻)   **A Turn Of The Wheel**
[no date] Ground Swell (RCCD-101)

WildRose; Farmer's Daughter/High Reel; A Turn Of The Wheel; Mountainside; MacPherson's Lament; Colleen; Mac's Fancy/Give Me A Drink Of Water; Shaken Up; Ghost Of Love; Sleepy Maggie/Gravel Walk/Little Beggarman *32:18*

✻✻✻   **Crossing The Border**
[no date] Ground Swell (RCCD-102)†

Legendary; Chessboard Dancer; Nightfall; Israel Got A Rabbit; Eleventh Hour; Stray Cat; Blues For You; O'Neil's March/Haughs Of Cromdale; Peace On The Inside; Memory Waltz; Sound Of Sleat/Ale Is Dear; Open Road *41:06*

✻✻✻✻✓   **Reel 'N' Roll**
1993 Ground Swell (GSR-67)†

Reel 'N' Roll; Don't You Be The One; It'll Have To Wait; Long Wait; The Wedding Gift; Pedestrian Again; Mystery Tonight; Dance Hall; Ghost Of Love; A Turn Of The Wheel; Colleen; MacPherson's Lament *46:28*

Loretto Reid & Brian Taheny
IRISH-CANADIAN CELTIC

Loretto Reid & Brian Taheny emigrated to Canada in 1988 from County Sligo, Ireland. Celtic musicians with a distinctive style, they have performed at many of Canada's folk festivals and frequently offer workshops on Celtic instruments. Loretto and Brian are former members of the Toronto Celtic band TIP Splinter. Their premier album *The Golden Dawn* features a lively collection of Irish jigs, reels, and airs composed by Loretto. She plays flute, tin whistle, and concertina while Brian adds guitar, dobro, fiddle, banjo, and mandolin. The performances are sumptuous—it's a pity the album is so short.
  See also TIP Splinter.

❋❋❋(❋)✔ **The Golden Dawn**
    1993 Willow (WPCD9301)

> Jigs: Mick And Mary Carr's/Trip To Kingswood; Reels: The Ivy Leaf/The Bank Of Ireland/Sean Sá Cheo; Rowena The Child; The Wind And The Willow; Ballisodare: Reels: Seamus Reid's Delight/The Five Hansom Daughters; Reels: Kate's New Shoes/Farewell To Sligo; The Golden Dawn: Reels: Sunrise/Sunset *24:32*

Tracy Riley
FOLK/POP; SINGER-SONGWRITER

On *Only Once*,Tracy Riley, a singer-songwriter from the Northwest Territories, delivers an outstanding debut album featuring her big, bluesy voice and acoustic guitar on original material such as "Three Wishes," "I Wonder," "Joliffe Island," and "Hear The Drum."

❋❋❋(❋) **Only Once**
    1994 Drum Song (TAR:001)†

> Three Wishes; When You Know; I Wonder; Joliffe Island; Pick Your Feet Up And Dance; Only Once; Wild Women Don't Have The Blues; P.M.S. Rap; Children With Fire; Hear The Drum *34:05*

Nancy Roach
MARITIMES FIDDLE

Nancy Roach, who began studying classical violin at the age of nine, later started playing the traditional repertoire. She is the winner of eight Maritime fiddle titles in Scottish class, Oldtime fiddling, and Waltz competitions. She has travelled extensively through the Maritimes and the United States studying fiddle styles. *Footnotes* is an album of dance tunes from across a broad spectrum of styles that includes Maritime and country traditions.

❋❋❋ **Footnotes: The Dancing Fiddle**
    1990 Nancy Roach (NRE 102)

> St. Ann's Reel/McNabb's Hornpipe; River John Sunset Waltz; Cabra Féidh/Bonny Lass Of Fisherrow; Maple Sugar/La Joyeuse Québécoise; Fisher's Hornpipe/Archie Menzie; Poor Girl's Waltz; Heather On The Hill/Princess Reel/Paddy On The

Turnpike; Faded Love/Maiden's Prayer; Big John MacNeil/Mason's Apron/
Growling Old Man And Woman; San Antonio Rose/Silver And Gold Two-Step; Cape
Blomidon Reel/The Shelburne Reel; Silver Wedding Waltz; Don Messer's Break-
down/Woodchopper's Breakdown *35:37*

Ian Robb

FOLK; SINGER-SONGWRITER

Ottawa-based Ian Robb, besides being a singer-songwriter and long-time member of
Friends of Fiddler's Green, also writes a literate, insightful column, "The British-
North America Act," in *Sing Out!* Robb's pre-CD work includes a series of albums for
Folk Legacy. *From Different Angels*, his first CD recording, refers to three of Robb's
musical influences—Stan Rogers, Peter Bellamy, and Ewan McColl. He pays tribute
to Rogers with "Make And Break Harbour" and "Mary Ellen Carter." From McColl
he has selected "The Big Hewer" and "The Lag's Song." From Bellamy's repertoire
Robb learned "Green Groves" and "A-Roving On A Winter's Night." The album also
includes Robb's infamous parody of "Barrett's Privateers," called "Garnet's Home-
Made Beer." Robb's clear, strong singing makes this album a clear-cut "must have"
for folkies.
See also Friends of Fiddler's Green.

※※※(※)✓ **From Different Angels**
1994 Fallen Angle (FAM 01CD)

> The Santa Fe Trail; Farmer's Boy; The Moving Cloud/Miss Thornton/Skepper
> Schotish; The Big Hewer; Make And Break Harbour; Ye Mariners All; Garnet's
> Home-Made Beer; The Last Minute Waltz/Midnight On The Water; A-Roving On A
> Winter's Night; Green Groves; Charlie Hunter/McGuire's/Cape Breton Dream; The
> Lag's Song; D-Day Dodgers; They're Taking It Away; Cattle In The Cane/Vladimir's
> Steamboat; The Mary Ellen Carter *61:38*

Dyhan Roberts

FOLK/POP; SINGER-SONGWRITER

On *Angel On The Shoreline*, British Columbia singer-songwriter Dyhan Roberts combines pop and country elements with folkish lyrics and acoustic guitar playing. Highlights of the album include "Angel On The Shoreline," "Little Bird," "One By One,"
"Undeniable Heat," and "Flying High On One Wing." James Keelaghan is guest vocalist on "Firelight." Roberts has a fine voice, but her very electric arrangements may
lean too heavily into pop for some folkies.

※※※ **Angel On The Shoreline**
1993 Arpeggio (DJ1703)†

> Angel On The Shoreline; Angry Hearts; Firelight; Little Bird; One By One;
> Undeniable Heat; Candle Of Love; Flying High On One Wing; Crackling Like Fire;
> Until Their Eyes Shine; In The Thick Of It; Bridges That Are Dreams *49:58*

Robbie Robertson & The Red Road Ensemble
FIRST NATIONS MUSIC; SINGER-SONGWRITERS

Robbie Robertson, of The Band, is half Mohawk and was raised on the Six Nations reserve near Hagersville, Ontario. His involvement in creating the music for a six-hour documentary, *The Native Americans*, led him on a musical journey in which he wrote and collaborated with a number of First Nations artists, including Kashtin (Innu), sisters Rita and Priscilla Coolidge (Cherokee), The Silver Cloud Singers (Hopi, Winnebago, Lumbee Flathead and Saponi Tuscarora), Douglas Spotted Eagle (Lakota), Ulali (Saponi Tuscarora and Mayan/Apache), Jim Wilson (Choctaw), Dave Carson (Choctaw), Benito (Taos Pueblo), Mazatl (Aztec/Mayan), and Bonnie Jo Hunt (Lakota). Robertson decided to call his contributors The Red Road Ensemble. "It's just a way of me saying I worked with some wonderful other people. It's my way of acknowledging them. The Red Road, in native talk, means the cool way, the righteous way—done with really honorable intentions"—Robbie Robertson, interview in *Network*, November 1994. Robertson received a "Producer of the Year" Juno for this album in 1995.

❋❋❋(❋)✓ **Music For The Native Americans**
1994 Capitol (C2-7243 8 28295 2 2)†

> Coyote Dance; Mahk Jchi (Heartbeat Drum Song); Ghost Dance; The Vanishing Breed; It Is A Good Day To Die; Golden Feather; Akua Tuta; Words Of Fire, Deeds Of Blood; Cherokee Morning Song; Skinwalker; Ancestor Song; Twisted Hair *54:28*

Georges Rodriguez
HAITIAN MUSIC; SINGER-SONGWRITER

Montreal resident Georges Rodriguez, originally from Haiti, is considered to be *the* Haitian percussionist. Rodriguez, who has been recording for over twenty years, is a musician and folklorist who has preserved the Haitian tradition of drums and drumming. *Tambours "Rada"* provides the listener with an overview of different Haitian styles. The musicians and vocalists on this very fine album are Fritz Pageot, Steve Pageot, Léopold Molière, Kesnel Hall, Michel Dubeau, Gary Crèvecoeur, Carole Stines, and Marie-Carmelle Millien.

❋❋❋❋ **Tambours "Rada"**
1993 George Rodriguez (GR-CD 1313)

> Anbatonel #1; Mazaka Lakwa; Maskaron; Van Van Van; Rabòday; Anbatonel #2; Bal Chanpèt; Iwa Zaou; Kontredans; Fi-a; Anbatonel #3; Vyèj Mirak; Solo Tambou *53:49*

Garnet Rogers
FOLK; SINGER-SONGWRITER

"The narratives of singer/guitarist Garnet Rogers bore down upon you like a brisk winter wind, tingling your soul long after they're passed"—*Performing Songwriter*. Raised in and around Hamilton, Ontario, Garnet Rogers may be Canada's quintessential folksinger-songwriter. An excellent musician who performed with his brother Stan for many years before embarking on an independent musical career, Garnet has a fine, strong voice and an uncanny ear for talent.

His debut album, *Garnet Rogers*, features Roy Forbes' "Woh Me," Doug McArthur's "Break The Law" and "Black Eyed Susan," Willie P. Bennett's "Music In Your Eyes," Connie Kaldor's "Bird On A Wing," and Archie Fisher's "Final Trawl." This is an album that wears well. *The Outside Track* features Ralph McTell's "Gypsy Song," Doug McArthur's "Ain't Goin' Home," James Keelaghan's "Jenny Bryce," Henry Lawson's "The Outside Track," Rod MacDonald's "American Jerusalem," Archie Fisher's "Denbrae," and Enoch Kent's "The Farm Auction." It also includes some original tunes by Rogers—the start of a successful songwriting career. *Speaking Softly In The Dark* continues in the same vein as *The Outside Track* with Rogers covering songs by other songwriters and adding a bit of his own to the mix. Highlights of the album include Mary Chapin Carpenter's "Goodbye Again," and Phil Ochs' "Crucifixion." This time around, the formula was not quite as gripping—it was time for Rogers to move on, which he did on his next release.

Small Victories may be Rogers' most popular album. While it includes a few covers, such as "The King Of Rome" by David Sudbury, this is the first album that is really Rogers' own. His songwriting bursts out all over on memorable tracks like "Small Victory," "One More Ride," "His Father's House," "Stars In Their Crown," "Off The Rails" and "Sleeping Buffalo." By *At A High Window* Rogers has developed the voice and style that characterizes his concert performances today. Confident and sure, Rogers delivers his songs with a mix of acoustic and electric arrangements. He has also developed the knack of writing *long* songs, such as the beautiful twelve-minute classic, "A Row Of Small Trees." Other highlights include "Through The Cracks," "At A High Window," and "Election Night: North Dakota." *Summer Lightning*, released in late 1994, was recorded live at Annie and Carl Grindstaff's house concert in London, Ontario and at the Commercial Tavern in Maryhill, Ontario. The ambiance is warm and intimate and Rogers performs a fine mix of covers and original material. New Rogers' songs on this album include "The Beauty Game," "What's Wrong With This Picture," "Frankie And Johnny," "Let Me Count The Ways," and "Summer Lightning."

❊❊❊(❊)✓ **Garnet Rogers**
    1984 Snow Goose (SGS-1111CD)†

> Woh Me; Break The Law; Music In Your Eyes; Carrickfergus/Final Trawl; Westlin Winds; Black Eyed Susan; Bird On A Wing; Farewell To Music; Thanksgiving Eve *46:07*

❊❊❊(❊) **The Outside Track**
    1986 Snow Goose (SGS 1113CD)†

> Gypsy Song; Green Eyes; Ain't Goin' Home; Jenny Bryce; The Outside Track; American Jerusalem; Denbrae; The Farm Auction; Blind Mary; Archie Gets A Leg Up; John O'Dreams *45:07*

❊❊❊ **Speaking Softly In The Dark**
    1988 Snow Goose (SGS 1115 D)†

> Dear Grandfather; The Sliprails And The Spur; McArthur's Farewell To The West; The Enfolding; Like A Diamond Ring; Hallelujah! (The Great Storm Is Over); Goodbye Again; Lament For Henry Chapin; Crucifixion; After All *44:37*

✳✳✳✳✓ **Small Victories**
1990 Snow Goose (SGS 1117)†

The King Of Rome; Small Victory; One More Ride; His Father's House; Stars In Their Crown; Off The Rails; One Bullet; Sleeping Buffalo; The Lost Ones; For Herself *59:04*

✳✳✳(✳) **At A High Window**
1992 Snow Goose (SGS 1121CD)†

Through The Cracks; Come From The Heart; Last Of The Working Stetsons; At A High Window; Willie Short; The Joy Of Living; Young Willie; A Row Of Small Trees; Election Night: North Dakota *53:47*

✳✳✳✳✓ **Summer Lightning**
1994 Snow Goose (SGS1123CD)†

Give The Fiddler A Dram; The Beauty Game; This Shirt; What's Wrong With This Picture; Frankie And Johnny; Let Me Count The Ways; Sleeping Buffalo; Sammy's Bar; A Row Of Small Trees; The Outside Track; Summer Lightning; The King Of Rome; O'Neil's Dream *66:33*

Stan Rogers
FOLK; SINGER-SONGWRITER

Many fans consider Stan Rogers the greatest Canadian folksinger ever, and the loss due to his death in an airline disaster in 1983 is still felt deeply. Every folk collection should contain a selection of Stan Rogers recordings. With assistance from his wonderful musicians, especially his brother Garnet, who adds magic to song after song with his fiddle playing, Stan created some of the finest folk music on record. If you're like most people who discover his music, you'll probably end up purchasing all the albums in his too-brief discography. Rogers is a memorial member of the Porcupine Awards Hall of Fame.

Rogers' ascent in popularity began with his discovery of the songwriting potential of the Canadian Maritimes, his ancestral home. He plumbed the history and character of Maritimes fishing and mining villages in his outstanding debut album, *Fogarty's Cove*. The album is filled to the brim with what are now Stan Rogers classics, such as "Forty-Five Years," "Fogarty's Cove," "Barrett's Privateers," and "Make And Break Harbour." Rogers' second album, *Turnaround*, is a little patchier, containing such gems as "The Bluenose" and "The Jeannie C.", but also containing some rougher, early material that shows a developing Stan Rogers rather than the later, mature artist. *Between The Breaks...Live!*, one of two live albums in Rogers' discography, is a classic that provides a good blend of Stan's original material mixed well with that of other songwriters. His cover of Archie Fisher's "Witch Of The Westmorland" is one of the album's highlights. The version of "Barrett's Privateers" on this album is considered by many to be definitive.

From the opening, achingly beautiful a cappella "Northwest Passage" to the gently lingering "California" that rounds out the album, *Northwest Passage* may be Rogers' finest work. It continues his exploration of the songwriting possibilities of Canada, this time the Canadian prairies and Canadian West. The album features some of his strongest lyrics: "Lies," "Free In The Harbour," "The Field Behind The Plow," "The

Idiot," and, of course, "Northwest Passage." Interspersed between *Northwest Passage* and *From Fresh Water* is Stan's "fun" album, *For The Family* on which he performs the traditional music his musically-talented family grew up on. A tribute to his roots, *Family* provides an insight into the direction Rogers might have taken. This was the first, and only, album he produced himself. He dispensed with the background strings, returning to a plainer, more traditional folk sound. *From Fresh Water*, released posthumously, was Rogers' last major project—a set of songs he wrote about the Great Lakes region of Canada where he was raised. His song cycles about Canada had come full circle, back to his home. The album includes some great Rogers' compositions, including "Lock-Keeper," "White Squall," "The Last Watch," and "The Nancy." It also displays a rarer side of Rogers—a pair of protest songs: "Tiny Fish For Japan," and "The House Of Orange." Ten years after Stan's death, Fogarty's Cove Music posthumously released a concert recorded in 1982 in Halifax, Nova Scotia. *Home In Halifax*, a superb live recording, preserves the essence of a Stan Rogers concert performance, including snatches of stage patter. It catches Garnet Rogers' engaging humour, and, arguably, the best version of "Barrett's Privateers" on all of Stan's albums. It also includes a previously unrecorded Stan Rogers song, "Sailor's Rest."

❋❋❋❋✓ **Fogarty's Cove**
1977 Fogarty's Cove (FCM-P/1001D)†

Watching The Apples Grow; Forty-Five Years; Fogarty's Cove; The Maid On The Shore; Barrett's Privateers; Fisherman's Wharf; Giant; The Rawdon Hills; Plenty Of Hornpipe; The Wreck Of The Athens Queen; Make And Break Harbour; Finch's Complaint; Giant: Reprise *39:30*

❋❋❋ **Turnaround**
1978 Fogarty's Cove (FCM 001D)†

Dark Eyed Molly; Oh No, Not I; Second Effort; Bluenose; The Jeannie C.; So Blue; Front Runner; Song Of The Candle; Try Like The Devil; Turnaround *40:57*

❋❋❋❋✓ **Between The Breaks...Live!**
1979 Fogarty's Cove (FCM-002D)

The Witch Of The Westmorland; Barrett's Privateers; First Christmas; The Mary Ellen Carter; The White Collar Holler; The Flowers of Bermuda; Rolling Down To Old Maui; Harris And The Mare; Delivery Delayed *43:30*

❋❋❋❋✓ **Northwest Passage**
1981 Fogarty's Cove (FCM 004D)†

Northwest Passage; The Field Behind The Plow; Night Guard; Working Joe; You Can't Stay Here; The Idiot; Lies; Canol Road; Free In The Harbour; California *39:39*

❋❋❋(❋) **For The Family**
1983 Folk Tradition (R002)†

Lookout Hill; Cliffs Of Baccalieu; Strings And Dory Plug; The Badger Drive; Cape St. Mary's; Two Bit Cayuse; Scarborough Settler's Lament; Yeastcake Jones; Up In Fox Island; Three Fishers *36:10*

❋❋❋(❋)✓ **From Fresh Water**
1984 Fogarty's Cove (FCM 007D)†

White Squall; The Nancy; Man With Blue Dolphin; Tiny Fish For Japan; Lock-Keeper; Half Of A Heart; MacDonnell On The Heights; Flying; The Last Watch; The House Of Orange *42:04*

❋❋❋❋✓ **Home In Halifax**
1992 Fogarty's Cove (FCM 010D)

Bluenose; Make And Break Harbour; The Field Behind The Plow; Shriner Cows (dial.); Night Guard; Morris Dancers (dial.); The Idiot; Lies; Free In The Harbour; Band Introduction (dial.); Workin' Joe; The Legend Of Fingal (dial.); Giant; Forty-Five Years; The Mary Ellen Carter; Barrett's Privateers; Sailor's Rest *64:01*

The Rose Vaughn Trio
FOLK/JAZZ/POP; SINGER-SONGWRITER

"[Rose Vaughn's albums] immediately set up an elegant and almost austere mood which never lets up ... the Rose Vaughn trio performs songs that are cordial and sometimes melancholy and the music is always captivating, if not downright luminous"— *Dirty Linen*. A regular act at folk venues across Canada, the Halifax-based, jazz-influenced Rose Vaughn Trio presents its atmospheric blend of music on *Sweet Tarragon*, with Rose Vaughn, the group's songwriter on lead vocals, Catherine Porter on piano, keyboard, flute, and Pam Mason on acoustic bass. Highlights include "Song Of The Fog," "Sally's Song," "Runaway Day," "Sweet Tarragon," and "Take Me Down To The River." The trio continues its unique music on the 1993 *Fire In The Snow*. Highlights include "Restless As A River," "Stone And Sand," "Fire In The Snow," "Stones," and "Seashell Boat."

❋❋❋(❋) **Sweet Tarragon**
1991 WildRose (102)†

Song Of The Fog; Sally's Song; Man/Maid Moon; Runaway Day; Out Of The Darkness; One Way Street; Cuu Cuu Viu; Sweet Tarragon; White Stretch Limo; Shopkeeper (Gina); Isabelle's Lament; Take Me Down To The River; Thyme On My Windowsill/Chaucer's Strut *44:08*

❋❋❋(❋) **Fire In The Snow**
1993 WildRose (103)

Restless As A River; Stone And Sand; Fire In The Snow; Shadow; Small; Celina; Ella May; My Jemmie; Stones; Equally In Love; Coming Home; Seashell Boat *40:48*

Don Ross
ACOUSTIC GUITAR; SINGER-SONGWRITER

With hands that move with the speed of a Cuisinart, Toronto guitar virtuoso Don Ross carries six-string acoustic folk guitar into the stratospheric regions usually reserved for flamenco, jazz, and classical. His compelling compositions delight the ear, propelling you from track to track with innovative delights and surprises. If you like guitar instrumentals, add Don Ross to your music collection and dive into his unique soundstream.

"First Ride," the first track on Ross's debut CD, *Bearing Straight*, may send you in search of your seatbelt. In a few short bars Ross establishes himself as one of the finest acoustic guitarists around as he launches into passages that take you around musical corners at breakneck speed. The sweet "Catherine" that follows is a slower, jazz-flavoured piece that combines violin and acoustic bass. The remainder of the album presents track after track of highly-pleasurable listening as Ross works his way through his imaginative compositions. This very long album was recorded "live" in the studio with no dubs or edits. Simply amazing. The eponymous album, *Don Ross*, continues the adventure with compositions like "Groovy Sunflowers," "Zarzuela," "Thin Air," "Bluefinger," and "Little Giants." This is guitar lovers' heaven.

Three Hands takes Ross in a different direction. Ross, who is half Scottish and half Micmac, displays a good, though not distinguished, singing voice on songs like "Spirit Wars" and "A Child Must Grow," songs about human relations Ross wrote after the events in Oka, Quebec in 1990 involving a clash between native and non-native cultures. With *This Dragon Won't Sleep* Ross began recording for Columbia. The album is a mix of instrumentals and vocals. Opening with the lush instrumental, "Godzilla," Ross explores diverse moods and styles. "Head & Heart," for instance, is a pop-oriented song with syncopated rhythms and ornamentation. Re-makes from earlier albums include "Groovy Sunflowers," "Catherine," and "Zarzuela."

❀❀❀❀✓ **Bearing Straight**
1989 Duke Street (DSRD 31054)

The First Ride; Catherine; Midnight March; Silversmith; That'll Be The Phone; Patmos; The Is-Ought Controversy; Goby Fish; King Street Suite; Ginger And Fred; In From The Cold; New Aaron; Slow Burn *65:42*

❀❀❀(❀) **Don Ross**
1990 Duke Street (DSRD 31065)

Groovy Sunflowers; Zarzuela; Thin Air; Bluefinger; Carolan's Quarrel With The Landlady/Michael And Juliana; Lucy Watusi; Wall Of Glass; Enka; August On The Island; Little Giants *46:36*

❀❀❀(❀) **Three Hands**
1992 Duke Street (DSRD 31084)

Spirit Wars; Hoover The Musical Dog; Island Of Women; A Child Must Grow; Hands; Run, Don't Walk; Sugar; Kehewin; Big Buck; Everybody Lies; 39 Weeks; Léger De Main *48:26*

❀❀❀(❀) **This Dragon Won't Sleep**
1995 Columbia (CK 80221)†

Godzilla; Head & Heart; Obrigado (Egberto); This Dragon Won't Sleep; Yoyomama; Any Colour But Blue; Groovy Sunflowers; Afraid To Dance; Tierra Maya; Catherine; Au Jardin D'Amour; Big Steps; Little Shoes; Zarzuela *60:14*

Wayne Rostad
FOLK/COUNTRY; SINGER-SONGWRITER

Ottawa singer-songwriter Wayne Rostad is well known as the host of the popular CBC TV series *On The Road Again* which travels across Canada focusing on unusual facets of Canadian life. In some ways, the TV show is a mirror of Rostad's 1991 album, *Storyteller*, a recording that, in song, tells the story of some of the interesting characters Rostad has met. The album includes "Noisy Jim's Cafe," about a popular little café and its proprietor just outside Saskatoon, "Ruby And Rose," a song about two ladies from Quebec who travelled one summer in a wagon pulled by a Belgian mare, and "Sonny, Pull With Me," about a pair of world champion dory racers in Lunenburg, Nova Scotia. The songs are tributes to real people, and the pen-and-ink drawings that accompany the lyrics add to the overall charm. Rostad's homespun voice will not win any awards, but the album is fun.

❋❋❋ **Storyteller**
1991 Stag Creek (SCR-CD 1013)

Stories To Tell; Transition To Trinity Bay; Ruins Of British Harbour; Passage To Grand Manan; King Of Dulse; Ruby And Rose; Noisy Jim's Cafe; Schubenacadie Tinsmith Man; Back To The Slocan; Sonny, Pull With Me; Clarence The Caribou; Song Of The Orcas; When I Grow Up *45:20*

Karl Roth
JAZZ

Calgary violinist Karl Roth, a member of The Cold Club and backup musician for many Calgary artists, steps out front and centre on *Everybody Wants To Be A Cat*, a top-notch jazz-oriented release that features Roth's excellent violin and voice. Guest musicians include Loni Moger, Neil Bentley, Dave Hamilton, Craig McCaul, Ian Grant, Dave Wilkie, and Ron Casat.
See also The Cold Club.

❋❋❋❋ **Everybody Wants To Be A Cat**
1994 Too Hot Music (THM CD 0001)

Everybody Wants To Be A Cat; Minor Swing; My Favourite Things; I've Got The World On A String; Swing 42; L'Accordéoniste; It Don't Mean A Thing; In A Sentimental Mood; When You Wish Upon A Star; Built For Comfort; Minor Swing; Two Sleepy People *42:30*

Denis Ryan
CELTIC FOLK

Denis Ryan, the founder of the popular group Ryan's Fancy, delivers an album of old favourites on *Mist Covered Mountains*. His Irish tenor voice is featured on songs like "Tiree Love Song," "Newport Town," "Mist Covered Mountains Of Home," "Will You Go Lassie Go," and "Dark Island." Ryan is joined by guest musicians and vocalists including Raylene Rankin, Tony Quinn, Scott Macmillan, and Dave MacIsaac.

※※※ **Mist Covered Mountains**
1991 Brookes Diamond (DRCD 228)†

Paddy's Green Shamrock Shore; Tiree Love Song; Newport Town; Sweet Forget Me
Not; Cape Breton Sunrise; Let Me Fish Off Cape St. Mary's; Mist Covered Moun-
tains Of Home; Will You Go Lassie Go; For Now I'm Sixty-Four; I'll Take You
Home Again, Kathleen/Isle Of Innisfree; Dark Island *42:35*

Buffy Sainte-Marie
FOLK/COUNTRY/POP; FIRST NATIONS MUSIC; SINGER-SONGWRITER

Saskatchewan-born Buffy Sainte-Marie inducted into the Juno Awards Hall of Fame
in 1995 for her lifetime achievement in the field of music. A dual citizen of Canada
and the United States, Sainte-Marie's career took flight in the 1960's when her uncanny songwriting talents and striking voice brought her to the forefront of the 60's
folk revival. Sainte-Marie may be Canada's most diverse songwriter—her material
ranges effortlessly from protest songs to love songs to country, pop, and rock. *It's My
Way*, from 1964, is a treasury of early Sainte-Marie material including protest "Now
That The Buffalo's Gone," "Cod'ine," "The Universal Soldier," "It's My Way," "He
Lived Alone In Town," "The Incest Song," and "Eyes Of Amber." On "Cripple Creek"
Sainte-Marie sings to the accompaniment of mouth bow. *Little Wheel Spin And Spin*,
from 1966, contains "My Country 'Tis Of Thy People You're Dying," "Poor Man's
Daughter," the countryish "Sometimes When I Get To Thinkin'," and the title track,
"Little Wheel Spin And Spin."

By the close of the 60's every folk act was making a Nashville album, and Sainte-
Marie was no exception. She has a knack for writing country/folk and for many fans
the 1968 recording, *I'm Gonna Be A Country Girl Again*, is simply her best. High-
lights include "He's A Pretty Good Man If You Ask Me," "A Soulful Shade Of Blue,"
"The Piney Wood Hills," "Tall Trees In Georgia," "Take My Hand For Awhile," and
"Gonna Feel Much Better When You're Gone." *Illuminations* is as different from
Country Girl as it is from *It's My Way*. This haunting, often beautiful, album was
Sainte-Marie's first experiment with electronics, combining acoustic guitar and voice
with synthesized sound. Her arrangement of Leonard Cohen's poem "God Is Alive,
Magic Is Afoot" is one of the album's highlights.

The Best Of Buffy Sainte-Marie was originally issued as a Vanguard "Twofer"—
two vinyl LP's in one package. The problem with this CD is that while Sainte-Marie's
wide-ranging songwriting sounds right on her individual albums where the tracks are
carefully sequenced, the *Best Of* collection turns them into a hodgepodge. The individual albums are more satisfying, but this collection is the only place you'll find CD
copies of songs like "Many A Mile," "Los Pescadores," and Joni Mitchell's "The
Circle Game." *She Used To Wanna Be A Ballerina* is one of Sainte-Marie's least successful albums—a move into pop music that doesn't ring true. *Moonshot*, on the other
hand, succeeds moderately well as a pop album. Backed by a congenial band, Sainte-
Marie introduces a new sound and includes some new material written for the occasion: "He's An Indian Cowboy In The Rodeo," "Moonshot," and "Native North American Child." In 1992 Sainte-Marie stunned the music industry by releasing her first
album after a hiatus of over fifteen years. *Coincidences And Likely Stories* is an album

for the 90's with 60's-like sentiments. Sainte-Marie has lost none of her songwriting magic—the album ranks among her best.

✳✳✳✳✓ **It's My Way**
1964 Vanguard (VMD 79142)

Now That The Buffalo's Gone; The Old Man's Lament; Ananias; Mayoo Sto Hoon; Cod'ine; Cripple Creek; The Universal Soldier; Babe In Arms; He Lived Alone In Town; You're Gonna Need Somebody On Your Bond; The Incest Song; Eyes Of Amber; It's My Way *40:35*

✳✳✳(✳) **Little Wheel Spin And Spin**
1966 Vanguard (VMD 79211)

Little Wheel Spin And Spin; House Carpenter; Waly, Waly; Rolling Log Blues; My Country 'Tis Of Thy People You're Dying; Men Of The Fields; Timeless Love; Sir Patrick Spens; Poor Man's Daughter; Lady Margaret; Sometimes When I Get To Thinkin'; Winter Boy *40:55*

✳✳✳✳✓ **I'm Gonna Be A Country Girl Again**
1968 Vanguard (79280-2)

I'm Gonna Be A Country Girl Again; He's A Pretty Good Man If You Ask Me; Uncle Joe; A Soulful Shade Of Blue; From The Bottom Of My Heart; Sometimes When I Get To Thinkin'; The Piney Wood Hills; Now That The Buffalo's Gone; They Gotta Quit Kickin' My Dawg Around; Tall Trees In Georgia; The Love Of A Good Man; Take My Hand For A While; Gonna Feel Much Better When You're Gone *34:02*

✳✳✳(✳) **The Best Of Buffy Sainte-Marie**
1987, 1970 Vanguard (VCD-3/4)

A Soulful Shade Of Blue; Summer Boy; The Universal Soldier; Better To Find Out For Yourself; Cod'ine; He's A Keeper Of The Fire; Take My Hand For A While; Ground Hog; The Circle Game; My Country 'Tis Of Thy People You're Dying; Many A Mile; Until It's Time For You To Go; Rolling Log Blues; God Is Alive, Magic Is Afoot; Guess Who I Saw In Paris; The Piney Wood Hills; Now That The Buffalo's Gone; Cripple Creek; I'm Gonna Be A Country Girl Again; The Vampire; Little Wheel Spin And Spin; Winter Boy; Los Pescadores; Sometimes When I Get To Thinkin' *71:04*

✳✳✳(✳) **Illuminations**
1970, reissued 1992 Vanguard [FNAC—France] (WM 321/ 662115)†

God Is Alive, Magic Is Afoot; Mary; Better Find Out For Yourself; The Vampire; Adam; The Dream Tree; Suffer The Little Children; The Angel; With You, Honey; Guess Who I Saw In Paris; He's A Keeper Of The Fire; Poppies *35:57*

✳✳ **She Used To Wanna Be A Ballerina**
1971 Vanguard (VMD 79311)

Rollin' Mill Man; Smack Water Jack; Sweet September Morning; She Used To Wanna Be A Ballerina; Bells; Helpless; Moratorium; The Surfer; Song Of The French Partisan; Soldier Blue; Now You've Been Gone For A Long Time *35:00*

✳✳✳ **Moonshot**
1972 Vanguard (WM 321/662140)

Not The Lovin' Kind; You Know How To Turn On Those Lights; I Wanna Hold Your

Hand Forever; He's An Indian Cowboy In The Rodeo; Lay It Down; Moonshot; Native North American Child; My Baby Left Me; Sweet Memories; Jeremiah; Mister Can't You See *32:12*

✳✳✳✳✓ **Coincidence And Likely Stories**
1992 Chrysalis/Ensign (F2 21920)†

The Big Ones Get Away; Fallen Angels; Bad End; Emma Lee; Starwalker; The Priests Of The Golden Bull; Disinformation; Getting Started; I'm Going Home; Bury My Heart At Wounded Knee; Goodnight *43:23*

Trichy Sankaran
SOUTH INDIAN DRUMMING

Toronto-based Trichy Sankaran is a virtuoso *mrdangam* player—the double-headed barrel drum from South India. A disciple of the late Sri Palani Subramania Pillai, Sankaran made his public debut at age thirteen. A professor of Indian Music Studies at York University, Toronto, his techniques have been filmed and documented by the CBC. Sankaran's writings include a textbook on mrdangam performance and rhythmic theory. Sankaran has performed widely throughout Asia, Europe, and North America. On *Laya Vinyas* he is accompanied by Karaikkudi Subramaniam, a leading proponent of the vina (a string instrument from South India), Lalitha Sankaran on taboura, and Andrew Timar on finger cymbals.

✳✳✳✳ **Laya Vinyas**
1990 Music Of The World (CDT-120)

Mrdangam Solo In Adi Tala (8 Beat Cycle); Mrdangam Solo In Misra Chapu Tala (7 Beat Cycle); Kriti: Padavini (Adi Tala); Kanjira Solo In Khanda Eka Tala (5 Beat Cycle); Talavadya Kacceri In Khanda Eka Tala; Kavadichindu In Misra Chapu Tala *42:13*

Sazacha Red Sky
FOLK/BLUES; SINGER-SONGWRITER

Red Sky Rising has been the subject of controversy since its release. The album claims that Sazacha Red Sky, the stage name of Vancouver session singer Nancy Nash, is the "spiritual" daughter of Vancouver's Chief Dan George. Can a non-native person do First Nations music? Controversy aside, this is a powerful album with some wonderful singing and slide guitar.

✳✳✳(✳) **Red Sky Rising**
1993 Sazacha Red Sky (SRS9313)

Wolf/Dolphin Welcoming Song; Stuck In The Middle; The Prayer Song; All Of My Love; Grandma's Comin; Roy's Song; Mr. Velvet Blue; Little Drum; Red Sky At Night; A.I.M. Song/The Prayer Of Silence *47:20*

Scatter The Mud

CELTIC FOLK; SINGER-SONGWRITERS

A Calgary-based Celtic pub band, Scatter The Mud puts a lively spin on traditional numbers and tunes written by band members. The group combines tight harmonies and well-played instrumentals on *In The Müd*. The album includes numbers like "Wavy Creek," described as "a body of water in Manitoba where you can skate, swim and augment your mosquito collection." Despite the light-hearted atmosphere, there is some seriously good Celtic music on this album. Scatter The Mud is Phil O'Flaherty, Cam Keating, Greg Hooper, and Conan Daly.

❋❋❋(❋) **In The Müd**
1994 Müd Music (MMCD0051)

> Leis An Lurigan/The Ingleneuk; Sleive Russell/The Swaggering Jig; Diamantina Drover; The Scotsman Over The Border/The Peeler And The Goat; The Old Mountain Road; Wavy Creek; A Bad Day For Brittany/Flying Plate/Whelan's Reel; Red Is The Rose; The Rakes Of Kildare/Stuart Chisholm's Walkabout/Famous Ballymote; As I Roved Out/Galdowyn's Reel/The Blacksmith; At The Ball And Chain *53:43*

Lesley Schatz

FOLK/WESTERN; SINGER-SONGWRITER

Calgary artist Lesley Schatz has put together an unusual set of albums on the Bear label from Germany. The first two albums, *Coyote Moon/Run To The Wind* and *Walls, Hearts & Heroes*, are collections of Schatz' songwriting, well sung in a "western" style with sparkling, outstanding backup musicianship from some of Calgary's best, including David Wilkie, Stewart MacDougall, Nathan Tinkham, and Cindy Church. The next three albums, *Hello Stranger*, *Banjo Pickin' Girl*, and *Brave Wolfe*, appear to be part of a project on the Bear label to do modern recordings of North American folk classics. The instrumentation on these recordings is stark—often just a simple guitar or banjo—and Schatz' effervescent, but somewhat fragile, voice doesn't always have enough depth to carry the tunes successfully. She does her best interpretations on faster-paced material, particularly Appalachian tunes. Unfortunately for Canadian folkies, CDs from the Bear label are imported into Canada at premium prices, seriously limiting the audience for Schatz' work. Schatz has a large following in Europe and the former Soviet Union.

❋❋❋(❋) **Coyote Moon/Run To The Wind**
1990 Bear (BCD 15513)†

> It's About Time; Alberta Blue; Freight Train Bound; The Way She Would Sing; Printed Word; Coyote Moon; Boppin' At The Gamle; Goin' Home; Old Tin Pot; Les' Wish; Alberta Waltz; Molly And Tenbrooks; To Each His Own; I'll Be On The Road Again; Run To The Wind; Chinese Silver; Slow Dance; Wind (Stay Away); The Only Sound You'll Hear; Empty Hands *72:24*

❋❋❋(❋) **Walls, Hearts & Heroes**
1992 Bear (BCD 15674)†

> Walls And Borders; Gotta Go (Bremen Train); Dryland; Lonely Bird; Back To Your

Arms; Girl Gone Wild; Old, Old Doll; Take A Stand (For The Children); I Can Hear Ya Callin'; Foothills Lullabye; My Heart Stands (At Your Door); Gypsy Blue; Wastin' The Moon; Merlin And The Cowboy; I Can Dance (Like Arthur Murray); New Crescent Moon; Once A Dream; Way Of Walkin' (She's Sure Got Away With My Heart); Old Wooley; A Christmas Wish; Christmas In The Cabin; Un Canadien Errant *78:05*

❋❋❋ Hello Stranger
1993 Bear (BCD 15725 AH)†

Hello Stranger; Shenandoah; The Wayfaring Stranger; Apple Blossom Time; Beautiful River Valley; The Sweetest Gift; The Water Is Wide; Somewhere In Tennessee; Froggy Went A-Courtin'; Farewell To Nova Scotia; Home On The Range; Down In The Valley; Whiskey In The Jar; The Girl I Left Behind; The Lily Of The West; Did He Mention My Name; Spanish Is A Loving Tongue; Cancion De Cuna; La Source; Brahm's Lullaby *57:57*

❋❋❋ Banjo Pickin' Girl
1993 Bear (BCD 15729 AH)†

The Winter It Is Past; Troubled In Mind; Cruel Sister; Barbara Allen; Little Joe, The Wrangler; Zebra Dun; Streets Of Laredo; Jesse James; Tom Dula; Banjo Pickin' Girl; Early One Morning; Arthur McBride; Jack O'Hazlegreen; Great Silkie; Silver Dagger; Rowan Tree; White Coral Bells; Flor Del Pino; Tumbalalaika; Will The Circle Be Unbroken *62:22*

❋❋❋ Brave Wolfe
1993 Bear (BCD 15735 AH)†

Red River Valley; Gypsy Davy; Oh Susanna; Brave Wolfe; The Banks Of The Ohio; I Never Will Marry; Greensleeves/Greenpeace; I Ride An Old Paint; Shady Grove; Rising Sun Blues; The Train That Carried My Man From Town; Shortenin' Bread; Cripple Creek; Mole In The Ground; Old Joe Clark; Nine Pound Hammer; Turkey In The Straw; Sinner Man; Careless Love; Pretty Little Horses *57:02*

Oliver Schroer
FIDDLE

The ubiquitous Oliver Schroer, a Toronto-based fiddler, is a popular session musician and producer. His concert performances are always wonderful and slightly wacky. Schroer's first CD, *Jigzup*, is an album of contemporary fiddle music that draws from a background of traditional fiddling and adds overtones from various musical cultures, including a touch of rock and a few bars of trumpet playing. It's a little offbeat, but it comes off well, with Schroer's fiddle providing a core that keeps everything centred. His second CD, *Whirled*, may have pushed the envelope a little too far. A few of the tracks are very difficult to listen to, which is a shame because most of the album is engaging. Highlights include "Into The Sun," "Whirled," "Blue Sun In A Yellow Sky," and "The Humours Of Aristotle." *Whirled* received an "Offbeat Folk Award" Porcupine in 1994.

❋❋❋❋✓ Jigzup
1993 Big Dog [no catalogue number]

Victory Of Love; Toby's Reel/The Job; Laughing In Her Sleep; Horseshoes And Rainbows; Far Away By The Sea/Lady Diane Laundy/Seanaghan Kennedy's;

Ansgar's Jig/Kari's Jig; Blow November Wind/Sea Of Change; The Devil And The Little Faces; The Hub Of The Wheel; Jump Up/Ghost Dance; Roro; December 16th/ The Shooting Star; If Geese Could Sing; Bright Eyes *51:47*

✳✳✳(✳) **Whirled**
1994 Big Dog [no catalogue number]

Into The Sun; Whirled; Blue Sun In A Yellow Sky; The Humours Of Aristotle; The Humours Of Plato; Early In The Morning/Irkuzan; Gurka's Retreat; Sit By Me; Deep Water; Marcie's Dzygh; Christmas With Poncho/Last Call; The Western Door; Handgames *51:32*

The Schryer Triplets
FIDDLE

Ontario's Schryer Triplets—Dan, Louis, and Pierre—thoroughly dominated Ontario fiddling contests for over a decade. *Triple Fiddle*, which showcases their ability to range effortlessly from traditional Celtic to Texas Swing, is a must purchase for all fiddle lovers. On this upbeat album the Schryers combine as a fiddle trio on some tracks and play solo on others. Guest musicians include Julie Lefebvre, piano; Denis Lanctôt, accordion, piano; Jamie Gatti, bass; Ann Downey, double bass; Rob MacLeod, drums; Al Bragg, pedal steel; Brian Pickell, guitar; Bobby Lalonde, guitar; Nathan Curry, cittern, mandolin, bodhran; Pat McLaughlin, guitar; Steve Piticco, guitar; and Kerry Vaillancourt, guitar.

✳✳✳✳✓ **Triple Fiddle**
1993 Schryer Triplets (CD 930702)

French Reels: La Sauvagesse/Reel À Rémi/Reel De L'Enfant/Reel Du Printemps; Panhandle Rag; Clog, Jig And Reel: Spellan's Inspiration/Sir Wilfred Laurier Quadrille/Donnell Leahy's Breakdown/Timmins Reel/Dan's Hornpipe; My Lily/The Sweetness Of Mary Strathspey/Hughie Jim Paul's Reel; Black And White Rag; Tennessee Waltz/Down Yonder; Waiting For Emilie; Irish Tunes: Maids Of Castlebar/The Flower Of The Flock/Farewell To Old Decency; Tico-Tico; McHattie's Waltz; Beaumont Rag; Jammin' Live: Cape Breton Dream/Chelsey's Jig/ Sally Goodin'/Fisher's Hornpipe/Sherbrooke Reel/Pointe-Au-Pic/Moving Cloud/ White Fish In The Rapids/Reel Du Faubourg/Schryer's Breakdown/Snowflake Breakdown/Indian Reel/Mason's Apron/High Road To Linton *47:11*

Sandy Scofield
FIRST NATIONS MUSIC; FOLK; SINGER-SONGWRITER

"Some tan the hides / some sew the beads / some live and die on skid row / cheap for pills and booze democracy"—from "Lil' Wat Man." On *Dirty River*, British Columbia singer-songwriter Sandy Scofield delivers a set of hard-hitting contemporary lyrics wrapped in tight acoustic/electric folk arrangements. Highlights include "Angels," "Dirty River," "Lil' Wat Man," "Geronimo," and "Fool's Gold." Scofield's strong, countryish voice drives the lyrics home on track after track.

✳✳✳(✳)   **Dirty River**
1994 Arpeggio (SP659)†

Angels; Dirty River; Sylvia; Sweet Talk; Lil' Wat Man; Kahnestake; Geronimo; Fool's Gold; Big House; Come The Spring *37:10*

Seanachie

CELTIC FOLK; SINGER-SONGWRITERS

Seanachie (pronounced *shawn-a-key*) is a Calgary Celtic-folk band that combines original songs with traditional jigs and reels on pipes, fiddle, and whistles. Their debut album, *Shouting At Magpies*, presents a mix of original material, such as Gordon McCulloch's "Faith In Rhetoric," "Leaving The Banks," and "Dieppe," alongside traditional tunes like "The Drunken Landlady," "Primrose Girl," and "Sleepy Maggie." The pace is gentle and the singing is intimate. Members of Seanachie are Gordon McCulloch, former member of the Calgary Celtic band First Draft and Seanachie's main songwriter, vocalist, and guitarist, Ann Gray, a piping champion, whistle player, and former member of the Barra MacNeils, Jackie Bell, who is also a member of Kilgore Trout, on vocals, violin, piano, and guitar, and Richard Gullison, a former member of Prairie Oyster on bass.

✳✳✳   **Shouting At Magpies**
1995 Seanachie (TBA)

Faith In Rhetoric; Leaving The Banks; Te Bheag; Fitzy's Birthday Present/ Skyeman's Jig/The Moose/The Drunken Landlady; Do You Remember; Go To Hell/ Duncan Johnstone; Dieppe; South In Autumn; Malts In The Optics/Forest Lodge/ Primrose Girl/Sleepy Maggie; Eyes That Laugh The Same

Seventh Fire

FIRST NATIONS MUSIC; FOLK/ROCK; SINGER-SONGWRITERS

A kind of First Nations Rap 'n' Roll band, Ottawa's Seventh Fire combines snappy lyrics with chants, electric instruments, and sax in a driving mix on *The Cheque Is In The Mail*. The band rips its way through numbers like "Where The Buffalo Roam," "Radiation Heat," and "Caught Up In The Smiles." Traditionalists may find the album too rock-laced for their tastes.

✳✳✳   **The Cheque Is In The Mail**
1994 First Nations (7621-10016-2)

Round Dance; Where The Buffalo Roam; Radiation Heat; The Cheque Is In The Mail; Caught Up In The Smiles; They Got It Made; Panic City; Days Of Anger; Think About The Children; My Home; Chi Meegwetch; Freedom Train; Round Dance (Reprise) *48:46*

Ron Sexsmith
FOLK/POP; SINGER-SONGWRITER

"Sexsmith's appeal is his utterly sincere voice and way with a tune; his unassuming manner carries the insights of an Everyman trying to remain optimistic in a tough world"—*Toronto Star*. Raised in St. Catharines, Ontario, Ron Sexsmith was equally influenced by Buddy Holly and Leonard Cohen. His voice has been described as "fragile" but older folkies will be excused if Sexsmith's voice reminds them of a young Phil Ochs. After several years of playing coffee houses, Sexsmith was signed by a major record label and his debut recording, *Ron Sexsmith*, is a solid effort that highlights his spare, understated, penetrating lyrics. Highlights include "Secret Heart," a song about the importance of expressing yourself, "Words We Never Use," inspired by watching a couple on the subway holding hands but not speaking, "Speaking With The Angel," a song written while observing his own child, and the poignant "From A Few Streets Over," about not having enough money to buy his kids ice cream from a street vendor.

❊❊❊(❊)   **Ron Sexsmith**
         1995 Interscope (CD 92485)†

> Secret Heart; There's A Rhythm; Words We Never Use; Summer Blowin' Town; Lebanon, Tennessee; Speaking With The Angel; In Place Of You; Heart With No Companion; Several Miles; From A Few Streets Over; First Chance I Get; Wastin' Time; Galbraith Street; There's A Rhythm *43:02*

The Sharecroppers
FOLK; SINGER-SONGWRITERS

A Pasadena, Newfoundland trio, The Sharecroppers consist of Guy Romaine, Ed Humber, and Mike Madigan. On *Natural*—so named partly due to the "natural" recording method with the trio performing in a church—The Sharecroppers deliver a set of nostalgic, downhome lyrics over a fabric of acoustic instrumentation and simple harmonies.

❊❊❊   **Natural**
      1993 Ibycus (SHC 001 02)

> One Room School; The Mill Whistle; Engineer's Song; Katie's Tune; The Kyle; The Legionnaires; Newfoundland Autumn; Freddie's Tune; Yesterday's Fishermen; My Grandfather's Fiddle; Newman's Reel; Mermaid; Twenty-Five Miners *46:20*

Sho Do Man
AFRICAN-CARIBBEAN FUSION; SINGER-SONGWRITER

Toronto-based Sho Do Man, born in Kinshasa, Zaire, launched his musical career at age seventeen. Since immigrating to Canada in 1987, his songs and compositions range from the Zairian dialect to English, French, and Spanish. On *Trouble, Trouble*, Sho Do Man's fine voice blends well with the catchy rhythms of his band in a mix of songs that range from Zairian-oriented material to Caribbean-style reggae. The musicians on this album include Adomo Ndaro Solomon, Bishop Okele, and Ossie Gurley.

✳✳✳(✳)   **Trouble, Trouble**
1994 Dark Light (DL 6001)

Trouble Trouble; Let's Change The Beat; Billy Part 1; Nadia; Itebe; Masiandoki; Baby Girl; Anto; Nathy; Billy Part 2

Simani
COUNTRY FOLK; SINGER-SONGWRITERS

The Newfoundland duo Simani (Bud Davidge and Sim Savory) perform rootsy, countryish songs written mainly by Davidge. Mixing acoustic guitar with fiddle and accordion accompaniment, Simani will be enjoyed by those who like "old country" music—simple, heartfelt, earthy, and (mostly) acoustic. Highlights from *Some Things I Cherish* include "Keep Our Spirit Alive," "Out Of My Sight," "Some Things I Cherish," "Watch The Flowers Grow," and a bouncy instrumental version of Emile Benoit's "Emile's Jig." *Home And Native Land* provides a similar mix of material. A takeoff on "I'se The B'y" called "I'se Da Boy" is a commentary on changes in the fishing industry. *Promises* is clearly their best-produced album to date. The sound is cleaner and Bud and Sim get a boost from some excellent session musicians.

✳✳✳   **Some Things I Cherish**
1990 SWC (SDCD 5159)

Keep Our Spirit Alive; Out Of My Sight; Emile's Jig; Some Things I Cherish; Whose Heart Is It; The Loveliest Day In June; Garden Of Eden; Bay Boy's Jig; Love Me Now; Watch The Flowers Grow *30:14*

✳✳✳   **Home And Native Land**
1992 SWC (SDCD 749212)

Island Of Mine; You Know Full Well; Cory's Jig; You're My Best Friend; Look At Her Blow; The Rose In The Hair; Nose To The Grindstone; In The Bushes With You; I'se Da Boy; Home And Native Land *31:57*

✳✳✳(✳)   **Promises**
1994 SWC [no catalogue number]†

The Promise; Said And Done; It Could Be Worse; B.J.; Take That; The Ballad Of Mildred Baxter; Every Blue Moon; Rock Valley Jig/Little Burnt Potato; A Tribute To Don And Al; I'll Send My Love With Roses *30:01*

Siren's Whisper
FOLK/POP; SINGER-SONGWRITERS

Siren's Whisper is a Newfoundland singer-songwriter duo consisting of Kathy Phippard and Esther Squires. *The Spell Is Cast* is a folkish, poetic collection of songs that, as the title implies, explores the spell of moments and the lyrical underpinnings of experience. The songs abound in water and ocean imagery.

✳✳✳ **The Spell Is Cast**
1992 Sirens (SW-001-02)†

Young At Heart; The Spell Is Cast; Here's To Life; Running Wild; Night Journey;
Faceless Angel; Deadman's Cove; Unmasked; You Walk Alone; Child Of The Sea;
Stranger; Looking To Dawn; Weather Inside; Towered In The Night *53:31*

Six Mile Bridge
CELTIC/FOLK; SINGER-SONGWRITERS

Six Mile Bridge is an Ottawa group that includes musicians from the Angstones and
Fat Man Waving. A traditionally minded, yet experimental, band, Six Mile Bridge
likes to blend world rhythms into their Celtic-based music, as featured on "Bombay
Revisited/Marioro," the opening track from *Six Mile Bridge*. The band consists of
Nathan Curry, Peter Kiesewalter, Ian Mackie, Ross Murray, James Stephens, and John
Wood.
See also The Angstones; Fat Man Waving

✳✳✳(✳) **Six Mile Bridge**
[no date] Canal (CANAL 259 CD)

Bombay Revisited/Marioro; The Banks Of Lough Gowna/More Power To Your
Elbow; Temagami; Yapper's Reel/My Darling's Asleep; Flowing Tide/Tommy
Sullivan's Polkas; Bound For India; The Wee Room; Killen's Fairy Hill/Ms.
McLeod/The Foxhunters; Go And Sit Upon The Grass; Blarney Pilgrim/President's
Choice; The Gravel Walk To Stravinsky's House; The Promise *55:30*

Laura Smith
FOLK/POP; SINGER-SONGWRITER

"I'm not a storytelling songwriter. I don't follow the tradition of telling stories about
losing cows. I'm talking about being a person, having questions. I'm documenting
being human"—Laura Smith, Interview, *Toronto Star*. Laura Smith, a singer-songwriter born in Ontario and a resident of Nova Scotia since 1984, brings a clear, bluesy
voice and insightful lyrics to her debut album, *Elemental*. Those who enjoy good
poetry in song will revel in this slightly obscure recording and will find it worthwhile
to track down a copy. *B'tween The Earth And My Soul*, released in late 1994, should
bring Smith's slightly dusky voice to a wider audience. The production values are
high and the music is memorable. Highlights include "Shade Of Your Love," "Four
Letter Word," "No Call For Mercy," "Duine Air Call," and an absolutely smashing
version of "My Bonny."

✳✳✳(✳) **Elemental**
1989 CBC Variety Recordings (VRCD1001)

Bells; Elemental; The Tides After Shifting; Faceless Wonder; Jordy; Shorelines;
Matt's Song; So Far From Home; Diggin'; It Works Great On Paper *33:51*

✱✱✱(✱) **B'tween The Earth And My Soul**
1994 Atlantica (02 77657 50235 21)†

Shade Of Your Love; Four Letter Word (For Lonesome); My Bonny; So Close To
My Knees; Two Steps; No Call For Mercy; Duine Air Call; I Go There; Gypsy
Dream; Clean Up Your Own Backyard; Whirlaround *48:13*

Charlie Sohmer

FOLK/COUNTRY/POP; SINGER-SONGWRITER

Ontario singer-songwriter Charlie Sohmer's expressive, sometimes gritty, voice
matches his wide range of songwriting styles on *Spirit Jewels*—an album that moves
effortlessly from folk to blues to country. Highlights include "All Your Tears," "Lilies
In The Valley," "I Who Would Run," "Crossing The River," and "Needle Of Love."
Fans who like Willie P. Bennett will find parallels in Sohmer's voice and lyrics.

✱✱✱(✱) **Spirit Jewels**
1994 Snowy River (SRR-S33)†

All Your Tears; Lilies In The Valley; I Who Would Run; Crossing The River; Inch By
Inch; The Lover And The Lady; Needle Of Love; Please Don't Let Me In; With
Grace; And Laugh *43:28*

Isidore Soucy

FRENCH CANADIAN FIDDLE

Isidore Soucy, born in Ste-Blandine, Québec in 1899, was the best fiddler in his home
town by his teens. By the time he moved from the Gaspé to Montréal, he was a remarkable fiddler and dancer who knew older dances such as quadrilles and schottisches which were different from the prevailing waltzes and reels. Soucy, who called
himself a "folkloriste" began playing on radio shows and eventually formed three
popular recording groups: Vive-la-Joie, the Trio Soucy, and, his most famous band,
the Famille Soucy. The Famille Soucy consisted of family members Eugène, Thérèse,
Marie-Ange, and Fernando. The family made its radio debut in 1956 and in 1960
launched the immensely popular TV show, *Chez Isidore*. After his death in 1963, the
band continued under his son, Fernando. According to the *Encyclopedia of Music in
Canada*, Soucy is said to have made some 1200 recordings, including 78's for Columbia, Starr, and Bluebird, and LP's for Dominion. Some of these historical recordings
have been captured on the CD *Isidore Soucy*, an MCA Héritage Québécois reissue.
There are no liner notes with this fine recording. Soucy was inducted into the Porcupine Awards Hall of Fame as a memorial member in 1994.

✱✱✱✱ **Isidore Soucy**
[no date, reissued 1991] MCA (MCAD-10489)

Gigue À Ti-Zoune; Reel Rêve Du Diable; Grande Gigue Simple; Set Canadien; Reel
À Manda; Valse De La Cuisine; Polka Piquée; Reel Des Esquimaux; Valse Du
Vieux-Québec; Marche Domino; Reel Du Pendu; Reel De Rimouski; Reel À Fi-Fine;
Reel Des Poilus; Reel Du Président *43:22*

Spirit Of The West

CELTIC FOLK; FOLK/ROCK; SINGER-SONGWRITERS

Vancouver band Spirit Of The West started out as a Celtic-influenced folk group similar to the Pogues, but, with shifting personnel, and changes in musical direction, the
group evolved into a popular rock band. Spirit Of The West has two distinct audiences: folkies, who tend to prefer their earlier material and young music fans who
prefer their later work. The focus of the group, throughout, has been the joint
songwriting of Geoffrey Kelly and John Mann. The earliest, and folkiest, material
available on compact disc is *Old Material*, a collection of songs from 1984-1986. On
this album Spirit Of The West does a convincing set of Celtic-oriented songs like
"Rocks At Thieves Bay," "To A Highlander Unknown," "Aberdeen," "Ships In Full
Sail," and "General Guinness." The second half of the album, recorded live, suffers
from poor recording quality. On this album the band consists of Geoffrey Kelly, J.
Knutson, and John Mann. *Tripping Up The Stairs* continues in a Celtic spirit, with the
same personnel. With *Labour Day* Spirit of the West changes musical directions. There's
still a rootsiness about the material but there's a tilt away from Celtic and towards
rock. Knutson has been replaced by Hugh McMillan.

Many Spirit Of The West fans list *Save This House* as their favourite album. The
lyrics are more exploratory and introspective than those on *Labour Day* and the tempo
has swung strongly towards the rock side of the spectrum. The band has added Linda
McRae and they've made a successful transition to their new sound. Highlights in-
clude "Save This House," "Last To Know," "Dirty Pool," "Not Just A Train," and
"Swingin' Single." The 1991 release, *Go Figure*, loses some of the edge of *Save This
House*. The band has added Vince Ditrich to bring the number to five. Of *Faithlift* one
reviewer says, "I enjoy this album for its sound and the rich imagery of its lyrics, but
I also miss the old Spirit of the West"—*Dirty Linen*. If you're a dedicated Spirit Of
The West fan, you may find the album either wonderful or disappointing, depending
on your expectations. If you're a marginal fan, this one may tax you.

❋❋❋(❋)   **Old Material: 1984-1986**
1984, 1989, reissued 1994 Stony Plain (SPCD 1141)

> Rocks At Thieves Bay; To A Highlander Unknown; Doin' Quite Alright; Down On
> The Dole; John Goodman; Aberdeen; Ships In Full Sail; Be Right; Time To Ring Up
> Some Changes; General Guinness *43:06*

❋❋❋(❋)   **Tripping Up The Stairs**
1988 Stony Plain (SPCD 1098)

> An Honest Gamble Jig/Tripping Up The Stairs; Our Station; Peacetime; Room
> Without A View (Stella); The Crawl; Homelands Jigs: The Kesh/The Blackthorn
> Stick; The Mists Of Crofton; Till The Cows Come Home; When Rivers Rise; Be
> Right/Pigeon On The Gate *39:39*

❋❋❋(❋)   **Labour Day**
1988 Stony Plain (SPCD 1123)†

> Darkhouse; Political; Profiteers; The Hounds That Wait Outside Your Door; Runboy;
> Drinking Man; Expensive/Cinema Of Pain; Gottingen Street; Take It From The
> Source *40:55*

❄❄❄❄ **Save This House**
1990 WEA (CD-70971)†

Save This House; Home For A Rest; Last To Know; Roadside Attraction; Dirty Pool; Not Just A Train; (Putting Up With) The Joneses; Turned Out Lies; Sentimental Side; Water In The Well; Wrecking Ball; Loaded Minds; Swingin' Single; The Old Sod *58:30*

❄❄❄(❄) **Go Figure**
1991 WEA (CD 74692)†

D For Democracy (Scour The House); Big Head; Spot The Difference; Pulling Lame; Let's Make A Mystery; Goodbye Grace; Just Another Day; Polaroid; Political; Ship Named Frank; Far Too Canadian *53:44*

❄❄❄ **Faithlift**
1993 WEA (CD 93642)†

5 Free Minutes; Sadness Grows; Is This Where I Come In; Bone Of Contention; Slow Learner; And If Venice Is Sinking; Mum's The Word; Death On The Beach; Sincerely Yours; God's Apprentice; Guildhall Witness; 6th Floor *50:09*

Starb'ard Side
CELTIC FOLK; SINGER-SONGWRITERS

The Nova Scotia group, Starb'ard Side, performs a sparkling mix of traditional and contemporary songs punctuated with original material. On their debut album, *Starb'ard Side*, they switch from instrumentals like the "Over The Starb'ard Side/Kilmoulis Jig/ Belle Dune Reel" medley to original material like "Wooden Ships And Iron Men," "Fisherman's Farewell," and songs like the Dave Mallet composition, "Light At The End Of The Tunnel." Starb'ard Side is Jim Pittman, Jim Hanlon, John Hanlon, Wayne Hiltz, and Bill Plaskett.

❄❄❄(❄) **Starb'ard Side**
1994 Slumgullion / CBC Maritimes (NGOLD 2002-2)†

Over The Starb'ard Side/Kilmoulis Jig/Belle Dune Reel; Light At The End Of The Tunnel; Wild Rose Of The Mountain; Wooden Ships And Iron Men; Pittman's Polka; The Shores Of Botany Bay/Speed The Plough; Will You Be Waiting; Morrison's/ Swallowstail/Tobin's; Home Dearie Home; Carleton County/Big John MacNeil/ Dusty Miller; Fisherman's Farewell; Johnny I Sure Do Miss You/Cheese/My Love Is A Lassiette; Down North; Debbie's Waltz; Hard Times *49:45*

Bob Stark
FOLK/POP; SINGER-SONGWRITER

Ottawa singer-songwriter Bob Stark's pleasant voice and bluesy guitar combine with consistently good songwriting to make *Levels Of Survival* an album worth exploring. Highlights include "Monopoly World," "Big City Movie," "Wasteland To Blue," "Don't Keep Breaking My Heart," and "Bigger Chill." *One Candle Burning*, produced by Ian Tamblyn, kicks off with the title track, "One Candle Burning," a haunting song about the Kurds escaping the military might of Saddam Hussein. The album presents a more countryish Stark on cuts like "This Side Of Dreamland" and "Funny Old World."

The poignant "Irish Dust" is a song about three teenagers in Northern Ireland mistakenly killed in a bomb attack.

***　　**Levels Of Survival**
　　　　1990　Snowy River (SRR-S29 CD)†

> Monopoly World; Big City Movie; Wasteland To The Blue; Soul Of My Life; Don't Keep Breaking My Heart; Don't Let 'Em Fool Ya; Bigger Chill; The 1990's; Medal For The Blues; Between Outrage And Fantasy; And We Stand *44:40*

***　　**One Candle Burning**
　　　　1994　Snowy River (SRR-S32)†

> One Candle Burning; In The Shadows Of Others; Tous Les Matins; This Side Of Dreamland; Funny Old World; Irish Dust; It Holds Your Name; If You Should Ask Me; One More Dance; What About Love; This Love For Thee *47:59*

Ben Sures

FOLK; SINGER-SONGWRITER

"Quirky with twists and unusual turns of phrase"—Festival Distribution *Newsletter*. On *No Absolutes* Winnipeg singer-songwriter Ben Sures has released a debut album sure to catch your attention with its combination of unusual lyrics and excellent musicianship. The album has a solid backup cast, including Ron Casat on accordion, Tim Williams on guitar and mandolin, and supporting vocals by Jane Hawley and Jennifer Gibson. Highlights include "Things A Fella Won't Do," "Tired," "Everything I Do," and "No Absolutes."

***　　**No Absolutes**
　　　　1994　Frozen Bandicoot (BSO4CD)

> Things A Fella Won't Do; Tired; Dear Sarah; Everything I Do; Breathe; Single Again...Almost; Patches; No Absolutes; Roll With The Punches; Two Little Boys; Plenty Of Pride; The Hippo And The Canary *43:10*

Suroît

FOLK/CAJUN/CELTIC; FRENCH-CANADIAN; SINGER-SONGWRITERS

Suroît is a Quebec band from Iles-De-La-Madeleine that writes original compositions based on traditional music. They rock them up blending Celtic, bluegrass, Cajun, and country elements with their Acadian sensibilities. Their debut album, *Suroît*, is an infectious recording that will have you asking for more. The smooth vocals and sparkling musicianship make this a good "road" album—put this one on in your car next time you're heading down the highway. The band consists of Félix Leblanc, Réal Longuepée, Kenneth Saulnier, Henri-Paul Benard, and Alcide Painchaud.

***(*)　**Suroît**
　　　　1994?　Gestion Son Image (SUR C 997)†

> Mystificoté; Léo; Beau Robert; Les Filles De Larochelle; Hé Yaille, Yaille (Disco Fait Dodo); Salut Cap Breton; M'En Allant Par Saulnierville Station; Saint-Sauveur; Les Bons Souvenirs; L'Amour Est Dur; La Rose; La Danse Du Samedi Soir; Quand Deux Violons Chantent *41:53*

Ruth Sutherland

CELTIC HARP; SINGER-SONGWRITER; COMPOSER

Ruth Sutherland, a Celtic harpist and vocalist based in Hamilton, Ontario, has been a member of Punkie Willie and Tight Little Island. A session singer for Luba and Jane Child, Sutherland has stepped forward to lend her stark, expressive voice and harpistry to *Rantin' & Rovin'*—a solo album that mixes traditional Celtic material with elements of Gregorian chant and African drums. The result is a recording that ventures beyond the usual soothing, meditative effects of harp music into something spunkier and more exotic. Sutherland's flute-like voice carries her material well through both the traditional and experimental tracks.

✳✳✳　　**Rantin' & Rovin'**
　　　　1994 FPVB Productions (RSCD-0194)

　　　　Chi Mi Na Morvheanna; Piping Jamie; O'Keefe's Slide/Kid On A Mountain; Down By The Sally Gardens; Ae Fond Kiss; Les Gendarmes; 3 Breton Dances; Strath Ban; À La Stivell; Dance To Your Shadow; Piping Jamie Reprise; Fleasgaich Oig; Paddy Be Easy; Chrò Chinn T'Sàile *43:30*

Sylvi

FOLK/POP; SINGER-SONGWRITER

Vancouver singer-songwriter Sylvi combines a career in music with a career in family and children's theatre. She also makes masks for visual art, clowning, theatre, and dance. As a songwriter, Sylvi writes and composes contemporary material with elements of folk, rock, and pop. Her second album, and first CD, *The Colour Of Compassion*, highlights the expressive voice of a growing songwriter dealing with the themes of relationships, injustice, individual empowerment, and the environment.

✳✳✳　　**The Colour Of Compassion**
　　　　1995 See Through (TBA)

　　　　Break My Heart; Catch Me I Am Falling; Doin' Time; The Feather; Full Moon Nightmare; I Thought I Saw You Again; Looking Into Space; 100 MPH; Phoenix; Why?

Tamarack

FOLK; SINGER-SONGWRITERS

"Songs that reflect this country's early years, sung with skill and enthusiasm, energy and charm"—*Canadian Composer*. Based in Guelph, Ontario, Tamarack is a folk group that has been around for over sixteen years and has produced eight albums (four of which are available on compact disc). Tamarack's specialty is writing songs based on Canadian history. Although there have been many changes in personnel over the years, co-founder James Gordon still anchors the group, writing much of the material. Tamarack CD's are simultaneously issued on the Canadian SGB and the American Folk Era labels.

　　　The first Tamarck album on CD is the 1991 *Fields Of Rock And Snow*, featuring James Gordon, Alex Sinclair, and Gwen Swick. Highlights include the Tamarack classics, "Harvest Train," "Fields Of Rock And Snow," "Teamwork," "Stuart And Lillian," and "Lonesome Cowboy's Lament." *Fields Of Rock And Snow* received a Porcupine Award for "Album of the Year" in 1991. *Frobisher Bay*, features Gordon, Sinclair, and Swick on songs like "Days Of Sun And Wind," "The Hangman's Eyes," "Loyal She Remains," "No Herring Left In The Bay," "The Greenland Whale," and Tamarack's signature song, the a cappella "Frobisher Bay." *Frobisher Bay* received a "Canadian History Award" Porcupine in 1994. *On The Grand: The Story Of A River* is the result of a commission by the Elora Festival to celebrate the naming of the Grand River in Ontario as a Canadian Heritage River. Part way through the album there's a personnel change: Gwen Swick is replaced by Carole LeClair. Today's Tamarack is Gordon, Sinclair, and LeClair. Highlights of the album include "Pawpine," "The Elora Mill," "The Virginia Brand," and "Pioneer Tower Road."

A group as established, popular, and award-winning as Tamarack deserves a good party, and they threw one in Guelph on September 24, 1993 when various members of Tamarck and close friends over the years got together in a live and, fortunately, recorded concert—*The Fifteenth Anniversary Concert*. Although the recording quality is less than ideal, the album captures the spirit of the event. The liner notes contain an elaborate and essential Tamarack family tree. Appearing on this album, on instruments or vocals are: David Archibald, Andrea Barstad, Ian Bell, Jeff Bird, the Bird Sisters, Shelley Coopersmith, Wendy Davis, Melanie Doane, Sarah Farquahar, James Gordon, David Houghton, Anne McKenzie, Tony Quarrington, Goldie Sherman, Jane Siberry, Alex Sinclair, Randy Sutherland, Gwen Swick, Chris Terhune, Margo Timmins, and David Woodhead.

See also James Gordon.

❀❀❀(❀)✓ **Fields Of Rock And Snow**
　　　1991, reissued 1993　Folk Era (FE1407CD)

> Harvest Train; Home To You Once More; The Kitty Friel; Black Rapids Girl; Far From Home; Fields Of Rock And Snow; Hangin' In The Barn; Teamwork; Aultsville; Stuart And Lillian; Lonesome Cowboy's Lament *38:24*

❀❀❀(❀) **Frobisher Bay**
　　　1993　Folk Era (FE1409CD)†

> Days Of Sun And Wind; Oh, Klondike; The Hangman's Eyes; Frobisher Bay; Loyal She Remains; The Vacuum Song; Charlie Fox; Pamela; No Herring Left In The Bay; Alaska Highway Driver; Logging Camp Christmas; The Greenland Whale *45:22*

❀❀❀ **On The Grand: The Story Of A River**
　　　1994　Folk Era (FE 1421 D)†

> Our White Man's Word; Pawpine; The Song My Paddle Sings; Lochaber No More/ Skirl Of The Pipes; The Elora Mill; The Virginia Brand; The Grand River Canal; She Is Fickle; Lancashire Lasses; Brant County Roads; Buried Treasure; Dufferin County; Pioneer Tower Road *48:16*

❀❀❀(❀) **The Fifteenth Anniversary Concert**
　　　1995　SGB (SGB 25)

> The Old Ragadoo; Wild Mountain Thyme; The Scarborough Settlers Lament; Grey County; The Swallowtail Jig/Morrison's Jig; Billy Boy; Harvest Train; Les

Raftsmen; Frobisher Bay; #1 Northern; Mining For Gold; Pamela; Teamwork/ Redwing; Lonesome Cowboy's Lament; Farther Along; Saturday Night Up The Gatineau/Fiddle Medley *67:31*

Ian Tamblyn

FOLK; SINGER-SONGWRITER; COMPOSER

"One of the most creative singer-songwriters in Canada"—Scott Merrifield, on the occasion of presenting Ian Tamblyn with the Jackie Washington Award at the Northern Lights Festival, 1990. Based in Old Chelsea, Quebec, near Ottawa, Tamblyn has composed music ranging from contemporary folk to avant garde. In addition to penning over 1500 songs, he is an avid naturalist, serving as artist-in-residence on scientific missions to the Arctic and Antarctica. His earlier folk material has been collected into a retrospective CD anthology: *Through The Years ['76-'92]*. As a composer, Tamblyn frequently adds textured layerings of keyboard to the tracks. Other tracks are simple, acoustic guitar numbers. Highlights include "Ghost Parade," "Paris Afternoon," "Campfire Light," "Cold Wind In The Cariboo," "First Nation," and the classic "Woodsmoke And Oranges." The rest of Tamblyn's CD's are instrumental compositions based on nature themes, incorporating recorded animal and bird sounds. While not exactly traditional folk, they are delightful, relaxing albums to listen to by the fireside. They include *Magnetic North*, *Over My Head*, and *Antarctica*.

✳✳✳(✳)✓ **Through The Years ['76-'92]**
    1976-1992, Issued 1992 North Track (CD NT 14)

> Ghost Parade; Paris Afternoon; Finding Myself At Your Door; Campfire Light; Woodsmoke And Oranges; Slate Islands Song; Cold Wind In The Cariboo; North Vancouver Island Song; First Nation; The Declaration Of Human Rights; Green And Firewood; One Horse Town; Turlutte; Love Will Away; 25th Hour Of The Day; Scene Through A Mirror *50:46*

✳✳✳(✳) **Magnetic North**
    1991 True North (WTNK 78)

> Raven And The Clam—Haida Creation Story; Kodiak Evening; The North Shore— Rainy Day; Nahanni; Gargantua Dawn; Big Sky; Lancaster Sound; Magnetic North; The Return *49:38*

✳✳✳(✳) **Over My Head**
    1991 True North (WTNK 79)

> Knock On Wood—Winter Piece; At The Feeder; Crawley Fields/April Showers; Early Morning May; Soaring; View From A Window; Loon Lake; Heading South *42:41*

✳✳✳(✳) **Antarctica**
    1994 North Track (NTCD3)

> The Bell Birds; Sastrugi; The Weddell Planet; Erebus Ice Caves; Out On The Ice Fields; The Penguin Came From Pittsburgh; Ed's Still Diving; New Life At Hutton Cliffs; Still Life For A Woodpecker; Labrador Dawn; The Bloodvein *54:10*

Tanglefoot
FOLK; SINGER/SONGWRITERS

Based in Peterborough, Ontario, Celtic-oriented Tanglefoot writes and performs original material drawn from Canadian history. *A Grain Of Salt*, their first recording available on CD, presents a collection of songs about Irish ancestors, incidents on Canadian lakes, Laura Secord's legendary warning about the impending American attack on Canada, and Abigail Becker ("The Angel Of Longpoint"), a strong pioneer woman credited with saving the lives of many sailors. On this captivating recording Tanglefoot consists of Joe Grant, Steve Ritchie, and Bob Wagar. *Saturday Night In Hardwood Lake* continues the historical material and adds a new member to the group: Al Parrish. The transition from a trio to a quartet hadn't fully gelled at the time of recording— some of the timing and energy of *A Grain Of Salt* is missing and the harmonies don't always merge as tightly. Highlights include "Traighli Bay," "The Last Breakdown," "Jones ¼ Line," and "Walls Of Pine."

✻✻✻✻✓ **A Grain Of Salt**
1992 Tanglefoot (ORM11-1192CD)

Jack The Green; Selkirk Settler's Lullaby; Waltzin' Willie Warkworth; A Grain Of Salt; Roll With The Tide; The Floating Bridge Of Ennismore; The Angel Of Longpoint; Instrumental Medley: Up And Down The Stairs/Drums At The Fair/ Wag's Jig; Sullivan's Shivaree; Below, Below; Secord's Warning; Keppel Township Love Song *45:22*

✻✻✻ **Saturday Night In Hardwood Lake**
1994 Tanglefoot (TML12-1194CD)

Traighli Bay; Motherlode; The Last Breakdown; Jones ¼ Line; No Smoke, No Baloney; Immigrant's Tears; Walls Of Pine; Longjohns In Summer; The Drunken Dummer Survey; Fire And Guns; Losing Sight; Paddy's Finger; Blow To The Heart *50:39*

Pat Temple And The High Lonesome Players
FOLK/BLUES; SINGER-SONGWRITER

Toronto singer-songwriter Pat Temple started the band High Lonesome with Reno Jack of the Jack family in 1988. Since then he has gone on to front the band and has taken them to Europe and across North America. Blending hillbilly rhythms with a strong dose of Texas swing, Temple delivers intense, intelligent songs like "Twenty-Nine Hands," "Feathers And Wind," and "Medicine Pipe Bag." On *Connecting Lines* The High Lonesome Players are Joe Haag, Steve McKinnon, Andy Grafitti, Chris Ward, Longevity John, Spencer Evans, Dave Allen, Charlie Hase, Willie P. Bennett, John MacMurchy, Tom Walsh, and Michelle Rumball.

✻✻✻ **Connecting Lines**
1991 Latent (LATEX CD10)

Twenty-Nine Hands; I'll Be Back; Salamander Bones; Cloud Walking; Beyond The Watershed; Feathers And Wind; Medicine Pipe Bag; Love Is Calling; Connecting Lines *51:04*

Oscar Thiffault

FRENCH CANADIAN

Quebec singer Oscar Thiffault is featured on the historical recording, *Oscar Thiffault*—an MCA Héritage Québécois reissue. The selections are fun—reminiscent of early La Bottine Souriante. With no liner notes, one cannot tell if Thiffault is playing guitar or whether he's the fine fiddler we hear on track after track.

✹✹✹✹　**Oscar Thiffault**
[no date, reissued 1991] MCA (MCAD-10492)

> Le Rapide Blanc; Le Rocket Richard; Si Tu Maries Ta Fille; Le Fréquentations; L'Enterrement D'Nicodème; La Cabane À Sucre; C'Était Un Capitaine; Les Petites Patates; Je Parle À La Française; En Passant Par Matawin; J'Ai Fait Une Banqueroute; Le Nouveau Wing En Hein; Au Pays De Bill Wabo; J'Ai Perdu Ma Blonde; Embarque Dans Ma Voiture *38:02*

Three Sheets To The Wind

FOLK; A CAPPELLA; SINGER-SONGWRITERS

Ottawa-based Three Sheets To The Wind is a trio consisting of Mary Burns, Rebecca Campbell, and Beverley Wolfe. Their debut album, *Grace Under Pressure*, was recorded one weekend at a cottage in the Ottawa Valley. Primarily an a cappella album, the material ranges from traditional to songs by Gordon Lightfoot and Ferron, to original songs by Rebecca Campbell, who is also a member of Fat Man Waving. Highlights include "The Hundred Acre Field," "The Flower Of Magherally," "Magdalene," "Grace Under Pressure," "Woodsmoke And Oranges," and a smashing version of Ferron's "The Cart," overlaid with a prayer song composed by Campbell.

See also Fat Man Waving.

✹✹✹(✹)✓　**Grace Under Pressure**
1994 Canal (Canal 264)†

> The Hundred Acre Field; The Flower Of Magherally; Ocean Art Piece; Magdalene; The Cart; Things In Life; Grace Under Pressure; Awake Ye Drowsy Sleeper; White Petals; Woodsmoke And Oranges; Female Rambling Sailor; Silver Threads And Golden Needles; The Way I Feel; Stay Home *49:07*

Tickle Harbour

CELTIC FOLK

Tickle Harbour is a group made up of three Newfoundlanders, three Irishmen, and an American. They offer, as the liner notes state, "a blend of music through which one can discern the strains of Irish melodies and hints of the sounds of the Newfoundland kitchen time. Influenced by both traditions, it is slavishly imitative of neither; it is Newfoundland/Irish music, with the distinct flavour of the folk music revival about it." While *The Brule Boys In Paris* "has something of the feel of friends getting together to play ... the musicianship is of a high calibre and the tunes while mostly traditional are not the usual ones found on all too many Irish albums"—*Dirty Linen*. Tickle Harbour on this album (there was a previous incarnation of the group) consists of Seamus Creagh, fiddle; Paddy Mackey, bodhran; Rob Murphy, flute; Bob

O'Donovan; Scott Schillereff, hammer dulcimer; Gerry Strong, tin whistle; and Don Walsh, guitar/bouzouki.

❋❋❋❋✓　**The Brule Boys In Paris**
　　　1991　Pigeon Inlet (PIP7235CD)

> Paddy Gavin's Reel/Last Night's Fun/Olde Cuffe House Reel; Eavesdropper Jig/ Humours Of Corofin/Martin Byrnes; O'Connell's Trip To Parliament/Lucky In Love/Patsy Minter's Reel; The Waterford Boys; The Night Before Larry Got Stretched/Humours Of Kinvara/Ratigan's Reel; Flatbush Waltz; The Rising Sun/ Freshwater Reel/Shrinking Reel; St. John's Mazurka/The Brule Boys In Paris; The Dionne Reel; Memory Waltz; Polkas; Kitty Yates Turn/Rawlins Cross Reel/Paddy Ryan's Dream/The Boys Of Laois *44:13*

TIP Splinter
IRISH-CANADIAN FOLK

Listening to TIP Splinter sets your feet tapping and makes your heart long to be Irish, even if your grandmother came from the Ukraine. The group's unusual name derives from a Toronto theatre group called the Toronto Irish Players (TIP). The singers were a group that splintered away from the original troupe to pursue music. There have been many changes in the personnel of the group since its inception. The only original member left is Jonathan Lynn, host of the Ontario Cable-TV folk music show *Highway 10*, for which Lynn received a "Builder of Canadian Folk" Porcupine Award in 1993. TIP Splinter received a "Canadian Celtic Song" Porcupine Award in 1990 for "Fields Of Saskatchewan."

The group's sole CD—*A Living Tradition*—is a compilation of material from their first four albums and tapes, arranged from most recent to oldest: *Takin' The Floor* (1992), *The Jumping Irishman* (1990), *Mooncoin* (1988), and *TIP Splinter & Friends* (1986). The quality of the group varies over the years, with the most recent cast providing the best tracks, but overall this long-playing album is a gem for anyone who loves Irish-Canadian music. Over the years, the following musicians have been members of TIP Splinter: Joe Byrne; James Ediger; Henry Geraghty; Patrick Hutchinson; Jonathan Lynn; Jim McGee; Eamonn O'Loghlin; Madeleine O'Loghlin; Loretto Reid; Jamie Snider; Brian Taheny; and Kieran Wade.

See also Loretto Reid & Brian Taheny.

❋❋❋(❋)✓　**A Living Tradition**
　　　1986-1992, reissued 1993　TIP Splinter (TS005)

> The Shores Of Newfoundland/Traveller's Reel; Tanernagee Was You Ever In Quebec; Dr. Gilbert's/The Queen Of May/The Red-Haired Girl/The Dark-Eyed Lassie/Lord McDonald's/The Laurel Tree/The Sandymount; Takin' The Ferry; Hector The Hero/Neil Gow's Wife/The Chicago/The Concert/The Magherafelt; For Better Or Worse; The Jig's Up: Daddy's Little Girl/The Long Road Home/The Ringsend Cowboys; The Hills Of Glenshee; Paddy When You Die/The Bird In The Bush/The Maid Of Mt. Cisco; The Fields Of Saskatchewan; McRory; Johnny From Hazlegreen; Castle Kelly/Farewell To Connacht/The Teetotaller; Rathdrum Fair; Kitty's Slip/Bobbin' Pearls; Loving Hannah; Polkas From Hell: Okeefe's/John Ryan's/Mickey Chewing Bubble-Gum *74:28*

Brent Titcomb
FOLK/POP; SINGER-SONGWRITER

Ontario singer-songwriter Brent Titcomb drew a large following in the 1970's. In 1993 he released a CD of his past recordings, *Healing Of Her Heart*, that also includes the new title track, "Healing Of Her Heart." Titcomb fans will delight in once again hearing Titcomb's soft, gentle vocals on songs like "Sing High, Sing Low," "No Walls At All," "Cassandra," "Flow On The River," and "Tibetan Bells."

❊❊❊　**Healing Of Her Heart**
　　　1977-1993　Manohar (MR102)

> Healing Of Her Heart; Sahajiya; Sing High, Sing Low; Now Walls At All; I Still Wish The Very Best For You; Cassandra; Full Moon In Pisces; Oh Great Provider; Flow On The River (Let Yourself Be); Tibetan Bells; A Falling Star *42:49*

Hugo Torres
LATIN AMERICAN FOLK; SINGER-SONGWRITER; COMPOSER

Winnipeg Latin American guitarist Hugo Torres began performing professionally in his native Chile when he was a teenager. Upon his arrival in Canada he formed Retaguardia, one of the first Latin American folk groups in Canada. An extremely accomplished solo guitarist, Torres also plays, composes, and arranges pieces for the charango, zampona, tarka, bombo, recorder, and keyboard. Torres' playing and fine singing voice is highlighted on *A Compilation*, a CD reissue of two of his previous albums, *Latin America In My Guitar* and *Condor Of Love And Fire*. This easy-listening, highly satisfying CD is well worth tracking down if you enjoy Latin American music.

❊❊❊(❊)✓　**A Compilation**
　　　　　1992　Rearguard [no catalogue number]†

> The Highlands (Altiplano); The Three Lands (Los Tres Pueblos); Unity For All (Unidad De Todos); Slogans For Peace; The People Without A River Of Love (El Pueblo Sin Un Rio De Amor); Latin America In My Guitar (America Latina En Mi Guitarra); The Black Pimpernel; Where Are You, Grandfather? (Donde Estas, Abuelo?); My Country (Mi Pais); Let's Think Again (Volvamos A Pensar); Condor Of Love And Fire (Condor De Amor Y Fuego); Far From Here (Lejos De Aqui); The Sailboat Of Sadness (El Barco De Tristeza); Island Of Hope (Isla De La Esperanza); Alive Again (Me Siento Vivo De Nuevo) *67:16*

Eleanor & Graham Townsend
FIDDLE

Two of Ontario's fiddle champions on the same CD—*Canada's Champion Fiddlers*—is a huge treat for fiddle fans. The album is divided roughly in half with Graham Townsend on the first half, ending with "Angus Campbell," and Eleanor Townsend playing from "Moon River Hornpipe" to the album's closer, "Wildwood Waltz." Each fiddler contributes grace and style to these recordings. The immaculate playing ranges from sweet waltzes to uptempo jigs and reels. The album received a "Don Messer Canadian Fiddle" Porcupine Award in 1993 and both Eleanor and Graham Townsend have been inducted into the Porcupine Hall of Fame for their lifetime contributions to Canadian fiddling.

✳✳✳✳✳✓ **Canada's Champion Fiddlers**
[no date] Heritage Music (HCD 4402)

Clear The Track; Liberty Two Step; Larry O'Gaffe; Father O'Flynn; Newlywed Reel; Rustic Rig; Peter's Favorite; Operator's Reel; Ste. Anne's Reel; Angus Campbell; Moon River Hornpipe; McDowell's Breakdown; The Jewel Waltz; Maggie Mawhinney's Jig; Little Bob River; Cowboy's Reel; Wildwood Waltz; Forester's Hornpipe *41:38*

Graham Townsend

FIDDLE

Ontario fiddle champion Graham Townsend won the CNE fiddle contest at age nine, and at age thirteen he made his first recording. A frequent guest on the *Don Messer Jubilee* TV show, Townsend won the Canadian Open Old Time Fiddler's Contest in 1963, 1968, 1969, and 1970 before retiring from competition. An active folklorist, Townsend has been active in documenting Canadian fiddle traditions. A master of every style, Townsend has been inducted into the North American Fiddlers Hall of Fame, the Ottawa Valley Country Music Hall of Fame, and the Porcupine Award Hall of Fame. *100 Fiddles Hits* was recorded primarily as a study aid for young fiddlers, providing them easy access to a broad range of traditional fiddle tunes. It also makes great listening for any fiddle lover. The only criticism of this fine album is that the liner notes do not indicate which sets are on which tracks of the CD. This prevents you from easily accessing tunes of interest.

✳✳✳✳ **100 Fiddle Hits: 35th Anniversary Collection**
1990 Dino (512 995-2 / RSP 236)

Crooked Stovepipe; Arkansas Traveller; Old Joe Clark; Soldier's Joy; Girl I Left Behind; Joys Of Quebec; Loggers Breakdown; Ragtime Annie; Down Yonder; Kingdom Come; Mittons Breakdown; Rubber Dolly; Debbie's Waltz; Black Velvet Waltz; Country Waltz; Tennessee Waltz; Wilson's Clog; Gray's Second Change; Whalen's Breakdown; Big John MacNeil; Bonnie Dundee; Major Mackie; First Western Change; The Blackthorn Stick; Orange Blossom Special; Patronella; Rakes Of Mallow; Don Messer's Breakdown; Liberty Two Step; Back Up And Push; Turkey In Straw; The Eighth Of January; Sugarfoot Rag; Road To The Isles; Cock Of The North; Smash The Window; Scotland The Brave; Up Jumped The Devil; Ricketts Hornpipe; Bowin' The Strings; Mississippi Sawyer; Old Barndance; My Little Girl; Climbing Up The Golden Stairs; Spanish Cavalero; Maytime Swing; Devil's Dream; Swamplake Breakdown; Chinese Breakdown; Maple Sugar; Pigeon On The Pier; Wind That Shakes The Barley; Wake Up Susan; Plaza Polka; Fisher's Hornpipe; Sailor's Hornpipe; Old Man And Old Woman; Miss McCloud's Reel; Rippling Water Jig; Old Red Barn; Rock Valley Jig; Hundred Pipers; Norwegian Waltz; Waltz Quadrille; Over The Waves; Peek-A-Boo Waltz; Flowers Of Edinburgh; Chicken Reel; Sally Goodin; Flop Eared Mule; Road To Boston; Redwing; Dusty Miller's Reel; Silvery Bells; Mocking Bird; Snowflake Breakdown; Angus Campbell; Tennessee Wagoner; Lightning Hornpipe; Hi-Lo Schottische; Rochester Schottische; Buffalo Gals; Golden Slippers; Bill Cheatum; St. Anne's Reel; High Level Hornpipe; Cripple Creek; Uncle Jim; Joys Of Wedlock; Bride Of The Wind;

Haste To The Wedding; Texas Quickstep; Kiley's Reel; Snow Deer; Lorn McDonnald's Reel; Little Brown Jug; Darling Nelly Gray; Circassion Circle; Boil The Cabbage Down; Draggin' The Bow *65:12*

Travels With Charley
FOLK/POP/BLUEGRASS; SINGER-SONGWRITERS

Vancouver-based Travels With Charley began as a trio consisting of Jackie Janzen on lead and backup vocals, Steve Mitchell on acoustic guitar, and Doug Cox on dobro, slide instruments, accordion, and banjo. The group performs a mix of original material and covers. Their debut CD, *Uncle Herb's Amusements*, includes a number of Steve Mitchell originals, including "What Do You Think?," "Your Key Won't Never Fit My House Again," "Girl From Medicine Hat," and "I Got A House." Jackie Janzen delivers an inspired cover of Joni Mitchell's "Carey"—you might even like her version better than Joni's. On their second album, *Red Rome Beauty*, James Young joins the group on string bass. The delightful, almost whimsical, interplay between dobro and six-string continues and Janzen's earthy voice finds a home on numbers like "Some Other Town," "Up To Me," and a smashing version of "Make Me A Pallet On Your Floor."

See also Doug Cox.

❊❊❊(❊) **Uncle Herb's Amusements**
[no date] Malahat Mountain (MMM-CD-002)

What Do You Think?; Carey; Your Key Won't Never Fit My House Again; Who's Behind The Door?; Girl From Medicine Hat; When You Come Back Again; Saved; Just At This Moment; Wonderful Tonight; If I Could Be There; I Got A House; Angel Band; Little Willie *48:29*

❊❊❊(❊) **Red Rome Beauty**
1995 Malahat Mountain (MMM-CD-003)

Red Rome Beauty; Some Other Town; The Thrill Of Her; Up To Me; Great To Be Gone; Make Me A Pallet On Your Floor; Grassy Knoll; Stop Breaking Down; How Did You Live; I Got To Travel; Old Emotions; Trouble, You Can't Fool Me *42:14*

Lucie Blue Tremblay
FOLK/POP; SINGER-SONGWRITER

"Lucie Blue Tremblay embodies many of the noble elements of folk music's hopes and aims: authentic multiculturalism (she mixes songs in English with songs from her French Canadian heritage); solid singing (her voice is like a mountain lake—clear, deep, pure); passion (her romantic focus on real-life processes powers her writing); and the unusual (her stunning whistle is one example)"—Laura Post, *Sing Out!* Quebec singer-songwriter Lucie Blue Tremblay performs her unusual mix of French and English songs on *Tendresse*. An easy-listening, poetic, album, its highlights include "Absence," "Tour Song," "Montréal," "Daddy's Song," and "Goodbye Song." *Transformations* is a similar album with Tremblay originals and two covers: Suzanne McGettigan's "A Place In The Woods" and Shari Ulrich/Jean Roussel's "With Or Without You." Tremblay's contributions include "Chez Nous," "The Little One," "There Was A Time," and "Getting Old."

❋❋❋(❋) **Tendresse**
1989 Olivia (ORCD955)†

Absence; Tour Song; Montréal; Daddy's Song; The Water Is Wide; Two Lives; Politique; Peaking; Jour Après Jour; Seventh House; Goodbye Song *44:37*

❋❋❋(❋) **Transformations**
1992 Olivia (ORCD967)†

Chez Nous; The Little One; The Guilty One; There Was A Time; A Place In The Woods; Transformations; Homeless; With Or Without You; Sailing Away; All Out Of Love Tonite; Getting Old; All It Takes *50:59*

Triple Threat
ACOUSTIC BLUES

Calgary acoustic blues band Triple Threat consists of Rusty Reed, Johnny V, and Tim Williams. *Terra Firma Boogie* showcases the group's fine musical talents on original material and covers, including "Bring it On Home," "On Down The Road," "San Francisco Bay Blues," "Statesboro Blues," and "Terra Firma Boogie." Driven on the rhythms of Johnny V's acoustic guitar, Williams' guitar and mandolin, and Reed's dynamic harmonica playing, Triple Threat's strong singing and great picking make *Terra Firma Boogie* a must purchase for blues fans.

❋❋❋(❋)✓ **Terra Firma Boogie**
[no date] Triple Threat [no catalogue number]

Bring It On Home; On Down The Road; Custard Pie; Borderline Runner; San Francisco Bay Blues; The Bottle's Gone; In Rehearsal For The Blues; Try And Kill Yourself; Caravan; Open Book; Au Contraire, Mon Frère; Harmony Grits; Take It Slow And Easy; So Now You Know; Statesboro Blues; Won't Go On; Terra Firma Boogie *63:48*

Terry Tufts
FOLK/COUNTRY; SINGER-SONGWRITER

Ottawa singer-songwriter Terry Tufts straddles the line between folk and country. *Transparent Blue* blends acoustic folk guitar with an electric country sound. Tufts' lyrics are highlighted on songs like "Stand 'Neath My Window," "The Bloom Falls Off The Rose," "Where Do I Go?" "Azelie," "Hanging Roses From Her Door," and "Approaching Cordelia."

❋❋❋ **Transparent Blue**
1990 Snowy River (SRR S28 CD)

Stand 'Neath My Window; The Bloom Falls Off The Rose; Candy Calls For Water; Where Do I Go?; Azelie; Don't Think I Want Your Lovin'; Hanging Roses From Her Door; Heart Of The Beholder; Holdin' On; Approaching Cordelia; Ocean Of Tears; Never No More *49:25*

Paddy Tutty

FOLK; SINGER-SONGWRITER

Saskatoon singer-songwriter Paddy Tutty is a consummate interpreter of traditional material from Britain, Ireland, and North America. An accomplished musician on guitar, fretted dulcimer, and fiddle, her albums are finely crafted creations that delight, play after play. Her third album, and first CD, *Prairie Druid*, presents a mix of traditional Celtic material interspersed with some original Tutty compositions. For those who love traditional music, this album, featuring Tutty's captivating voice and instrumental work, is a "must." Guest musicians include Ian Mackie on tablas, berimbau, tambourine and tabor; John Geggie on double bass and fretless bass; Ian Robb on English concertina and Morris bells; Pippa Hall on backup vocals; John Henderson on bodhran and vocals; Peter Kiesewalter on shawm; and Ian Tamblyn on keyboards and hammered dulcimer.

✳✳✳(✳)✓ **Prairie Druid**
   1992 Prairie Druid (PA03CD)

   Island Spinning Song; Lough Erne; George Sand's; All Among The Barley; The Prairie Pagans; The Tankard Of Ale; The Man Behind The Plough; Wild Hog; Mina's Waltz; Fair Annie; Woodland; Land On The Shore *45:26*

Two-Penny Opera

FOLK/POP; SINGER-SONGWRITER

The Toronto band, Two-Penny Opera, put together a solid contemporary folk/pop album with *Dead & Crazy People*. Featuring lyrics by the group's chief songwriters, Mary-Ellen Anderson and Sandy Stubbert, the album's highlights include "Do You," "Frankie Met Sally," "Nothing Else," "Silver Surfer," "Quicksand," and "Blind Eye." Two-Penny Opera is Mary-Ellen Anderson, Sandy Stubbert, Ken Purvis, and Frank Baraczka. The group has disbanded.

✳✳✳ **Dead & Crazy People**
   1992 Two Productions (TWO CD-2)†

   Change; Tears; Frankie Met Sally; Nothing Else; Silver Surfer; Rickie; Tomorrow; Quicksand; Not Up To You; Keep It Inside; Do You; Blind Eye *47:30*

Ian Tyson

FOLK/WESTERN/COUNTRY; SINGER-SONGWRITER

Juno Award Hall of Famer Ian Tyson grew up in British Columbia. Influenced in childhood by the horse stories of Will James, Tyson eventually drifted into cowboy life and the rodeo. A gifted songwriter and performer, Tyson teamed up with Sylvia Fricker in the 1960's to form the enduring and popular sound of Ian & Sylvia. After the 1960's folk revival, Tyson hosted a weekly country music television show for CTV that ran for five years, first as *Nashville North* and later as *The Ian Tyson Show*. In the late 70's Tyson divided his time between music and his ranch in Alberta. He met new success as a solo performer on the western circuit. Ever a strong lyricist, Tyson's later works celebrate "cowboy culture"—the folk culture of the west. Tyson's rich, soft baritone voice has been his signature from his early Yorkville coffeehouse days in Toronto to his latest "western" albums. "Tyson's voice works ... like a pull of good whisky; rich and carrying, it edges close to the nasal passage before retreating safely, riding that fine country line that so very few voices find"—Roy MacGregor, *The Canadian*.

Ol' Eon, from 1973, was Tyson's first solo album after the breakup of Ian & Sylvia. Tyson is in good voice on this work that features many fine songs, including "Some Kind Of Fool," "Blueberry Susan," and "The North Saskatchewan." *One Jump Ahead Of The Devil*, from 1978, was one of Tyson's solo albums on Boot Records, later reissued on CD by Stony Plain. The recording is muddy—Tyson's voice sounds distant and the sidemen and background vocalists are less than inspired. Despite some good lyrics this is one strictly for dedicated Tyson fans.

Old Corrals And Sagebrush, from 1984, has been reissued by both Stony Plain and Vanguard. The sequence of the songs is different on each and the Vanguard reissue includes an extra song, "Diamond Joe." The Vanguard recording has been used for this guide. This excellent album is the first of the soft-edged cowboy recordings that have become Tyson's trademark in recent years. Highlights include "Alberta's Child," "The Old Double Diamond," "Leavin' Cheyenne," "Gallo De Cielo," "Diamond Joe," "Night Riders Lament," and "Murder Steer." *Cowboyography*, from 1986, is an all-Tyson album that continues the cowboy music started on *Old Corals*. A bonus is a remake of the Tyson classic, "Summer Wages." The album also introduces background vocalist, Cindy Church, who became a regular on subsequent Tyson recordings. The 1989 *I Outgrew The Wagon* features songs like "Cowboys Don't Cry," "Casey Tibbs," "I Outgrew The Wagon," "Adelita Rose," "Since The Wind," and a remake of "Four Strong Winds." *And Stood There Amazed*, from 1991, showcases the prolific Tyson on another strong album. Highlights include "Black Nights," "Lights Of Laramie," and "Springtime In Alberta." A reviewer in *Dirty Linen* calls *Eighteen Inches Of Rain*, from 1994, "an exceptional release from a man who has put the western back into country music." Tyson just keeps on writin' and singin' fine cowboy songs. Highlights include "Horsethief Moon," "Eighteen Inches Of Rain," "Chasin' The Moon," and "Til The Circle Is Through."

See also Ian & Sylvia.

❋❋❋(❋) **Ol' Eon**
1973 A&M (CD-69820)

Some Kind Of Fool; Bad Times Were So Easy; Blueberry Susan; Sam Bonnifield's Saloon; If She Just Helps Me; Lord, Lead Me Home; Great Canadian Tour; She's My Greatest Blessing; Spanish Johnny; The Girl Who Turned Me Down; The North Saskatchewan; Love Can Bless The Soul Of Anyone *33:39*

❋❋(❋) **One Jump Ahead Of The Devil**
1978, reissued 1978 Stony Plain (SPCD 1177)

What Does She See; One Jump Ahead Of The Devil; Beverly; Turning Thirty; Newtonville Waltz; Lone Star And Coors; One Too Many; Texas, I Miss You; Goodness Of Shirley; Freddie Hall; Half Mile Of Hell *37:41*

❋❋❋(❋)✓ **Old Corrals And Sagebrush & Other Cowboy Culture Classics**
1984, reissued 1994 Vanguard (151/52-2)†

Alberta's Child; The Old Double Diamond; Windy Bill; Montana Waltz; Whoopee Ti Yi Yo; Leavin' Cheyenne; Gallo De Cielo; Old Corrals And Sagebrush; Old Alberta Moon; Diamond Joe; Night Rider's Lament; Tom Blasingame; Sierra Peaks; Colorado Trail; Hot Summer Tears; What Does She See; Rocks Begin To Roll; Will James; Murder Steer *74:26*

❋❋❋(❋)✓ **Cowboyography**
1986 Stony Plain (SPCD 1102)†

Springtime; Navajo Rug; Summer Wages; Fifty Years Ago; Rockies Turn Rose; Claude Dallas; Own Heart's Delight; The Gift; Cowboy Pride; Old Cheyenne; The Coyote And The Cowboy *43:28*

❋❋❋ **I Outgrew The Wagon**
1989 Stony Plain (SPCD 1131)†

Cowboys Don't Cry; Casey Tibbs; I Outgrew The Wagon; Arms Of Corey Jo; Adelita Rose; Irving Berlin (Is 100 Yrs Old Today); Since The Rain; The Wind In The Fire; Four Strong Winds; The Banks Of The Musselshell; The Steeldust Line *40:57*

❋❋❋ **And Stood There Amazed**
1991 Stony Plain (SPCD 1168)†

Black Nights; Lights Of Laramie; Jaquima To Freno; Springtime In Alberta; Non-Pro Song; Milk River Ridge; Rocks Begin To Roll; Jack Link; You're Not Alone; Magpie; Home On The Range *41:05*

❋❋❋(❋) **Eighteen Inches Of Rain**
1994 Stony Plain (SPCD 1193) / Vanguard (79475)†

Horsethief Moon; Heartaches Are Stealin'; Eighteen Inches Of Rain; M.C. Horses; Big Horns; Rodeo Road; Chasin' The Moon; Nobody Thought It Would; Old House; Alcohol In The Bloodstream; Old Corrals And Sagebrush; Til The Circle Is Through *42:04*

Sylvia Tyson
FOLK/COUNTRY; SINGER-SONGWRITER

Juno Award Hall of Famer Sylvia Tyson, née Fricker, knew by age fifteen that she wanted to be a folksinger and moved to Toronto as soon as she finished high school in Chatham, Ontario. In 1959 she met Ian Tyson and they teamed up to form Ian & Sylvia, one of Canada's most enduring folk duos. After the Ian & Sylvia years, Sylvia hosted the CBC radio show *Touch The Earth* for five years, beginning in 1974. The show provided important exposure for Canadian performers and established Sylvia as an independent personality. With her unique, instantly-identifiable voice and strong songwriting, Sylvia pursued a solo career in country music. "Her songs, while written in a faithful down-home style, have a sophistication that I would like to think comes from her Canadian roots ... They aren't hung up on the blues or on defining right-of-middle-of-the-road; they usually have simple stories to tell ... topics usually left un-sung in the country vein"—Paul McGrath, *Globe and Mail*. In recent years Sylvia has also taught herself button accordion, which she uses to accent her material. Sylvia's early solo albums have not yet been reissued on compact disc.

The first CD available from her country period is *You Were On My Mind*, featuring songs like "Pepere's Mill," "Rhythm Of The Road," "River Road," and two of her classics, "Trucker's Cafe" and "You Were On My Mind." Her 1992 release, *Gypsy Cadillac*, includes "Heart Disease," "Remain A Child," "Deeper Waters," "The Sound Of One Heart Breaking," "I Walk These Rails," "Chocolate Cigarettes," and "Gypsy Cadillac." Her most recent activity has been anchoring the outstandingly successful collaboration of four singer-songwriters called Quartette.

See also Ian & Sylvia; Quartette.

❋❋❋(❋) **You Were On My Mind**
1989 Stony Plain (SPCD 1140)†

> Pepere's Mill; Slow-Moving Heart; Rhythm Of The Road; Walking On The Moon; Thrown To The Wolves; The Night The Chinese Restaurant Burned Down; You Were On My Mind; Sleep On My Shoulder; Trucker's Cafe; River Road; Last Call; Le Moulin À Pépere; Reprise; The Blind Fiddler's Waltz *48:47*

❋❋❋ **Gypsy Cadillac**
1992 Silver City (SCD 2266)†

> Heart Disease; Remain A Child; Deeper Waters; Feeling Seventeen Again; The Sound Of One Heart Breaking; I Walk These Rails; String Too Short To Save; Chocolate Cigarettes; Diamond Love; So Quiet Now; Hearts On The Faultline; Gypsy Cadillac *45:14*

Tzimmes

SEPHARDI-KLEZMER; SINGER-SONGWRITERS

"Tzimmes was formed in 1986 in Victoria, B.C. They are a quartet who specialize in both secular and spiritual songs performed in Yiddish. A number of the songs are traditional Sephardic love songs with a backdrop of Arabic drumming"—Festival Distribution *Catalogue*. *Sweet And Hot* features the gentle voices of Yona Bar-Sever, Moshe Denburg, Myrna Rabinowitz, and Julian Siegel. Even non-Yiddish-speaking folkies can appreciate the lovely music on this album.

❋❋❋(❋) **Sweet And Hot**
1993 Tzimmes (TZ-1)

> Yossel Yossel; Hashem Yishmorcha; Morenica; Laner Velivsamim; Adio Querida; Vechitetu; Shein Vi Di Levone; Odessa Bulgarish; Rozhinkes Mit Mandlen; Gib Mir A Heym; The Book Of Life; Adon Olam; Matai Tagia Eit Lashalom *56:05*

UHF

FOLK/COUNTRY/POP; SINGER-SONGWRITERS

A musical collaboration similar to Quartette, but preceding it in time, UHF stands for Ulrich-Henderson-Forbes, as in Shari Ulrich, Bill Henderson, and Roy Forbes. The three British Columbia singer-songwriters took time out from their solo careers to team up for one concert and the result was so successful that the project continued into the studio where *UHF* was recorded. The tracks alternate among original songs from each artist. Forbes' songs are the folkiest. Highlights include "Holding Out For You," "Keep Lightin' That Fire," "Golan Boys," "Running Back To Her," and "When Life Explodes." *UHF II* is the inevitable followup to *UHF*. Same formula, same results: excellent music.

See also Roy Forbes; Shari Ulrich.

✳✳✳(✳)   **UHF**
1990 Tangible (TR 102)

When I Sing; Holding Out For You; Keep Lightin' That Fire; Day By Day; Golan Boys; Running Back To Her; House Up On The Hill; Can't Go Home; When Life Explodes; One Step Closer To The Light; Wings For The Sky; Do I Love You *47:41*

✳✳✳(✳)   **UHF II**
1994 Tangible (TR CD243)†

Lifting My Heart; Watching The River Run; Wild One; Don't You Cry; There Must Be Some Way; Changed Forever; Boiling River; Stand; I'm On Edge; Time Will Take Its Toll; Goodbye; Call Up An Old Friend *47:10*

Uisce Beatha

FOLK/ROCK; SINGER-SONGWRITERS

Uisce Beatha (pronounced *ishka-baha*) is a Gaelic expression for "water of life." Uisce Beatha is a young Halifax band with Celtic and alt-rock influences. The original songs of *The Mystic Of The Baja* present a somewhat bleak landscape, without the levity, charm, or hope one often finds in Celtic music. *Voice Of The Voyager* follows in the same vein. "For all the uptempo arrangements, most of the 16 songs are rather dark accounts of people at various crossroads and dead ends, where the whiskey flows freely but it's not at all a pleasant world"—*Dirty Linen*. Uisce Beatha excels at instrumentals, but the vocals are weak—the uninflected voices don't provide a particularly interesting vehicle for the lyrics. Uisce Beatha is Alan Glen, John Glen, Paul Meadows, Damian Morrissy, Doug Watt, and Marty Coles.

✳✳✳   **The Mystic Of The Baja**
1993 Uisce Beatha (UBCD01)

Whose Child Is This; Promises; Lose That Skin; Maggie Coulter; Where The River Meets The Sea; Take Me Now; Rod And Reel/The Rattlin' Bog; This Is The Story/Coleman's Cross; Strangers; Working Man; Purple Heather; Tenderness Behind The Rage; Preparation For A Wake/Off To California *45:07*

✳✳✳   **Voice Of The Voyager**
1994 Uisce Beatha (94759CD)†

If You Have To Laugh; I Won't Give Up; Heartbeat; Boys Night Out; Mercy Hotel; Peterings; Bottle's End; Dream Reader; Drinkin' With The Lord; Idle Mind; Weathered By The Whiskey; Company Of Ghosts; Old South London; Johnny; The Fool Has Parted; Road Less Travelled *57:37*

Shari Ulrich

FOLK/POP; SINGER-SONGWRITER

Vancouver singer-songwriter Shari Ulrich, who writes insightful lyrics sung in a pop style, is part of the UHF project. The *Best Of Shari Ulrich* is a compilation of songs from her first three out-of-print solo albums: *Long Nights* (1980), *One Step Ahead* (1981), and *Talk Around Town* (1982). Ulrich's 1989 release, *Every Road*, includes strong lyrics on songs like "Legacies," "Someday," "Looking For Me," and "Every Road." Ulrich plays a violin instrumental on "Inside Passage."

See also UHF.

❋❋❋ **The Best Of Shari Ulrich**
1980-82 Esther (CD 627)

She Remembers; Somethin's Gotta Give; The One And Only; I'm Not The One; Long Nights; Oh Daddy; Romeo; The Lion; Mysterious Child; Bad Bad Girl; Save It; With Or Without You; Starlight; Flying *52:45*

❋❋❋ **Every Road**
1989 Esther (UPCD 80144)†

Legacies; Someday; Looking For Me; Inside Passage; The Heartland; House Up On The Hill; Only The Heart; The Jig; It's Not Love; Every Road *39:46*

Uzume Taiko Ensemble

PERCUSSION; TAIKO DRUMS

Time to put away those hammered dulcimers, banjos, guitars, and fiddles. The drums are coming! Uzume Taiko's first CD, *Chirashi*, gets things going nicely, but their second CD, *In Your Dreams*, recorded live at the Vancouver East Cultural Centre, launches them into full flight. The powerful, yet lyrically expressive, taiko drums put new meaning to the expression "back to basics."

❋❋❋(❋) **Chirashi**
1990 Aural Tradition (ATRCD 115)

Q; Grace; Spring On Heavenly Mountain; Sammai; Trap (A Love Song); Chirashi; Night Of The Torch Festival; Lullaby For Taiyo (Komori Uta); The Secret Of Life; Sazanami ("Ripple") *54:33*

❋❋❋❋✓ **In Your Dreams**
1994 Oo Zoo May (ZOOM 001)

In Your Dreams; One Step Forward—Two Thousand Years Back; Stepping Stones; Shadowing The Moon; 5 to 5; Fast Life On A Lazy Susan; Taiyo Goes To Camp *56:46*

Valdy

FOLK/POP; SINGER-SONGWRITER

At the 1994 Ottawa Folk Festival, British Columbia performer, and former Ottawa resident, Valdy was presented with a lifetime achievement award. Valdy's popular, laid-back music is an indelible part of the aural landscape for anyone who listened to radio in the 70's. *Classic Collection* brings it all back, including the prescient "Rock'N'Roll Song" that correctly tracked the shift in tolerance from folk music to rock: "Play me a rock'n'roll song / don't play me songs about freedom and joy / play me a rock'n'roll song / or don't ya play me no songs at all." *Heart At Work* extends Valdy's songwriting into the present. This 1993 release features fresh songs with better production values than those on his *Classic Collection*. Highlights include "When Peace Came To The Valley," "Magdalena," "Link In A Chain," "First Time Around," and "After All."

❋❋❋(❋)✓ **Classic Collection**
1988 A&M (CD 9147)

> Peter And Lou; Rock'N'Roll Song; A Good Song; Dirty Old Man; Yes I Can; The One You Love; Hot Rocks; Simple Life; Leaving Ain't The Only Way To Go; Weather'd Hands; Whirl And Twirl And Swirl; Easy Money; Sonny's Dream; Renaissance; Hometown Band; I'd Rather Be; Landscapes; Chocolate Goodnight *55:02*

❋❋❋(❋) **Heart At Work**
1993 PEG (PMK 012)†

> When Peace Came To The Valley; Magdelena; Link In A Chain; How Could It Be Better; Dreams About You; Atlantic Blue; First Time Around; Runaway; Hey Hey Mama; Double Solitaire; Shining Times; After All *41:46*

The Wakami Wailers

FOLK; SINGER-SONGWRITERS

The Wakami Wailers were formed by the chance meeting of individual musicians who met at a park rangers' school at Ontario's Wakami Lake Provincial Park. From jamming together in the evenings after classes, they went on to become a recording group. Their first album, *Last Of The White Pine Loggers: Songs From The Lumbercamps*, available only on cassette, was well received. Their second album, and first CD, *Waltz With The Woods*, was "inspired by the natural beauty and stories of Ontario's provincial parks"—liner notes. Similar to Tamarack and Tanglefoot, the Wakami Wailers write songs based on Ontario history. The solid playing and earthy vocals make this a very charming album. Highlights include Wade Hemsworth's "Log Driver's Waltz," "The Riverman," "One Last Spike," "Land Of The Silver Birch," "White Lake Swamp Stomp," and "Waltz With The Woods." The Wakami Wailers are Robert Hollett, guitar, vocals; Michael Bernier, fiddle, mandolin, vocals; Mark Despault, guitar, banjo, concertina, vocals; and Jeff Allen, spoons, story telling. Guest musicians include Andy Thompson, bass, accordion, keyboards, and Bernie Martin, accordion, bodhran.

❋❋❋ **Waltz With The Woods**
1993 Wakami Wailers [no catalogue number]

> Log Driver's Waltz; John Denison; The Riverman; Wakami; The Castle Of White Otter Lake; One Last Spike; Take This Land; A Legend Of Nanabozho; Land Of The Silver Birch; Run To The Bay; Shan's Song; White Lake Swamp Stomp; Waltz With The Woods *47:02*

Len Wallace
TRADITIONAL FOLK; SINGER-SONGWRITER

"Len Wallace may be the lone ambassador for the use of accordion as a solo instrument for a singer-songwriter"—*Dirty Linen*. Wallace writes in the tradition of Pete Seeger and Woody Guthrie—populist songs about working people. With virtuoso accordion, powerful songs, and Wallace's passionate vocal delivery, *Midnight Shift* may be one of the strongest old-style folk albums in the guide. Highlights include "Men Of The Working Shift," a song about the Nova Scotia Westray mine disaster in 1992, "Mama Said," a Terry Jones song about being forced off the family farm by foreclosure, "Leaving The Fishing Behind," about the closing of the cod fisheries, and "Cold Piece Of Steel," which Wallace describes as a "sea chantey about life on the factory floor."

✹✹✹✹✓ **Midnight Shift**
1994 Len Wallace (LEW-02-001)

Men Of The Midnight Shift; Mama Said; Never Tire Of The Road; Celto-Slavic Fusion I; Leaving The Fishing Behind; Back Breaking Day; If They Come In The Morning; Celto-Slavic Fusion II; Takin' Care Of Business; Cold Piece Of Steel; Sing The Eagle Home *41:09*

Peggy Ward
FOLK; SINGER-SONGWRITER

Calgary singer-songwriter Peggy Ward brings a strong social conscience to her writing. Her first CD, *We Are The Dance*, includes "Bring 'Er Around Lass," a feminist song about what sailing would be like on an all-woman ship, "People Belong To The Land," written for the Lubicon Cree of northern Alberta, "Song To A New York Poet," an insight into misplaced perceptions, and "Sophie's Song," the story of a mistreated native woman. *Songs To Clean Your House By* continues along the same lines, with anti-war songs, thoughts about AIDS victims and their friends, and several songs about the abuse of women. Ward is not an easy-going songwriter—her spare arrangements pack a punch.

✹✹✹ **We Are The Dance**
1990 Laughing Out Loud (DWCC-9001)

Bring 'Er Around Lass; People Belong To The Land; Song To A New York Poet; Driftwood Hunting; Sophie's Song; Boat Harbour's Lament; One Of Those Days; And When You Go; We Are The Dance *42:08*

✹✹✹ **Songs To Clean Your House By**
1992 Laughing Out Loud (LOLM2)

Yes Means Yes; These Thoughts; The Swimming Song; Dance The Dance; You Never Know; How Then Shall We Live; Let It Rain; Yes We Will; 1 800 345 Mary; Miss You Like 90; Momma; The Canticle Of The Kindred Spirits *58:59*

Baxter Wareham
MARITIMES/CELTIC FOLK

"Baxter is one of my generation of outport Newfoundlanders who, despite the dates on our birth certificates, were born in the eighteenth century—a time some forty or fifty years ago when the way of life was much as it had been in the time of our grandparents. Before we were 'dragged kicking and screaming into the twentieth century,' we had lived long enough to be forever aware of the gulf that separates us from the life of those who came before us. Only memory can bridge the gulf. Music jogs the memory. The music preserves something of what might have been passed on to the next generation, but has been left 'to the wind and the rain and the sea'"—Pat Byrne, liner notes to *Buffett Double*. After performing with groups for years, *Buffett Double* is Baxter Wareham's first solo album. Celebrating the music of Placentia Bay, the album is a collection of traditional songs arranged by Wareham, with the exception of "Tragedy Of Resettlement," by Sam Butler, and Wareham's own composition, "Harbour Buffett Waltz." Wareham is joined on the album by a strong cast of Maritime musicians: Leeland Wareham, Kelly Russell, Bryan Hennessey, Noel Dinn, Kathy Phippard, Don Walsh, Jim Payne, and Pat Byrne.

❋❋❋(❋)   **Buffett Double**
1989 Pigeon Inlet (PIPCD-7324)

> Mickey Relligan's Pup; The Old Smite; Mac Master's Tune/Herb Reid's Tune; Jennie On The Moor; Down By The Riverside; Killiecrankie; Tragedy Of Resettlement; Buffett Double; Donald Munroe; Harbour Buffett Waltz; The Yankee Privateer
> *36:26*

Jennifer Warnes
POP ARRANGEMENTS OF LEONARD COHEN

Jennifer Warnes is an American singer who was Leonard Cohen's backup singer for several years. Her outstanding tribute album, *Famous Blue Raincoat*, has gained widespread popularity. For those who don't enjoy Cohen's delivery, the versions on Warnes' album are a slick, well interpreted alternative to Cohen himself. Cohen makes a guest appearance on "Joan Of Arc."
See also Leonard Cohen.

❋❋❋(❋)   **Famous Blue Raincoat: The Songs Of Leonard Cohen**
1986 Attic (ACDM 1227)

> First We Take Manhattan; Bird On The Wire; Famous Blue Raincoat; Joan Of Arc; Ain't No Cure For Love; Coming Back To You; Song Of Bernadette; A Singer Must Die; Came So Far For Beauty *41:36*

Buddy Wasisname & The Other Fellers
CELTIC FOLK/COMEDY; SINGER-SONGWRITERS

Buddy Wasisname & The Other Fellers is an unusual Newfoundland group that switches effortlessly between comedy and traditional jigs, reels, and waltzes. The group consists of Kevin Blackmore, Ray Johnson, and Wayne Chaulk. Highly talented musicians and songwriters, they liven up the dance floor with numbers like "Jesse Collins' Slipway" and "Devil's Own Hoof" and then have you rolling on it with comic songs like "Peein' In The Snow" and "The Miracle Cure." These albums are just the thing when you've maxed out on seriousness. And the "straight" tracks provide perfectly timed relief from the comic relief. Any album will do—they're all fun.

✱✱✱ **Flatout**
1990 Third Wave (TWPCD003)

Sarah; Jesse Collins' Slipway; Flatout; Glory Be; Yodelling Song; The Bay Is My Home; Dragger Song; Devil's Own Hoof; Saltwater Joys; Seamus O'Brien; M'Auld Dudeen; Dear Mister Ford; Kitty Jones Reel; Rock Yourself On The Ocean; Row Boys Row; Peein' In The Snow *41:37*

✱✱✱ **The Miracle Cure!**
1992 Third Wave (TWPCD005)

Goin' Up With Brudder; Wattle Hill Turnoff; Miracle Cure; Banks Of Island Pond; Little Ditty; Men Of The Bay; Spring On The Island; Put A Bit Of Powder On A Doo; Chainsaw Earle; Ladies In The Centre; Peggy Gordon; Carry Me Home To Me Granny's; Comforts Of Home; Me Car; The Pits; Rum Ri Row *43:14*

✱✱✱ **100% Pure**
1993 Third Wave (TWP006)

Make N' Break Hornpipe; Ogis Blogis Mogis; Shinny On The Ice; Thank God For Drugs; Technicolour Love; The Missus; Noises And Faces; Me And Bill; The Hillside In September; Hector's Tune; Fitted For The Helm; On The Government Wharf; By The Glow Of The Kerosene Light; Take The Old Squeeze Box; On The Deep Blue Sea; Song For Newfoundland; Two Good Reasons; The 'Vette *52:52*

✱✱✱ **Salt Beef Junkie**
1995 Third Wave (TWPCD 007)†

Salt Beef Junkie; Uncle Tim's Two Stepper/Rock The Rodney; Still More Time To Go; The Light Of The Western Stars; An Islander's Lament; A Hurtin' Song; Where Fishermen Used To Be; Is You 'Appy?; He's A Part Of Me; Did You Hear Dis One?; My Inco Hat; Goodbye Old Friend, Goodbye; Da Yammie *51:20*

Bobby Watt

FOLK; SINGER-SONGWRITER

Based in Whitby, Ontario, Bobby Watt, who organizes Ontario's Horseshoe Valley Folk Festival, is a balladeer who specializes in the songs of his native Scotland. Watt has had a checkered career, working as a labourer and as a diver for the Toronto police force, helping locate and reclaim drowning victims. In recent years he has become a full-time musician. *Homeland*, produced by Garnet Rogers, is an album with the theme of immigration and longing for home. Watt's soft, accented voice is featured well on songs like "Indiana," Don McGeoch's "Homeland," "The Call," "Black Douglas," and "The Joy Of Living." *C'est Watt*, also produced by Rogers, is another strong album, though not as thematically unified as *Homeland*. It contains original Watt compositions, such as "Alabaster Lady," "Papillon," and "Just Another Mile." Watt received a Porcupine "Songwriting Award" for "The Call" in 1991.

✳✳✳(✳) **Homeland**
1991 Snow Goose / Glenashdale (SGS 1118)†

> Indiana; Homeland; The Girl I Left Behind; Black Douglas; The Journey; The Call; Lovely Arran Maid; Deep In My Heart; Hush Hush; The Flittin' Day; Heart Of Your Home; Buffalo Jump; The Joy Of Living; Auld Lang Syne *52:05*

✳✳✳(✳) **C'est Watt**
1994 Snow Goose / Glenashdale (SGS 1122)†

> Alabaster Lady; Rolling Hills Of The Borders; The Cruel Brother; My Love Is Like A Red Red Rose; Papillon; Jamie Raeburn; Reflections; Just Another Mile; Every Living Thing; The Gaudie Runs/Welcome Bobby Back/The Watts Return To Otter Creek; Footprints *43:30*

Minnie White
ACCORDION SQUARE, SET AND STEP DANCE TUNES

One of Newfoundland's cultural icons, Minnie White has been called "first lady of Newfoundland accordion" in tribute to her lifetime contributions to traditional accordion interpretation. *The Hills Of Home*, her fourth album, and first CD, was produced by Jim Payne. This album is essential—every cut is a gem—and your feet will be tapping from the first track to the last. The album received a "Harry Hibbs Award for East Coast Music" Porcupine in 1994. Additional musicians on the recording include Rick Hollett, piano, flute, tambourine; Fergus O'Byrne, banjo, mandolin, tin whistle, 12-string guitar, bodhran, spoons; Dave Panting, bass, mandolin; Jim Payne, guitar, mandolin. Vocals: Linda Byrne; Eleanor Dawson; Jean Hewson; Christina Smith; Esther Squires.

✳✳✳✳✓ **The Hills Of Home**
1994 Singsong (SS 9478)

> Rambling Jig; Waltz To The Hills Of Home; Coastal Memories; Irish Jig/Viking Jig; Sammy's Hornpipe; Me Mother Won't Let Me Marry; Polly's Jig/French Reel; Southern Sounds; Rock The Baby; Dance With The Girl With The Red Dress On; Valley Echoes; Fiddler's Jig; Green Grow The Rushes-O; Irish Breakdown; Johnny Mac's Jig; Rock Island Waltz; MicMac Square Dance Tunes; Fisherman's Reel; Larry O'Gaff; Cooper's Hornpipe; Blue Skirt Waltz; Pushthrough Jig *50:25*

Nancy White
HUMOUR/SATIRE/SOCIAL COMMENTARY; SINGER-SONGWRITER

Ontario singer-songwriter-satirist Nancy White is Canada's answer to Tom Lehrer. Her biting, self-deprecating wit ranks her alongside the Royal Canadian Air Farce for pricking balloons and levelling the mighty. *Momnipotent: Songs For Weary Parents* is a collection of songs inspired by 80's Yuppie-ism. From "Memo To Droola" and "Everything Turn To Ratshit In My Life" to her wicked imitation of Leonard Cohen on "Leonard Cohen's Never Gonna Bring My Groceries In," White's humour is refreshing and delightful. The album includes her classic, "Daughters Of Feminists." *Pumping Irony* is a collection of satirical songs White wrote for the CBC Radio's public affairs show *Sunday Morning*. Americans may have difficulty following these Canadian topical songs. To fully appreciate "Canada's Sweetheart Joe Clark,"

"Nouveau Calgary," "Geezers In Love," (Brian Mulroney and Ronald Reagan), and "Viva Papa Pierre," you had to be there!

❋❋❋(❋) **Momnipotent: Songs For Weary Parents**
1990 Children's Group (SANCD 1025)

> I'm Babbling; It's So Chic To Be Pregnant At Christmas; Memo To Droola; Child On Board; Suzie Money Gone Away; Everything Turn To Ratshit In My Life; Momnipotent; Stroller Ladies; Daughters Of Feminists; Leonard Cohen's Never Gonna Bring My Groceries In; Mammas Have A Secret; The Children's Entertainer; Open That Can *41:25*

❋❋❋(❋) **Pumping Irony: Songs Of The 90's**
1993 CBC Radio/Mouton [no catalogue number]

> Bambi The Refugee; Senator Lawson At The Motel Cucaracha; Canada's Sweetheart Joe Clark; What An Embarrassing Mayday; Nouveau Calgary; Royal Couch Potato; Vienna Rap; Barnacle Betty And Psycho Pike; Gods Of America; Saving Francis' Bacon; Geezers In Love; The Auld Alliance; Cute For A Tory; Viva Papa Pierre; Baby On The Potty All Day; Hurray For Bobbi Bondar; Hall Of Hosers *55:30*

The Whiteley Brothers
BLUES

Two of Toronto's consummate musicians, Ken and Chris Whiteley began performing professionally in 1965. Influenced by the blues since early in their careers, they have put together a concise history of the blues on *Bluesology*—"a highly-polished work of entertainment and celebration"—*Dirty Linen*. *Bluesology* features the Whiteley brothers on twenty different instruments, plus a number of outstanding guests including Colin Linden, Gene Taylor, Jackie Richardson, and Chris's son Dan Whiteley. The album is an obvious labour of love that blues fans will want to add to their collection.
See also Chris Whiteley; Ken Whiteley

❋❋❋(❋) **Bluesology: A Journey Through The Blues**
1992 Pyramid (PD007)

> Before This Time; Crazy Blues; M&O Blues; Memphis Jug Blues; When The Train Comes Along; Custard Pie; Got Me Worrying; Feel Like Going Home; Crawdad Hole; In The Night; Sugar Sweet; Sneaking Around; Don't Start Crying Now; We Don't Talk; Wee Wee Baby *49:42*

Chris Whiteley
SWING/BLUES; SINGER-SONGWRITER

Toronto multi-instrumentalist and singer-songwriter Chris Whiteley has been performing, writing, and recording swing and blues music for over twenty years. He has received four Juno award nominations in addition to acclaim for two albums of original songs with wife Caitlin Hanford (currently part of Quartette). Whiteley has performed throughout North America at festivals, clubs, and concerts. Most recently he has been recording with his son, Dan Whiteley, who plays lead guitar. In addition to vocals, Chris plays trumpet, harmonica, guitar, and pedal steel. On *Second Look*, the Whiteleys have rolled out another fine album—"a bountiful mix of original material, peppered

with just the right amount of classic swing and blues outings"—*RPM Chart Weekly*.
When you're ready for some jazzy, swing-style blues, put this one on and enjoy.
See also The Whiteley Brothers.

✳✳✳✳ **Second Look**
1994 Pyramid (PD011)

> Cherry Red; Second Look; When Push Comes To Love; A Smooth One; Change
> Your Point Of View; Can't Get Enough; Mean To Me; She Walks Right In; Swing
> 42; Another Day Without You; Mother Earth; On The Other Line; The Light
> Descends From Heaven; Total Eclipse *52:51*

Ken Whiteley
SWING/BLUES/GOSPEL/CHILDREN'S; SINGER-SONGWRITER

Toronto musician and producer Ken Whiteley has been called a "playing encyclopedia" for his vast repertoire, command of a variety of styles, and prodigious ability on over a dozen instruments. He has appeared on over 100 albums and has produced over 50. The children's recordings he has produced have sold over four million copies. His own recording for children, *All Of The Seasons*, draws from a variety of musical traditions, including folk, calypso, gospel, and the blues. The twenty songs range from traditional and classic kids tunes to songs written by Whiteley, Raffi, Tom Paxton, and Pete Seeger. In characteristic fashion, Whiteley plays eighteen instruments on the album. A lively collection for the kids—and adults will enjoy it too.
See also The Whiteley Brothers.

✳✳✳✳✓ **All Of The Seasons**
1993 Alcazar (ALA 1010)†

> Catch Hold Of My Hand; The Hippopotamus; The Wiggle Song; Goes To Sleep; Big
> Beautiful Planet; Little Drops Of Water; Frosty Weather; I Can't Wait For Spring;
> Clouds; One More River; Calypso Stomp; Up Like A Rocket; Teddy Bear's Picnic;
> Get Along Home; I Heard The Water Singing; All Of The Seasons; Maple Syrup
> Time; Swimming, Swimming; I Like Picking Apples; Goodbye Waltz *50:30*

Ken Whiteley, Jackie Washington, Mose Scarlett
OLD-STYLE SONGS

Toronto musician Mose Scarlett, with "a velvet baritone that could smooth the scales off an armadillo" specializes in music of the 20's, 30's and 40's. An internationally acclaimed guitarist, his first album, *Stalling For Time*, was produced by Bruce Cockburn. Scarlett has toured internationally and has appeared on numerous radio and television programs.

Born in 1919, Jackie Washington has been a staple of the Canadian music scene since the age of five when he sang with The Four Washington Brothers. With a repertoire that extends from the days of slavery to the present, Washington knows well over 1400 songs. In his career he was worked with Duke Ellington, Lionel Hampton, Clark Terry, Joni Mitchell, Gordon Lightfoot, Sonny Terry, Brownie McGhee, and Lonnie Johnson. A recipient of the Lifetime Achievement Award from the Ontario Arts Council, he is held in such high regard by the Ontario music community that several Jackie Washington awards have been created to honour his outstanding musicianship.

Where Old Friends Meet, produced by Ken Whiteley, and including Whiteley on instruments and backup vocals, features all three of these outstanding performers on a comfortable, relaxed album that was culled from recordings done over five years. As Whiteley says in the liner notes, the music "falls outside of today's market-driven industry ... Call this music what you will, it is timeless, sincere, and lots of fun." Whiteley received a Porcupine "Dream Award" in 1991 for his production of this recording. The album was also nominated for a Juno award in the "Roots & Traditional" category in 1992. The album is a must for those who love "old-time" music.

✻✻✻✻✓ **Where Old Friends Meet**
1991 Pyramid (PD006)

> A Little Street Where Old Friends Meet; Go Where You Go; I Wish I Could Shimmy Like My Sister Kate; Alone In The Dark; I Won't Cry Anymore; It Must Be You; The Three Bears; You Say The Sweetest Things; On The Sunny Side Of The Street; Blind Barnabas; I'm So Sad; Fool's Paradise; Makin' Whoopee!; My Very Good Friend The Milkman; I'll See You In My Dreams; We'll Meet Again *50:34*

WhiteTail Singers

FIRST NATIONS MUSIC; SINGER-SONGWRITERS

WhiteTail Singers is a drum group of North Ontario native musicians who have created a set of original songs influenced by the singing styles of drum groups in western Canada and the United States. As the liner notes explain, "the songs, the dance, and the drum hold special meaning in social aspects of their culture. The drum in particular represents The Heartbeat of Mother Earth." The songs and dances emphasize community interaction and include social commentary. "What Happened To The River Where I Used To Live?" was "inspired by the hydro dams being put up in the James Bay area in Northern Quebec, and about how it has altered the Cree People's homelands, which have been in existence for thousands of years." Those who collect pow-wow recordings will welcome this album.

✻✻✻(✻) **Forever Dancing: Pow Wow Songs**
1994 First Nations Music (Y2 77621-10019-2-2)

> Drum Theme; Fast Young Boy's Dance Song; What Happened To The River Where I Used To Live; Women's Fancy Shawl Dance Song; Come Together Song; Old Women's Dance Song; Dance Like This; Children's Dance Song; Men's Fancy Dance Song; Forever Dancing *37:18*

David Wiffen

FOLK/POP; SINGER-SONGWRITER

Ottawa singer-songwriter David Wiffen was one of the best-known Canadian folk performers in the late 1960's, early 70's. By the mid-70's he came off the road and went home to Ottawa where he's been living since. He had virtually dropped out of music until an appearance at the 1994 Ottawa Folk Festival where he was greeted with thunderous ovations. His landmark album, *Coast To Coast Fever*, co-produced by Wiffen with friend Bruce Cockburn was reissued in 1994. In addition to classic Wiffen songs like "Skybound Station," "Coast To Coast Fever," and "Full Circle," the album includes Willie P. Bennett's "White Lies," Murray McLauchlan's "You Need A New Lover Now," and Bruce Cockburn's "Up On The Hillside." The album features Cockburn as a guest musician. For those who have worn out their Wiffen vinyls, this is a must purchase.

✹✹✹(✹)   **Coast To Coast Fever**
1973, reissued 1994 EMI (S2-0777-7-26707-2-4)

Skybound Station; Coast To Coast Fever; White Lines; Smoke Rings; Climb The Stairs; You Need A New Lover Now; We Have Had Some Good Times; Lucifer's Blues; Up On The Hillside; Full Circle *39:43*

David Wilkie
FOLK/COUNTRY/WESTERN; MANDOLIN

Alberta mandolin player and singer-songwriter David Wilkie, widely known for his collaboration with Stewart MacDougall as The Great Western Orchestra, also made some earlier recordings that were nearly lost when the original companies went out of business. Wilkie managed, eventually, to get the tapes back and has released them on CD as *Shoebox*. Part one of the disc is a reissue of Wilkie's 1977 instrumental album, *The Mandoline Kid*. Part two has never been released before—Wilkie refers to these cuts as *The Used Car Sessions (1984-85)*. This part of the CD includes vocals from Diamond Joe White and Texas artist Katy Moffatt, as well as Ron Casat among the guest musicians. The mandolin sessions are a treat and the recovered vocals of White and Moffatt are a bonus. This is an excellent album for fans of country folk.
   See also The Great Western Orchestra.

✹✹✹(✹)   **Shoebox**
1977, 1984-85, reissued 1991 Centerfire (CFA003)

Lleñyo Grande; Stoney Waltz; Melody From Raymond; Avalon; Toulouse Tango; Duck On A Junebug; I've Never Loved Anyone More; Turkey Knob; Variations On The Theme Of Huckleberry Finn; Chanson D'Amour; Old Cowhand; There Stands A Glass; Jersey Bounce; Freight Train Boogie; Cold, Cold War; Too Many Bridges; I Gotta Have My Baby Back; Eager Beaver; Sugar Mountain; Don't Get Around Much Anymore; Along The Navajo Trail *70:51*

The Willies
FOLK/POP; SINGER-SONGWRITERS

The Willies are a Toronto folk trio that blends a 60ish three-part harmony with contemporary lyrics. The liner notes to *Sacred And Insane* express this thought: "In trying to achieve our goals in life, we discover the need of others—thus we become incompetent. Because of our incompetence, we try and fail and learn that everything takes 3 times as long and costs 3 times as much as we thought—thus we become crazy. In learning to enjoy our craziness, we begin to hear the voice of God and see the work of men and women...thus we get...The Willies." Thankfully the song lyrics are less cryptic than the liner notes and the Willies deliver some catchy, well-played tracks that bear repeated listening. The Willies are Philip Küntz, also known as "Brother Philip," vocals, mando/guitars, writer; Suzanne Belanger, vocals, percussion; and Paul Harris, vocals, bass.

❋❋❋ **Sacred And Insane**
1993 Permanent (PW CD301)†

Pallisade Of Dreams; Best Revenge; What About Me; Your Love; Unity Song; Free Today; Nice Place Here; Can't Say No; So Bad; False Drugs; Desert Sky; Who; Annabelle *51:23*

Johnny Wilmot
CAPE BRETON FIDDLE MUSIC

In another project to preserve Cape Breton fiddling history, Breton Books & Music has issued *Another Side Of Cape Breton*, a re-mastering of older recordings from LP's and 78's featuring Johnny Wilmot, a Cape Breton fiddler from the Northside. As with their Winston Fitzgerald CD, this recording ensures that the fine fiddling of Johnny Wilmot can be heard by today's generation of fiddle lovers. A huge thank you!

❋❋❋❋ **Another Side Of Cape Breton**
[no date] Breton Books & Music [no catalogue number]

Tom Ward's Downfall/Jackson's Reel; Baddeck Gathering/The Girls Of Banbridge; Dr. Gilbert's Reel/The Queen Of May; The Jug Of Punch/Ships Are Sailing/Green Fields Of America; Lord Gordon's Reel; An Inverness Jig; Basker's Rambles; Maid Behind The Bar/Flax In Bloom; Maids Of Tramore; Orange And Blue/Kitty Of Oulart; Jackson's Polka; King's Jig/An Irish Jig; Boys Of The Loch/The Devils In Dublin/Roaring Mary; Geese In The Bog; Woman Of The House; Old Grey Goose/ The Clay Pipe; Nova Scotia Barn Dance; The Frost Is All Over/Lark In The Morning; Bird In The Tree/The Mourne Mountains; Devine's Favourite/The Rambler; Flannel Jacket; Cape Breton Favourite/The Whiskey Jig; Hughie Shorty's Reel/Walker Street Reel *68:55*

Tom Wilson
COUNTRY FOLK; SINGER-SONGWRITER

Calgary singer-songwriter Tom Wilson was born and raised in West Virginia where he grew up listening to the bluegrass music of Flatt & Scruggs and the radio classics of Hank Williams. From these influences he has developed a warm, honest style of folkish country music that is modern but still true to its traditional Appalachian roots. Set against the backdrop of southern Alberta's prairie, foothill, and mountain imagery, his first CD, *Another Blue Sky Day*, is a collection of songs about love, loneliness, and the lure of the highway. Highlights include "The Harvest Dance" and "Rockies In The Rain." Additional musicians include Cindy Church, Phil Hall, Jeff Bradshaw, and Kelvin Bell.

❋❋❋ **Another Blue Sky Day**
1994 Blue Rockies (BRM001CD)

Blue Sky Day; Long Gone And Lonesome; The Harvest Dance; I Go Crazy; Rockies In The Rain; Don't Cross That Line; Makin' Some Time For You; As Far As Love Goes; All That's Left (Is The Leavin'); Baby's Big Brown Eyes *34:47*

Jesse Winchester
FOLK/COUNTRY/ROCK; SINGER-SONGWRITER

Widely acknowledged as one of the music industry's outstanding songwriters, as well as a fine singer, Montreal-based Jesse Winchester is a reclusive figure who rarely gives public performances. A draft exile from the United States who elected to stay in Canada after President Carter's general amnesty, Winchester's songs are touched with a longing for the South. Songs like "Yankee Lady" and "Brand New Tennessee Waltz" are modern-day classics performed by artists and groups across North America. Winchester's older recordings are being reissued by Stony Plain, Sugar Hill, and Rhino. *Jesse Winchester*, a sought-after 1970 recording produced by Robbie Robertson was reissued in 1994. This was followed by his second album, *Third Down, 110 To Go* with its reference to a hopeless situation in Canadian football. *The Best Of Jesse Winchester*, a good cross section of Winchester's work, and a better buy in terms of CD duration, was released in 1989. *Humour Me*, a 1988 recording, has been reissued by Sugar Hill with two additional songs, "Pushover" and "Love Is Fair," not included on the original LP and cassette.

❋❋❋(❋) **Jesse Winchester**
1970, reissued 1994 Stony Plain (SPCD 1198)

Payday; Biloxi; Snow; The Brand New Tennessee Waltz; That's A Touch I Like; Yankee Lady; Quiet About It; Skip Rope Song; Rosy Shy; Black Dog; The Nudge *35:03*

❋❋❋(❋) **Third Down, 110 To Go**
1972, reissued 1994 Stony Plain (SPCD 1199)

Isn't That So?; Dangerous Fun; Full Moon; North Star; Do It; Lullaby For The First Born; Midnight Bus; Glory To The Day; The Easy Way; Do La Lay; God's Own Jukebox; Silly Heart; All Of Your Stories *30:19*

❋❋❋(❋) **The Best Of Jesse Winchester**
1972-89, reissued 1989 Rhino (R2 70085)

Tell Me Why You Like Roosevelt; Mississippi, You're On My Mind; Yankee Lady; The Brand New Tennessee Waltz; Biloxi; Talk Memphis; Bowling Green; Do It; Defying Gravity; Say What; I'm Looking For A Miracle; Do La Lay; Skip Rope Song; Everybody Knows But Me; Rhumba Man; A Showman's Life; Dangerous Fun; All Of Your Stories *56:02*

❋❋❋(❋) **Humour Me**
1988 Sugar Hill (SH-CD-1023)

If I Were Free; Thanks To You; They Just Can't Help Themselves; Too Weak To Say Goodbye; Let's Make A Baby King; Well-A-Wiggy; I Don't Think You Love Me Anymore; Willow; Humour Me; I Want To Mean Something To You; Pushover; Love Is Fair *52:19*

Richard Wood
MARITIMES FIDDLE

Young Prince Edward Island fiddler Richard Wood fiddles up a storm on *All Fired Up!*. Having only taken up fiddle a few years ago, Wood is already demonstrating virtuoso talents that put him in a category with other young fiddlers such as Natalie MacMaster and Ashley MacIsaac. Fiddle lovers should track down a copy of this album!

✻✻✻✻ **All Fired Up!**
1994 Richard Wood [no catalogue number]

Flowers Of Edinburgh/Trip To Windsor/Ste. Ann's; Ferry/River Bend/Traditional/ Paddy In London/George MacPhee's; Lady Caroline Montague/Lady Loudon/Reel/ Blind Nora O'Neil/Miss Taylor; Flowers Of Hope; Fram Upon Him/Miss Catherine Ann Lamey's/Charlie Hunter's/Peggy's; Highland/Dick And Marlene Cardiff's/ Daryl Poirier's/Allan McKinnon's/Bud And Anne Watson's; Joey And Angela Beaton's/Mrs. MacAuley's/Eric McEwen's/Carigoim/Traditional; Clan Munro/Frank Sutherland's/Marquis Of Huntley; Treviot Bridge/Stool Of Repentance/John Allan's; The Awl Man/Castle/The Ice Man's; Sea Sound; Vendome Clog/Earl Marischal's/ The Fisher's Wedding/Howie MacDonald's; Lament For Glencoe/The Cape Breton Symphony's/Miss Susan Cooper/Grant's/The Four Stroke *53:43*

Scott Woods
COUNTRY-STYLE FIDDLE

On *Fiddle Magic*, Ontario fiddler Scott Woods, winner of the Canadian Old Time Fiddle Championship in 1993, performs primarily in a country/swing style on tunes like "Down Yonder," "In The Mood," "Dixie Blossoms," and "Pat's Country." His lyrical, winsome playing will have you waltzing in time for the duration of this graceful, lively recording.

✻✻✻✻ **Fiddle Magic**
1992 McLeod Music (MMP-20292)

Down Yonder; Sarah's Waltz; In The Mood; Dixie Blossoms; Pat's Country; Meryl Anne's Waltz; Step Dance Medley: Ariel/Deep River Jig/Liverpool Hornpipe/Fergus Reel; Lassie's Jig; Once In A While; Strathspey/Reel Medley: My Sister's Weddin'/ Old Doc Woods/Flowers Of Edinburgh/De'il Amang The Tailors; Fergus Rag; Kendra's Wedding; Bye Bye Blues; The Ninety And Nine *41:23*

The Wyrd Sisters
FOLK/JAZZ; SINGER-SONGWRITERS

The Wyrd Sisters are not really weird, though they may lay claim to being unusual, unique, original, and provocative. According to their bio sheet, they take their name from "the ancient Triple Goddess who represented the circular nature of life and the phases of the moon. A form of her has existed in almost every known culture—the three fates, the three phases of life—(re)birth, maturity, death; the maiden, the mother and the crone; She who was, she who is and she who will be." With top-notch songwriting and vocal harmonies, this Winnipeg group has brought its unique blend of folk music to folk festivals and clubs across Canada and the United States. Their second album, and first CD, *Inside The Dreaming*, features songs like the moody, evocative title song, "Inside The Dreaming," the jazz-influenced "3000 Million," and the environmental plea, "Farewell To Clayoquot." The Wyrd Sisters are earning a reputation as one of the important new voices in Canadian folk music. The group consists of singer-songwriters Nancy Reinhold and Kim Baryluk and singer Lianne Fournier.

❊❊❊(❊) **Inside The Dreaming**
1995 Wyrd Sisters (Wyrd CD2)†

Inside The Dreaming; By Our Own Fear; 3000 Million; One Hip Shaking; No Simple Explanations; Farewell To Clayoquot Sound; Another Dreamless Sleep; Dance, Little Brother; Warrior; If It Ain't Here; The Edge Of Grace *45:32*

Yakudo
TAIKO DRUMS

The name Yakudo means "to be full of life and energy." When this Toronto ensemble performs on Japanese taiko drums on *Yakudo*, they fully live up to their name. The drummers, as the liner notes indicate, are able to "create a variety of sounds as quiet as a gentle rainfall to as loud as a raging thunderstorm." The group also incorporates flutes and gongs. The expressive drums of Yakudo underscore the poetry that is possible with one of the world's oldest folk instruments. Members of the ensemble include Sam Baba, Chris Hano, Craig Hayama, Randy Hayama, Darren Miyasaki, Gary Nagata, Miyako Panalaks, and Mark Sano.

❊❊❊ **Yakudo**
1994 Yakudo (YCD 1092)

Narukami Bayashi; Harukoma; Ko-Ryo No Mai; Shudan; San-Nin Kyoku; Sanmyaku Daiko; Fujin *46:44*

Kathleen Yearwood
FOLK/POP; SINGER-SONGWRITER

"[*Book Of Hate*] is a very strange album ... I just wish her message was a little less oblique"—*Dirty Linen*. Many listeners may be as perplexed as the *Dirty Linen* reviewer in trying to understand and appreciate *Book Of Hate*. The aggressive guitar work contrasts sharply with her soft, lilting soprano vocals. Yearwood is a talented singer and there are some strong moments on the album, which is a mix of traditional material like "Peggy Gordon" and "Tam Lin" and original material, all delivered in a highly unorthodox style. The angry, sometimes pointed, lyrics, the strange, smouldering delivery, and the sudden explosions of electric guitar imitating industrial noise make this a difficult album to assimilate.

❊❊(❊) **Book Of Hate**
1994 Amatish (SW0394-2)

Peggy Gordon; Tam Lin; Who Killed Phillip?; Night Falls; Pastorale; By Any Other Name; Lost My Way; Panik In The Cattle-Pen; Louis Riel's Farewell; Amsterdam Street; For Jesse Bernstein; Fiery Heart *55:01*

Lesley Young

FOLK/POP; SINGER-SONGWRITER

Ontario singer-songwriter Lesley Young combines her expressive alto voice, jazz-tinged acoustic guitar, and fresh lyrics into a contemporary folk/pop mix on *Symphony For Two*. Highlights include "That's The Jazz," "Dangerous," "So Long," "Symphony For Two," "Shades Of Blue," and "Song To The Wilderness."

✳✳✳ **Symphony For Two**
1994 BlueSong (BSM101)†

Laughing In The Wind; That's The Jazz; Dangerous; So Long; Picture A Sea; He Came Waltzing; Smoke And Ashes; East To West; Symphony For Two; He's Grown; Shades Of Blue; Flying Straight To You; Song To The Wilderness *58:34*

Neil Young

FOLK/ROCK; SINGER-SONGWRITER

Ontario singer-songwriter and Juno Hall of Famer Neil Young has been a mainstream rocker since the mid-60's when he teamed up with Stephen Stills and Richie Furray to form Buffalo Springfield. Later he collaborated with Crosby, Stills, and Nash. Afterwards, he pursued a solo career, forming bands like The Rockets, Crazy Horse, and The Stray Gators. Despite his rock orientation, he has skirted close to folk at several points with folk/rock songs and lyrics that have become deeply associated with the singer-songwriter spectrum of folk music—songs like "After The Gold Rush," "Only Love Can Break Your Heart," "Southern Man," "Heart Of Gold," "Harvest Moon," and "Helpless." Deciding which of Young's albums to highlight in this guide was put to a vote on the *rec.music.folk* Internet newsgroup. The consensus among Neil Young fans was that the following are the most "folkish" of Young's albums: *Neil Young*, *After The Gold Rush*, *Harvest*, *Old Ways*, *Harvest Moon*, and *Unplugged*. His purely rock albums are not listed.

See also Crosby, Stills, Nash & Young.

✳✳✳ **Neil Young**
1969 Reprise (CD 6317)†

The Emperor Of Wyoming; The Loner; If I Could Have Her Tonight; I've Been Waiting For You; The Old Laughing Lady; String Quartet From Whiskey Boot Hill; Here We Are In The Years; What Did You Do To My Life?; I've Loved Her So Long; The Last Trip To Tulsa *36:10*

✳✳✳✳✓ **After The Gold Rush**
1970 Reprise (CD 2283)†

Tell Me Why; After The Gold Rush; Only Love Can Break Your Heart; Southern Man; Till The Morning Comes; Oh, Lonesome Me; Don't Let It Bring You Down; Birds; When You Dance You Can Really Love; I Believe In You; Cripple Creek Ferry *35:13*

✳✳✳✳✓ **Harvest**
1972 Reprise (CD 2277)†

Out On The Weekend; Harvest; A Man Needs A Maid; Heart Of Gold; Are You
Ready For The Country?; Old Man; There's A World; Alabama; The Needle And The
Damage Done; Words (Between The Lines Of Age) *37:31*

✳✳✳ **Old Ways**
1985 Geffen (GED24068)

The Wayward Wind; Get Back To The Country; Are There Any More Real Cowboys?; Once An Angel; Misfits; California Sunset; Old Ways; My Boy; Bound For
Glory; Where Is The Highway Tonight? *36:54*

✳✳✳(✳) **Harvest Moon**
1992 Reprise (CDW 45057)†

Unknown Legend; From Hank To Hendrix; You And Me; Harvest Moon; War Of
Man; One Of These Days; Such A Woman; Old King; Dreamin' Man; Natural
Beauty *51:57*

✳✳✳(✳) **Unplugged**
1993 Reprise (CDW 45310)†

The Old Laughing Lady; Mr. Soul; World On A String; Pocahontas; Stringman; Like
A Hurricane; The Needle And The Damage Done; Helpless; Harvest Moon;
Transformer Man; Unknown Legend; Look Out For My Love; Long May You Run;
From Hank To Hendrix *65:35*

Record Company Addresses

A&M RECORDS OF CANADA LTD., dist. by Polygram

AGLUKARK ENTERTAINMENT INC., dist. by EMI

AKA RECORDS, Box 86013, North Vancouver, British Columbia V7L 4J5 Fax:
(604) 986-5077

AKASHIC RECORDS, PO Box 178, Bragg Creek, Alberta T0L 0K0, dist. by Festival

ALCAZAR PRODUCTIONS, PO Box 429, Waterbury, VT, USA 05676

ALLAN PATRICK, Contact at: (514) 485-3490

ALPHA YAYA DIALLO, dist. by Festival

AMATISH MUSIC, 6840 14th Ave., Markham, Ontario L6B 1A8 (905) 294-9618

AMBER MUSIC, Box 156, Topsail, Newfoundland A0A 3Y0 (709) 834-1705

ANALEKTA DISTRIBUTION INC., 841, rue Querbes, Outrement, Québec H2V 3X1

ANDERSON & BROWN, PO Box 292, Fergus, Ontario N1M 2W8

APPALOOSA - I.R.D., Via G.B. de La Salle 4, 20132 Milano, Italy [North America:
David Essig, Thetis Island, British Columbia V0R 2Y0 (604) 246-9424]

AQUARIUS RECORDS LTD., 1445 Lambert Clossa, Suite 200, Montreal, Quebec H3H
1Z5, dist. by 1-800-JOE-RADIO (563-7234)

ARPEGGIO RECORDS, 12271 Bridgeport Road, Richmond, British Columbia V6V 1J4
(604) 273-7232

ARRANDALE, c/o 560 10th St. 'A' W., Owen Sound, Ontario N4K 3R6

ARTIST RESPONSE TEAM, 3112 W. 5 Ave., Vancouver, British Columbia V6K 1V2
(604) 731-7808

ASHÉ DISCS, dist. by Festival

ASHMORE AUDIO PRODUCTIONS, PO Box 613, Sutton West, Ontario L0E 1R0, dist. by
Holborne

ASYLUM / ELEKTRA, dist. by WEA

Record Company Addresses

ATLANTIC RECORDING COMPANY, dist. by WEA

ATLANTICA MUSIC, 1819 Granville St., 4th Floor, Halifax, Nova Scotia B3J 3R1 (902) 422-7000

ATTIC RECORDS LIMITED, 102 Atlantic Ave., Toronto, Ontario M6K 1X9

AURAL TRADITION RECORDS, Vancouver Folk Music Festival Society, 3271 Main St., Vancouver, British Columbia V5V 3M6, dist. by Festival

AUVIDIS, 47 av. Paul Vaillant-Couturier, F-94250 Gentilly, France

AVA MUSIC, 2255-B Queen St. E., Suite 128, Toronto, Ontario M4E 1G3

AZIMUTH RECORDS, 1028 Hamilton St., 3rd Floor, Vancouver, British Columbia V6B 2R9 (604) 488-1551

B&R HERITAGE ENTERPRISES, PO Box 3 Iona, Cape Breton, Nova Scotia B0A 1L0

BACK ALLEY JOHN, 332 24th Ave. SW, Calgary, Alberta T2S 0K2 (403) 245-6172

BACKBURNER RECORDS INC., 7715-154 A St., Edmonton, Alberta T5R 1V3 (403) 228-1327, dist. by Festival

BALL OF FLAMES PRODUCTIONS, 3126 W. 13th Ave., Vancouver, British Columbia V6K 2V3

BARB MATTIACCI, 197 Hunter St. W., Suite 16, Peterborough, Ontario K9J 2L1

BARBED WIRE RECORDS, 852 Bird St., Birmingham, MI 48009 USA (810) 540-9031

BEAR FAMILY RECORDS, PO Box 1154, D-27727 Hambergen, Germany (04794) 1399

BEDLAM RECORDS, RR#3, Belfast, Prince Edward Island C0A 1A0 (902) 838-2973

BERTHA NORWEGIAN, Box 261, Fort Simpson, Northwest Territories X0E 0N0

BERTINA CELINA PRODUCTIONS, Box 217, Stn. B, London, Ontario N6A 4V8

BIG DOG MUSIC, 589 Markham St., Toronto, Ontario M6G 2L7

BIG POND PUBLISHING AND PRODUCTION LTD., Madison Centre, 4950 Yonge St., Suite 1008, Toronto, Ontario M2N 6K1

BILL GALLAHER, #4 - 1275 Pembroke St., Victoria, British Columbia V8T 1S7 (604) 382-7531

BIRD SISTERS, PO Box 433, Guelph, Ontario N1H 6K5

BLACK JAGUAR, Contact Marcos at (416) 537-1201 or (604) 253-6377

BLASPHEMY MUSIC, PO Box 21586, 1850 Commercial Drive, Vancouver, British Columbia V5N 4A0

BLUE OCEAN RECORDS, 128 Evanson St., Winnipeg, Manitoba R3G 1Z9

BLUE ROCKIES MUSIC, 7355 Silver Springs Road N.W., Calgary, Alberta T3B 4L3 (403) 288-0051

BLUESONG MUSIC, Box 59118, 2238 Dundas St. W., Toronto, Ontario M6R 3B5

BMG MUSIC CANADA, 2245 Markham Road, Scarborough, Ontario M1B 2W3

BOB QUINN, No address listed. Try Atlantica

BONANZA CREEK RECORDS, 135 Britannia Road, Ottawa, Ontario K2B 5X1

BOYING GERONIMO, dist. by Festival

BRAKIN' TRADITION, PO Box 553, Waverly, Nova Scotia B0N 2S0

BRAZEN HUSSY RECORDS, 404 Tenth St. E., Saskatoon, Saskatchewan S7N 0C9 Fax: (309) 653-3245

BRETON BOOKS & MUSIC, Wreck Cove, Cape Breton Island, Nova Scotia B0C 1H0

BROOKES DIAMOND PRODUCTIONS, Suite 507, World Trade & Convention Centre, 1800 Argyle St., Halifax, Nova Scotia B3J 3N8 (902) 422-7000

BUDDY MACDONALD, North Shore, RR #1, Englishtown, Victoria County, Nova Scotia B0C 1H0 (902) 929-2041

BUTTER AND SNOW PRODUCTIONS, c/o Shirley Montague, Norris Point, Newfoundland A0K 3V0

CANAL RECORDS, PO Box 57029, 797 Somerset St. W., Ottawa, Ontario K1R 1A1

CAPE BRETON CHORALE, University College Of Cape Breton, PO Box 5300, Sydney, Nova Scotia B1P 6L2

CAPITOL RECORDS, dist. by EMI

CAPTAIN TRACTOR, 184 1033-121 St., Edmonton, Alberta T5N 1L1 (403) 488-1638, dist. by Festival

CBC RADIO CANADA, Box 500, Station A, Toronto, Ontario M5W 1E6 (800) 363-1530

CBC VARIETY RECORDINGS, Box 6000, Montreal, Quebec H3C 3A8 (514) 547-4429

CBS MUSIC PRODUCTS, dist. by Sony

CEILIDH FRIENDS, 208 Nordic Arms, Yellowknife, NT X1A 1E4

CENTERFIRE MUSIC, Box 868, Turner Valley, Alberta T0L 2A0 (403) 933-2210

CHACRA ALTERNATIVE MUSIC INC., 3155 Halpern, St. Laurent, Quebec H4S 1P5

CHEEKY DISC, 2908 Manitoba St., Vancouver, British Columbia V5Y 3B4

CHERRYWOOD STATION, Box 871, Vashon Island, WA, USA 98070, dist. by EarthBeat!

CHESTER RECORDS, 238 Augusta Ave., 2nd Floor, Toronto, Ontario M5T 2L7

CHILDREN'S GROUP INC., 561 Bloor St. W., #300, Toronto, Ontario M5S 1Y6 (416) 538-7339

CHIPPED ROCK MUSIC, dist. by Brookes Diamond

CHRYSALIS/ENSIGN, dist. by EMI

CIRCLE 'M' RECORDS, 289 Fergus St., South Mount Forest, Ontario N0G 2L2

COLCANNON, 1 Collins Place, Mount Pearl, Newfoundland A1N 1E5

COLD CLUB RECORDS, Box 1048, Turner Valley, Alberta T0L 2A0 Fax: (403) 933-2210

COLLEGE OF PIPING AND CELTIC PERFORMING ARTS OF CANADA, 619 Water St. E., Summerside, Prince Edward Island C1N 4H8 (902) 436-5377, dist. by Attic

Record Company Addresses

COLUMBIA, dist. by Sony

CONDOR, dist. by Heritage

COUNTRY MUSIC STORE, Ossie Branscombe, Proprietor, 2889 Danforth Ave., Toronto, Ontario M4C 1M3 (416) 690-5564

COYOTE ENTERTAINMENT GROUP, PO Box 84631, 2336 Bloor St. W., Toronto, Ontario M6S 4Z7 (416) 530-4333

CULTRUN MUSIC, PO Box 273, St. B, Ottawa, Ontario K1P 6C4

DARK LIGHT MUSIC, 51 Bulwer Street, Toronto, Ontario M5T 1A1 (416) 977-9859

DAVID CRAIG, 266 Prince William St., Saint John, New Brunswick E2C 2C1 (506) 642-2244

DEBOLT PRODUCTIONS, Box 284, Sudbury, Ontario P3E 4P2

DENON CANADA INC., 17 Denison St., Markham, Ontario L3R 1B5

DINO MUSIC, dist. by Polytel

DISQUES BROS, LES, dist. by Fusion III

DISQUES KAPPA, 86, Chemin de la Côte Ste. Catherine, Outremont, Québec H2V 2A3 (514) 270-9556, dist. by Distribution Select

DISQUES STAR, C.P. 72, Verdun, Québec H4G 3E1 (514) 766-8785, dist. by Distribution Select

DISTRIBUTION SELECT, 500 Ste. Catherine Est, Montréal, Québec H2L 2C6

DJOLÉ, PO Box 5613, Victoria, British Columbia V8R 6S4

DONALD McGEOCH, 22 Spartan Drive, Brantford, Ontario N3R 6C7

DORIAN RECORDINGS, 8 Brunswick Road, Troy, NY 12180-3795 USA (518) 274-5475

DOUG WEBSTER, PO Box 744, Yarmouth, Nova Scotia B5A 4K3

DRAGONWING MUSIC, 4818 Dalhousie Dr. N.W., Calgary, Alberta T3A 1B2, dist. by Festival

DRUM SONG PRODUCTIONS, Box 71514 Hillcrest P.O., White Rock, British Columbia V4B 5J5 (604) 535-2214

DUCKWORTH DISTRIBUTION, 198 Duckworth St., St. John's, Newfoundland A1C 1G5 (709) 753-9292

DUKE STREET RECORDS, Div. of Horsefeathers Music Company, 121 Logan Ave., Toronto, Ontario M4M 2M9, dist. by MCA

DULCIMER TRADITIONS, PO Box 26, Fordwich, Ontario N0G 1V0 (519) 335-3182, dist. by 1-800-JOE-RADIO (563-7234)

ÉDITIONS DES FRÈRES LABRI, LES, no address on liner notes; occasionally dist. by Country Music Store, Toronto

EARTHBEAT!, PO Box 1460, Redway, CA, USA 955560

ECO ANDINO, Montréal, Québec (514) 387-8648 (514) 733-1299

ELEKTRA, dist. by WEA

EMI MUSIC CANADA, 3109 American Drive, Mississauga, Ontario L4V 1B2

ENERGY DISCS RECORDS, 15262 MPO, Vancouver, British Columbia V6B 5B1 (604) 255-4575

ESTHER RECORDS, Box 152, Bowen Island, British Columbia V0N 1G0

EVANS & DOHERTY, Box 31234, Halifax, Nova Scotia B3K 5Y1 (902) 852-5323

FALLEN ANGLE MUSIC, 285 Spencer St., Ottawa, Ontario K1Y 2R1 (613) 722-0482

FANTASY OF LATIN STRINGS, contact: The Murri Agency, PO Box 586, Hadley, MA, USA 01035 (413) 527-8180

FAT UNCLE RECORDS, 60 Rupertsland Blvd., Winnipeg, Manitoba R2W 2M8

FESTIVAL DISTRIBUTION, 1351 Grant St., Vancouver, British Columbia V5L 2X7 (604) 253-2662, (800) 633-8282

FEYGELE, 17 Hearthstone Cres., Willowdale, Ontario M2R 1G2 (416) 633-6558

FIDDLESTICKS MUSIC, Box 7, Margaree Harbour, Nova Scotia B0E 2B0

FIENDISH RECORDS, Denman Place PO, PO Box 47023, Vancouver, British Columbia V6G 3E1

FIRST NATIONS MUSIC INC., Box 1180, 16 Fifth Ave., Sioux Lookout, Ontario P8T 1B7

FLATLAND 6, PO Box 47069, Vancouver, British Columbia V5Z 4L6 (604) 873-4420, dist. by Festival

FLYING BULGAR RECORDINGS, 90 Ilford Rd., Toronto, Ontario M6G 2H5

FLYING FISH RECORDS, 1304 W. Schubert, Chicago, IL, USA 60614

FOFG PRODUCTIONS, 26 Noble St., Unit 12, Toronto, Ontario M6K 2C9

FOGARTY'S COVE & COLE HARBOUR MUSIC LTD., 23 Hillside Ave. S., Dundas, Ontario L9H 4H7

FOLK ERA PRODUCTIONS, 705 S. Washington St., Naperville, IL USA 60540-3535 (800) 232-7328

FOLK TRADITION, dist. by Valerie Enterprises

FOLK-LEGACY RECORDS, INC., Box 1148, Sharon, CT, USA 06069 (800) 836-0901

FOLKLORE IN SONG, P.O. Box 2235, Station B, Scarborough, Ontario M1N 2E9 (416) 299-8502

FPVB PRODUCTIONS, 24 Hyde Park Ave., Hamilton, Ontario L8P 4M5 (905) 526-8908

FRANTIC MUSE PRODUCTIONS, PO Box 93558, Nelson Park Post Office, Vancouver, British Columbia V6E 4L7

FROZEN BANDICOOT MUSIC, PO Box 27271, Winnipeg, Manitoba R3B 3K2

FUSION III, 5455 rue Pare, Suite 101, Montréal, Québec H4P 1P7

GATHERING PRODUCTIONS, 68 Churchill Ave., Toronto, Ontario M6J 2B4

GEFFEN RECORDS, dist. by MCA

GESTION SON IMAGE ET SUROÎT, 839 Sherbrooke Est, Suite 101, Montréal, Québec H2L 1K6 (514) 522-1716

GIGS & REELS, 6159 Leeds St., Halifax, Nova Scotia B3K 2T9

GLENASHDALE MUSIC, P.O. Box 70504, 1615 Dundas St. E., Whitby, Ontario L1N 2L1

GRD RECORDINGS (CANADA), 102 - 2339 Columbia St., Vancouver, British Columbia V5Y 3Y3

GREAT BIG SEA, c/o NRA Productions Ltd., 32 Cherrington St., St John's, Newfoundland A1E 4X6

GREAT NORTH PRODUCTIONS, #012, 11523 - 100 Ave., Edmonton, Alberta T5K 0J8 (403) 482-2022

GREEN LINNET RECORDS, INC., 43 Beaver Brook Road, Danbury, CT 06810 (203) 730-0333

GREENTREE MUSIC, PO Box 434, Walkerton, Ontario N0G 2V0

GROUND SWELL RECORDS, P.O. Box 245, Central Station, Halifax, Nova Scotia B3J 2N7 (902) 492-0447, (800) 563-7935

GROUPE CONCEPT MUSIQUE, dist. by Sony

GUERNSEY COVE PARLOUR PRODUCTIONS, Guernsey Cove, Prince Edward Island C0A 1V0 (902)-962-3204

GUIGNOLÉE, Contact: Gilles Cantin (514) 752-1917

GUMBOOTS, 3505 Ingraham Drive, Yellowknife, North West Territories X1A 2E8

GUN RECORDS, PO Box 8391, Station A, Halifax, Nova Scotia B3K 5M1 (902) 423-8434

GYPSALERO PRODUCTIONS, Contact: Carrie Riches Artist Management, 1850 W. 1st Ave., Vancouver, British Columbia V6J 1GS (604) 734-5305

HAPI RECORDS, 159 Thornberry Lane, Waterloo, Ontario N2T 2C9

HEARTSONG RECORDS, 2820 Albert St., Regina, SK S4S 3N5 (306) 779-1200

HERE AND NOW RECORDS, dist. by Festival

HERITAGE MUSIC, 41 Antrim Cres. #311, Scarborough, Ontario M1P 4T1

HIMA HOSS, 3816 rue De Bullion, Montréal, Québec H2W 2E1 (514) 844-1950

HOLBORNE DISTRIBUTING CO., PO Box 309R, Mt. Albert, Ontario L0G 1M0

HUED PRODUCTIONS, 1255 rue Main, C.P. 1172, Moncton, New Brunswick E1C 8P9

HUGHBOY RECORDS, PO Box 223, Wemindji, Quebec J0M 1L0

HYPNOTIC RECORDS, dist. by Amber

IADY MUSIC, 168 Foster Ave., Belleville, Ontario K8N 3P9 (613) 968-3895

IBYCUS MUSIC, 11 Ross Ave., Pasadena, Newfoundland A0L 1K0 (709) 686-5101, dist. by Duckworth

IMPROBABLE MUSIC, PO Box 16010, Bellwoods Postal Outlet, Toronto, Ontario M6J 3W2 (416) 603-0384

INCONNU PRODUCTIONS, Box 5514, Whitehorse, Yukon Y1A 5H4   Fax: (403) 633-4788

INGOLD/PARADIGM, no address listed; (905) 455-3810, dist. by CBC Maritimes

INTERDISC DISTRIBUTION INC., 27, Louis Joseph Doucet, Lanoraie, Québec J0K 1E0 (514) 887-2384

INTERNATIONAL MUSIC, dist. by Auvidis

INTERSCOPE, dist. by WEA

INTERSOUND, INC., 1 Select Ave., Scarborough, Ontario M1V 5J3

INTREPID RECORDS, 205/65 Jefferson Ave., Toronto, Ontario M6K 1Y3, dist. by EMI

INVINCIBLE MUSIC (CANADA), dist. by GRD

ISBA MUSIC ENTERTAINMENT, 5046 Chambord St., Montreal, Quebec H2J 3N2   (514) 522-4722, dist. by Sony

JABULA RECORDS, Box 91699, West Vancouver, British Columbia V7V 3P3   (604) 926-4602

JACKSON DELTA, PO Box 2384, Peterborough, Ontario K9J 7Y8

JAM PRODUCTIONS, dist. by Atlantica

JERRY ALFRED, c/o David Petkovich, Box 5514, Whitehorse, Yukon Y1A 5H4   (403) 633-4788, dist. by Festival

JIMMY BOYLE RECORDS, 358 Danforth Ave., Box 65068, Toronto, Ontario M4K 1M0

JIMMY EKHO, No address listed; try Nakasuk School, Iqaluit, Northwest Territories X0A 0H0

JOHN MCLACHLAN, 950 Belvedere Drive, North Vancouver, British Columbia V7R 2C1   (604) 980-6904

JR RECORDS, 1412 39 St., Edmonton, Alberta T6L 2M7

JUBA!, 9662 86th Ave., Edmonton, Alberta T6C 1J9

JUSTIN TIME RECORDS INC., 5455 rue Pare, Suite 101, Montréal, Québec H4P 1P7

KATARI TAIKO DRUM GROUP ASSOCIATION, Suite 100, 1062 Homer St., Vancouver, British Columbia V6B 2W9   (604)-683-8240

KILGORE TROUT, PO Box 61154, Kensington Postal Outlet, Calgary, Alberta T2N 4S6   (403) 270-3124

KILLIECRANKIE, PO Box 27016, Cambridge, Ontario N1R 8H1

KINETIC RECORDS, 431-67 Mowat Ave., Toronto, Ontario M6K 3E3

KLAASEN CONNEXION, PO Box 4897, Ville Saint-Laurent, Québec H4L 4Z5   (514) 333-1852

L.Q. PRODUCTIONS, 7239-112 St., Edmonton, Alberta T6G 1J4   (403) 430-0686

LAPPLAND, PO Box 8223, Victoria, British Columbia V8W 3R8

LARRY JENSEN, c/o Fromager's Music, 221 8th St. E., Owen Sound, Ontario N4K 1L2

LATENT RECORDINGS, dist. by BMG

LAUGHING OUT LOUD MUSIC, Chinatown, PO Box 77060, Calgary, Alberta T2G 5J8

LEN WALLACE ENTERPRISES, 346 Randolph, Windsor, Ontario N9B 2T6

LITTLE GIANT RECORDS, 23 Knappen Ave., Winnipeg, Manitoba

LOOKOUT MUSIC, [no address listed]

LOWRIDER RECORDS, 2969 E. Seventh Ave., Vancouver, British Columbia V5M 1V2 (604) 255-7814, dist. by Festival

LUPINS RECORDS, PO Box 3130, Halifax, Nova Scotia B3J 3G6, dist. by Big Pond

MALAHAT MOUNTAIN MUSIC, Box 30033, Saanich Centre PO, Victoria, British Columbia V8X 5E1 (604) 479-4741

MANOHAR RECORDS, no address listed; try Festival Distribution

MARGAREE SOUND, 225 Lake Driveway W., Ajax, Ontario L1S 5A3 (416)-683-5680

MARIPOSA FOLK FOUNDATION, 60 Atlantic Ave., Suite 106, Toronto, Ontario M6K 1X9 (416) 588-8371

MARIPOSA IN THE SCHOOLS, 68 Broadview Ave., Suite 401, Toronto, Ontario M4M 2E6

MARK BRACKEN MUSIC, Box 2193, Sidney, British Columbia V8L 3S8

MARK HAINES, 166 Wallace St., Woodbridge, Ontario L4L 2P4 (905) 851-3234

MAY IP, 44 Chester Le Blvd, Unit 7, Scarborough, Ontario M1W 2M8

MCA RECORDS CANADA, 2450 Victoria Park Ave., Willowdale, Ontario M2J 4A2

MCLEOD MUSIC PRODUCTIONS, 610 St. David St. S., Fergus, Ontario N1M 2L9. (519) 843-3173

MEN OF THE DEEPS MUSIC, 3202 MacLeod Ave., New Waterford, Nova Scotia B1H 1J7

MERCURY, dist. by PolyGram

MILL STREET RECORDS, no address listed; dist. by 1-800-JOE-RADIO

MILLES PATTES, dist. by Musicor

MKM MUSIC PRODUCTIONS LTD., 556 Laurier Ave. W., Suite 503, Ottawa, Ontario K1R 7X2 (613) 234-5419

MOIRA CAMERON, 617 - 5310 -44th St., Yellowknife, Northwest Territories X1A 1K3

MOKA MUSIK, 12 Fielding, Moncton, New Brunswick E1A 3T6 (506) 383-1483

MONGREL MUSIC CORPORATION, Box 667 Station A, Prince George, British Columbia V2L 4S8

MOOSE RECORDS, no longer active; try used CD bins for Moose recordings

MORIA CAMERON, 617 - 5310 - 44th St., Yellowknife, NT X1A 1K3

MOTHER OF PEARL RECORDS INC., Woodmore, Manitoba R0A 2M0 (204) 427-2605

MOUTON RECORDS, Box 128, Station E, Toronto, Ontario M6H 4F2

MÜD MUSIC, Box 36035 Lakeview Postal Outlet, Calgary, Alberta T3E 7C6

MUSA RECORDS, 859 Wolseley Ave., Winnipeg, Manitoba R3G 1E1

MUSIC OF THE WORLD, PO Box 258, Brooklyn, NY, USA 11209-0005

MUSICOR, 2620 Route Transcanadienne, Pointe-Claire, Quebec H9R 1B1

MUSICWORKS INC., #207, 1501 - 17th Ave. S.W., Calgary, Alberta T2T 0E2

MUSIQUE MULTI-MONTRÉAL, 4372 rue Marquette, Montréal, Québec H2J 3X6 (514) 872-0023

NANCY ROACH ENTERPRISES, PO Box 8473, Halifax, Nova Scotia B3K 5M2

NATALIE MACMASTER, RR 1, Port Hastings, Cape Breton Island, Nova Scotia B0E 2T0 (902) 625-1344

NAZKA, 2 Bloor St. W., Suite 100-262, Toronto, Ontario M4W 3E2 Fax: (416) 968-9417

NEMESIS PUBLISHING, see Cherrywood Station

NETTWERK PRODUCTIONS, Box 330-1755 Robson St., Vancouver, British Columbia V6G 3B7 (604) 654-2029

NEW EARTH MUSIC PUBLISHING, 118 Wildwood Ave., Victoria, British Columbia V8S 3V9 (604) 589-5662

NGOMA, PO Box 579, 545 E. Broadway, Vancouver, British Columbia V5T 1X4 (604) 253-7228

NICK RECORDS, Bob Bossin, Site 24, Box 22, Gabriola Island, British Columbia V0R 1X0 (604) 247-7476

NIGHT SUN, Box 1024 Iqaluit, Northwest Territories X0A 0H0 (819) 979-4204

NORTH TRACK RECORDS, Box 68, Station B, Ottawa, Ontario K1P 6C3

NORTHERN DANCER MUSIC, 11 - 2453 Queen St. E., Toronto, Ontario M4E 1H7 (416) 699-7220

NORTHERN SKY RECORDS, Box 790, Smithers, British Columbia V0J 2N0, dist. by Festival

NORTHUMBERLAND RECORDS, RR1, Campbellford, Ontario K0L 1L0 (705) 942-2142

NORWEGIAN, BERTHA, Box 261, Fort Simpson, NWT X0E 0N0

NRA PRODUCTIONS LTD., 32 Cherrington St., St. John's, Newfoundland A1E 4X6

OASIS PRODUCTIONS, 76 Cadorna Ave., Toronto, Ontario M4J 3X1 (416) 467-8820

OLESIA PRODUCTIONS, PO Box 2877, Winnipeg, Manitoba R3C 4B4

OLIVE HOUSE, 179 Olive St., Victoria, British Columbia V8S 3H4

OLIVIA RECORDS INC., 4400 Market St., Oakland, CA 94608 USA

ON TAP RECORDS, Jughead, 998 Bloor St. W, PO Box 10526, Toronto, Ontario M6H 4H9

OO ZOO MAY RECORDS, dist. by Festival

OPEN MIND, PO Box 89084, Westdale Postal Outlet, Hamilton, Ontario L8S 1B0 (905) 527-8146

ORQUESTA BC SALSA, 62 Oriole Walk, Vancouver, British Columbia V5W 2J8 (604) 327-5324

OTTAWA FOLKLORE CENTRE LTD., 744 Bronson Ave., Ottawa, Ontario K1S 4G3 (613) 238-7222

OVERTOM PRODUCTIONS LTD., 20-B Dominion St., Glace Bay, Nova Scotia B1A 3M6 (902) 849-1005

PAGE PUBLICATIONS INC., 800 Steeles Ave. W., Suite B10-138, Thornhill, Ontario L4J 7L2

PEG MUSIC, A division of Oak Street Music, 1067 Sherwin Road, Winnipeg, Manitoba R3H 0T8

PERMANENT RECORDS, 612 Yonge St., Toronto, ON M4Y 1Z3

PHILIPS, dist. by Polygram

PIGEON INLET PRODUCTIONS LTD., PO Box 1202, Station C, St John's, Newfoundland A1C 5M9 (709) 754-7324

PIPER STOCK PRODUCTIONS, Torbay, Newfoundland A0A 3Z0 (709) 437-6326

POCHEE RECORDS, 47 Kelsonia Ave., Scarborough, Ontario M1M 1B2 (416) 595-1515

POLYDOR, dist. by PolyGram

POLYGRAM, 1345 Denison St., Markham, Ontario L3R 5V2

POLYTEL, Polygram Distribution, 6000 Cote de Liesse, St-Laurent, Quebec H4T 1E3

PRAIRIE DRUID MUSIC, 219-11th St. E., Saskatoon, Saskatchewan S7N 0E5

PRIVATE, INC., dist. by BMG

PYRAMID RECORDS, 512 Roxton Road, Toronto, Ontario M6G 3R4 (416) 533-9988

QUALITY SPECIAL PRODUCTS, 1-480 Tapscott Road, Scarborough, Ontario M1B 1W3

QUINLAN ROAD, PO Box 933, Stratford, Ontario N5A 7M3 (519) 273-3876, dist. by WEA

RATTLE FALLS PUBLISHING, c/o John Prince, 17 Draper St., RR #1 Box 17, Keswick, Ontario L4P 3C8

REARGUARD PRODUCTIONS, 39 Stinson Ave., Winnipeg, Manitoba R3L 2S3 (204) 453-8581

REPRISE, dist. by WEA

RESOURCE RECORDS, 2803 W. 4th Ave., PO Box 74656, Vancouver, British Columbia V6J 1K2

REVENANT RECORDS, Hunter River, RR3, South Rustico, Prince Edward Island C0A 1N0 (902) 963-2005, dist. by Sony

RHINO RECORDS INC., 2225 Colorado Ave., Santa Monica, CA, USA 90404

RICHARD WOOD, 13 Wescomb Cres., East Royalty, Prince Edward Island C1C 1B6 (902) 894-3836

RIVER RECORDS, dist. by Festival

ROCKY COAST MUSIC INC., 7 Purcell's Cove Road, Halifax, Nova Scotia B3N 1R2 (902) 477-3130

RODEO RECORDS, dist. by Holborne

ROUNDER RECORDS CORP., One Camp St., Cambridge, MA 02140, USA

ROVER RECORDS, Box 85, Madrono Drive, British Columbia V0R 2R0 Fax: (604) 468-7502

RTP PRODUCTIONS, Box 6245, Station J, Ottawa, Ontario K2A 1T3

RYKODISC USA, 530 N. 3rd St., Minneapolis, MN 55401, USA

RYNDE RECORDS LTD., PO Box 6213, Innisfail, Alberta T4G 1S9, dist. by Festival

SAKATCHEWAN INDIAN CULTURAL CENTRE, dist. by Festival

SAZACHA RED SKY, PO Box 65156, 348 Danforth Ave., Toronto, Ontario M4K 3Z2 (310) 289-3197

SCHRYER TRIPLETS, 1559 Alta Vista Drive, PO Box 59024, Ottawa, Ontario K1G 5T7

SCUTTLEBUTT RECORDS, 123 S. Turner St., Victoria, British Columbia V8V 2J9 (604) 386-8143

SEA-CAPE MUSIC LTD., R.R. 2 Marion Bridge, Cape Breton, Nova Scotia B0A 1P0

SEADANCE MUSIC, PO Box 184, 36 Adelaide St. E., Toronto, Ontario M5C 2J1

SEALED WITH A KISS RECORDS, P.O. Box 52091, Edmonton Trail P.O., 311 - 16th Ave NE, Calgary, Alberta T2E 8K9

SEANACHIE, 1635 Broadview Road NW, Calgary, Alberta T2N 3H2

SEE THROUGH RECORDS, PO Box 48510, Vancouver, British Columbia V7X 1A2 (604) 253-1240, dist. by Festival

SELECT 500, 500, rue Ste. Catherine Est, Montréal Québec H2L 2C6 (514) 940-6201

SELF-PROPELLED MUSIC, Tom Lewis, PO Box 501, Fruitvale, British Columbia V0G 1L0

SGB RECORDS, Box 714, Guelph, Ontario N1H 6L3

SILVER CITY RECORDS, dist. by Sony

SILVERWOLF RECORDS, Contact: Fleming Artists' Management, 5975 av. du Parc, Montréal, Québec H2V 4H4 (514) 276-5605

SINGSONG PRODUCTIONS, P.O. Box 6371, Station C, St. John's, Newfoundland A1C 6J9 (709) 726-8622

SIRENS, PO Box 1421, Station C, St. John's, Newfoundland A1C 5N8, dist. by Duckworth

SLUMGULLION PRODUCTIONS, PO Box 1633, Lunenburg, Nova Scotia B0J 2C0

SNOW GOOSE RECORDS, dist. by Valerie Enterprises

SNOWROSE RECORDS, 3017 St. Clair Ave. #302, Burlington, Ontario L7N 3P5

SNOWY RIVER RECORDS, PO Box 4655, Station E, Ottawa, Ontario K1S 5H8

Record Company Addresses

Sony Music Canada, 1113 Leslie St., Don Mills, Ontario M3C 2J9

Sound On Sound Records, 97 Victoria St. N, 2nd Floor, Kitchener, Ontario N2H 5C1 (519) 745-1092

Soundwright, dist. by Ottawa Folklore Centre

Stag Creek Music Inc., dist. by RTP

Stephen MacDonald Productions, 29 Royal Ave., Sydney, Nova Scotia B1P 4M1

Stony Plain Recording Co., PO Box 861, Edmonton, Alberta T5J 2L8 (403) 468-6423

Strange Pagan Recordings, 3135 Upper Place NW, Calgary, Alberta T2N 4H2

Strictly Country Records, PO Box 91, Coventry, CT, USA 06238

Sugar Hill Records, PO Box 4040, Duke Station, Durham, NC USA 27706-4040

Summertime Productions Society, 440 George St., Sydney, Nova Scotia B1P 1K3

Sunshine Records Ltd., 275 Selkirk Ave., Winnipeg, Manitoba R2W 2L5

Surucuá Art Production, #G-2404 Guelph St., Vancouver, British Columbia V5T 3P3, dist. by Festival

SWC Productions, PO Box 77, English Harbour West, Newfoundland A0H 1M0 (709) 888-5151

Sweetwater Music, General Delivery, Alberton, Ontario L0R 1A0

Tangible Records, Box 152, Bowen Island, British Columbia V0N 1G0 Fax: (604) 947-0505

Tanglefoot Media Ltd., Box 2263, Peterborough, Ontario K9J 7Y8 (705) 639-2129

Tchaka Productions, C.P. 48015, 5678 ave. Du Parc, Montréal, Québec H2V 4S8, dist. by Musicor

Theatre Erebus Inc., #4-125 Melrose Ave. S., Hamilton, Ontario L8M 2Y7 (905) 527-4260

Third Wave Productions Ltd., Box 563, Gander, Newfoundland A1V 2E1 (709) 256-8009

TIP Splinter, 8 Hewitt Ave., Toronto, Ontario M6R 1Y3

Too Hot Music, dist. by Musicworks

Tranquilla Music, dist. by Valerie Enterprises

Transit, dist. by Interdisc

Triple Threat, 2, 1511 - 21st Ave SW, Calgary, Alberta T2T 0M8

True North, dist. by Sony

Turtle Records, #202-1505 W. 2nd Ave., Vancouver, British Columbia V6H 3Y4

Two Productions And Publishing, PO Box 73564, 509 St. Clair Ave. W., Toronto, Ontario M6C 1A4

TZIMMES, #12 - 719 E. 31st Ave., Vancouver, British Columbia V5V 2W9 (604) 879-8415

UISCE BEATHA, 10 Lundy Lane, London, Ontario N6C 3G5

UNITY ARTS INC., PO Box 760, Manotick, Ontario K4M 1A7

VALERIE ENTERPRISES, Woodburn Road, R.R. #1, Hannon, Ontario L0R 1P0 (905) 692-4020

VANGUARD RECORDS, 1299 Ocean Ave., Suite 800, Santa Monica, CA, USA 90401

WAKAMI WAILERS, c/o Box 2349, Picton, Ontario K0K 2T0

WALTER OSTANEK, 41 Geneva St., St. Catharines, Ontario L2R 4M5 (905) 684-2961

WARNER ARCHIVES, dist. by WEA

WARNER BROS. RECORDS, dist. by WEA

WART RECORDS, Toad Productions, 14 Mt. Hope St., Kitchener, Ontario N2G 2J2

WAXY SKIN PUBLISHING, 6-155 O'Connor St., Ottawa, Ontario K2P 1T3

WEA MUSIC OF CANADA, 1810 Birchmont Rd., Scarborough, Ontario M1P 2J1

WENDY MAcISAAC, RR #1, Port Hastings, Inverness County, Nova Scotia B0E 2T0 (902) 625-1340

WESTPARK MUSIC & PUBLISHING, PO Box 260, 227 D-500, Koeln 1, Germany (0221) 24-76-44, dist. by Cultrun

WIDE-EYED MUSIC, PO Box 268, Station P, Toronto, Ontario M5S 2S8, dist. by Festival

WILDROSE RECORDS, 2873 Agricola St., Halifax, Nova Scotia B3K 4E7 (902) 455-9928

WILLOW PRODUCTIONS, 1561 Williamsport Drive, Mississauga, Ontario L4X 1T7 (905)-625-7387

WINDWARD PRODUCTIONS & PUBLISHING, 339 Wellesley St. E., Toronto, Ontario M4X 1H2

WINGNUT PRODUCTIONS, 508 Aylmer St. N., Peterborough, Ontario K9H 3W5

WORD OF MOUTH, PO Box 429, Station P, Toronto, Ontario M5S 2S9

WYRD SISTERS, Box 26062 - 116 Sherbrook St., Winnipeg, Manitoba R3C 4K9 (204) 775-5543

YAKUDO, PO Box 86041, Oakville, Ontario L6H 5V6

Folk Festivals In Canada

The number of folk festivals in Canada has grown from a small handful twenty years ago, to dozens of festivals with representation in every province. Festivals are ideal places to see large numbers of artists in a small space of time. In addition to folk music, most festivals also have wonderful craft exhibits and excellent children's facilities. The following list of festivals in Canada was extracted from the Canada Council Touring Office *Jazz, Folk, World Music Presenters Directory*. The full directory, which includes clubs, societies, associations, and publications, may be obtained from the Canada Council at 1-800-263-5588, extension 4292. The telephone and fax numbers of the festivals are subject to change.

Alberta

CALGARY FOLK FESTIVAL, Calgary, Alberta (403) 233-0904, Fax: (403) 266-3373

CANMORE FOLK FESTIVAL, Canmore, Alberta (403) 678-2524

DREAMSPEAKERS NATIVE ARTS FESTIVAL, Edmonton, Alberta (403) 439-3456, Fax: (403) 439-2066

EDMONTON FOLK FESTIVAL, Edmonton, Alberta (403) 429-1899, Fax: (403) 424-1132

JASPER FOLK FESTIVAL, Jasper, Alberta (403) 852-5187, Fax: (403) 852-5781

British Columbia

HARRISON FESTIVAL OF THE ARTS, Harrison Hot Springs, British Columbia (604) 796-3664, Fax: (604) 796-3188

ISLANDS FOLK FESTIVAL, Duncan, British Columbia (604) 748-3975

MIDSUMMER FESTIVAL, Smithers, British Columbia (604) 846-9331

MISSION FOLK FESTIVAL, Mission, British Columbia (604) 826-5937

Folk Festivals In Canada

ROCK AND TWANG FESTIVAL Rossland, British Columbia (604) 362-3366

VANCOUVER FOLK FESTIVAL Vancouver, British Columbia (604) 879-2931, Fax: (604) 879-4315

WOMEN IN VIEW FESTIVAL Vancouver, British Columbia (604) 665-6684, Fax: (604) 685-6649

Manitoba

BRANDON FOLK MUSIC & ARTS FESTIVAL Brandon, Manitoba (204) 727-3928

WINNIPEG FOLK FESTIVAL Winnipeg, Manitoba (204) 231-0096, Fax: (204) 231-0076

New Brunswick

FESTIVAL BY THE SEA St. John, New Brunswick (506) 632-0086, Fax: (506) 632-0994

MIRAMICHI FOLK SONG FESTIVAL Newcastle, New Brunswick (506) 773-4469

Newfoundland

NEWFOUNDLAND FOLK FESTIVAL St. John's, Newfoundland (709) 576-8508

Northwest Territories

FESTIVAL OF THE MIDNIGHT SUN Yellowknife, Northwest Territories (403) 920-7118, Fax: (403) 873-5939

FOLK ON THE ROCKS Yellowknife, Northwest Territories (403) 920-7806, Fax: (403) 873-4114

GREAT NORTHERN MUSIC FESTIVAL Inuvik, Northwest Territories (403) 979-3536

Nova Scotia

CENTRE BRAS D'OR FESTIVAL OF THE ARTS Baddeck, Nova Scotia (902) 295-2787

LUNENBURG FOLK FESTIVAL Lunenburg, Nova Scotia (902) 634-3180, Fax: (902) 634-3572

Ontario

ALL FOLKS FESTIVAL Kingston, Ontario (613) 548-6525, Fax: (613) 548-6514

BLUE SKIES FESTIVAL Clarendon, Ontario (613) 384-1014

EAGLEWOOD EARTH FESTIVAL Pefferlaw, Ontario (416) 481-5506, Fax: (416) 481-9319

EARTH, AIR, FIRE & WATER: CELTIC ROOTS FESTIVAL Goderich, Ontario (519) 524-2400

EARTHSONG FESTIVAL Hamilton, Ontario (905) 525-6644, Fax: (905) 525-8292

FESTIVAL OF FRIENDS Hamilton, Ontario (905) 525-6644, Fax: (905) 525-8292

HILLSIDE FESTIVAL Guelph, Ontario (519) 763-6396

HOME COUNTY FOLK FESTIVAL London, Ontario (519) 645-2845, Fax: (519) 645-0981

HORSESHOE VALLEY FOLK FESTIVAL Barrie, Ontario (905) 434-1714, Fax: (905) 434-8302

MARIPOSA FOLK FESTIVAL Toronto, Ontario (416) 588-8371, Fax: (416) 588-8974

MILL RACE FESTIVAL OF TRADITIONAL MUSIC Cambridge, Ontario (519) 621-7135

NORTHERN LIGHTS FESTIVAL BORÉAL Sudbury, Ontario (705) 674-5512, Fax: (705) 671-1998

OTTAWA FOLK FESTIVAL Ottawa, Ontario (613) 788-2898, Fax: (613) 788-4060

PETERBOROUGH FOLK FESTIVAL Peterborough, Ontario (705) 749-3157

QUINTE FESTIVAL Picton, Ontario (613) 476-5828

SONGS OF SAIL Penitanguishene, Ontario (705) 534-3881

SUMMERFOLK FESTIVAL Owen Sound, Ontario (519) 371-2995, Fax: (519) 371-2973

WYE MARSH FESTIVAL Midland, Ontario (705) 526-7809, Fax: (705) 526-3294

Prince Edward Island

NATIONAL MILTON ACORN FESTIVAL Charlottetown, Prince Edward Island (902) 894-8766

Québec

FESTIVAL D'ÉTÉ Québec, Québec (418) 692-4540, Fax: (418) 692-4384

WORLD FOLKLORE FESTIVAL Drummondville, Quebec (819) 472-1184

Saskatchewan

NESS CREEK FESTIVAL Big River, Saskatchewan (306) 652-0897

REGINA FOLK FESTIVAL Regina, Saskatchewan (306) 757-7684, Fax: (306) 779-1200

Yukon

DAWSON CITY MUSIC FESTIVAL Dawson City, Yukon (403) 993-5584, Fax: (403) 993-5510

Artist Index

C

S

X

Y

Z

Song Index

Song Index

256

Song Index

261

D

F

H

I

Song Index

L

M

O

P

Q

Song Index

U

W

X

Y

Z